ADRIFT ON THE EARTH

ADRIFT *on the* EARTH

Caribbean Romanticism and Geopoetics

KIR KUIKEN

STANFORD UNIVERSITY PRESS
Stanford, California

Stanford University Press
Stanford, California

© 2026 by Kir Kuiken. All rights reserved.

No part of this book may be reproduced or transmitted in any form or by any means, electronic or mechanical, including photocopying and recording, or in any information storage or retrieval system, without the prior written permission of Stanford University Press.

Library of Congress Cataloging-in-Publication Data
Names: Kuiken, Kir, author.
Title: Adrift on the Earth : Caribbean Romanticism and geopoetics / Kir Kuiken.
Description: Stanford, California : Stanford University Press, 2026. | Includes bibliographical references and index.
Identifiers: LCCN 2025050176 (print) | LCCN 2025050177 (ebook) | ISBN 9781503645981 (cloth) | ISBN 9781503646827 (paperback) | ISBN 9781503646834 (epub)
Subjects: LCSH: Caribbean literature—History and criticism. | Political ecology in literature. | Romanticism. | Earth (Planet)—In literature.
Classification: LCC PN849.C3 K85 2026 (print) | LCC PN849.C3 (ebook)
LC record available at https://lccn.loc.gov/2025050176
LC ebook record available at https://lccn.loc.gov/2025050177

Cover design: Michele Wetherbee
Cover design: Lilian Garcia-Roig, *Moving Subject-Action Painting, Water and Rock Flows, WA, 2010*, 48"x48", oil on canvas
Photo credit: Alec Kercheval
Private Collection-Dallas

The authorized representative in the EU for product safety and compliance is: Mare Nostrum Group B.V. | Doelen 72 | 4831 GR Breda | The Netherlands | Email address: gpsr@mare-nostrum.co.uk | KVK chamber of commerce number: 96249943

For Miles and his Earth

CONTENTS

ACKNOWLEDGMENTS

This book was first conceived as an island of ideas about European Romanticism; it eventually transformed into an archipelago of concepts connecting Romanticism with the Caribbean. It is to Branka Arsić that I owe the gratitude for this move: the many conversations we had over the years encouraged me to venture into some of the unorthodox associations and arguments that make this book what it is.

Other conversations and exchanges helped it immensely along the way; some I am able to trace here, others remain subterranean, silently imprinted on the book's pages without my knowing. I would especially like to thank Deborah Elise White, my coeditor of a collection on Romanticism's engagement with the Haitian Revolution: During our collaboration on that volume's introduction, some ideas for this book began to crystallize. Joseph Albernaz, Anna Ezekiel, Amanda Goldstein, and Frédéric Neyrat, the contributors to the issue of *Romantic Circles* on "Romanticism and Political Ecology" that I edited, have been important cothinkers. The discussions I have had with the members and graduate students of the Derrida Seminars Translation Project over the past sixteen years have contributed beyond measure to my work in general, and to my thinking about Earth and world in particular. The project's careful attention to language has also been an enduring inspiration. Richard Barney offered his time and gave helpful suggestions on my first chapter. My exchanges with John E. Drabinski, including an interview he conducted with Deborah Elise White and myself on his podcast, helped me rearticulate some of the book's arguments, particularly on Glissant.

A portion of chapter 3 is drawn from an essay titled "Günderrode's Earth:

On the Political Ecology of 'Life'" previously published in the *European Romantic Review* 34, no. 3 (2023), which is reprinted here in modified form with the permission of Taylor and Francis Ltd. This same chapter was fleshed out thanks to an invite from Andrew J. Mitchell to attend a week-long symposium on Karoline von Günderrode at Emory University.

A portion of chapter 4 is drawn from an article previously published in *Romantic Circles* 1, no. 2 (2024), titled "Hölderlin: From the Death of Nature to the Earth"; it is reprinted here in modified form under Creative Commons license CC-BY-NC-ND.

I would also like to thank Sébastien Pierrot-Minnot for granting permission to include his photograph of an Amerindian stone in Martinique's Montravail Forest in chapter 4; Sir John Soane's Museum for permission to include an image of Joseph Michael Gandy's 1798 painting "Architectural Ruins, A Vision"; and Jean Jonassaint for connecting me to the Frankétienne family to access images of his paintings. Mary Grace Albanese kindly helped with translation from the Creole. I would also like to thank the administration at the University at Albany, SUNY, for two separate one-semester research leaves that were instrumental in allowing me to complete the manuscript.

My editor at Stanford, Erica Wetter, has made the whole production process unexpectedly smooth and easy: I am grateful to her for finding thoughtful readers and for guiding me through the labyrinthine protocols of review and copyrights. Caroline McKusick's help in manuscript preparation was as important as were her early suggestions on how to reshape it. I couldn't be happier with the press's choice of anonymous readers: their detailed comments, pointed criticism, intellectual precision and generosity honed the book's argument in important ways.

During the pandemic years, when work on this book nearly ground to a complete halt for some time, friends and neighbors stepped forward to help in so many ways. I would like to thank my local neighborhood "Mombsquad" in Albany, New York, for creating a semblance of normalcy and community in those difficult times.

Now for two people to whom this book owes its current shape most directly: David Wills, a colleague, mentor, collaborator, cothinker, close reader and close friend, read the draft in its entirety and offered numerous suggestions. His dorsal thinking and linguistic brilliance worked stealthily behind my own writing, enabling me to see what I was (and wasn't) actually saying, gently nudging a different phrase that then somehow made the whole paragraph work differently. Vesna Kuiken spent many hours with the manuscript, making suggestions on how to improve it, and then offering still others that helped improve those improvements. I could not have completed this book without David's and Vesna's support.

And while it is, in many ways, about the past, the book is also about and *for* the future, particularly a future that is not mine. That future is Miles Jasper Kuiken and the Earth I wish to leave him.

ABBREVIATIONS

Full sources given in notes and references.

A	John Clare, "The Ants"
AT	John Clare, "Address to Time"
B	F. W. J. Schelling, *Bruno, or on the Natural and the Divine Principle of Things*
BE	Jacques Roumain, "Ebony Wood"/"Bois-d'ébène"
CF	Patrick Chamoiseau, *Crusoe's Footprint*
DE	Friedrich Hölderlin, *The Death of Empedocles*
EC	Heinrich von Kleist, "Earthquake in Chile"
ET	John Clare, "Eternity of Time"
F	F. W. J. Schelling, *First Outline of a System of the Philosophy of Nature*
FC	Daniel Maximin, *Les fruits de la cyclone*
GT	Olive Senior, *Gardening in the Tropics*
HG	William Wordsworth, "Home at Grasmere"
IE	Karoline von Günderrode, "Idea of the Earth"
LT	Karoline von Günderrode, "Letters of Two Friends"
M	Friedrich Hölderlin, "The Main"/"Der Main"
MA	Patrick Chamoiseau, *La matière de l'absence*
MD	Jacques Roumain, *Masters of the Dew*
MP	Karoline von Günderrode, *Muhammed: Prophet of Mecca*
MV	Frankétienne, *Melovivi ou le piège suivi de brèche ardente*
PI	Édouard Glissant, *Poetic Intention/L'intention poétique*
PN	G. W. F. Hegel, *The Philosophy of Nature*

PR Édouard Glissant, *Poetics of Relation/Poétique de la relation*
PW Friedrich Hölderlin, *Sämtliche Werke und Briefe*, vols. 1–2
R John Clare, "Remembrances"
RA John Clare, "Recollections After an Evening Walk"
RM Erna Brodber, *The Rainmaker's Mistake*
RS John Clare, "Rural Scenes"
S Olive Senior, "Shell"
SB Karoline von Günderrode, "Story of a Brahmin"
SM Patrick Chamoiseau, *Slave Old Man*
ST John Clare, "Shadows of Taste"
SW John Clare, "Lament of Swordy Well"
WH G. W. F. Hegel, *Lectures on the Philosophy of World History*
WJ William Wordsworth, *Poems in Two Volumes*

ADRIFT ON THE EARTH

INTRODUCTION

ON THE MORNING OF November 1, 1755, the vessel *Nancy* was suddenly so violently shaken that its captain believed it had run aground, despite the fact it was some distance from the shore. Quickly measuring the depth of the water with a plumbline, he determined that for some strange reason the shock to his ship had been caused by the water actually *rising* approximately thirty feet in two minutes. Initially unaware of why this would be the case, he was among the first to witness and experience just one of the devastating impacts of what later became known as "the Lisbon earthquake." The earthquake occurred along a roughly 500-kilometer stretch of fault line several hundred kilometers from the coast of Portugal. Though seismographs did not yet exist, the quake likely registered at least 8.7 and possibly more than 9.1 on the Richter scale, making it one of the most powerful earthquakes in human history. The forces it unleashed were incredible. The fault itself thrust a roughly 500-kilometer segment of the Earth as much as ten meters up from the ocean floor. It was at least ten times as powerful as the deadliest earthquake in human history: the one that destroyed Haiti in 2010. And its effects were felt as far away as the Caribbean—the tsunami caused by the earthquake traveled westward for ten days, eventually causing a wall of water four meters high to land on the shores of Martinique.[1]

The earthquake crushed the city of Lisbon in the most dramatic of ways, its destruction unfolding in three waves. The first, the earthquake itself, occurring as it did on the morning of All Saints Day, when most of the population was in church, likely killed nearly 10,000 residents instantly as cathedral and house walls caved in on them. When the dust had settled briefly as aftershocks continued to terrify inhabitants, the survivors, huddling by the port to avoid being buried under the crumbling edifices of the city center, were hit by an eastward moving tsunami that, having traveled 200 kilometers from the epicenter, produced a wall of water likely ten to fifteen meters high that drowned nearly everyone close to the shore. The final wave of destruction came in the form of a massive fire caused by the primary modes of heating and light in the city: fireplaces lit to cook the day's festive meal and candles lit to illuminate the interior of churches for those gathered to celebrate the holiday, quickly became the spark, and the scattered debris caused by the earthquake the fuel, for a massive inferno. As the fire spread from the north of the city to the south driven by a brisk dry wind, the temperature of the fire likely reached nearly 1000°C, consuming everything in its path as multiple smaller fires merged with the larger one. It was an unprecedented apocalypse that in a matter of a day leveled a major European capital.[2]

The story of the Lisbon earthquake has been told many times, and it is usually a story about a shift into a new form of modernity. But which one, exactly? Most often, as I will elaborate below, it is the modernity of scientific progress and rationality, as well as the story of human resilience in the face of natural catastrophe. The aftermath of the Lisbon earthquake, as Nicholas Shrady and more recently Mark Molesky have argued, involved a move from treating natural catastrophes as providential retribution for mankind's sins toward understanding them through scientific explanations that sought to find rational accounts for such occurrences, with the hope of avoiding their worst effects in the future. On this account, the Lisbon earthquake has figured as the catalyst for a tale of scientific and human progress—the harbinger of an exclusively European modernity.

There is, however, a different story to tell about its aftermath, one more relevant to our current moment located *in the wake* of this modernity. Though *Adrift on the Earth* is not about the Lisbon earthquake, the narratives that have been generated about it provide a useful heuristic for outlining the stakes of this book. For the quake's catastrophe revealed the terrible and destabilizing indifference of the Earth to human affairs: a nature thought to have been tamed by European humanity reasserted itself, showing with a vengeance that it was not specifically made "for" Man. This emergence of an indifferent Earth in the Lisbon earthquake, however, entailed much more than just the collapse of a belief in its divine creation. The Earth's indifference, rather, pertains to what happens when one wakes up one morning to an Earth that has become radically strange, having slipped its mooring in whatever cosmology or secular philosophy had heretofore given it meaning or made it a center of orientation. It is revealed when one is both abandoned *by* an Earth one thought one knew and abandoned *to* an Earth that has become foreign and destabilizing, no longer reflecting or anchoring current forms of human society or prevailing structures of meaning. It is that opening or transition that is at the heart of this book and that defines what it means to be "adrift" on the Earth. The Lisbon earthquake destabilized existing European conceptions of the Earth, either as a vast repository of material wealth waiting to be exploited, or as a natural force needing to be tamed by an autonomous subjectivity so as to rise above its materiality. The shock of the Lisbon earthquake revealed an untamed and untamable nature in the form of Earth forces capable of leveling human societies in a matter of mere hours. But in the emergence of an Earth entirely indifferent to, and therefore nullifying of, its locus as a resource base or space of conquest that could underwrite narratives of European progress and dominion of the globe, something else began to take shape: a "drift" toward alternative conceptions of the Earth. What might an indifferent or unconquerable Earth imply for ideas of community or historical memory? How would a new relation to the Earth challenge existing conceptions of subjectivity, collective belonging, or notions of progress? It is this understanding and rearticulation of the Earth that is central to the authors gathered in this book, from contemporary Caribbean writers—Édouard Glissant, Erna Brodber, Jacques Roumain, Olive Senior, Patrick Chamoiseau, Frankétienne, and Daniel Maximin—to European Romantics who were writing in the aftermath of the Lisbon event, including William Wordsworth, John Clare, Karoline von Günderrode, and Friedrich Hölderlin. What draws all these diverse authors together under a single banner is what I will call, drawing on Guadeloupian author Daniel Maximin's use of the term, a kind of writing called "geopoetics,"[3] a term whose precise use I will go on to define in more detail briefly, but which is a cousin to what has come to be known as "ecopoetics." Ecopoetics, on the one hand, constitutes an immense field running the gamut from writing concerned with a rearticulation of the relation between humanity and nature, to questions about the possibility of an ecological ethics, to the problem of the relation between ecology and aesthetics.[4] "Geopoetics," on the other hand, tends to privilege an encounter with a nonhuman or, better, *inhuman* Earth, as the means by which immersion in a prior horizon of meaning comes undone. Thus, whereas "geopoetics" signifies for Maximin a geological, cultural, and historical topography of the Caribbean, I employ the term more broadly to describe a form of writing that makes the Earth—and a new relation to it—a central motif.

Allow me to first outline the two conceptual orientations to the Earth that emerged in the wake of Lisbon so as to sharpen my own definition of geopoetics. The first is the well-known narrative about the Enlightenment's theories that framed the earthquake through the idea of humanity's dominance over nature, its right to "possess" the Earth and bend it to human will, or to treat it as a resource for the political and social structures reliant on it. In this narrative the Lisbon earthquake was proof of human rationality's superiority. The other reading of the earthquake, however, is decidedly different to the first and emerges in response to it. Indeed, I follow the old maxim: Romanticism was a response to the Enlightenment,[5] but this maxim is altered slightly here by starting out from their two very different responses to the effects of the earthquake and the emerging science of the time. *Adrift on the Earth* follows this lesser-known story by indexing an emerging awareness of the Earth's anteriority to every human society, every human community, along with the essentially asymmetrical relation between the Earth and human society entailed in that relationship. If the Lisbon earthquake revealed anything, according to this interpretation of the event, it was that human societies, human worlds, were intrinsically bound up with the Earth, dependent on it for their very existence. And the Earth? The Earth, on the other hand, could do quite well without us—it could just as easily turn against human habitation as support it. The Earth's indifference emerges, then, not just when it threatens to overturn human life, but also when it has ceased to occupy a place within a familiar framework of meaning, calling that framework fundamentally into question. This shock at what one might call the "epistemological level" is then followed either by the collapse of the privilege and legitimacy of the previous framework, or by a reintroduction of the Earth's indifference into a different horizon of meaning—or both. The emergence of an indifferent Earth, in other words, clears a space in which other relations to the Earth become possible. These other relations to the Earth are not necessarily identical with its indifference, but they are nevertheless predicated upon it. When, for example, Daniel Maximin in *Les fruits du cyclone: Une géopoetique de la Caraïbe* (Fruits of the cyclone: A geopoetics of the Caribbean) suggests that the Earth was an ally to marooning slaves in the Caribbean because it provided them with a form of subsistence external to the plantation system that allowed large and growing maroon communities to exist and persist,[6] this does not affect the Earth's indifference; it was neither for nor against the plantation system. But what the maroon's relation of subsistence to the Earth does—through an interaction with it that is no longer bound up with its status as a vessel or repository for European cash crops—is articulate a new understanding of the Earth that becomes the basis for a different *kind* of communal identity. The Earth's indifference, then, is the disruption necessary for the articulation of a new world or horizon of meaning, at least up to the point where its potentially destabilizing force leaves such a possibility open. As we will see, the historical configuration I call "Caribbean Romanticism" examined in this book covers a variety of responses to the Earth's indifference, from perceiving it as the basis for new forms of nomadic or postcapitalist community, to darker visions that regard the current iteration of an indifferent and at times destructive Earth as the potential end of *any* future horizon of meaning. In each case, rather than attempt to cordon off the Earth's indifference by situating it within a narrative of scientific progress, the geopoetics of the authors I examine forces an encounter with a destabilizing Earth that can no longer been seen as a ground to be possessed or mastered, or as the foundation for dominion and authority.

This is why it is important to differentiate what might be called the belated Romantic response to the Lisbon earthquake from its Enlightenment cousin. What, then, were the new scientific theories and conceptions of the Earth that emerged during and after the Lisbon earthquake that the Romantics responded to? How did they come about, what prompted them, and how did they enter the circulation of ideas? Enlightenment debates about the earthquake have usually been couched in terms of the advent of scientific explanations for natural disasters. When Voltaire pens his famous "Poem on the Lisbon Disaster," subtitled "An Inquiry Into the Maxim 'Whatever Is, Is Right,'" which questions the notion of a benevolent God; when Rousseau responds to Voltaire's poem with an essay condemning Lisbon's city planning and construction for the overall death toll; and when Kant explains the earthquake in terms of gas emissions in the Earth, likely inspired by the emerging field of volcanology, it is as though all the quintessential exemplars of the European Enlightenment had been deployed to frame the Lisbon earthquake as a natural and empirically accountable phenomenon.[7]

A seldom-noted ethical and political dimension permeates these views of the Lisbon earthquake, however. Even in the texts where Kant elaborated on what he thought were purely mechanical, scientifically measurable causes for the earthquake, he was compelled in the end to address the main *non*natural explanation: "We see that an infinite number of evildoers sleep in peace," he writes, "earthquakes have shattered certain countries since time immemorial with total indifference to the old and new inhabitants," while "cities that could not presume to be any less punishable than others" were similarly destroyed.[8] And although in his theory of earthquakes, as in his moral philosophy, God is merely a regulative principle—purely unnecessary as a precondition for understanding the event (or for moral action)—in his later aesthetic philosophy in which he addresses the concept of the sublime, Kant doesn't shy away from introducing the might and power of earthquakes as a touchstone. As Alexander Regier has shown, Kant tasked himself with cordoning off the disturbing prospect of an indifferent Earth through the experience of an aesthetic distance that reaffirms autonomous individual subjectivity.[9] His concept of the sublime in its various incarnations thus manages to reassert and fortify humanity's separation from the natural world at the precise moment it had seemed to be most overwhelmed by it.[10] In the *Third Critique*, written thirty-five years after the Lisbon earthquake, various natural calamities, including "thunder clouds towering up into the heavens . . . volcanoes with their all-destroying violence"[11] and earthquakes figure as conduits for the feeling of an internal sublimity and the infinity of reason it produces. The power of nature to destroy human habitation, to overwhelm its very physical existence, is redirected into a narrative of human autonomy that becomes the basis of humanity's "freedom" from natural constraints. When Kant explicitly excludes God as a source of the feeling of "awe" that arises from the sublime, he does so because that feeling points *solely* to the rational freedom of a human subject who, giving itself its own moral laws fundamentally distinct from the laws of nature, supersedes its physical need for survival in favor of principles worth more than its own natural life. In other words, for Kant the Lisbon earthquake triggers the reaffirmation of humanity's separation not only from God, but from natural forces as well.

The Romantics begged to differ—some more, or differently, than others. Heinrich von Kleist, a Romantic who explicitly wrote about the Lisbon earthquake, centered his short story "Earthquake in Chile" entirely on the collapse of biblical and moral explanations, and on the threat of human violence unleashed by the destruction of social laws.[12] What does not happen in the story, however, is any discussion of the indifference of the Earth to human concerns, except in the context of chance or the need to make sense of human suffering.

While "Chile" certainly joins with Kleist's many other explorations of what might be called "experiences of the extreme,"[13] it frames the significance of the earthquake entirely in terms of the ensuing collapse of social order and civil law. The story centers around two lovers—Jerónimo Rugera and Doña Josefa—whose illicit love affair is discovered by Josefa's father, "one of the richest noblemen of the city."[14] Though she is sent to a convent, their affair continues, issuing in a child born out of wedlock for which Josefa is sentenced to death and Jerónimo imprisoned. On the day her sentence is set to be carried out, an earthquake levels Santiago. As Jerónimo prepares to commit suicide, he is rescued by chance: the walls of the very pillar on which he had sought to hang himself collapse onto the buildings across the street, saving him from being crushed by the debris. Meanwhile Josefa is spared death at the scaffold and returns to the convent to collect her young child. Initially framing these events in terms of chance or accident, the story's conclusion centers on the question of what organizes a system of law and justice in the wake of the sheer contingency of events and social collapse. On the one hand, Josefa and Jerónimo find each other again and seem to be at least temporarily forgiven for their "sins" as the earthquake levels all social distinctions. People who are otherwise on the margins of society are now demonstrating "selflessness and more than human self-sacrifice" (EC 318/152), going so far as to endanger their own lives to save others in a quasi-Kantian gesture of transcendent moral values over and above mere survival.[15] On the other hand, the same appeal to transcendent justice animates a mob that, having been coaxed into believing that the earthquake was divine retribution for the community's tolerance of Josefa and Jerónimo's transgression, proceeds to kill them along with any innocents standing nearby. For Kleist, therefore, the earthquake is an occasion to examine the radical exigency of social and moral law, as well as the violence that subtends it once the social order has collapsed. Since there is no way of knowing whether the earthquake is accidental or preordained, we are left with the violent and murderous reaction of a mob trying to make sense of the catastrophe and needing a culprit. While Kleist's explanations, unlike Kant's, establish a realm of possible *moral* indifference, his main interest is in the earthquake's leveling effects and the violence that results from bestowing a divine significance on it. Where Kant's and Kleist's interpretations of the earthquake converge, in other words, is on the question of human freedom and the forces unleashed by this devastating event from the standpoint of human moral and social worlds.

It may seem surprising, then, that it is the Romantics on whom I focus in this study, and less the supposedly more scientific Enlightenment thinkers mentioned above, who dwelt on the more *de*stabilizing consequences of an indifferent and temporally prior Earth that was slowly being discovered in the science of the period. Whereas Enlightenment debates about the seeming indifference of the Earth to human moral and political realms prompted a kind of doubling down on the notion of the exceptionality of the human and its moral disconnection from the natural world, the science of the time was beginning to demonstrate that the history of the Earth simply did not coincide with the history of humanity *at all*. The Romantics I gather in this book lingered on these theories: If the history of the Earth is far longer than first thought, and if there is only one Earth, then perhaps there is more than one form of nature in its history. What had existed on the Earth in terms of flora and fauna prior to humanity was possibly fundamentally different from the present, and likely inhospitable to humanity's existence. As Alan Bewell has convincingly argued, the Romantics put serious pressure on the idea of nature as a concept in the singular, in part due to the period's growing awareness of the much larger expanses of time that constitute the natural history of the Earth.[16] One of the domains in which this was most evident was geological science, which was no stranger to the plurality of natures. The debate between "Neptunists," represented for instance by German geologist Abraham Gottlob Werner, who determined that the Earth was formed out of a vast ocean, and "Vulcanists" such as Italian geologist Scipione Breislak, who claimed the Earth's surface formations were created by the heat of volcanic energy, implied that the ancient Earth looked significantly different from its present constitution. Though the British preferred to name their own theories of deep time according to different gods, James Hutton's "Plutonist" theory, later popularized by Charles Lyell, intimated not only that the early Earth was far older and far different geographically and climactically than today's, but that its precise age was uncertain.[17] This spurred the further question of whether the Earth had changed gradually from the ancient past (a position known as "uniformitarianism," shared by Hutton and Lyell) or was shaped by catastrophic natural events such as massive floods, traces of which could still be found in the present landscape.[18] Either way, nature was becoming less and less singular, indeed more plural by the day as science understood that the singular planet Earth had its own nonhuman history.

This awareness was reinforced as some of these ideas began to filter into poetic and philosophical writing of the period. German *Naturphilosophie*, for example, attempted to account for the entirety of the natural world in terms of a developmental model in which nature's inherent rationality gradually unfolded. It thereby considered not just the logical but also the *temporal* dimension of nature's capacity to change and evolve. Across the channel in England, Charlotte Smith's poetry invoked the "late theories of the earth"[19] to explain the deposits of fossil shells too high up on the cliff walls to be there accidentally,[20] thus ushering into the literary imagination the idea that the Earth had once hosted not only bygone human societies but also vanished forms of nature. When Percy Shelley, famously musing on the sublime mountaintop of "Mont Blanc,"[21] asked "Did a sea / Of fire, envelope once this silent snow?," he ventriloquized Vulcanist arguments about the formation of the Earth. The nonreply that follows in the poem ("none can reply—all seems eternal now")[22] suggests less that nature is "eternal" than the possibility of a temporal disjunction between its deep past and its present formation.

The interest in and awareness of what might be called the sciences of "deep time," however, were not without attendant conceptualization (and poetic representation) of what this might mean for human societies. If natures rose and fell like empires, and if human societies in some fashion depended on a specific conception of nature for their existence, what then was the relationship between the indifferent and temporally anterior Earth and the many human societies and political formations that had materialized on its surface over the course of human history? While the notion of an indifferent Earth exists primarily in the realm of science and refers to a purely *geological* substrate for a broader history of nature, the *ideas* of nature on which human societies depend seem confined to a distinctly human history that represents the natural world in a specific way. Frédéric Neyrat's catalog of the various "deaths of nature" that constitute what he calls the West's "a-naturalist drive"—from nature's reduction to an instrument of God's will, to its mechanization in the seventeenth century, to its commodification with the rise of global capital[23]—outlines what nearly all the Romantic authors represented in this book sensed: not only is nature plural, significantly predating humanity and the present, but its imbrication with a historically determined human polity implies that each historical moment establishes its *own* conception of nature, its own cosmology or "world." To clarify: my use of the term "world" designates a nexus of meanings in which things emerge or signify in and through some system of value.[24] This includes nature of course, which, depending on the world with which it is associated, can appear, for example, as a source of energy, or as an object of scientific study, or as a territory to be conquered. A "world" can therefore also be understood as a network of relationships among different entities, as in Greek cosmologies that structured the relationships among gods, humans, and animals. When Keats's "Ode to Psyche," for instance, situates Psyche's past existence in the world of ancient Greece—"When holy were the haunted forest boughs / Holy the air, the water, and the fire"—it conveys two historically specific conceptions of nature. The first is the ancient Greek idea of nature as a set of elements (air, water, earth, and fire) animated by myth; the second is the modern scientific understanding of nature articulated at the end of the poem, by which point the Greek world has vanished and what remains is the "soft delight / That shadowy thought can win"[25] of the speaker's modern relation to nature.

An objection could be raised at this point: Doesn't the plurality of natures enabled by the deep time of the Earth's geological past at least preserve those various periods of natural history as themselves independent from or indifferent to human social structures? The fact that the Earth has had multiple climates or eras in its past in no way implies that its natural history is equivalent to the human history of successive *conceptions* of nature. By equating the two, doesn't one risk effacing precisely the Earth's indifference to human moral and political worlds? Bewell details this objection when he takes Phil Macnaghten and John Urry to task for their argument in *Contested Natures* that there is "only a diversity of contested natures; and that each such nature is constituted through a variety of sociocultural processes from which such natures cannot be plausibly separated"[26] by arguing that this perspective effectively "dissolves the materiality of the natural world into social forces and relationships."[27] However, to claim that there is an inextricable connection between social formations and the conception of nature on which they rely is not the same thing as claiming that there is *no* fundamental alterity or reality to the natural world outside of human social forces and relationships. As Louis Althusser has shown, ideology—in this case a particular human society's idea of nature—"represents the imaginary relationship of individuals to their real conditions of existence." That is, even the multiple conceptions of nature that are the historical product of social forces and relationships nevertheless "make allusion to reality."[28] There is the real and there is the imagined *relation* to that real that exists in specific material social and cultural practices. The financialization of nature, its transformation into an fungible commodity, for example, might very well imagine the reality of the Earth's limited resources from within an illusory conception of a "nature" capable, like the financial markets, of limitless growth, but that doesn't prevent financial capital from acting *as if* there were no material limits to its needs, with all the thoroughgoing consequences of the sixth mass extinction and the collapse of the biosphere we are experiencing today. In other words, to begin to call into question the imagined relation between a social formation and the conception of nature on which it depends is also to create room for *another* understanding of that relationship based on a form of nature it *does not* invent or constitute. This, in effect, was how the Romantics grouped in *Adrift on the Earth* positioned themselves: while there may have been a succession of different historically specific conceptions of nature built into the self-understanding of various human worlds at various moments in human history, these are all dependent on the history of an Earth that remains essentially distinct from that succession, while at the same time figuring as that history's condition of possibility. There is the indifference of the Earth, in other words, and then there is the elision or interpretation of that indifference in and through the history of the succession of human worlds.

What binds the Romantics gathered in this book together, therefore, is not just their belonging to a literary period known as Romanticism, but their common understanding of the Earth—namely, that it is external to every concept of nature and to every world that attempts to obfuscate or ignore it. The Earth, on one hand, cannot be pluralized like the various politically charged ideas of "nature" specific to particular human societies,[29] whereas the various worldly *relations* to the Earth's indifference, on the other hand, can be. As an un-constructible indifference, the Earth is the ground of the many other worlds or *cosmoi* that have come and gone on its surface, constituting what might be called their "unconditionality."[30] Localizing yet unlocalizable, ungrounded yet silently grounding, the Earth is the precondition for any and every particular world.[31] And yet, it could also suddenly unleash forces humanity could neither control nor master, fundamentally destabilizing those worlds. For the Romantics, this was an Earth even more external to civil society than the one society had invented as the "state of nature" from which it had supposedly emerged into the social contract. The fragility of human and animal life led these writers to quite different conclusions from Enlightenment narratives concerning the nature of progress, human history, and civil society. If the Earth was indifferent to human political and moral concerns, its independence or alterity suggested that it was more than simply an object that could be acquired or conquered. The Romantic countercurrent I examine here thus challenged central liberal ideas about the relationship between society and property as represented, for instance, by Locke's philosophy, which takes the Earth to be a material good or commodity that can be appropriated by mingling the autonomous subject's active labor with a supposedly inert nature.[32] Rather, the Earth, for the Romantics studied here, is ungraspable and therefore fundamentally inappropriable—a "sublime" far more inhuman than the Enlightenment's ideas about the individual self.[33] This was an Earth that emerges when the ostensibly stable ground under our feet begins to heave, shift, and cave, dislocating faith in rational progress along with humanity's ability to extricate itself from its enmeshment in forces beyond its control.[34] To cycle back to the example with which I began, the Romantics pick up on another legacy of the Lisbon earthquake that takes us in a decidedly different direction from the Enlightenment desire to stabilize the human subject in the face of the overwhelming power of nature. What entered the picture, post-Lisbon, was an awareness of the extent to which the conditions of a stable sense of self, a stable society, a stable metropole and its colonies, a stable conception of nature—in short, stability of *any* kind—are thoroughly dependent on a ground that is not so grounding after all and that, as Dipesh Chakrabarty puts it, "does not return our gaze."[35] That indifference produces an opening that not only displaces existing conceptions of the Earth and nature, but also opens up a new conception of the Earth that now must take into account its own contingent formation, as well as its belonging to a historically specific world.

While fears of the Earth turning against the possibility of human habitation may, until recently, have seemed distant to readers in the Western world,[36] these fears are not so remote to island communities—most notably small island nations threatened with inundation thanks to rising sea levels caused by global climate change. Of course, the difference between Lisbon and our own moment of the Anthropocene is that our fully global disaster is much slower moving and indisputably produced by human activity. And yet, the conceptual frameworks that turned Lisbon and other Western metropoles into major colonial powers—the understanding of the human and its freedom promoted by the Enlightenment, as well as the relation between political structures and the natural world that made the latter subservient to the former—generated the kind of modernity that still fuels the Anthropocene. These frameworks, moreover, were being consolidated in the eighteenth and nineteenth century in the aftermath of the Lisbon earthquake. And as Daniel Maximin puts it in *Fruits of the cyclone*, if the disaster of the Lisbon earthquake prompted reflection in Europe on the "innocence" of Man with regard to natural calamities, the cyclical nature of the natural disasters afflicting the Caribbean highlights instead "the secret laws of a logic of the living, alongside the disasters caused by humans."[37] In other words, while the European Enlightenment saw the Lisbon earthquake in terms of an innocent humanity faced with an unconcerned nature, for Maximin Caribbean geopoetics highlights the relation between an indifferent Earth and specifically *human* sociopolitical disasters, underscoring how European conceptions of nature and human freedom were intricately bound up with calamitous social forms such as slavery and the plantation economy. Because, as Maximin argues, regularly occurring natural disasters such as cyclones in many cases helped limit or impede the plantation system—even if only temporarily—Caribbean geopoetics tends to foreground an indifferent Earth that nevertheless often acts *as if* it is on the side of the "living," opening another kind of freedom different from the "freedom" of the Enlightenment autonomous subject to enslave others.

Of course, the Caribbean became, precisely during the Romantic period, the site of a world-historic event—the Haitian Revolution[38]—which directly challenged key Enlightenment ideas about what it means to be human, along with the notion of the rights-bearing subject as the center of political power. As the French Revolution collapsed into Napoleonic authoritarianism, it became clear that what Kant had interpreted as the promise of the former—the French Revolution as an "event of our time which demonstrates this Moral tendency in the human race"[39]—clearly hadn't been realized. Though the Haitian Revolution has often been interpreted as a tributary of its French counterpart, the partial (and racially determined) conception of universality from the Preamble to the French Constitution concerning the "Rights of Man" was in fact laid bare and a genuinely revolutionary promise was restored in the Haitian rather than the French event. Though the Jacobins abolished slavery in 1794, they did so grudgingly and in the hope of enlisting Haiti's rebelling slaves in their war against nearly every other colonial power in Europe, as Spain and England both vied for control of the colony. By the time the Haitian Revolution became a war for national independence—because it was clear that the French expedition sent by Napoleon in late 1801 was only going to restore slavery—it also became clear that the emancipatory promise of the French Revolution had shifted geographic locales. When the "unthinkable" finally happened in 1804 and the Haitian revolutionaries declared the first Black Republic, the shock of that unprecedented event was genuine and should not be underestimated, even though it was quickly suppressed in European historical consciousness in part because every Western colonial power, including the United States, had slave colonies and plantation economies threatened by the example of Haitian independence. The Haitian Revolution had exposed the material underbelly—slavery—that underwrote European emancipatory promises, while achieving something few had thought possible: actual emancipation. And it revealed the extent to which European liberalism—including Enlightenment conceptions of the social contract, its understanding of nature, the Earth and non-European peoples as a form of property—were all ideas and philosophies harnessed to a set of brutal exclusions that proclaimed "freedom" for select European rights-holders while subjecting Europe's colonies and the non-Europeans in them to forced migration, colonial subjugation, and enslavement. In short, the very Enlightenment ideas that had supposedly underwritten various emancipatory promises were at the same time crucial mechanisms in the art of colonial subjugation and expansion.

If the particular form of "humanity" Kant perceives as surmounting its natural confines in the face of natural catastrophes such as the Lisbon earthquake was the progenitor of its own catastrophes—from the global expansion of extraction economies to the systems of forced labor that made them possible—then it is crucial to look back at this period, and the one that followed from it, from the perspective of the present. How did we get here, and more importantly, how did a countercurrent to the triumphalism of the European liberal subject expanding itself across the globe present itself during this period in ways that are relevant *for* the present? What if the Haitian Revolution was just the beginning of a challenge to the modernity that had established itself across the globe in the late eighteenth and early nineteenth century? If the Lisbon earthquake, and by extension our Anthropocenic moment, were as much about the literal ground of the Earth giving way as it was about other grounds—economic, ecological, philosophical and conceptual—falling along with it, grounds that continue to come undone as the form of modernity that was taking shape then continues to unravel now, then Lisbon represents the arrival of a very different and much more precarious modernity than the one usually attributed to it.

What exactly is the link between our present moment and the indifferent Earth that so dramatically revealed itself in the Lisbon earthquake? The link is the *extent* to which human-made disasters (slavery and the plantation system) are inseparable from the supposedly natural disasters of the Earth (cyclones, sea-level rise, deforestation, and a host of other calamities induced by the modernity that was taking shape at the time of the Lisbon earthquake). To put it in familiar terms: if in the era of the Anthropocene humans have become the equivalent of a geological force, it is because our use of energy, the extraction of fossil fuels that powered the industrial and agricultural revolutions, threatens to raise the Earth's temperature well above the 1.5°C the Intergovernmental Panel on Climate Change has targeted as the point above which massive changes in the Earth's systems will have become unstoppable, as some of them already are. That this is the result of the continued expansion and insatiable energy needs of global capital is beyond any doubt. That these needs are an extension of the resource extraction that took place primarily in the global South during the period of colonial expansion, most significantly in the eighteenth and nineteenth centuries, is also beyond any doubt. The first forced migration of the Anthropocene is not today's environmental refugees fleeing the inundation of their lands by rising seas but the Middle Passage, when human labor was required to transform growing regions seized from indigenous populations in the newly colonized Caribbean into vast plantation economies that buttressed European metropoles. To say that a similar dynamic with a different form of slavery remains largely in place today would be saying too little. For when the earthquake swallowed Lisbon, Portugal was just entering its so-called second golden age of colonial expansion. It was the first European power to import slaves from West Africa in the fifteenth century, and its former colony Brazil was one of the last to abolish slavery in 1888. What must have seemed one of the most stable institutions on the Earth—a Western metropole—faltered under the weight of its own rubble. Indeed, in the years after the earthquake, Portugal lost an estimated 32 to 48 percent of its total GDP, relegating it to a secondary colonial power.[40] If the Lisbon earthquake revealed an indifferent Earth, that indifference nevertheless produced profound global political effects, as Caribbean geopoetics would underscore two centuries later.

To be clear: this book is not interested in charting the Anthropocene's beginning or its driving force since these questions seem either obvious (global capitalism) or irrelevant (should we trace it back to Columbus or to Thomas Savery?), attempting as they do to pinpoint an era that has no single origin but is instead a network of often anachronistic discourses and practices. However, one still ought to begin with obvious causality: no mass transformation of the globe into European-controlled growing zones for cash crops, no mass extraction of fossil fuels and other energy sources for the expansion of global capital, no enslavement of non-European peoples, no Anthropocene. This indisputable starting point should subsequently lead us into a set of intricacies that have to do with the shifting conceptual scaffolding underpinning these phenomena: racialized conceptions of the human, emerging notions of the social contract, and changing conceptions of nature among them. All these formed a nexus of ontological commitments essential for the colonial division of the planet and the extraction economies that ensued. In the case of the Earth, for instance, colonial expansion had to first make it a unified object or *thing* that could be appropriated and distributed into zones of influence. While the first wave of colonialism took place under the sign of divine right on an Earth bequeathed to those chosen by God, the eighteenth and nineteenth centuries would conceive of the Earth in terms of a partition and appropriation of land that founded not just the newly republican nation-state, but also its "right" to colonies. This understanding of the Earth—still prevailing today—conceived of it as a vast domain distributed between friend and enemy, an enormous globe waiting to be appropriated, allocated, or reassigned through the dispossession of indigenous inhabitants deemed inferior, or by any other means. In other words, the Earth became a "resource base," a commodity to be enclosed, possessed, and mastered in much the same way as the non-European inhabitants occupying those newly conquered territories.

In the chapters that follow, I focus on the emergence of this conceptual scaffolding and examine it from the perspective of two countercurrents I see as ensuing from it: on the one hand, in writers usually associated with European Romanticism as I have already detailed above, and on the other, in contemporary writers and thinkers of the Caribbean who respond to the legacies of that period and whose connection to the Romantics I detail in what follows.

Why these two traditions? And what does contemporary Caribbean thought and aesthetics have to do with, say, Wordsworth? As I have already suggested, Romanticism belongs to and ventriloquizes the time and place—late eighteenth- and early nineteenth-century Europe—when new scientific breakthroughs in geology and biology began to wrest the natural world, and specifically the Earth, from their anchor in religious dogma. The Romantics were well versed in contemporary geological theories, but they were also insistently creating alternative models of community, new ways of living with and on the Earth, in the era of high colonialism. But because these new scientific horizons went hand in hand with Europe's colonial expansion of its territorial horizons—let's not forget Hegel's injunction that geography determines a culture's historical "progress"—today's Caribbean authors, whose ancestors were silenced by that very concatenation of science and politics, find it imperative to respond directly to that period and therefore indirectly to some of its most radical thinkers. In engaging with the concepts, aesthetics, and politics of colonialism, Romanticism articulates a countercurrent view of the Earth and its inhabitants by disarticulating the conceptual scaffolding underpinning European exceptionalism. Contemporary Caribbean authors, I argue, deepen and extend that tradition, updating it for our contemporary moment.[41]

This brings me to my title and the seemingly strange neologism "Caribbean Romanticism." Needless to say, no such thing existed in the late eighteenth and nineteenth centuries—it is not a literary historical term. Seanna Sumalee Oakley's *Common Places: The Poetics of African Atlantic Postromantics*, the only major study to date to address the relation between twentieth- and twenty-first-century Caribbean authors and European Romanticism, claims that contemporary Caribbean authors updated several poetic forms and tropes first developed by French and English Romantic poets to revisit the themes of utopian desire, redemption, and the everyday. They did so, Oakley claims, while at the same time challenging what she sees as Romanticism's universalist pretensions and its "mystified individualism."[42] My approach is different: rather than tracing questions of influence, *Adrift on the Earth* rereads a countercurrent within Romanticism *through* the forms and ideas of contemporary Caribbean authors with the aim, on the one hand, of reimagining Romanticism from the standpoint of its suppressed colonial foundations and, on the other, of reading contemporary Caribbean literature as a response *to* that very suppression. In revising both, "Caribbean Romanticism" figures as an interpretative diplopia in that it designates a strain in Romanticism that becomes visible only once the poetic experiments to which its themes and forms have been harnessed are made explicit in the geopolitical context of the present, namely, in the perdurance of neocolonialism, its role in the acceleration of global warming, and the continued aftermath of the racial hierarchies that underpinned European colonial expansion—that is, the entirety of the liberal conceptual scaffolding to which the Romantics were reacting and which is central to the concerns of contemporary Caribbean authors. The result allows us to see affinities that might not otherwise be discernible and to make the case for a persistent geopoetics extending back at least to the late eighteenth century. As opposed to the universalism and individualism we are accustomed to seeing as central to Romanticism, a stranger version emerges here that encompasses what it means to be "adrift" on the Earth: unrooted or uprooted, without house or home, while nonetheless producing a poetic relation to an Earth that binds different communities together without reducing them to one another. Being "adrift" on the Earth thus means also taking up a different relation to identity than the idea of being anchored in a particular place or homeland. It means confronting an indifferent Earth as the starting point for a new conception of global relations between other peoples and other worlds. It means reconceiving human temporality in terms of the Earth's, and it means rethinking how the Earth functions as the foundation of human memory, history, and identity. More than just a cosmopolitanism or nomadism, being "adrift" involves a recognition of the fundamentally contingent relation between human societies and the Earth.

It is to these author's various geopoetic imaginings of the Earth that this book is directed. The term "geopoetics" is neither new nor my own and has a history that predates even Maximin's use of it. Mary Modeen and Iain Biggs ascribe it to American geologist Harry Hess, who coined it in one of the first papers on the science of plate tectonics.[43] Conversely, Kenneth White's Geopoetics Institute aligns the term with the development of a "potential world-culture," by which he means a kind of neocosmopolitanism.[44] In *Adrift on the Earth* this term is closer to Hess than White in that it has less to do with a global culture than with an Earth that is the immanent basis for all human worlds, cultures, and civil polities, while nevertheless remaining irreducible to them. In fact, in this definition of the Earth I am simply following the writers gathered in this book: for what binds them together, more so than the periods, traditions, or stylistic movements they belong to, is their general if unacknowledged consensus that the Earth precedes and potentially supersedes any specific world, any culture or national identity located in a particular geographic space. Each author I consider writes from within their own geographical locale but does so in the name of a set of nonhuman forces that constitute an Earth that cannot be owned—an Earth that destabilizes every distribution of geography into zones for resource extraction. Rather than attempting to express a distribution of the Earth, geopoetics in my sense conceives of the Earth otherwise.

To what ends? Those too are various: while they coalesce around a set of concerns that challenge existing and persisting forms of colonialism and land appropriation, the geopoetics in the book's title pertains to a writing that is not just *about* the Earth but *of* and located *in* the Earth. As I said, for the authors studied here, the Earth is circumscribed by its own history independent from human presence or action. It inscribes on its surface not only prehistoric traces, but also those of ancient or exterminated civilizations, some of which were deliberately effaced from historical narratives to vindicate the present social order. The Earth thus becomes, for some of these authors, reimagined as an archive, particularly in Caribbean writers like Chamoiseau and Senior, giving voice to cultures and peoples erased by the history of colonialism, allowing them to retroactively assert their defiance and persistence from within the neocolonialism of the present. For others—Roumain for example—a newly inappropriable Earth is conceived as a vast commons that resists enclosure, thereby enabling a new form of collectivity. In each case, geopoetics is a name for an attempt to rethink the present spatial and political organization of the planet in the face of its fundamental anteriority to every world on its surface, that is, its ultimate indifference to current conceptions of nature or autonomous subjectivity. This book articulates the multiple ways in which that indifference is redeployed to make other ways of relating to the Earth possible, ones that cannot be fully integrated into existing political formations.

Why then restrict the application of this term to a set of European Romantics and contemporary Caribbean poets? While geopoetics can certainly be found in other traditions and historical periods, the authors gathered in this book dramatize and emphasize an important nexus of problems that originated in Europe during the Romantic period but continue to resonate as the same problems today in the vulnerable island nations of the Caribbean, one of the first laboratories of European colonialism. Note, however: I am not suggesting that Caribbean thinkers were *influenced* by the Romantics in any direct literary or aesthetic way—that would be too reductive philosophically and too suspect politically. My wager instead is this: as they look back at the shifting conceptions of the Earth that were being forged in tandem with scientific breakthroughs and with political (democratic, revolutionary, abolitionist) narratives of the early nineteenth century, Caribbean writers often take the opportunity to respond to *that* era which had extinguished the voices of their ancestors. They do so by fostering their own geopoetics in which the Earth again appears in a lead role, this time as the subject of our *present* historical moment—the Anthropocene. Situated as they are in the space of an archipelago exposed to rising seas, the people of the Caribbean comprehend better than any continental nation the relation between those rising seas and the persistent geopolitical conception of the Earth and of the human that has brought us to this point.[45] And because they write from an archipelago, their Earth is one where the ocean is everywhere—an Earth ultimately in flux which, by its mobile nature, crafts alternatives to grounded or rooted forms of identity and property. In all these cases, in other words, pressure is being put on central tenets of the conceptual scaffolding grounding Western notions of identity as rooted in place—from the privilege of specific ideas about what defines the human, to the belief that any sense of identity takes shape only in relation to an other. To be "adrift" on the Earth for these modern Caribbean authors is thus also to allow the Earth's instability to become a starting point for forms of belonging no longer modeled on monolithic or autochthonous lines of filiation.

Adrift on the Earth is therefore neither a period nor a comparative study. It is both and neither—a study in elective affinities, if you will, in that it refracts the Romantics through contemporary Caribbean authors. While the Romantics in their turn respond to imperial conceptions of the Earth, each Caribbean writer here articulates a relationship between the Earth and the legacies of eighteenth- and nineteenth-century colonialism on the one hand, and the geopolitics of the present on the other, including the vast economic burdens levied on the global South in the accelerating ecological catastrophe of climate change. The Caribbean authors therefore extend and radicalize some of the Romantics' insights and conceptions about geology's relationship to the political by articulating anew the link between the civil polity and the Earth, allowing us to see the contemporary purchase of Romantic geopoetics. The ecological and colonial devastation the Caribbean witnessed, and under which it continues to suffer, is at the center of our current ecological concerns—a compressed microcosm of what is now a worldwide phenomenon. If the Caribbean authors I consider here invent their own geopoetics to respond to the legacies of this prior moment of colonial enslavement, they also link that past to our contemporary stage of global modernity when international capital envisions the Earth as a unified proprietorship, a notion that threatens various geographies, particularly small island nations and communities, with further devastation. To frame a Romanticist thinking of the Earth through Glissant, Brodber, Roumain, Senior, Chamoiseau, Maximin, and Frankétienne is not merely to show the contemporary relevance and continuity of

Romantic-era ideas of the Earth; it is also to allow the poetic traditions of the Caribbean, as the suppressed material ground of those ideas, to decide how they are interpreted.

How, then, do contemporary and Romantic geopoetics reimagine the relation between the Earth and various collectivities, both local and global? Focusing primarily on the concept of the social contract that underpins liberal conceptions of community, this book examines what happens in geopoetry when the supposedly fundamental distinction between the civil order and nature is disarticulated by something—the Earth—even more heterogeneous to the social order than the "state of nature" it supposedly left behind. Liberal or republican social contracts grant civil rights to individuals on the basis of their "natural rights," producing, in Bruno Latour's terminology, the "two houses" of modernity.[46] In the first house are the citizens of a polity who acquire rights by having acceded to a social contract, while the second house hosts everything that is excluded from the political, and from the rights granted to citizens, including slaves, women, animals, and, ultimately, nature itself, all of which become available for use or exploitation. Such notions of the social contract effectively generated a political ecology, that is, a particular understanding of the relationship between the social, and what lies outside of it, and is therefore bereft of political standing. Ecology, a term coined by Ernst Haeckel to designate the scientific study of an animal's relationship to its surrounding environment, takes on a new meaning here, particularly insofar as "ecology" is related to its etymological roots in the Greek word *oikos* (household or home). Latour's "two houses" of modernity is in fact a single *oikos*: an "ecology" that designates the proper place of belonging for various beings, whether they are inside the social space and thus given "rights," or are bereft of them due to their status as beings without social standing. Geopoetics, however, often frames its encounter with the Earth in relation to an experience of the *loss* of a world, the loss of a prior sense of orientation or belonging, a way of centering the self in a particular locale.[47] Its conception of the Earth comes to the fore in the context of the collapse of coordinates that set the Earth into a recognizable cosmology, locating our feet firmly on its solid ground or in a recognizable "home." When the Earth intervenes in the form of an earthquake, a tsunami, or when it indexes the death of an entire world, a more unsettling idea of it emerges—an idea we no longer recognize as a "homeland," a place of rest, or as the basis for a sense of rootedness. This is why I choose the term "geopoetics" over and against "ecopoetics"; the latter term still tends, for the most part, to privilege a relation to the *oikos*, an orientation that focuses on the desire for a relatively stable relation between human worlds and their surrounding environment. For most of the authors read here, the Earth is fundamentally, to begin with, *de*localizing, and only subsequently—if at all—*re*localizing.[48] In my conception of geopoetics, ecology thus becomes less a matter of a relation to, or circumscription by, a surrounding environment than an encounter with a materiality that disrupts our sense of self, our security of place or belonging. When coupled with the social contract's idea of the distinction between nature and the social, an indifferent Earth becomes the means by which to reconceive that relationship, thereby also reimagining who or what belongs to an *oikos* or home, and who or what remains systematically excluded from it.

Geopoetics thus becomes a *political* ecology in that it defines the social order's relationship to what is outside of it and therefore excluded from the "rights" granted to those who are recognized as belonging to the civil polity. It does this in two ways: first by showing that a particular society's conception of nature is anything but universal—it is instead a historically determined idea that every such grouping relies on to justify existing economic and social structures. Nature, in this sense, once again, is distinct from the Earth's indifference; it is a necessary *fiction* of the social, justifying how it is formed and who and what has value or rights. Secondly, geopoetics rearticulates the social exclusions built into that conception of nature *through* a recognition of the indifferent Earth. The list of noncitizens in Latour's "second house" is potentially wide-ranging and could include nonhuman entities of various kinds, from animals to humans who have been dehumanized by their position in a racial hierarchy. Geopoetics involves the reinvention of those conceptual coordinates through an encounter with a destabilized and destabilizing Earth.

Needless to say, the nonuniversality of the decision determining who has standing as a political entity and who does not was most brutally and directly exemplified in the Caribbean slave colonies. Elements of the Western imaginary had for centuries equated and treated indigenous cultures on colonized lands and African slaves as simply part of the landscape, beings still fully immersed in nature, understood at best as a version of Rousseau's "savage man,"[49] but more often as entities bereft of culture or history, either like a passive backdrop against which the drama of European history plays out, or like trees and rocks standing in the way of "cultivation" of the land. The Earth, as a form of nature distinct from these political formations deemed "natural," gave the lie to these universalizing claims about their naturalness, an ideology that went hand in hand with Western colonialism's fundamentally global ambitions. Once a political ecology—a "world" in the sense I described above—is established in the metropole it is exported to the colony, opening the land, the indigenous populations living on it, the resources imbedded in it—and any other spaces deemed external to the "natural" right of (European) subjects—to development, exploitation, and expropriation. The Earth's alterity to every social system attempting to master it thus becomes the experience through which a relation of asymmetry can be reconstructed between the natural and the social, thereby challenging any view of nature that relegates humans, and even in some cases nonhuman others, to the status of mere life without social standing.

Like the Romantics I consider in this book, the Caribbean authors I discuss highlight the explicitly political dimension of an Earth that no longer functions as a stable ground, that instead relativizes existing conceptions of nature as politically or racially charged, and that allows, through an encounter with its indifference, the possibility of articulating one's identity or the political otherwise. Roumain, for instance, reads the Haitian Revolution in his early writings effectively as a national liberation struggle for possession of the land. Yet, his final novel, *Masters of the Dew*, reconceives the Earth as a vast commons that, coupled with a set of Haitian peasant practices such as the *coumbite* (the collective act of tilling a neighbor's land), presents a vision of a new international for the global South's lumpenproletariat. For Chamoiseau, the indifference of the Earth reveals itself as an archive of various pasts—including ones that have been effaced by the transformation of the Earth into a globe divided by colonial powers. In his novel *Slave Old Man* about a marooning slave who passes beyond the border of the plantation on which he has lived his entire enslaved life, we discover a reconceived Earth in the forest outside the plantation that begins to transform the titular character into a different kind of subject. No longer defined by the internal exclusions and racial hierarchies of the civil polity ruling the plantation, outside of it he encounters a stone—a figure for the Earth itself—carved and inscribed by the many indigenous inhabitants who lived on the island before colonization exterminated them or turned them into mere "nature." These alterities—the stone and the Great Woods outside the plantation—undermine the conception of "nature" the slave economy invented for itself and point to both the plantation's enduring afterlife and to the possibility of its eventual downfall in the future, revealing that it has failed to fully efface its crimes and that it will one day enter the ash heap of history.

Unlike the Romantics, however, for each of the Caribbean authors discussed here, the Earth is an archipelago surrounded by the ocean and, as such, becomes a way of imagining the *creolization* of the planet, as Chamoiseau and others have suggested.[50] The figure of the archipelago—a series of islands seemingly distinct but connected to each other through ocean currents—provides a way of thinking through a shift away from social and communal formations grounded in blood and soil—relations that privilege the opposition between friend and enemy, master and slave, citizen and noncitizen, human and nonhuman—toward communal associations predicated on something closer to the law of the sea, an international zone owned by no one, open to all and regulated by laws of relation rather than belonging. The archipelago, in other words, becomes the starting point for a conception of being "adrift" on the Earth that is global in scope.

Finally, for the geopoets gathered here, the Earth is neither a metonym for the totality of worlds nor another name for "the globe" conceived as a whole. While there might be multiple natures, multiple societies, multiple worlds that are successive or simultaneous, intersecting or distinct, embedded in each other or not, there is only *one* Earth. But because it is irreducible to each world it makes possible, the only thing capable of totalizing the Earth as a single unified "globe" would be a world intent on absorbing all the others. In the eighteenth and nineteenth centuries, the idea of a fully integrated "globe" organized around European power was the objective of every national colonial project. In our own moment of the Anthropocene, that totalizing world is capital's general equivalence which, as Jean-Luc Nancy suggests, "virtually absorbs, well beyond the monetary or financial sphere but thanks to it and with regard to it, all the spheres of existence of humans, and along with them all things that exist."[51] Thus, if geopoetics imagines the Earth as an alterity to the worlds currently existing on its surface, it also necessarily contests any specific world's global or colonial ambitions by qualifying it as simply one among others, on the same immanent plane of the Earth as all the rest. In other words, geopoetics engages with what Gayatri Spivak insists is an injunction to think the Earth as an alterity, a challenge to the concept of a "globe"[52] that reduces the Earth to a vast depository of resources—and the global South to a labor camp for European goods and consumption economies. "The globe is on our computers," Spivak writes, "it is the logo of the World Bank. No one lives there; and we think we can aim to control globality. The planet is in the species of alterity, belonging to another system; and yet we inhabit it, indeed are it."[53] That last enigmatic identification—inhabiting the Earth but also *being* it—encapsulates another dimension of the Earth's political valence I find in the authors studied here: The Earth is the standpoint from which these poets imagine another form of globality, where the Earth is understood as an alterity to every world hoping to contain it. It thereby defines the basis upon which multiple worlds enter into contact with one another and opens a space for another relation to the Earth and our existence on it that could potentially allow us to address the global political and cultural consequences of the Anthropocene.

The chapters of this book are not aligned chronologically; instead, each begins with a reading of a contemporary Caribbean author through whose geopoetics I interpret their Romantic counterpart.

My first chapter explores the relation between political community and the Earth that makes it possible, opening with an analysis of Glissant's *Poetics of Relation* where community is seen as predicated on "relation" to an exteriority, rather than on rootedness to a place. Identifying the archipelago as "one of the places in the world where Relation presents itself most visibly,"[54] Glissant lays out a poetics that defines identity in terms of its relation to something outside of itself. Because it is an archipelago—islands dependent on ocean currents for their ties to the outside world, housing populations uprooted from their homelands—the Caribbean, Glissant argues, creates a community of drifters and nomads that acts as a model for the way global societies and cultures in general relate to one another. Glissant's philosophical argument prompts me to consider Erna Brodber's novel *The Rainmaker's Mistake*, in which the myth of rootedness in the Earth is both a fundamental feature of the plantation system and a recurring premise for national decolonial liberation struggles. True liberation, Brodber suggests, means relinquishing any notion of rootedness and embracing a thoroughly contingent relation to place that privileges the possibility of a continuous reinvention of the self. These two Caribbean geopoets allow us to see how Wordsworth's early poetry developed a similar conception of community's "archipelagic" relation to landscape. Two hundred years prior, together with Coleridge and Southey, Wordsworth was an early accomplice in the idea of creating a utopian society of equals on shared common land near the Susquehanna River in the United States. While this community never materialized, Wordsworth's early poetry, particularly

"Home at Grasmere," is framed by its principles. While Wordsworth's work is often read as being "rooted" in nature or a specific locality, his early poetry, when refracted though Glissant's argument, transforms England's Grasmere into an itinerant, unrooted community of humans and nonhumans—as opposed to an indigenous belonging to, or appropriation of, the land. As Glissant and Brodber advocate, Wordsworth's community is not defined by rootedness or possession of the land, but by a relation to otherness framed by the alterity of the Earth. Grasmere, for Wordsworth, is therefore also where the social and the natural are fundamentally intertwined. Wordsworth, the chapter claims, is the first Romantic poet to develop a geopoetics where the Earth cannot be owned, and where multiple communities, human and nonhuman alike, encounter one another meaningfully.

The second chapter explores how this notion of the Earth becomes the political idea of a vast commons, which in turn motivates postnational forms of resistance to colonialism. It pairs Jacques Roumain's novel *Masters of the Dew* with John Clare's protest poems to argue that the geopoetics found in their works is predicated on an indifferent Earth the inappropriability of which becomes the basis not just for new forms of community, but for resistance to the Earth's enclosure by global capital. Roumain's last great novel before his untimely death has often been read as an example of a postcolonial nationalism that locates an "authentic" Haitian culture in the peasant class, in contrast to the political classes compromised by American neocolonialism. However, by emphasizing the role the Earth plays in the novel—it has been ravaged by a drought brought about by systematic deforestation—Roumain creates a narrative with a much broader scope. Centering his novel on the collective task of finding and cultivating a source of water, Roumain goes on to suggest that the Earth, unlike the nearby American plantation which has reduced its workers to wage-slavery, is not owned by the peasants and therefore is capable of becoming the source of a new international collectivity that could unite the various peasant classes of the Caribbean, acting as a counterweight to American neocolonialism. Through the lens of Roumain's notion of the Earth as commons, we more readily see the broader conception of "class" in Clare's protest poetry. As an agricultural laborer, Clare's world was threatened by the enclosure acts, which privatized all available land in his native Helpston to extract as much abundance from each parcel as possible. His poetry witnesses the death of one concept of nature in favor of another that treats both the land and the laborers on it as assets to be exploited. Resistance to this order—

which is the heart of Clare's geopoetics—celebrates how different human and nonhuman worlds present an alternative relation to the Earth than the one imposed by the industrial system of agriculture coming into being at the time. His great protest poem, *The Lament of Swordy Well*, gives voice to an enclosed limestone quarry, revealing the extent to which the land's privatization engulfs other worlds—human and nonhuman alike. In this way, Clare's poetry, I argue, draws important connections between nonhuman worlds and the world of the peasant laborer, gesturing toward an "international" commons that spans multiple species.

Clare's posthuman internationale broadens the book's scope and opens it in the third chapter to two thinkers of the Earth who rearticulated the borders between life and nonlife, the organic and the inorganic, which is to say, the hierarchical dichotomy of life at work in colonial ideologies. I start from Olive Senior's collection of poems *Shell*, which considers how nonorganic "things" develop a life of their own by harboring the possibility of a memory of the world to which they formerly belonged, including the silenced voices of Senior's enslaved ancestors. The image of the shell becomes a way of addressing history, geography, and the interface between them "where memory thickens and pearls," and where the earthly lithic element of the shell "comes alive," giving voice to the dead. It thereby dislocates the ontological classifications that had suppressed and liquidated those ancestors. The shells denote at once the resonance of silenced voices in the empty chambers of the shell and a "space waiting for the choices we make,"[55] a new form of solidarity or community between the living and the dead in the present. For Senior even lithic formations have an afterlife, forming as they do new associations and new forms of life and memory in the present. Viewing Karoline von Günderrode through Senior's poetic vitalism draws important connections between Günderrode's theory of the Earth and her literary writings. For Günderrode, everything on the Earth—from plants and mountain ranges to human organisms—is alive because it is constantly decaying and being reorganized by the Earth. As in Senior, this fact disturbs the ontology that privileges certain forms of life over others, while also grounding Günderrode's politics by suggesting that human societies function according to the same logic. In other words, no particular society is privileged in relation to another: each rises and falls in its turn, and the Earth, rather than Western historical teleology, is the motor of history. In this way Günderrode differed substantially from her idealist male contemporaries working in *Naturphilosophie*, producing the first thoroughly *materialist* and uniquely vitalist conception of that genre, which challenged the understanding of global modernity found in her male contemporaries. Günderrode's *Naturphilosophie*, I argue, unsettles the notion of self-consciousness as the endpoint of nature, along with the Eurocentric hierarchy that idea implies. Examining her brief manifesto "Idea of the Earth," alongside her account of Hinduism in *Story of a Brahmin* and the rise of Islam in her play *Muhammed: Prophet of Mecca*, I show that her vitalist *Naturphilosophie* informs her understanding of history and politics because it implies that nothing on the Earth, whether human or nonhuman, has any privilege in relation to the ground out of which it emerges. Nor can anything leave the Earth behind to become self-organizing because it is into and out of the Earth that everything ceaselessly emerges and dissolves. These processes require an approach to the Earth and to human society that understands that humans are neither the central species on its surface, nor Western societies the apogee of their achievements.

Senior's and Günderrode's respective contemplations of the multiplicity of life on the Earth lead me in the fourth chapter to two geopoetic writers who explore the politics of extinction, or the end of any multiplicity, compressed in the allegorical image of an indifferent Earth that has seen various worlds come and go, and that threatens to extinguish ones that currently exist. In Patrick Chamoiseau's novel *Slave Old Man*, a runaway slave enters a forest in which he encounters a stone marked with the writing of bygone indigenous civilizations, which either predate the arrival of Europeans or were exterminated by them. "The Stone," as Chamoiseau puts it, "is many peoples. Peoples of whom only it remains."[56] The old slave's identification with the stone relativizes the world represented by his master through the anteriority of the Earth to that world. It does so both by inscribing in the Earth the memory of the many worlds the master helped destroy, and by gesturing toward the possibility that the master's world will suffer a similar fate in the future. Turning to Hölderlin's poetry—about the birth of modern Europe out if its relation to the extinct world of ancient Greece—and viewing it through the lens of Chamoiseau's more explicitly sociopolitical understanding of extinction sharpens not only the role that the Earth plays in Hölderlin, but also how it exposes modern Europe to the possibility of its own potential disappearance in the future. Guided by Chamoiseau's imaginary, I argue that Hölderlin's poetry and theoretical writings contemplate an Earth without any world—an Earth that *remains* despite the comings and goings of various worlds on its surface, including European ones. For Hölderlin, the Earth constitutes an indifferent ground that in the end exists beyond *every* world or cosmology it makes possible. His Earth is one that emerges through an experience of displacement from one world (ancient Greece) to another (modern Europe) where it is encountered as being *distinct* from either one, revealing every world's dependence on something entirely unaffected by attempts to position it within a particular history or cosmology.

I close my book with a conclusion that examines Haitian poet *Frankétienne* through Guadaloupian author Daniel Maximin's elaboration of what the latter calls a distinctly "Caribbean geopoetics." I focus primarily on Frankétienne's play *Melovivi ou le piège* (Melovivi or the trap), which describes what it calls a "zig-zagging planet" (*la planète zigzague*) that has been sent into disarray by a global modernity that has disrupted its "musical clockwork" (*l'horlogerie musicale*).[57] This disruption, the play suggests, threatens multiple worlds—animal, human, and spiritual. Through a series of poetic calls and responses between two voices, Frankétienne's play connects the destabilized natural forces of the Earth with the social disorder those forces produce, moving seamlessly from natural catastrophes to the problem of global hunger, from political corruption to the disasters of erosion. I argue that Frankétienne's "spiralist" writing is predicated on the figure of the spiral as a representation of the relation between forces of stability and tendencies toward chaos that can be found in both the natural world and in human societies. Hence, Frankétienne's conception of the Earth, framed through the figure of the spiral, destabilizes the border between the natural and the political. It does so, however, in view of the primarily destructive tendencies unleashed by climate change in our own contemporary moment of the Anthropocene, where the indiscernibility between natural and human-made disasters has become acute. He thereby reflects on a global modernity that has unleashed a mutually destabilizing relationship between an Earth in the midst of collapse and the fragile societies, particularly in the global South, this collapse threatens with destruction. I go on to argue that Daniel Maximin's conception of "Caribbean geopoetics"[58] emphasizes the idea that the indiscernibility between natural and human disasters provides space for a reconsideration of the way the Earth's destructive forces, now unleashed by the processes of climate change, can be seen as both a threat to, but also as the possibility of, a poetic and political reinvention of the present. The conclusion closes by arguing that Frankétienne and Maximin's writing constitutes a geopoetics of the future: an attempt to locate the possibility of new forms of creation, new forms of relation, in the midst of a progressively destabilized and destabilizing Earth.

ONE

LANDSCAPES OF RELATION

The Earth and Postnational Community in Glissant, Brodber, and Wordsworth

Never forget the place from which you depart but leave it behind and join the universal. Love the bond that unites your plot of earth with the Earth, the bond that makes kin and stranger resemble each other.

—MICHEL SERRES, *Natural Contract*

THE FIRST INSTANCE OF the historical configuration I'm calling "Caribbean Romanticism" includes seemingly strange bedfellows: Édouard Glissant and William Wordsworth. But in at least one significant respect they share a connection around their development of a geopoetics, which addresses two different yet related crises. The crisis Glissant addresses is the "abyss," as he calls it, of the Middle Passage in the wake of which a new kind of community must emerge. The crisis that preoccupies Wordsworth is the collapse of the French Revolution into colonial authoritarianism, which suggested that the nation-state was no longer the engine behind what he had hoped would become the universalizing project of a "human nature born again."[1] For both writers these are the crises of absolute beginnings, and as such elicit a response that entails a novel understanding of the Earth. This novel understanding of the Earth presupposes an alternative to the "global" conception Carl Schmitt designated as the European "nomos of the Earth,"[2] by which he meant the gradual construction in the eighteenth and nineteenth centuries of a European spatial order across nearly the entire planet. Each territorial zone developed by each

European colonial power connected colonial land acquisition with an original founding act constituting the metropole as a nation-state to which other territories could be appropriated. This "nomos of the Earth" also underpinned the Middle Passage by producing the nexus of land acquisition and extraction economies that were the lifeblood of European expansion across the globe. Glissant and Wordsworth both contest this nexus by articulating postnational forms of community that rethink the relationship between land and identity.[3] Against the "nomos of the Earth" that understands identity as monolinear, organized around a shared essence or a shared belonging to a territory, Glissant and Wordsworth propose communities that are itinerant and organized by their relation to something exterior, the Earth represented either as another geographic space or as a fundamental otherness.

The European "nomos of the Earth" entailed a specific conception of the relation between the Earth and law that comes undone in the wake of the emergence of an indifferent Earth. As Schmitt insists, "the earth is bound to law in three ways. She contains law within herself, as a reward of labor; she manifests law upon herself, as fixed boundaries; and she sustains law above herself, as a public sign of order. Law is bound to the earth and related to the earth." In other words, the Earth's solidity, its capacity to receive, bear, and sustain the trace of human labor, the fact that it supplies natural geographic borders, and its role as an orienting ground, creates an isomorphic relationship between the Earth and human law or the *polis*. The Earth's relative stability is the ultimate ground for "public order," a *polis* that has an inside and an outside, a defined and ultimately closed space in which not only a specific human society subsists, but an entire human world. As Schmitt insists, "every ontonomous and ontological judgment derives from the land," revealing the extent to which being and law, ontology and ontonomy (with its nod to Kantian human moral autonomy), become essentially indiscernible. There is effectively no distinction in the European "nomos of the Earth" between the Earth and the human world it makes possible, no distinction between what is and the law a particular world or society authorizes and imposes. Schmitt explicitly contrasts this solidity of the Earth with the law of the sea (which for him is not part of the Earth). The sea offers no similar unity of "space and law, of order and orientation" because it has no "character."[4] It immediately dissolves every sign of human labor, offers no fixed boundaries and therefore cannot act as a ground for law. This is why there can only be a "law of the sea" that involves a free use that is resolutely international, open to all, and external to the concept of state territory (except within a specific proximity to solid land).

The European "nomos of the Earth" thus necessarily *overrides* any notion of the Earth's indifference to human law: In this view, the Earth is the law's very foundation or possibility, an index of its solidity and legitimacy. It functions as the ground and spatialization of a "human" (in truth, European) sovereignty that is potentially global in scope. This spatialization of law also generates the precondition for collective identity by instantiating an inside and an outside, an "us" and a "them," rooting identity in and to a specific territory or land. It is only once this initial act of identification has been created by an original act of land appropriation that a movement outside that territory becomes possible. But that movement, grounded as it is on the imbrication of land and human law, is necessarily colonial: the exporting of an enclosed collective identity to other territories or geographic spaces.

What happens, however, if the isomorphism between land and law, or land and identity, starts to waver as an indifferent Earth intervenes to destabilize it? If the colonial order was predicated in part on a conception of an Earth that grounded rights of ownership, forms of national belonging, and European expansionism, how might postcolonial struggles be pressed to enjoin their emancipatory struggles to a new conception of the Earth and of territory?

While mid-twentieth century decolonization struggles all over the globe liberated enslaved people from direct exploitation, other forms of domination, structured by market forces, quickly asserted themselves after those struggles achieved national independence. Those other forms have by and large remained in place or have become even more acute. Because the very existence of the European nation-state as a form was grounded in the spatial ordering of the entirety of the Earth as a resource base for European capital, resistance to that entrenched global order fell into a trap. In some cases, liberation was too partial in scope, leaving intact forms of identity inherited from the colonial period; in others, decolonial resistance was forced to frame emancipation from colonial rule around yet another act of land acquisition, thereby leaving intact the spatialized European order that, while faced with territories now independent from its direct rule, reasserted itself postliberation in the form of enforced debt regimes. Take the Congo for example: When it was liberated from Belgian rule, it was forced to take on the repayment of loans Belgium had procured from the World Bank during its colonization which were used primarily to purchase goods from Belgium itself! Liberation was, therefore, entrapped by a cynical trajectory moving from outright extraction and slavery to indirect forms of exploitation such as the foreign acquisition of mineral rights to service debts, or through other "deeds" to the portion of the Earth now technically under the jurisdiction of the newly independent postcolonial nation, yet for all intents and purposes still under the thumb of foreign interests. Saddled with these legacies of colonialism, nations of the global South were then by and large forced to trade the only "property" they had left: the natural or human resources found within their borders. This trap was ultimately coupled with another impasse: If an understanding of the Earth as a vast resource base was still the dominant one postliberation, what was the way out? If ownership and "rootedness" to the land were integral to colonial mechanisms of domination, upon what new relation to the physical land could these newly founded national communities be grounded?

For Wordsworth, who witnessed how quickly the "emancipation" promised by the nation-state could degenerate into Napoleonic imperialism, the collapsed hopes attached to the establishment of a new republic prompted an urge to imagine alternative communal forms that could bring about the liberation of humanity by other means, through smaller communities whose primary mode of identification was a connection to the land itself. The idea that "man and nature are essentially adapted to each other" led him to turn toward the particularity of landscape and the force or sway it has on the development of the mind's sense of self.[5] For Wordsworth, it is nature not as abstract idea but as attachment to a particular place that connects the self with others, facilitating relations between members of the community through the externality of the land rather than through some shared native or national characteristics. And though Wordsworth's geopoetics is more explicitly local than Glissant's, there is nonetheless a latent Earth-wide dimension in his geopoetics. His early focus on the landscape of the English Lake District in and around Grasmere is situated in relation to other "nooks of earth" it is meant to represent, and Grasmere is made the whole of the Earth *in microcosm*.

For Glissant, a response to the impasse of the postcolonial "trap" had to be found, too, in a different relation to the Earth capable of generating a sense of community outside the confines of nation-state identification. If the Caribbean in particular was the site of new forms of identity no longer modeled on "rootedness" to the land, and if a genuinely postcolonial conception of a new "nomos of the Earth" had to find some other basis than the idea of the Earth as a spatialization of identity, a new "aesthetics of the Earth," a new way of situating the self in its relation to others, had to be generated. It is precisely that aesthetics in Glissant that helps illuminate the subterranean political dimension of Wordsworth's geopoetics, highlighting how challenges to identitarian structures predicated on belonging to the land or autochthony shape postnational forms of community. In the present context that means thinking about a relation between community and land that moves beyond conceiving the Earth as carved up into multiple resource bases to be traded on the world market. What happens, Glissant and Wordsworth both ask, when the Earth is no longer "ours" to own or sell, when it is no longer conceived of as a vast globe to be appropriated, and when land no longer authorizes hard and fast notions of us and them, instead becoming the condition of possibility of connection with others whom I have never met?

In what follows, I examine the role the Earth plays in Glissant's thought, beginning in his early *Poetic Intention* and leading up to its most elaborate expression in *Poetics of Relation*. Though Glissant's conception of the hybridity of Caribbean identity has received a great deal of attention, my reading is that *Poetics of Relation* must be seen first and foremost as a geopoetics, that is, a new way of understanding the relation between the Earth and human communities. Glissant develops some of these ideas in his novels, including and especially *Fourth Century* and *Overseer's Cabin*, but I find the most emphatic example of this strand of geopoetics in Erna Brodber's novel *Rainmaker's Mistake*, a Jamaican story about the transition from a slave state founded on myths of proximity to the land and rootedness in the Earth to an eventual emancipation from these myths. Like Glissant's *Poetics of Relation*, Brodber's novel suggests that the promise of emancipation must be coupled with the relinquishment of colonial ideas of autochthonous identity. One finds these ideas in Wordsworth's early poetry too; in fact, it is precisely through the lens of the role of the Earth in Glissant's *Poetics of Relation* that we can see in early Wordsworth an "archipelagic" imagination at work that treats the land in terms much more proximate to the "law of the sea." "Home at Grasmere" is a poetic rendering of the society Wordsworth hoped to create with Coleridge and others in the Lake District of England in the wake of the failure of both the French Revolution and of Coleridge and Robert Southey's plan to create an egalitarian "pantisocratic" community in the United States. While often read as a lament for older rural forms of community, Glissant's *Poetics of Relation* draws out the political consequences of Wordsworth's itinerant geopoetics in "Home at Grasmere," revealing a form of postnational community founded at the height and heart of the national. Early Wordsworth, in other words, ages well when read through Glissant: He's a poet of today's Earth, recognizing its indifference to human law though the contemplation of an itinerant community situated on an Earth that cannot be possessed.

Glissant's Earth: From Territory to Archipelago

Relative to the population of the planet, there has never been a period involving more human displacement on the surface of the Earth than the period of the Atlantic slave trade. As European colonial powers began to expand territorially and economically, and as more settlers arrived in what to them was the "new world," their insatiable need for slave labor accelerated, forcing millions from their native lands to toil and die in colonized territories seized from indigenous populations. Never before had so many people been displaced, nor had so many indigenous cultures been eradicated so rapidly. Moreover, European colonial powers were terraforming the Earth in unprecedented ways. Whole forests and jungles were razed to grow commodities prized in world markets. Evidence found in ice cores from Antarctica suggests that the genocide of the indigenous populations in the Americas, where human populations had been reduced to roughly 10% of their pre-Columbian size, intensified a small ice age lasting from about 1400 to 1850 that occurred thanks to reduced carbon emissions.[6] While it wasn't until well into the twentieth century that we began recognizing the sheer scale and interaction of the changes made in the land, population, and climate of the Earth during the expansion of this "nomos of the Earth," it is nevertheless clear that a fundamental transformation in the way communities and territories interrelated was also underway. As the Earth was being transformed, so too were conceptions of the possible itinerancy of human societies.

In the twentieth century, with decolonization, a rethinking of the relation between emergent nations and the land they occupied began to take shape. Once independence had been achieved, the question of what structures would form the "social glue" binding members of the community together became a central one for nascent postcolonial nations, particularly since they now housed multiple ethnic identities and cultures, many of which had been imported from elsewhere over centuries of European colonization. In the absence of other models, a relation to the land of the former colony itself would become one of the key means of achieving some sense of social cohesion. There was the question of the physical borders of the new nation, which were usually instituted by the colonizing metropole according to its own needs and aims. Would these borders be viewed as a legitimate homeland, or a vestige of colonial subjugation? Could one simply reconstitute the structures of community that had previously inhabited the land, especially since they had been replaced by European race and class hierarchies? Moreover, vast areas had been terraformed in ways that meant that there was no return to the way the land had existed, or had been inhabited, prior to colonialism. What relation might this newfound "people" or nation, riven as it was by various internal cultural, class, and racial differences, have to the territory it had liberated?

In the construction of the postcolonial state or nation, "the people" of a former colony come into being thanks to a set of narrative structures—the telling of tales, the formation of myths—that give the community its consistency. As Homi Bhabha suggests, "the people are neither the beginning nor the end of the national narrative; they represent the cutting edge between the totalizing powers of the 'social' as homogeneous, consensual community, and the forces that signify the more specific address to the contentious, unequal interests of identities within the population." In other words, the construction of a national community in the wake of colonial liberation often became the site of a "narrative struggle" involving not just relations with the former metropole but *internal* conflicts between, on the one hand, voices seeking to unify a heterogeneous population into a homogeneous whole and, on the other, those advocating for a heterogeneity to the dominant narrative through contending histories or myths. The relation of the nation or community to the land or territory it occupies is one of these narrative threads or myths that for Bhabha invokes "the recurrent metaphor of landscape as the inscape of national identity."[7]

The problem here is that the metaphor of the landscape as a parallel "inscape" is treated as if it were an already given, stable correlation à la Schmitt. The nation might engage in a narrative struggle over how or for whom the landscape becomes a means of identification, but its internalization as "one's own" requires a figurative solidity, stability, and reliability that founds community by instituting the homogenization of space and time necessary for the nation to take shape. As Benedict Anderson has shown, narratives of the nation are structured by the assumption of an empty homogeneous temporality that provides the unity and continuity necessary to imagine the nation's existence across long stretches of time.[8] The only way England, for example, can imagine its existence as beginning with the Anglo-Saxons and culminating in the present is if it assumes an unbroken continuity across time that allows the selfsame lineage to appear in each epoch, forming a consistent narrative of historical and cultural development. Over time, though, this collective identity is also *spatialized* in the land, constituting as it does a metaphoric grounding for an imagined autochthonous essence, a "belonging" to a particular geography that imagines filiation as a spatialization of the community around a shared territory.

But not every national or postcolonial narrative is the same. The former slave colonies of the Caribbean were riven by quite different histories and power dynamics than were India or Algeria, for instance, where indigenous populations remained largely intact after liberation. Jamaica's original indigenous Taíno population, by contrast, was exterminated, its few survivors having fled to the island's mountainous regions, where they eventually joined Jamaica's growing maroon communities. By the time Jamaica gained independence in 1962, well after slavery was abolished in 1834, its population consisted of the descendants of former slaves, mixed-race populations, and a white elite that had retained most of its colonial privileges. This meant, then, that in the aftermath of the country's liberation from Great Britain, the primary relation between the newly emergent people of Jamaica and the territory they occupied could not be easily centered around claims to nativity. Coupled with these demographics is the specificity of Caribbean geography: As part of an archipelago—a chain of islands divided into discrete island colonies—Jamaica was not the only Caribbean nation in a similar situation. All the island nations of the Caribbean, whether independent or not, housed similar populations—descendants of colonists, slaves, and indentured servants—who might be said to have as important historical and cultural ties with each other as they did to those on their own island.

For Glissant, the uniqueness of Caribbean identity and culture, what he calls "Caribbeanness," entails shifting attention from "unilateral" relations with a metropole to the "multidimensional nature of the diverse Caribbean"[9] found in its archipelagic geography. Framed around linguistic "hybridity"—the Caribbean after all is home to francophones, anglophones, and hispanophones as well as Creole-speaking peoples, among others—Glissant's early writings prompted Jean Bernabé, Patrick Chamoiseau, and Raphaël Confiant to develop the concept of *créolité*,[10] which argues that Caribbean cultural identities must be seen as fundamentally itinerant, hybrid, and structured by the vestiges of practices from multiple global communities past and present, from indigenous Amerindian cultures to African ones.

However, because it emphasizes cultural hybridity over a culture's geographic specificity, *créolité* in Glissant's view doesn't reflect the distinctiveness of Caribbeanness. That is, *créolité* for him risks taking the form of yet another exclusive identity, this time a hybrid one meant precisely to avoid that danger, because it does not sufficiently prioritize how that identity takes shape in relation to an otherness it cannot appropriate as "its own." Caribbeanness, for Glissant, can only be thought or experienced through the specificity of the Caribbean landscape or seascape. Rather than being rooted territorially in the solidity of a continental landmass, each island in an archipelago is related to an "elsewhere"[11] of some kind, whether that is understood as a metropole or as other Caribbean nations connected by their position within the chain of islands. Though each island may attempt to view itself as an independent nation, because it is part of an archipelago it is irreducibly bound up with the others, connected together by a "law of the sea" that relates each island to the other through what cannot be made its own. This geological arrangement institutes, for Glissant, a *geographic form of thought* without a single exclusive rooted identity, modeled on the movement of ocean currents and therefore on a fundamental itinerancy that characterizes not just the ancestors of the people displaced from their homelands in the eighteenth and nineteenth centuries, but the Earth itself as a *dynamic* rather than static milieu in which individuals or collectives enter into relation with one another. If the eighteenth century "nomos of the Earth" understood the Earth as a stable landmass waiting to be conquered, with the oceans as merely the means by which to do so, archipelagic thought understands the Earth as a dynamic system without solidity or stability, modeled *on* the movement of ocean currents. For archipelagic thought, in other words, the Earth is essentially oceanic, connecting even the most far-flung regions to the other, instituting a general Caribbeanness of relations across the entirety of the globe.

But this would entail fundamentally rethinking what a nation is, what communal identity is, and what the Earth is. Glissant, as one might expect in the context of the Caribbean, begins with the historical "abyss" of the Middle Passage, since it is there that the first opening to a different relation to the Earth, to land or territory, occurs. On the other side of that "abyss" lies an "*Antillanité*" (Caribbeanness) predicated on the complete deracination of a world or a horizon of meaning that can no longer be fully recuperated. When enslaved Africans were brought to the Caribbean, they were torn away from a familiar world and thrown into the space of what Glissant in *Poetics of Re-*

lation calls a "non-world" (*non-monde*).[12] If a world is the space of meaning where things makes sense and truths are legible, as they are in a cosmology or religion that orders the relationships among gods, animals, and humans, the nonworld is a fall into absolute senselessness where that horizon of meaning is completely dissolved. One arrives in a nonworld when one is wrenched violently away from one's "familiar land, away from protecting gods, and a tutelary community" (PR 5/17). The nonworld the enslaved African encounters in the "abyss"[13] of the Middle Passage is a radical rupture with a past world of sense and meaning, and a movement toward an unknown and violent elsewhere:

> The asceticism of crossing this way that land-sea that, unknown to you, is the planet Earth, feeling a language vanish, the word of the gods vanish, and the sealed image of even the most everyday object, of even the most familiar animal, vanish. (PR 7/19)

The ship's passage here involves an impossible encounter with an unknown and unknowable "planet Earth" that strips the enslaved African of any recognizable bearings. He encounters not just a "new land"—a *terre* in the usual sense of landscape or territory—but a *terre-mer* (a "land-sea") or ocean that unbeknownst to him is also *la planète-terre* (the planet Earth). The *planète-terre*, or Earth, is a totality completely outside the scope not just of any prior cosmology defining a familiar *terre* (a land or territory), but an experience that collapses one's relation to the everyday, to anything recognizable, to one's own sense of self. It is, in other words, an Earth outside of *any* horizon of meaning whatsoever, indifferent to any world or cosmology that might have in the past provided a point of orientation.

Paradoxically though, this first terrifying elsewhere marks the starting point for another form of "shared knowledge" (formed around the experience of displacement). There is no return to the previous world, of course, but out of this encounter with an indifferent Earth without a world to give it meaning, a new relation to "an unknown that does not terrify" (PR 9/21) and an Earth that is no longer the "unknown" in quite the same way, becomes possible. For another world,[14] another horizon of meaning, another form of community, emerges on the other side of the shared experience of an unknown Earth, one now located in a new land (*terre*), making concrete the community's relation to an "elsewhere."[15]

This relation to an elsewhere is the fundamental component of archipelagic thought, for Glissant, because it weds a relation to a new land with the itinerant movement of being adrift on the Earth as a fundamental relation to an elsewhere—*la planéte-terre*—that cannot be summed up into a homogeneous totality. The experience of displacement and the loss of world Glissant examines in the first section of *Poetics of Relation* grows in the second half of the book into a geopoetics that takes the "totality" of the Earth as the starting point for understanding "Relation" as a vast interconnected whole that is nevertheless not the unitary "globe" of the eighteenth century "nomos of the Earth." Glissant's planet Earth, distinct from the "totality" of the Earth understood by European colonialism as a globe to be parceled up by empires and nation-states, becomes instead a principle of differentiation for evanescent encounters between groups and cultures, an interconnected surface without exteriority where various relations, becomings, or "creolizations" occur.[16] Crucially, for this new world—which is not yet a nation-state—the planet Earth is *nothing but* an exteriority, an "elsewhere" that is the condition of possibility for relations with others, rather than a vast resource base or principle of collective identity.[17] Any Relation worthy of its capitalized name thus entails being situated in a particular place, a geographical position: "Relation exists in being realized, that is, in being completed in a common place" (PR 203/219). The archipelago is the Earth is the condition of Relation. There is no genuine relation to the other without a Relation to the Earth; the planet-Earth as the first terrifying encounter with the unknown is eventually transposed into a (nonterrifying) *Relation* to the unknown.

The idea of a geographic form of thinking, or a geographic basis for cultural identity, is not unique to Glissant, but his articulation avoids a determinism that understands the relationship between identity and geography in terms of lineage, or as a naturalization of culture. Hegel, whose ideas about geography's relation to culture I will explore in more detail in chapter 3, famously claimed in *Lectures on the Philosophy of World History* that geography defines the "national spirit" of a people, producing actual differences between specific cultures and races.[18] While Glissant doesn't deny the intimate bond between culture and locale, he differs from Hegel, for whom geographical determination is the "natural" component of a community's cultural worldview. For Glissant, by contrast, there is nothing intrinsic about the relationship between land and people—the link between them is purely accidental.

What matters for Glissant, then, is the *mutability* of the relation to the Earth. The itinerancy of the cultures that emerge in the Caribbean, for instance, are contrasted through their archipelagic thinking of the Earth with other itinerant cultures such as the "Huns," whose nomadism is ultimately "a devastating desire for settlement" (PR 12/24). Theirs is a nomadism, in other words, that starts by voyaging to an "elsewhere" only in order to reinstall the same rooted relation to the land in that space. This form of nomadism, which Glissant calls "arrowlike nomadism" (*nomadisme en flèche*), must be contrasted with other kinds of nomadism, for example what he calls "circular nomadism" (*nomadisme circulaire).* What distinguishes them is how a culture or community relates to the land—and ultimately the Earth as a whole—thereby forming its development and *raison d'être.* Without a relation to the Earth as the unknown and as what is fundamentally *distinct* from one's own world, "arrowlike" nomadic cultures become essentially colonial, importing their preexisting structures of meaning from one territory to another without undergoing any transformation—"New World" same as the "Old World." Arrowlike nomadism simply *expands* its own existing world onto other territories, conceiving the Earth as one vast extension of the unity of its own world, a homogenized replica of itself.

The communities of former slaves, however, are circularly nomadic; that is, they are nomadic without recourse to any prior world or homeland. To them, the Earth is fundamentally unknown, and as such, once the less terrifying relation to that unknown becomes possible postslavery, becomes linked with a "search for the Other" (PR 18/30). Because they have lost their home world and must create another, theirs is an itinerancy at once geographic *and* cultural. Exiled from indigeneity, the former slaves brought much of their earlier cultures with them, yet they did so, Glissant argues, in a purely syncretic fashion, adapting and adopting the beliefs and practices of many cultures. No longer the people of a single root, but of multiple nonhierarchized derivations in shifting relation to each other, the former slaves also developed a novel archipelagic relation to the Earth as a whole: "Errant, he challenges and discards the universal—this generalizing edict that summarized the world as something obvious and transparent, claiming for it one presupposed sense and one destiny. He plunges into the opacities of that part of the world to which he has access" (PR 20/33). In other words, the errant or circular nomad takes up a relation to the totality of the Earth but does so in a way that insists on the otherness or "opacity" of other lands and peoples, refusing to reduce them to itself. Circular nomadism develops, Glissant argues, until a new poetic relation to the Earth emerges that "makes every periphery into a center" and ultimately "abolishes the very notion of center and periphery" (PR 29/41). Today, in the wake of colonialism, nation-states continue to vie to increase the scope and range of their "zone of influence," the region of the globe in which they have economic or military sway, either directly or through proxies. Glissant's circular nomadism attempts to challenge these colonial logics by articulating a theory of cultural identity through a relation to the other that shatters the notion of center and periphery, dominant and dominated. There is no longer the notion of a "Russian world"—parts of the globe with a historical or spiritual tie to Russia—or an American Monroe Doctrine declaring the Western Hemisphere to be its own proper domain. Rather than a geography of zones of influence, the Earth becomes a set of relations to other lands that are fundamentally irreducible to any center, enacting a relation to the other through the unknown "*planète-terre*."

Though this requires a postnational conception of the Earth, since the nation-state form is a relation to land that is necessarily "arrowlike" in Glissant's terms, conceiving of the Earth in this way also requires a shift in the conception of its "totality." Unlike the totality of the European "nomos of the Earth" under which we still live, the Earth in Glissant is a fundamentally *unknown* totality. In the European spatial order, that unknowability vanishes, becoming a unity or homogeneity. As such, it approximates what Glissant in *Poetic Intention* calls "the One,"[19] which can be approached in at least two different ways: as a unified "harmony," the dream of every colonial and neocolonial project, or as a unity that emerges in the wake of decolonial liberation movements when "half the world came out of the nights, the half that until then had been marked to be the dark face of the globe" (PI 9/13). The totality of the Earth that preceded this moment was a false one, the dream of a harmonious totality effacing actual totality, which Glissant calls the "concrete unity of the Earth" (*l'unité concrète de la terre*): "What the unity of the world needs is that part of the world which, shivering in its being, is saddled with non-existence" (PI 9/13). Framed here in the language of "world," Glissant is essentially arguing that there is no such thing as "the world" in the singular. Rather, the world as the "concrete unity of the Earth" includes what Jacques Rancière calls those who "have a part in the act of governing" and those who do not, worlds recognized as such, and those denied existence.[20] Transposed to the planetary scale, the totality of the Earth is thus not just the unity of the Earth as a planet, but a distribution of geographies or "lands" placed in relations not of trade or power, but of alterity and difference: "There are so many lands (*terres*): totality results (much more than their sum) from their relation to come. It is not possible to conclude" (PI 80/90). Glissant's unknown Earth, in other words, is a *differentiated* totality rather than a sum total of nation-states, and it cannot be fully known or made transparent to itself.

Glissant's description of "the One" may sound abstract, but its deployment as a different conception of totality is not just a claim about the Earth as a planet; in the context of decolonial struggle it acquires a distinctly political valence, occurring when the "half of the world" of the global South "came out of the nights" after liberation, when "the earth became one, and in this density the One, mandated by the imaginary, was confirmed. The poetic ecstasy of the One is untied by militant unity" (PI 9/13). The Earth is "one" here in a very different sense from the colonial "One," for it becomes so only once national liberation movements begin to challenge the global hegemony of the European "nomos of the Earth." With the emergence of independent postcolonial states, two things happen simultaneously: the hegemonic notion of the One is "confirmed" in the enmeshment of every part of the globe in a web of market forces, yet at the same time another conception of the unity of the Earth begins to take shape thanks to the "militant" unity presented by an emergent global South that insists on the Earth as a totality of relations at war with the totalizing wholeness of the Earth as "the One."[21]

While the Earth is the condition of possibility for the multiplicity of worlds or "lands," the *way* in which a world defines itself in relation to an "elsewhere," to the alterity of those other lands, depends on its conception of the Earth as a totality. With the proliferation of various determinations of the world in Glissant's later work—from the "whole-world" (*tout-monde*)[22] to the "chaos-world" (*chaos-monde*)—it is tempting to see him use the term "Earth" as just another name for the "global community," the domain of international relations. But that understanding of global relations already determines the Earth as the homogenized version of "the One," as a single world, even if the relations between cultures or nations are defined by conflict and competition. The point is that there is no world, no horizon of meaning, out of which *a* world in the singular, however globalized, could be said to come into being because the Earth is external, an "elsewhere" to each and every world on its surface. It exists only as the Relation between *multiple* worlds on its surface.

This is why whenever Glissant tries to articulate the totality of Relation independently from the Earth, he resorts to hyphenated concepts to attenuate what is usually understood by "world" as a unified horizon of meaning.

Take, for example, his concept of the "whole-world," which would seem to function in similar ways to his notion of the Earth's totality. However, the idea of the "whole-world" captures the chaotic[23] and heterogeneous *result* of the Earth's totality, which is not identical with the "whole-world." The term "whole-world" is a kind of shorthand for a perspective Glissant's thought de-activates in advance but nevertheless needs if it is to contrast its consequences with other relations to the Earth as totality. The "whole-world" would at first seem to imply a perspective *outside* the multiplicity of worlds on the Earth's surface, capable of grasping their relation to each other in a single fantasized image, similar to the homogenized "One" of *Poetic Intention*. And yet the "whole-world" indexes that multiplicity without subjecting it to the perspective of an assumed expansion of *a* world, in the singular, across the entirety of the planet. Glissant's "whole-world," thus, is made up of incompatible worlds whose only common denominator is each one's specific relation to the Earth, to the particular territory it occupies. An early version of this idea emerges through a description of what it means to be "born to the world" (*naître au monde*) in *Poetic Intention*:

> For a long time the world was thus an idea of the world, world-as-solitude, or as-identity, enlarged from the sole evidence of the known particular and enclosing the All as a pure extension of that particular. He who went far from home, the Discoverer, and he who remained on his land, the to-discover, shared that common belief. To be born into the world, is at last to conceive (to live) the world as a relation: as a composed necessity, a consenting reaction, a poetics (and not a morality) of alterity. (PI 15/20)

"To be born to the world" thus does not mean being born into a particular world that attempts to extend its already "known particularity" to other worlds. "To be born to the world," like his later concept "the whole-world," involves encountering the relations between worlds as one does the "unknown Earth," as something completely heterogeneous to one's own.

In a sense, then, Glissant extends the disorienting experience of the loss of the world and the encounter with the unknown Earth of the enslaved African in the first section of *Poetics of Relation* into a model for a new relation to the Earth, a new relation to land, a new relation to the other, and thus to a new form of community. The enslaved African is not the only one to encounter the unknown Earth, but the kind of culture, the kind of community and world he and his descendants construct on the other side of that terrifying encounter transforms it into the condition of possibility of Relation with others, becoming a generalized model of community. At the very heart of the colonial and racial hierarchies carving the Earth into a set of fiefdoms, and rigidly defining relations between self and other, emerges another relation to the Earth, and a new conception of its globality.

While the Earth is everywhere in Glissant's work, it is only in *Poetics of Relation* where the connection between it and postnational forms of collectivity is most clearly articulated. In *Poetic Intention* the Earth is primarily juxtaposed to the colonial dream of "the One," a desire for a unity and transparency of the world that cannot be realized but is nonetheless the objective of every world structured by expansionist colonialism. In *Poetics of Relation*, however, Glissant relates the Earth to a totality that has already *relinquished* the desire for transparency and homogeneity, and that has accepted what he calls the fundamental "opacity" (*opacité*) not just of every other land, but of every culture or identity's relation to itself. This term enters his discourse whenever it is a question of describing the unknowability of other peoples, lands, or worlds, or of articulating the internal differences to itself found *within* a particular world.[24] The term "opacity" thus indexes alterity but does so through the unknowability of the Earth: a relation to its nontransparency, its unknowability, founds each world's opacity to itself and to the other.

Because the unknown Earth requires thinking anew the link between communal identity and land, Glissant insists that a world (culture or community) is irreducible to the nation-state.[25] As he puts it in "Punctuations" in *Treatise on the Whole-World*, "the 'realization' of the earth-totality has changed the perception or the imagination that each community has of 'its' land. The physical frontiers between nations have been made permeable to cultural and intellectual exchanges, to the hybridization of sensibilities, which has meant that the nation-state is no longer powerful enough to barricade from the inside everyone's relation to *the earth*."[26] In other words, because it is not a question of ownership, the Earth cannot be appropriated and is therefore never a birthright.

Moreover, if the Earth is not simply a collection of "lands" (*terres*), if it is first the condition of possibility for any relation to the other, then it is also the first (and primary) relation of *any* kind, defining as it does one's place within a cosmology or a religion, within a politics and within a culture. A world, each world, in all its aspects, is defined by how it relates to the Earth: through land acquisition and a totalizing and colonizing of other worlds, or by a recognition of the profoundly chaotic totality of associations and links between them, for instance. In either case, the Earth anchors a world's relation to the other. And in a more down-to-Earth fashion, as it were, how a world treats others is how it treats the Earth. This is why Glissant insists in *Poetic Intention* that the "earth is different to each":

> The earth is the supreme argument (whose "return to the earth" was sometimes its miserable caricature). . . . Man is indeed given to the future, because, a poet, he cannot here fulfill his wish; so he presents himself in his earth: it becomes (it is) the eternal wager, behind so much furtiveness, whose aroma is never enclosed. It is the poverty in which he nourishes himself. But the earth is different to each. (PI 80/90)

If "the earth is the supreme argument" and Man "presents himself in his earth," this implies that the Earth is neither an object, nor a mere space of habitation. It is instead the condition of possibility for a world, or a poet's, habits and beliefs, his relation to the future and to himself. Hence the reason for the strange possessive "his earth": by "presenting himself in his earth," Man as poet takes as a starting point a relation to the Earth's unknowable opaque totality. Out of this relation emerges a world, a way of presenting himself, "his earth"—his particular relation to its opacity. For Glissant, poetics and poetry must be understood not just as a form of writing but in their original Greek sense as a mode of production. Every world and every poetics produces its own relation to the Earth's totality, which defines who or what that world is, how it interacts with the alterity of others and with the Earth itself.

As we have seen, Glissant privileges "circular nomadism's" relation to land over "arrowlike nomadism's" expansionism. The mechanism of that expansionism now becomes clearer: the arrowlike nomad's self-identity and its construction through an opposition to the other creates an isomorphic relation between land and monolinear configurations of identity, as in Schmitt's discussion of the "nomos of the Earth." The arrowlike nomad sees the "homeland" as grounding the self in an autochthony it can export. For instance, "France for the French," the slogan of the far right *Solidarité Française* prior to the Second World War, was more than a declaration of some essence of what it means to be French. It explicitly connected nativity, land, and identity as basically interchangeable. Anyone not "rooted" in the soil, the fruit of France's single lineage, could not claim belonging to that community. It also *implicitly* took up a relation to the Earth: France was seen as a stable homeland with a singular identity; as such, the nomadism of its colonial aspirations meant exporting that stability abroad, colonizing the globe as part of France itself (which is the reason why Algeria was considered a French *département*, essentially making it a province of the country). This colonial export of French identity did not make native Algerians French—but it did mean that France as a territory could theoretically encompass the entirety of the Earth.

In contrast to this nationalist model and its notion of autochthonous rootedness in the land, Glissant proposes a different conception of rootedness that dovetails with his description of the relation to the unknowable opaque Earth represented by "Caribbeanness." Drawing on a Deleuzo-Guattarian concept, Glissant suggests that the rootedness at work in Caribbean communities is essentially "rhizomatic,"[27] eschewing notions of national filiation understood as being structured around a single unique lineage, essence, or history. Rhizomatic roots have no arborescent core, are nonlinear, are resistant to hierarchical genealogy, and privilege horizontal rather than hierarchical forms of propagation, like the syncretic religion of Vodou, which combines Amerindian, Catholic, African, and other belief systems into a unique graft privileging none of the various "roots" from which it derives. This rhizomatic structure allows heterogeneous links between different "plants" growing on the same territory, as it were, as in Jamaican Rastafarianism which welds together Christian and African beliefs with notions of a "living prophet" to form a new kind of theology.

In what way do these cultures produce a different relation to the Earth? Since they eschew a monolinear rootedness to the land, the communities that emerge from them are trans- or postnational in the sense that they no longer grasp the Earth as a set of territories "owned" by a people through natural right. Caribbean nations, Glissant insists, are organized around itinerant or "adrift" relations to land rather than filiation thanks to the fact that, whatever form the community might take after liberation from colonial rule, no one remaining on it could claim any privileged autochthony. The nation-state does not vanish in Glissant, but it is recontextualized by a de-essentialized conception of national identity that emphasizes becoming and displaces fixed or monolithic forms of national identity.

Glissant calls this shift to postnational community an "aesthetics of the Earth" (*esthétique de la terre*) by which he means not just a regime of representation,[28] but "an art of conceiving, imagining and acting" (PR 155/169). A community or culture's "aesthetics of the Earth" is not just how it represents its relation to a particular geographic space but is a way of being that affects how *everything else* appears for members of that community: the way one acts in the world, the way one participates in social life or politics, and so on. But it is also, he claims, an "aesthetic of disruption and intrusion" (*esthétique de bouleversement et de l'intrusion*) (PR 151/165) suggesting that it is primarily oppositional in its effects:

> Almost everything is said in pointing out that under no circumstances could it ever be a question of transforming land into territory again. Territory is the basis for conquest. Territory requires that filiation be planted and legitimated. Territory is defined by its limits, and they must be expanded. A land henceforth has no limits. That is the reason it is worth defending against every form of alienation. (PR 151/166)

To conceive of the Earth as a "territory," as opposed to a "land," is to understand the relation between geography and "the people" as an arborescent rooted filiation structured by defined limits between self and other. The limits of a territory are not just borders in the geographic sense, but are also an aesthetics, a sensibility that enacts a particular kind of spatialized distinction between inside and outside, "us" and "them." Glissant's "aesthetics of the Earth" contests this by introducing a relation to land, as opposed to territory, that "has no limits." This lack of limits does not mean that the community exists in a space without borders, only that those borders are essentially porous and shifting rather than discrete and protectionist.

However, articulating a community through "land" rather than "territory" is meaningless for Glissant unless the relation—the interstice—between different lands makes something happen or involves a mutual becoming "where each is changed by and changes the other" (PR 155/169).[29] And so the original relation to the Earth as territory begins to be unsettled by a new one: the "thought of the Other" (*la pensée de l'Autre*) must be coupled with "the other of Thought" (*l'autre de la Pensée*) (PR 154/169), whereby each side of a relation is *altered* in the encounter or exchange:

> Thought of the Other is the moral generosity disposing me to accept the principle of alterity, to conceive of the world as not simple and straightforward, with only one truth—mine. But thought of the Other can dwell within me without making me alter course, without "prizing me open," without changing me within myself. . . . The other of Thought is precisely this altering. Then I have to act. That is the moment I change my

> thought, without renouncing its contribution. I change, and I exchange. (PR 155/169)

Obviously, then, Glissant has in mind cultural exchanges that involve more than the importing and exporting of goods or the creation of tourism bureaus. An aesthetics of the Earth essentially shifts registers to a different kind of exchange, where something other than commodities are traded, an exchange "that isn't just sand and coconut trees but, instead, the result of our creative activity. Integrate what we have, even if it is sea and sun, with the adventure of a culture that is ours to share and for which we take responsibility" (PR 153/167). This aesthetics is thus simultaneously an "intrusion" into concepts of culture seen as homogeneous, and into concepts of land as territory or as a commodity to be exchanged on the market, like a tourist destination or a depository of raw materials. The community that would emerge in the wake of this new aesthetics has yet to take shape, but rather than propose a specific model for a postnational community, Glissant poses a set of guiding questions for it:

> How have cultures—Chinese or Basque, Indian or Inuit, Polynesian or Alpine—made their way to us, and how have we reached them? What remains to us of all the vanished cultures, collapsed or exterminated, and in what form? What is our experience, even now, of the pressure of dominant cultures? (PR 153–54/168)

Glissant's native Martinique is just one of many lands situated in the exchanges of the (chaotic) totality of the Earth, but the questions he poses for any community suggest a network of relations between lands both near and far, as well as cultures that have vanished. All of these questions circle around how others—including "dominant" cultures in positions of power—have shaped the collective "we." How have various others, near or far, with us or vanished, constructed that "we," and how do they continue to enact a form of becoming, both in themselves and in "us"?

A concrete example of this aesthetics of the Earth can be found in Glissant's examination of the differences between a collective "we" constructed through national memory, and one constructed through what he calls the "cultural memory of the Earth community" (*la mémoire culturelle de la collectivité Terre*).[30] In a text—*Mémoires des esclavages* (Memories of slavery)—written on the occasion of the opening of the National Center for the Memory of Slavery and Its Abolition in Paris, France, in 2007, Glissant sees the center as representing a new postnational sensibility enabling forms of community that cross national borders. Parallel to his distinction between territory and land, Glissant distinguishes between two forms of memory related to each one: the "memory of the tribe" (*la mémoire de la tribu*),[31] which is connected to a particular nation-state, and the "cultural memory of the Earth community" connected to the Earth. The former entails only the historical relation of a community to its sense of self, through the narratives it gives itself concerning its past, in this case through the history of France and its culpability for slavery. The latter is a "memory of the future" that is not specific to a particular nation, not filtered through a particular territory, but instead interpreted through the open-ended *interrelation* between different "lands." In other words, the opening of this center on French "territory" concerns not just its own national history but a broader form of terrestrial memory connected with archipelagic thought and the Earth. The center, Glissant writes, represents "an archipelago thought, which invents at each moment the effect of Relation, disperses and scatters the identities into relation, nevertheless reinforcing each one and safeguarding them from the autism of identity, trembling with the dazzling world. . . . Through what we would call the memory of the Earth community, we think with the world."[32] National memory, which only begrudgingly acknowledges its role in the system of slavery, and even then only as an event of the past, cannot integrate the kind of memory and its co-relative community Glissant claims the center represents. Slavery was multinational in every sense of the word and so too is its memorialization, which stages encounters between lands and people who activate, and are structured by, a memory that exceeds the national and remains "independent of the official action of states."[33] The cultural memory of the Earth is archipelagic not only because it is irreducible to a specific national story, but also because it is relationally oriented toward the future rather than the past. It situates the memory of slavery and its abolition within a constant reinvention of communal and national relations in the present, not at the level of the nation-state, but at the level of peoples—the African diaspora—whose identity remains irreducible to the territory in which they find themselves, but who are nevertheless tied together through the memory of the Earth.

Glissant's aesthetics of the Earth takes as its starting point what he calls the "tortured geography"[34] of the Caribbean: a land deforested, riven by violence past and present, yet now suitably positioned to reconceptualize a "global" community to come that might originate from a different relation to the Earth—an Earth no longer organized by arborescent roots, belongings, and identities. An Earth no longer traded or exchanged as a commodity. An Earth understood as an open totality for relations that have yet to exist, or that are in the process of being constructed. An Earth that, essentially exterior to the worlds and communities that subsist upon it, places them in relation to each other, defining each land only in and through its relationality rather than through the arrowlike nomadism of an identification of the Earth with human law. This is an Earth that is the starting point for a worldwide community, provided that by this term something more is meant than the "community of nations" or the global market. If, as Glissant insists, "relation exists in being realized, that is, in being completed in a common place" (PR 203/219), that common place, in both the literal and figurative senses, is this Earth here and now.

One of the clearest examples of Glissantian geopoetics emerging out of the Caribbean's "tortured geography" is Erna Brodber's masterful *Rainmaker's Mistake*, a novel narrating Jamaica's transition from slavery and its abolition to the former colony's independence.[35] It allegorizes a shift that occurs in a community's understanding of itself over the course of this history as it is forced to confront the myths of rootedness and autochthony that have formed it and worked to normalize its enslavement.[36] Brodber's novel is therefore an account of what happens when the narratives that have buttressed slavery and shaped the community after its independence are cast aside in favor of a different relation to land and cultural identity—a new aesthetics of the Earth in Glissant's sense—that could therefore be viewed as truly *post*colonial.

Because *Rainmaker's Mistake* has been out of print for some time, I begin with a brief synopsis, interspersed with analysis of the significance of the novel's allegory. The novel opens on a plantation owned by "Mr. Charlie" who, in his need for labor to harvest sugarcane, concocts an origin myth involving the Earth, digs a hole in the ground and plants "a wash of seed from his body."[37] The result, so his story goes, is that this seed sprouts yams, which then grow into a number of slaves at various stages of development, from children and young adults to the fully grown. At the outset the novel deliberately abjures narrative sequence:[38] all of the action initially takes place in a timeless space of myth where every slave, with the sole exception of the overseer Woodville, believes themselves to be "of the Earth," having sprung up as yams harvested from the seed of the Father—a perverse allusion to the garden of Eden where neither history, in the sense of human temporality, nor sexual reproduction, yet exist. None of the slaves age or die, and absolute fidelity to the Father is sacrosanct.

This asexual world at a complete standstill gives way, in the wake of the abolition of slavery, to a dispersion of the community after the disappearance of Mr. Charlie, which coincides with Isis, one of the adult women on the plantation, giving birth to a pale-skinned child who has obviously not descended from a yam! Seeing this, Woodville begins to laugh so hard that he generates a wind destroying the plantation. The community splits in two, each settling in one of two places, "the Future" and "the Norm." "The Norm" lies between both "the Past"—the old plantation that has now been abandoned—and "the Future," where some of the former slaves settle in what is ultimately not a geographical elsewhere but a temporal one. Those in the Norm take soil from the Past to cultivate the land for their own purposes, trading with those in the Future while waiting for the return of the Father, Mr. Charlie. Though the names of these places suggest a fall of sorts into time or history, those in the Norm soon discover a disquieting fact: they are still not developing or aging. While seemingly "free," they have stagnated, effectively reproducing elements of the plantation system in new forms by maintaining the same division of labor and the same organization of the community that had existed in the period of slavery. When one of the characters, Queenie, discovers that even though no one in the Norm has aged at all but that Isis has in fact died, she sets out to the Future to understand why, while her brothers, Essex and Little Congo, have chosen to return to the Past. When they do so, an even more substantial break with the yam myth of origins occurs when, back on the original plantation, they discover not only the graves of children left behind after the group's dispersal, but also the interred bodies of Mr. Charlie and Woodville.

This discovery obviously invalidates the myth of patrilineal autochthony constructed by Mr. Charlie, but it also begins to shift the Norm community's relation to the land: If they are not yams from the seed of their Father, what are they? And if (Lord God) the Father and master has been discovered to be nothing more than a rotting corpse, how does this fact shift the community's perception of itself as being "of the Earth"? A new aesthetics of the Earth redefines the group once the yam myth and the way it narrates the community's rootedness in the soil begins to crumble. Elizabeth De Loughrey makes a crucial point about the symbolism of the yam, a staple food for African descendants and an important source of sustenance for both marooning slaves and those on the plantation who were allowed by their masters to cultivate them in the provision grounds. However, her assertion that, because yams are a rhizome, they must be read as a "natural metaphor for African regeneration in a new soil, the root (of Africa) in a creolized, rhizomatic Caribbean,"[39] neglects that in the novel the yam is primarily a figure for a monolinear origin, not a rhizomatic trope of creolized identity. The figure of the yam is not what produces the rhizomatic turn toward a different conception of identity; instead, it is the discovery of a divided origin marked by sexual difference that ushers in a realization of the community's itinerant derivation, a "Motherland" that is also an "elsewhere" in Glissant's sense that most of the former slaves have never known: Africa.

What takes shape in the novel, then, is a relation to an internal opacity and a geographical "elsewhere" that produces a more nuanced, though unsettling, understanding of the community's relation to the land on which it finds itself. For this relation to be possible, two things must happen: first, the death of God (or the Father, Mr. Charlie) and, second, the collapse of the idea of the Earth as a feminized "native soil" out of which the community springs autochthonously. The discovery of Mr. Charlie and Woodville's corpses means that the Earth is now not just a site of endemism and origins, but of dispersal and death[40]—a *terra incognita*, if you will, forcing the Norm community to discover its own mortality. "Are we to become stiff and be put in a hole in the earth; why, we were raised from it, how go back?" asks one of the characters. The narrator replies simply: "I see the question on their faces, even if none give it voice. I do not know the answer" (RM 121).

The Norm community's exposure to its own finitude is also its exposure to a different history or genealogy from which the yam myth of autochthony had cut it off. It slowly becomes clear that it was not Mr. Charlie, but in fact Woodville, the eponymous rainmaker, who sired most of the community and collaborated in the enslavement of his own people in a metaphoric act that echoes the novel's title. Collaborating in the "migration of forty choice fruits of mother's nation" (RM 138), Woodville—whose indigenous name is Tayeb—and who the group thinks could never make a mistake—uses this trust to condemn his entire family to slavery. When Tayeb realizes his mistake, it is too late: Africa as the Mother has been usurped by the false myth of the Father, an original dispersion the community is now forced to confront for the first time. In the face of this humiliation, and in an act of repentance, he tries to make it rain: "not just to give us water, but to let them see that we knew how to do great things that they had never dreamt that human beings could do" (RM 140). His capacity to remember how to do so, however, appears to fail him: "He tried to remember; tried to remember Mother; he tried to remember how you did it" (RM 140). The deluge that does come though—it is unclear whether of his volition or not—reveals his crimes:

> The rains came. No God, no rod, not a cent. Just the rains. I told you. They surely came. They showed us our mother's body swept away by the tide of Tayeb's rains. Drowned. They had a word for that they said—matricide. He had committed matricide. He had failed, he said. He had given her no comfort, he said. Had abandoned her nation. Separated her people, he said, had turned his back on her, and would not be consoled. Genosuicide he called it. My brother cried and cried and cried, full of water now, water rushing from every aperture of his frame. (RM 140)

The "rooted" myth of origins now fully shattered, the community must confront its forced abandonment of a motherland it has never known. It must come to terms with its orphaned itinerancy caused by the collusion of one of its members. Woodville's act of matricide (or "genosuicide"—the extermination or cutting off of indigeneity or origins)—and the discovery that God is dead under the soil of the plantation and through the rains revealing Tayeb's crimes—place the community into a different relation with its "roots,"[41] which are now revealed to be multiple, divided, and fundamentally itinerant. Woodville/Tayeb is an ambivalent character in the end: both a collaborator with the European system of slavery and someone who restores the community to its postemancipation, postmythic understanding of itself, returning the former slaves back to their "naturalness" (RM 146) which involves a recognition of the community's finitude, its multiple lineages, its multiple fathers and absent "Mother." Uprooted and adrift, this is a community without a model: "Here we are. No brother; no mother to teach us. Not even a father whose memory could challenge us into action. No Maker, no Preserver. No models to pursue" (RM 146). As a community without model, it is now free to *become* whatever it wants, in relation to a "root" it didn't even know it had, outside the kinship structures it has inherited, through an articulation of its own sense of community without precedent.

It is this transition from rootedness in the earth to itinerancy *on* the Earth, Brodber's novel implies, that constitutes the condition of possibility for a genuine emancipation from slavery and colonialism. Involved here is an aesthetics of the Earth in Glissant's sense that enacts a refashioning and reshaping of the community out of a new relation to the land—both the one on which it finds itself and an "elsewhere" from which it has been exiled. Rather than frame the question of postcolonial identity around double consciousness à la Du Bois[42] or the psychopathology of formerly colonized subjects forced to reconcile multiple affiliations and filiations à la Fanon,[43] Brodber views postcolonial emancipation as a break with mono-cultural concepts of filiation rooted in the soil. The novel's various narrators—a device that enacts the novel's theme of itinerancy by dispersing the narrative into a multiplicity of voices—all insist that what remains in the land must be considered "sacred," a place only the Father may access. That conception of the sacrality of the Earth masks a totalitarian desire for an arborescent root bound up with a belief in the land's capacity to ground unilinear filiation. In the collapse of that myth, however, the community becomes connected to several "elsewheres" that are temporal ("the Future") as well as spatial (Africa) but otherwise occluded. What does it mean, then, to be "in the free" (RM 150), the novel's final words? It means being open to a future *absent* the myth of filiation, as well as absent any model not permeated by a relation to alterity, including one's own. That alterity is encountered through an Earth that has become unknown and archipelagic, but at the same time unfettering, permitting a community to *come into being* rather than to endlessly reconstitute itself around a single identificatory lineage.

"Nooks of the Earth": Wordsworth's "Home at *Grasmere*"

While the abyss of the Middle Passage is absolutely central to a rethinking of community's relation to the Earth, the transatlantic slave trade was not the only way itinerancy began to challenge the idea of the nation, the global European "nomos of the Earth," and its relation to the land. In fact, serious attempts to rethink the Earth's centrality to every community's self-understanding can be found at the height of European colonial expansion and during the rise of the nation-state in Europe's revolutionary period. Clearly, these two contexts are not commensurate, yet the fact that they unfolded precisely when a particularly rooted, fusional conception of the nation was taking shape in Europe and being expanded across the globe is not accidental. As Saree Makdisi has argued, "England in the years around 1800 was not what would today be called a Western country, nor was it possible to neatly and cleanly distinguish it as a metropolitan space from the various colonial sites—both near and far—over which it sought to project political economic and cultural power." Makdisi points out that the particular construction of the national "we" or collective identity emerging at this point did not operate solely along the native/foreigner divide, which suggests that the particular construction of white Englishness emerging at the time was articulated internally as much as externally, and that "the borders between 'here' and 'there,' 'us' and 'them,' were for some time rather more amorphous, even porous, than we might have imagined."[44] Makdisi's examples show how the same rhetoric of "othering" that took shape around foreign others (the Irish, Africans, Arabs, the Chinese, West Indians, etc.) also captured the way Scottish highlanders or the urban poor in England were depicted such that a new specifically white, English identity could emerge. However, during this period there were also experiments with forms of community that aimed to reconfigure the relation between land and nation, geographic space and the construction of "the people" in their relation to others both internally and externally. These precedents, though less obviously pro- or anti-colonial than many of Makdisi's examples (including Wordsworth, who will be my own main example here),[45] nonetheless form a nexus with contemporary geopoets of the Caribbean, particularly Glissant, insofar as they—perhaps unwittingly (but does it matter?)—express an itinerant and unrooted conception of the relationship between land and community. This rearticulation was a way of creating new kinds of collective life that might challenge the hegemony of the nation as the primary form by which the people's sovereignty and identity could emerge. In the wake of disillusionment with the French Revolution, British Romantic poets such as William Wordsworth searched for alternative collective modes, albeit on a smaller scale than the nation, to carry the torch of democracy and liberation forward in the wake of its near total collapse in Europe. Seeing the French Revolution as a return to older forms of autocracy with a new veneer, Wordsworth sought to develop a poetics attentive to the way individual relations—through the externality of nature and the Earth—might become the basis of a new kind of collectivity by articulating the supposed universality of those relations and the modes of feeling they induced.

While this places Wordsworth squarely within the traditional liberal tradition that sought to understand the basis of collective life through the assumed starting point of atomized individuals who coalesce into a "whole"—first as family and smaller communities, then as nations—there is an element of his early poetry that advances some unexpected elements that link it to the nascent lineage of geopoetics, the most important expression of which is contemporary Caribbean literature, since it was connecting these ideas with *actually emergent* nations. The dominant trajectory of Wordsworth's writing generates an understanding of community through the individual, as attested by the epic structure of *The Prelude*—an autobiographical poem of roughly nine thousand lines. The poem's autobiographical sequence that leads up to the French Revolution and Wordsworth-as-narrator's subsequent disillusionment with its outcome is followed by his return to England and his taking up residence in the Lake District near Grasmere. Wordsworth's early poem "Home at Grasmere" is the first part of what was supposed to be his great "philosophic song," "The Recluse," a poetic project prefigured in *The Prelude* but which was never completed, and which was supposed to describe the vicissitudes of human nature from the standpoint of the isolated individual. But "Home at Grasmere" goes farther in that it envisages forms of community that would reconstitute the failed hopes of the French Revolution by other means, that is, by grounding such hopes in smaller nonnational communities capable of articulating a relation to the other as something different than the identification of a universal "citizen." What "Home at Grasmere" evinces, then, is a slightly stranger Wordsworth than the one to which we're accustomed. In this poetic experiment, his otherwise insistent focus on how individuals are formed into collectives is placed on hold, while another issue is addressed via the landscape of Grasmere: a poetic exploration of the way particular "nooks of the earth," as Wordsworth calls them, form the basis of collective life rather than some general "human nature." For unlike the many references to "human nature" that populate Wordsworth's other poetry, "Home at Grasmere" is an example of a geopoetics that articulates collective life through the specificity of a landscape.

With the help of Glissant's "aesthetics of the Earth," this collective can be seen as constitutionally itinerant, and defined by connections with a wide variety of others, including nonhumans. Wordsworth thereby becomes a Romantic-era poet concerned with a form of belonging to the Earth that acts as an alternative to the nation because it is structured by a contingent relation to a particular landscape that cannot be owned and that features relations to others more akin to the "law of the sea." Through that connection the "archipelagic" dimension of Wordsworth reveals itself: In lieu of a traditional nation-state or local parish that governs relations between human "citizens," a latent Glissantian "aesthetics of the Earth" in Wordsworth activates a community that goes beyond national belonging and exposes itself not just to other lands, other "nooks of Earth," but also to a variety of *nonhuman* geographic "elsewheres."[46] Wordsworth's community is itinerant in the sense that neither its human members, nor even its nonhuman ones, can claim any autochthonous relation to the land, and yet they share a bond with each other in and through their common chosen dwelling. Through that choice, those communal bonds are imaginatively extended to other communities and parts of the Earth that are not necessarily determined by the borders of nation-states. This "archipelagic" Wordsworth also draws out a specific moment in history when a specific conception of Englishness was being correlated to a "united" kingdom and when community in whatever form couldn't be conceived otherwise than as organized around a common possession—a national territory or land.[47] In that sense, Glissant's thought helps us to identify Romanticism's important, albeit all too brief, imaginative experimentation with the Earth (which I call geopoetics) that appeared in the early nineteenth century to challenge not only various nationalisms organized by filiation and territory, land, blood, and soil, but also their expansionist aims. While this ended up ultimately being a road not taken by Wordsworth, who later became nationalist and conservative, it nonetheless lives on as a latent trajectory within the Romantic period, suggesting a historical configuration that leads up to the twentieth and twenty-first centuries.

Wordsworth's early poetic interest in rural communities has often been taken as nostalgia for a kind of community living closer to nature or a return to a more rooted relation to the land, distinct from the mass migrations into the cities that took place in the wake of the collapse of rural economies that had organized agricultural production for centuries.[48] While I explore the legacy of the commons and its understanding of the Earth in the writings of Jacques Roumain and John Clare in the next chapter, it is only with the help of Glissant's poetics of Relation that we can begin to see how Wordsworth, Clare's better known contemporary, took up the idea of an ownerless Earth as the basis of community, rendering it in quite different terms than nostalgia for the immediacy of a long-lost rural past or rootedness in the soil. Unlike Clare, who worked the land, Wordsworth was not an agricultural laborer, so his views of the British rural working class were decidedly more abstract, framed by Rousseau's ideas of "natural man"[49] and the hope that the precise contours of human nature could be mapped by close observation of the rural poor. What Glissant allows us to see about Wordsworth is not just his conception of land as unpossessable, but also how the specificity of a community's relation to land shapes that community, and more precisely how a nontraditional relation to land acts as the precondition for any postnational form of community.[50] Grasmere may exist as a region internal to England, yet for Wordsworth its status is not defined by its relation to that particular "whole"—that is, the nation as the fundamental relational structure. Though not presented in terms of ocean currents and the interconnection between lands, Wordsworth's early geopoetics presents Grasmere as the local instance of what Wordsworth envisions as a planetary phenomenon. In this sense, the global for Wordsworth can only be accessed through the local, almost as if Wordsworth, for a moment, substitutes the question of how isolated individuals form larger collectives for a poetry interested in the question of how relations to local landscapes translate into a broader sense of community shared *across* national borders, a community he still uses the term "mankind" to describe despite the fact it includes the possibility of nonhuman members.[51] And while the itinerancy Wordsworth depicts is one of choice rather than forced migration, it becomes a central feature of the community.

At the end of 1799, Wordsworth moved into a small cottage in Town End with his sister Dorothy, under the assumption that Coleridge and others would soon follow to create a version of the community they had imagined taking shape in America. "Home at Grasmere" becomes a poetic account of that never realized community, situated now in the middle of England, with Wordsworth and Dorothy (named "Emma" in the poem) figured as migrants to the valley. In fact, the valley itself becomes the poem's central character, providing sanctuary for all life-forms and creatures finding a temporary home in it, acting as a kind of refuge from other communities because it is quite literally bordered on two sides by hills forming a valley that Wordsworth calls a "Concave":

> Within the bounds of this huge Concave; here
> Should be my home, this Valley be my World.
> From that time forward was the place to me
> As beautiful in thought as it had been
> When present to my bodily eyes; a haunt
> Of my affections[52]

If typical Wordsworthian themes are embedded here, particularly the landscape being gradually transposed into an internal one, the poem still insists on the valley's materiality as it enfolds various inhabitants within its physical space. Grasmere becomes a site for their interactions, encounters, and alliances; it becomes both their world and a relation to the Earth.

And even though he is with Emma, Wordsworth-as-narrator emphasizes his solitude as coextensive with the valley's material enclosure. Joined in their solitude, the two siblings reflect on the relation between the external landscape of Grasmere and the internal one, but this link reveals more than just a connection between nature and the mind. It reveals instead how connection to the land in fact *breaks* this solitude in advance because the land activates a bond to every inhabitant of the valley. This relation, for Wordsworth, is more than just imaginative or mental since it is grounded in the material existence of the valley. The land itself, its physical reality, becomes the means by which the mind experiences its connection with others, who all take up a relation to this particular nook of the Earth. In this way, Grasmere becomes a "center" and a "small abiding place of many men" (HG 48:165) by which its inhabitants, human and nonhuman alike, are placed in relation to one another. And yet that relation goes beyond simply residing in the same place. For Wordsworth this shared connection to Grasmere is a "sensation"—"the one sensation that is here" (HG 46:156)—specific to the valley itself. As we'll see, that "sensation" is not simply how the valley appears to human perception, but an affective connection providing a common feeling of being possessed *by* the land, embraced by its capacity to provide a sense of "home," a shared dwelling space that is not purely one's own and that cannot be possessed. The point of "Home at Grasmere," then, like Wordsworth's great unfinished "philosophical poem" "The Recluse," is not individual isolation for its own sake, but a reduction of enforced or artificial forms of sociality (which Wordsworth associates with the increasingly crowded streets of the city where people have been forced to live together out of purely economic necessity). This reduction of the social is achieved at first through solitude and isolation but eventually arrives at a genuine sense of connection with one's surroundings, including the co-inhabitants of that milieu, through the "one sensation" specific to Grasmere.

How, then, does that "one sensation" create a new form of sociality between both humans and nonhumans? The initial sense of seclusion the valley generates allows the uniqueness of its terrain, and the "sensation" allied to it, to create a relation, first to the valley itself, then to other inhabitants of the valley, and finally to other "nooks of the Earth" such as Grasmere:

What want we? Have we not perpetual streams,
Warm woods, and sunny hills, and fresh green fields,
And mountains not less green, and flocks and herds,
And thickets full of songsters, and the voice
Of lordly birds—an unexpected sound
Heard now and then from morn to latest eve,
Admonishing the man who walks below
Of solitude and silence in the sky?
These have we, and a thousand nooks of earth
Have also these, but no where else is found—
No where (or is it fancy?) can be found—
The one sensation that is here; (HG 46: 145–56)

The uniqueness of the "sensation" specific to Grasmere does not foreclose the possibility that other similar "nooks of earth" have their own sense of belonging or "home" articulated in the title. The one that exists in Grasmere is cultivated by the reality of the landscape, from the "perpetual streams" and "mountains not less green," to the sounds of fellow inhabitants including the "lordly birds" that "admonish the man who walks below." Wordsworth's repeated use of the locative "here" to define the precise whereabouts of the "sensation" suggests that the "sensation" and "here" are effectively indiscernible. The parenthetical question ("or is it fancy?") is not about the reality of the sensation but, coupled with the repeated phrase "no where else," concerns the reality of its *location*, and perhaps some doubt on the part of Wordsworth-as-speaker about whether the sensation is as unique as he thinks it is. The sensation, a sense of "here" irreducible either to the land or to some internalized landscape of the mind, is nothing but the *relation* between the two, a "here" that "abides by day / By night, here only; or in chosen minds / That take it with them hence, where'er they go" (HG 46: 158–60). The "or" in the second line defines the relation between "chosen minds" and the land by articulating Grasmere's "here" as what at first defines something, a feeling, that remains persistent—night or day—thanks to the physical landscape, but which then becomes something its inhabitants take with them when they leave. In other words, "here" indexes a Relation, in Glissant's sense, to a specific landscape that has irreducibly *shaped the self* while maintaining its material distinctness and its relation to an "elsewhere." Hence the reason for the uncertain locality of the sensation: it is both "here" and "elsewhere" simultaneously.

The specific locality of the "sensation" is therefore ambiguous—it is "here only" in the sense that it is generated by being enfolded in Grasmere's valley yet continues to define a collective belonging in the absence of that landscape. The nature of the sensation, therefore, is difficult to define given its liminality between the mind and the physical reality of the landscape, its status as a tangible "nook of earth" with its intellectual and emotional dimensions. In a famous passage that defines the nature of the "sensation" binding every inhabitant to the land, Wordsworth couches it in the language of the sublime:

> 'Tis (but I cannot name it), 'tis the sense
> Of majesty, and beauty, and repose,
> A blended holiness of earth and sky
> Something that makes this individual Spot,
> This small abiding-place of many men,
> A termination, and a last retreat,
> A Centre, come from wheresoe'er you will,
> A Whole without dependence or defect,
> Made for itself, and happy in itself,
> Perfect Contentment, Unity entire. (HG 46–48: 161–70)

The sensation the speaker cannot quite identify but which is tied to the specificity of the landscape (a "blended holiness of earth and sky") is meant to give meaning to the idea of "home" in the title of the poem. That sense of home, however, apart from being portable, is also available to anyone "whereso'er" they may happen to come from. In other words, as with the speaker and Emma, the idea of home associated with Grasmere is not predicated on native belonging but on something more akin to a receptivity, an attunement to the beauty and tranquility proffered by the landscape, a "sensation" open to anyone and everyone.

Of course, Wordsworth's description of the relational sensation specific to Grasmere as well as the way it enables the totality of connection with others is somewhat different from Glissant's geopoetics. In Wordsworth, the "Whole without dependence or defect" of Grasmere, which he also calls a "unity entire," implies that totality is situated within a particular locale, in other words, that Grasmere is itself a totality; for Glissant, on the other hand, totality is the differentiated unity of the entire Earth. In short, Wordsworth's totality prioritizes a determinate set of relations that a *specific* landscape makes possible, whereas Glissant's archipelagic totality emphasizes relations to other lands and islands, other "nooks of earth" in Wordsworth's words.

The difference, though, is one of scale rather than structure. For Wordsworth, Grasmere is a totality he hopes will eventually become a globality. The shared "sensation" of unity the speaker and Emma experience in Grasmere enables relations and encounters with the valley's other inhabitants, such as the pair of swans on which the poem focuses, who come and go from within its confines. That this community might eventually take up a relation to other lands is left as an undeveloped thought for a "hereafter" in which "all the Vales of earth" might one day be formed around the "portion of blessedness" and "knowledge" represented by Grasmere:

> A pair seceding from the common world,
> Might in that hallowed spot to which our steps
> Were tending, in that individual nook,
> Might even thus early for ourselves secure,
> And in the midst of these unhappy times,
> A portion of the blessedness which love
> And knowledge will, we trust, hereafter give
> To all the Vales of earth and all mankind. (HG 52: 249–56)

In part because of his liberal commitments, Wordsworth's Earth is conceived of as a collection of "nooks," or regions, each of which has its own sensation and, at some point, can be related to the others through that shared singularity. A relation to the local landscape is for Wordsworth the starting point for a broader globality, a connection to "all the Vales of earth and all mankind," and so what binds inhabitants to a particular landscape could potentially become the source of a broader universality. The fact that this "trust" is contextualized by the "unhappy times" of England's involvement in the war against revolutionary France suggests that Wordsworth's political hopes have been transferred to articulations of smaller communities organized around a shared relation to land that, through its eventual extension to "all the Vales of earth," might in the future become an alternative source of universality distinct from the abstraction of the "citizen" that defines belonging to the nation. Of what, Wordsworth's poem asks, are we citizens, if not primarily of the "nook" of earth we have chosen as our own? In what way does the land itself introduce a sense of belonging or "sensation" that translates into a form of society with others that is neither organic nor strictly speaking "natural,"[53] but is instead a relation to the land as the condition of a chosen community with others? And how might this sense of community be translated into a broader universality of "love of man"[54] that transcends the national?

The answer to all these questions for Wordsworth is compressed in an understanding of land as more than a matter of ownership or property rights.[55] I don't mean to suggest that Wordsworth is a Marxist *avant la lettre*; the emphasis for this claim lies elsewhere. For him, a community doesn't possess a particular land or territory but is instead possessed *by* it. We can see this ostensibly counterintuitive idea in "Home at Grasmere" when it describes the "ownership" entailed in the speaker's and "Emma's" relation to the sensation specific to Grasmere. Because this sensation cannot be properly located—is it in the land itself or the minds of its inhabitants?—it is also in-appropriable, un-possessable either as a parcel of land or as an individual experience because it is more than a physical object:

> The unappropriated bliss hath found
> An owner, and that owner I am he.
> The Lord of this enjoyment is on Earth
> And in my breast. What wonder if I speak
> With fervour, am exalted with the thought
> Of my possessions, of my genuine wealth
> Inward and outward? (HG 42: 85–91)

The language of "ownership" Wordsworth uses here reverberates through the rest of the poem as the sensation of totality the valley represents is developed in various ways, but always with a view to the notion that it is a form of "wealth" that cannot be hoarded or privatized, and that, like Glissant's "aesthetics of the Earth," is not an exchangeable commodity. The "unappropriated bliss" described above is instead something that overtakes or overcomes the speaker, offering him a "genuine wealth" not entirely his own.

Paradoxically, however, this initially individual unpossessable "bliss" is shared with the other inhabitants of the valley. It thus becomes a kind of common property and a form of relation to one another so long as "property" is understood here as something other than a material good or even a "commons."[56] A commons entails a specific legal structure, as I will explore in the next chapter when discussing Clare, and can too easily be misconstrued as simply collectively owned land. The shared, unlocalizable "sensation" of Grasmere, its flickering between external materiality and mental content, as the tie that binds the members of the community to each other—this is what matters to Wordsworth. And it is also where he locates something approximating the Glissantian Earth—a totality that cannot be homogenized and as a result connects the self with the other. Except that in Wordsworth, the connection with the other explicitly extends beyond purely human inhabitants of the valley. A flock of birds, residents of Grasmere the speaker had earlier remarked were invisible companions, are present through their songs but not by sight. Then suddenly many of them appear over the lake with the arrival of an unseasonably warm day in the middle of winter. They, much like Wordsworth and Emma, are rapt by the "sensation" that is Grasmere:

> They are jubilant
> This day, who drooped, or seemed to droop, so long;
> They shew their pleasure, and shall I do less?
> Happier of happy though I be, like them
> I cannot take possession of the sky,
> Mount with a thoughtless impulse, and wheel there
> One of a mighty multitude, whose way
> And motion is harmony and dance
> Magnificent. Behold them, how they shape
> Orb after orb, their course still round and round
> Above the area of the Lake, their own
> Adopted region, girding it about
> In wanton repetition, yet therewith—
> With that large circle evermore renewed (HG 54: 284–97).

The notion that the birds, like Wordsworth, display their pleasure, bliss, or joy invokes a cluster of similarities between them and other residents of the valley: the birds, like the speaker and Emma, cannot take possession of their "adopted region"—it is not theirs to own. And yet, the space of the sky is what allows them to "wheel" and "dance" in such a way that they become a single "mighty multitude." Grasmere, an "adopted region" for the two humans, is a space like the sky "above the area of the Lake" wherein relations become possible, including with the birds. If the land in whatever form—earth or sky—cannot be appropriated, it is because this "property" is precisely what renders it a condition of possibility, like Glissant's Relation, for relations with others.

This connection to Grasmere's nonhuman inhabitants grows more explicit right after the description of the flock when the speaker notes that the two swans who would normally be seen gliding on the lake are gone. The fact that they are missing sparks a kind of crisis as the poem explicitly identifies Wordsworth and Emma with the swans. The worst possibility comes to mind: Maybe a shepherd of the valley has shot one or both, and so the idyllic sense of "home" that has until now infused Grasmere is potentially shattered by the possibility of violence. The poem's identification of its two human protagonists with the swans becomes a meditation on the fact that, while Grasmere may create the *possibility* of relations between its human and nonhuman inhabitants, those associations are not necessarily benevolent. Like the birds above the lake, identification with the swans is predicated on their shared choice of Grasmere as their home:

> They came, like Emma and myself, to live
> Together here in peace and solitude,
> Chusing this Valley, they who had the choice
> Of the whole world. (HG 58: 326–29)

Again, the specificity of the land binds the swans to the speaker and Emma: they are two "pairs" who have made Grasmere their adopted home. Like the human duo, the swans have chosen the valley in the name of a shared solitude; both Wordsworth and Emma, as well as the two swans, have already formed the most minimal of all communities: a couple. Wordsworth, however, repeatedly emphasizes that the swans are a pair not just because he and Emma resemble them ("They strangers, and we strangers; they a pair, / And we a solitary pair like them") (HG 58: 340–41), but because his meditation on the possible killing of the swans is also a reflection on how the forms of relation engendered by the shared "bliss" of the valley are potentially insufficient to ward off other imperatives—such as the shepherd's need to supply food for his family—that threaten to make those relations potentially predatory.

Critics often discuss the role of the swans, some even insisting that it is the poem's pivotal episode.[57] Raimonda Modiano, for instance, suggests that "Wordsworth fears that he may become a sacrificial victim, encountering the same fate as the two swans killed by the shepherds of Grasmere."[58] Yet what critics often neglect is the fact that the poem actually directs its concern back to Grasmere, as if Wordsworth's conjecture about the fate of the swans had somehow "wronged" the valley itself. This, then, is less a personal identification with the swans than a potentially wavering faith in the capacity of the valley to generate necessarily *compassionate* relations among its inhabitants. In fact, the rest of the poem is little else than an attempt to reconstitute a faith in the land's inherently benevolent status, an insistence that "they who are dwellers in this holy place / Must needs themselves be hallowed" (HG 60: 366–67), that the valley imparts to those inhabitants "an overflowing love / Not for the creature only, but for all / Which is around them" (HG 60: 375–77).

Another important difference between Wordsworth's and Glissant's geopoetics merges here, then: Wordsworth insists, despite the potential for violence represented by the missing swans, that the *kinds* of relations between a particular nook of the earth, such as Grasmere, and its inhabitants are necessarily affirmative or ameliorating. Shattered hopes, and their reconstitution, are a pattern found through Wordsworth. In *The Prelude*, for instance, disillusionment with the French Revolution leads to the question of how the imagination is initially "impaired" in its full capacities, but eventually "restored" through a connection with the natural world.[59] In "Home at Grasmere" the contemplation of the absent swans leads to a similar crisis as the threat of violence enters the otherwise idyllic community until a renewed "faith" in its capacity to bind inhabitants together is likewise restored. In other words, because he is committed to the idea that the mind and nature are fitted to each other, Wordsworth advances a geopoetics that emphasizes mutually reinforcing relations meant to bring about an improvement of "mankind" or "human nature" in general. Even relations to the nonhuman inhabitants of the Earth are articulated through this connection, potentially reestablishing a recalcitrant humanism precisely at the place—his articulation of community with nonhuman others—where Wordsworth seems most ready to break with it. His geopoetics is ultimately universalist, articulated through a "mind" potentially shared by all, in relation to a nature with purely progressive dimensions, through relations that are essentially restorative, unlike the possibly conflictual power relations found in Glissant. Wordsworth's revolution and his conception of the totality of the Earth attempt to bring about this new form of community (and new relation to the Earth) without struggle, and certainly without violence, a privilege afforded to one whose very survival has not been threatened, and whose world has remained essentially intact, despite shattered hopes. This universalist dimension in Wordsworth constitutes the most significant distinction between his and Glissant's geopoetics since, for Glissant, no conception of the totality of the Earth is possible until the homogenized European "nomos of the Earth" has been fundamentally challenged by decolonial struggle.

And yet, despite these decidedly nineteenth-century humanist trappings, Wordsworth's geopoetics, by understanding totality—and therefore the Earth—through a connection to a specific landscape, challenges other ways of founding community, including those that view the Earth through a "nomos of the Earth" that centralizes the nation-state, private property, and autochthony. Though Wordsworth's humanist-universalist tendencies might be seen as leading to a rehomogenization of the totality he articulates through Grasmere, it is nonetheless this element of his geopoetics that aligns him with the more direct critiques of the (rooted) nation-state form found in contemporary Caribbean geopoetics. Though Wordsworth believed in the abstraction of "human nature," the complex relations he establishes through the land between humans and fellow nonhuman inhabitants nevertheless cannot be reduced to a whole or "One" that standardizes or homogenizes them. The totality of relations, for Wordsworth, may not yet be global or planetary, but it is also not uniform either. Certainly, in the less globalized world of the nineteenth century, Wordsworth's poetics merely gestures at the full-fledged idea of totality one finds in Glissant. Yet it echoes it by suggesting that, even out of the most profound solitary isolation, one is always necessarily bound up with others through one's own, and through their own, relation to the Earth:

> We shall not scatter through the plains and rocks
> Of this fair Vale, and o'er its spacious heights,
> Unprofitable kindliness, bestowed
> On Objects unaccustomed to the gifts
> Of feeling, that were cheerless and forlorn
> But few weeks past, and would be so again
> If we were not; we do not tend a lamp
> Whose lustre we alone participate,
> Which is dependent on us alone,
> Mortal though bright, a dying, dying flame.
> Look where we will, some human heart has been
> Before us with its offering; not a tree
> Sprinkles these little pastures, but the same
> Hath furnished matter for a thought; perchance
> To some one is as a familiar Friend.
> Joy spreads and sorrow spreads; and this whole Vale,
> Home of untutored Shepherds as it is,
> Swarms with sensation, as with gleams of sunshine (HG78: 649–66).

It is not the abstraction of "human nature" or the imagination here that conveys to Wordsworth and his sister that they are "not alone"; it is the physical land (the "plains and rocks / Of this fair Vale") that register the many "gifts of feeling" bestowed on it. The land, then, is not a static "object," a mere background against which the drama of humanity plays out. It figures instead as a Glissantian archipelago, opening access to others and to spatial and temporal elsewheres of various kinds, from other nooks of Earth to places where "some human heart has been / Before us with its offering." Each of these features of the landscape, swarming with "sensation," provides not just "matter for thought" but the condition of possibility for an encounter with others—human or otherwise—who, despite being a stranger, could become a "familiar Friend," rendered so through the shared relation to the land. Grasmere is for Wordsworth a field of relations to other inhabitants, even if they never meet "in person" as it were, regardless of whether or not there is a person there of which to speak.

It is that sense of a chosen belonging—for the swans as much as the Wordsworths—to a "nook of earth" that governs Wordsworth's articulation of a community capable of surpassing what he perceives as the purely arbitrary and haphazard relations between people and cultures characterized by rapid urbanization in the early 1800s. London in *The Prelude*, for instance, is a space organized by forms of relation to others that provokes an even more profound solitude than the one that exposes the speaker and Emma to their surroundings, and thus to all the others around them. It is not that Grasmere, as a rural land, offers a communal model of immediate face-to-face relations, or an "organic" community grounded in some "closer" relation to nature. In both forms of solitude—the solitude of the city and the solitude of Grasmere—one is with others through one's relation to a place. But in the case of the city, the heterogeneity of the other is flattened out either into purely commercial relations Wordsworth views as too inessential to constitute anything resembling genuine community, or into an anonymity that renders every other interchangeable with any other.[60] The totality represented by the metropolis produces forms of relation and connection to others that have "no law, no meaning and no end"[61] akin to the homogeneous "One" in Glissant. The totality of Grasmere is contrasted with the totality of the city through the *kinds* of relations Grasmere facilitates by enabling what Wordsworth calls a "true community" through a relation to the unique "sensation" specific to it as a specific geographic place:

> Solitude is not
> Where these things are: he is truly alone,
> He of the multitude whose eyes are doomed

To hold a vacant commerce day by day
With that which he can neither know nor love—
Dead things, to him thrice dead—or worse than this,
With swarms of life, and worse than all, of men,
His fellow men, that are to him no more
Than to the Forest Hermit are the leaves
That hang aloft in myriads—nay, far less,
Far less for aught that comforts or defends
Or lulls or chears. Society is here:
The true community, the noblest Frame
Of many into one incorporate (HG 88–90: 807–20).

Though the city dweller is surrounded by "swarms of life," his "fellow men" are in fact "dead" to him because their associations with each other, framed by commercial necessity or anonymity, are as exchangeable and homogeneous as "the leaves / That hang aloft in myriads," each essentially the same as the last. The community of Grasmere too involves relations to fellow men whom one might never actually encounter, yet the community is "true" because the valley functions as an external basis of connection that joins inhabitants as different and as varied as Wordsworth, his sister, a pair of swans, a flock of birds, and a potentially murderous shepherd, together into one society. Each is different, even "opaque" to the other in Glissant's sense, and yet the landscape itself is their condition of relation, connecting them without privileging any of them, either through the categories of "species" or "filiation." Wordsworth's early poem is thus an example of a geopoetics not unlike Glissant's and Brodber's, all three exploring other forms of social existence that might be possible outside the frame of the nation-state and its rooted model of identity. These other forms of community become available, however, only once a new relation to the Earth takes center stage: a relation to an un-possessable Earth that is the condition of all relations to the other, rather than a property or condition of territorial and filial belonging.

We do not find Wordsworth's division between urban and rural communities in Glissant or Brodber, nor do we find his apparent idealization of the parochial. Nevertheless, what connects them is the way each of them predicates whatever form of community comes after the nation-state on a new relation to the Earth that is itinerant, mobile, and, ultimately, structured around shifting relations to a geographic locality rather than on fixed or rooted identities grounded on autochthony. They are all also united around a conception of the Earth that understands it as "archipelagic" in Glissant's sense: each place, land, or "nook of the earth" is irrevocably connected to, and defined by, its relation to others, through an ultimately unknowable Earth. In Glissant, geographic relations are figured by ocean currents, in Brodber's through the break instituted by the discovery of the diasporic status of the community, and in Wordsworth through the "sensation" specific to each locale that defines each inhabitant's connection to the other. Each writer, in their own way, concretizes a form of community *bound to the Earth*, based on a form of communal togetherness realized not by connection to a shared essence or identity, but through the fundamental contingency of one's relation to a specific geographic locale. A "nomos of the Earth" predicated not on an isomorphism between land and identity, Earth, and human law, but on an itinerancy grounded in a (nook of) earth that cannot be made one's "own," and is therefore a "homeland" of a very different kind.

In a diary entry composed during her stay in Grasmere (April 29, 1802), Wordsworth's sister Dorothy (the "Emma" of "Home at Grasmere") recounts taking a walk with William to "John's Grove," a place they had named after their brother. John Wordsworth was captain of the largest vessel owned by the East India Company, trading between Great Britain and China. He drowned when his ship sank in 1805. Prior to his death he visited his siblings and enjoyed strolling through the grove in the valley they had named after him. Dorothy remembers one of her walks with William in 1802:

> We then went to Johns Grove, sate a while at first. Afterwards, William lay, & I lay in the trench under the fence—he with his eyes shut & listening to the waterfalls & the Birds. There was no one waterfall above another—it was a sound of waters in the air—the voice of the air. William heard me breathing & rustling now & then but we both lay still, & unseen by one another—he thought that it would be as sweet thus to lie so in the grave, to hear the *peaceful* sounds of the earth & just to know that ones dear friends were near.[62]

Lying on the earth, each listening to its "peaceful sounds," William contemplates an impossible relation, after his death, to an Earth that maintains not only a connection with the various sensations it produces, but also with "ones dear friends," including Dorothy, whose shared proximity to those sensations is felt rather than seen. In a way, Dorothy ventriloquizes here a relation to the land Wordsworth articulates in "Home at Grasmere" as he imagines it now in an unattainable posterity. The fact that the name of this site would three years later be attached to an actual rather than imagined death, a death framed by and the result of colonial trade relations, only highlights the extent to which two different relations to the Earth are able to coexist in and be signified by the same plot of land. William Wordsworth's own poem on his brother's visit—"When I First Journeyed Hither," written before John's death—emphasizes the extent to which William was constantly visiting that "sequestered nook"[63] of the grove prior to his brother's visit. However, as the poem emphasizes, he was unable to locate a satisfactory path that would allow him to traverse it at his leisure. When his brother John arrived in Grasmere after they had been apart for fourteen years, William laments that they "knew little in what mold / Each other's minds were fashioned" and that there was little between them other than a mere bond of "common feelings of fraternal love" (WJ 565–66: 79–83). However, upon returning to the grove after his brother's departure, William discovers a path his brother had unearthed there "by pacing here / With that habitual restlessness of foot / Wherewith the sailor measures o'er and o'er / His short domain upon the Vessel's deck" (WJ 565: 70–74), a path that William was unable to discover despite his constant wandering in the grove. When John departs again for the sea, a new bond—one that is no longer of a common feeling of kinship—is created between them, in and through a relation to Grasmere. William images his brother once again pacing the deck "to and fro" (WJ 566: 107), the same mode of walking that had allowed John to discover the path in the grove. That step, cultivated at sea, is once again happening in "some far region, here, while o'er my head / At every impulse of the moving breeze / The fir-grove murmurs with a sea-like sound" (WJ 566: 108–11). Bound more intimately by a relation to the grove than any relation of blood or kinship, they become joined by an itinerancy shared through Grasmere, as William "tim[es] his steps" (WJ 566: 112) with his brother at sea in the grove, and as the trees mimic the sound of the ocean. The grove itself creates a relation between them that is not just imagined but grounded in a kind of itinerancy that, when transplanted to Grasmere, mirrors being adrift on the sea, and constructs a connection to the land even William could not have envisaged. John's death, bound up with the arrow-like nomadism of British colonialism, thus shares a space, quite literally, with a very different kind of being adrift. John's Grove, a name now forever bound up both with Wordsworth's geopoetic articulation of an itinerant community distinct from the nation-state, as well as with his brother's role in Great Britain's colonial expansion,[64] becomes a cipher of two different lineages: a thinking of the Earth as a relation to the other, and one that treats it as a site of trade or conquest.

In our present moment the former lineage could not have placed a more trenchant task before us, particularly in the era of the Anthropocene. That task is to understand how to produce a "people" beyond the nation-state that could take up the problem of relation not just as a question of international law, or of international trade and diplomacy, but as a condition of survival.[65] In the wake of Wordsworth, Brodber, and Glissant, this task entails not just reconceiving a worldwide community the totality of which must consist of something more than the sum of its parts: a set of independent nations with their own "people" and relation to a particular land. Rather, the perspective of collectivity must be generated out of a relation to the Earth as something that is no longer viewed as an object to be plundered, but that is instead seen as the very condition for, and possibility of, collective life itself, a collectivity beyond all "rooted" forms of identity, shared ownership of the land, or neocolonial dreams of expansion. A collectivity founded, that is, through a new kind of nomadism that finds us all adrift on the Earth, drifting toward the other and away from the self, made "one" only in and through a collective fidelity to an inscrutable and indifferent Earth.

TWO

ROUMAIN AND CLARE

The Earth as Commons

THE FIRST CHAPTER WAS a reflection on the way community takes shape in the context of itinerant, postnational relations to land or territory. This chapter explores how a geopoetics that conceives of the Earth as a vast commons—something fundamentally unpossessable and outside of any economic exchange—also provides the basis for forms of solidarity no longer framed by national or ethnic identity, by an internationalism still confined to the relations between nation-states, or by the ownership of collective "natural resources." In today's global marketplace, the Earth's capacity to support life is variously commodified: components of the Earth's systems once deemed part of the "public interest"—water for example—have been turned into a "resource" to be sold as a private stockpile for extraction. Meanwhile, individual nations, trapped by the corruption and collusion of their own political elites, are too enmeshed in the enforced structures of privatization to respond or resist. Effective answers instead come from grassroots environmental activism: Vandana Shiva, for instance, has undercut Monsanto's monopoly on seed distribution in India by resorting to the traditional peasant practice of simply saving it—keeping an amount of seed in reserve from each harvest sufficient to maintain a consistent stock for subsequent ones, reducing the need for multinational suppliers. Though some see these actions as resistance to modernization and the technologized practices required for mass-scale agricultural production, far more is stake. As I outline in this chapter, the move to pit traditional peasant agricultural practices against multinational encroachment is not new: we've seen it proposed in Haiti eighty years ago, and ever further back in England a hundred years before that. What is new, however, is the extent to which the conflicts between national and multinational agribusiness and the relation to the Earth figured in more traditional agricultural practices requires rethinking not just the connection between a particular geographic space and forms of community irreducible to the nation-state or the global market, but also how that community represents the nature of its collective life in relation to the Earth. Is the Earth a set of private plots of land organized around individual property rights, or is it a shared resource bequeathed to the collective for its safekeeping?

That opposition may seem less part of a postnational understanding of community than it may at first appear. Though the private model is clearly the one favored by most nation-states across the globe, even the notion of a shared resource has become recently framed in terms of nation-state relations. Take, for example, a 2016 report by the International Institute for Applied System Analysis titled "Global Commons in the Anthropocene: World Development on a Stable and Resilient Planet," an institute created during the Cold War to facilitate policy-driven research on large-scale projects including "sustainable development" and "energy security" across national lines, funded largely by scientific organizations within member states. In their "global commons" report, the authors propose distinguishing between various ways in which the Earth is divided into a series of different "commons"—aspects of the Earth, or the Earth's systems, upon which all nations depend, and which therefore require a set of multilateral agreements concerning their use or exploitation. Defining the goal of a "global commons" in terms of a "resilient and stable planet," the report suggests separating the Earth into a series of different commons zones, depending on the makeup of each one's respective "stakeholders." Defining these zones as "shared resources," the authors suggest distinguishing "local commons"—what are usually called "national resources" such as fishing stocks, irrigation systems, agriculture, and timber located within the borders of a particular nation-state—from the "global commons" which includes the "biomes, biodiversity and biogeochemical cycles that combine to form a dynamic equilibrium at the planetary scale."[1] The former are the managed domain of the nation-states in which they are located, the latter require every nation to apply the principle of collective "planetary limits" to the safeguarding of Earth-systems stability, which the authors contend is now imperative for all national economies.

Though no doubt well intended, the report's vision of the Earth as a commons remains bound—for obvious reasons—by its enclosure within national and global market frameworks that view the Earth's surface as carved up into either national or multinational "resource bases." While these individual nation-states must now, according to the authors, consider the global commons of the biosphere, they do so from within a conception of the Earth as enclosed, a vast repository one can access so long as one does not interfere with other extraction economies by destabilizing the broader biosphere on which they all depend. This liberal view of the commons essentially reduces it to a shared but parceled out storehouse that must be regulated to preserve the functioning of global markets; if there is no stable planet, there are no stable national economies. To remain stable, national economies must, for good fiduciary reasons, no longer treat the Earth as an externality to the economy but instead as intrinsically bound up with the market and its long-term sustainability. When the report turns to the underlying "principles" that must govern the "management" of the global commons, it describes the need to change a set of "worldviews" to "the idea of planetary stewardship for the global commons," in what it calls a "grand transformation" that will become a new "social contract for planetary stewardship," facilitating "technological, social and behavioral changes."[2] These behavioral changes, to put it simply, are only encouraged to maintain the stability of capitalism; a "grand transformation" to ward off a more radical one, and a conception of the Earth as commons in line with prevailing understandings of it as a "resource base," a property to be owned and distributed.

This chapter explores a different conception of the Earth as commons which, it argues, is more relevant, if not more necessary, for our contemporary moment than the current one ensnared by global capital. What if the Earth considered as a commons is *neither* a "shared resource" for humans *nor* the purview of national economies, but is instead the starting point for the articulation of other worlds that would include postnational solidarities among not just local or national peoples, but among species? A commons that would be the basis for a new international no longer organized solely along class lines, related to an Earth that can be no longer be understood as a property of any kind, whether private or collective. A notion of the commons that extends even beyond what had been legally recognized in England as a set of rights commoners had to certain uses of private land.[3] An understanding of the commons predicated on the *precedence* and indifference of the Earth to every human legal and economic system. A concept of the commons exemplified at various moments in the nineteenth and twentieth centuries by so-called peasant cultures and their collective relation to the land.

In this understanding of the Earth, it is not just that water or seed must remain "publicly owned," but that an entirely different relation to the Earth defined by what the community *cannot transform into its property* becomes central to its self-understanding.[4] The Earth in this sense becomes an unconditional "gift"[5] exceeding all modes of exchange, all forms of property, all economization of its status as the unconditional basis for human *and* nonhuman worlds of various kinds.

How that "gift" is received or conceived of, however, determines what that world looks like. In the Judeo-Christian tradition, for example, the "gift" of the Earth is framed by an economy of giver and receiver, with an original sovereign—God—bequeathing Earth to man's "dominion." Man is chosen for this role as the next best thing to God, the only creature created in God's likeness. As Genesis puts it: "And God said Let us make man in our image, after our likeness: and let them have dominion over the fish and the sea, and over the fowl of the air, and over the cattle, and over all the earth, and over every creeping thing that creepeth upon the earth."[6] The biblical isomorphism between God and Man enables allows God's sovereignty over the Earth to be substituted for Man's. A world defined by this theological relation to the Earth as divine gift is organized around the Great Chain of Being, wherein life is hierarchically ordered, with God as original proprietor occupying the apogee, humanity as God's proxy on Earth directly subordinate to Him, and every other inhabitant of the Earth—as well as the Earth itself—the subject of Man's "dominion." The gradations on the chain govern not just relations between human and nonhuman creatures, but also hierarchies *within* human societies, ordered by one's distance from God or proximity to nature. The gift of the Earth conceived of in this way creates a hierarchy of life that also became central to liberal theories of property, with the Earth and its less-than-human and nonhuman inhabitants available to humanity as raw material for its labor, even while the explicit theological underpinnings of this idea were transformed over time into a secular conception of private property.

Though this other notion of the commons is also organized around the idea of the Earth as gift, its aim couldn't be more different. If one had to identify its philosophical counterpart, it could be found in the concept of "givenness" (*Gegebenheit*) at work in the phenomenological tradition. Decidedly anonymous, Heidegger's *es gibt*[7] ("it gives'), for example, is a giving without donor or receiver and therefore without debt or exchange. It connotes what is "there" prior to its manifestation (or its being "enframed" through technological calculation) within a particular world or structure of appearance. What makes the Earth "there" is not God as transcendental signifier but rather the Earth's withdrawal from any economy of restitution, credit, debt, or property. As Jacques Derrida suggests, for there to be a gift in this sense the recipient must not "*recognize* the gift as gift. If he recognizes it *as* gift, if the gift *appears to him as such*, if the present is present to him *as present*, this simple recognition suffices to annul the gift." The gift is annulled, in other words, through its reinsertion into an economy, an exchangeability, the circulation of the gift of *something* from someone to someone else. In this circulation, the gift becomes a *thing* for which the recipient incurs at least a symbolic debt. On the other hand, a gift that would avoid this fate would be a "gift that gives not a given but the *condition* of a present given in general."[8] Translated to the language of geopoetics, the anonymous gift of the Earth is not the giving of something: an object, a planet, a property, a set of raw materials. Rather, the Earth is the giving of time and place, a background against which these things might appear, but which remains irreducible to the world or horizon of meaning that makes sense of it.[9]

The Earth's giving of time and place thus introduces the possibility of a different kind of world that would receive it. Worlds are possible because of the Earth's unconditional anteriority, a giving without object or remainder. But they also come into being thanks to the way they relate to the Earth's unconditionality, how their political, economic, cultural, and agri-cultural practices are intertwined with it. A key part of a world's relation to the gift of the Earth is therefore how it understands a collective's relation to what grants it time and place. If the unconditionality of the Earth located in seed, water, or land is not a *thing* to be claimed as one's own, a fact of nature that when mixed with one's labor becomes property,[10] then what binds a collective together is no longer a connection to some thing or essence in common either. Rather, it is a shared relation to the givenness of the Earth itself, a nonproperty, a non-thing that cannot be owned.

How, then, did the theological conception of the gift of the Earth transform into the ground for liberal property rights and the current conception of the commons as shared resources? John Locke in *Two Treatises of Government* argues that the Earth is initially a commons of a certain kind, one bestowed by God to Man: "God . . . has *given the Earth to the Children of Men*, given it to Mankind in common." The Earth might be a shared commons, but in line with biblical tradition, it is a commons for humanity only. What Locke needs to explain, however, is by what right humanity's proprietorship of the Earth transforms from common to private ownership, namely how: "Men might come to have a *property* in several parts of that which God gave to Mankind in common, and that without any express Compact of all the Commoners." How, in other words, does the Earth as commons get carved up into private fiefdoms, since no collective agreement to this effect has ever been made? The answer pertains to how God's sovereignty over the Earth is transferred to Man. In the biblical tradition, the transfer takes place via Man's likeness with God; in Locke and in the liberal tradition, the transfer takes place via *reason*: "God, who hath given the World to Men in common, hath also given them reason to make use of it to the best advantage of Life." Bestowed with reason, Man becomes the sole creature on Earth capable of claiming ownership over *himself*: "Though the Earth, and all inferior Creatures be common to all Men, yet every Man has a *Property* in his own *Person*. This no Body has any Right to but himself. The *Labour* of his Body, and the *Work* of his Hands, we may say, are properly his."[11] Now operating independently of God's blessing, humanity, endowed with reason, becomes the sole creature on Earth capable of *self*-possession. That capacity, when mixed—through labor—with what does *not* have reason, becomes by extension Man's "own." Now, rather than merely authorized by God as caretaker of his creation, Man becomes his own sovereign through what is proper to him.[12] The "law of reason," as Locke calls it, thereby becomes a "law of nature."[13] And as England's colonial expansion accelerated in the seventeenth century, this "law of nature" was wielded as a weapon to endorse land appropriation and slavery by at once defining certain humans as so insufficiently endowed with reason that they could therefore become property, and by claiming that, because indigenous populations had not sufficiently cultivated the land, that they could therefore be deemed not to properly "own" it.

Geopoetry's focus on the indifference of the Earth, however, challenges this interpretation of the gift-structure by rearticulating Earth's givenness in relation to a being-there that is not "for" any recipient, and therefore does not become the ground of human law and property. If the Earth is no one's from the beginning, neither God's nor man's, it does not enter any economy of exchange and ownership, a facticity that destabilizes the connection between the Earth and property. And since that connection is the organizing principle of global capital, past and present, another idea of the commons exemplified in the so-called peasant relation to the land I articulated above is opened through an encounter with an indifferent Earth that is no longer there "for" anyone or anything in particular. And this relation to a different understanding of an unconditional Earth also rearticulates the nature of the community or social order made possible by it. The turn to what I'll call for shorthand a "peasant relation to the Earth" is therefore not simply a valorization of precapitalist social relations; it makes the very thing on which the global market relies—the Earth—the starting point for a different kind of communism or communitarianism from below.

It is the specificity of that relation between the Earth as commons and new forms of community that this chapter elaborates by turning to two literary exemplars in its development—one an early twentieth-century Haitian writer—Jacques Roumain—whose novel *Masters of the Dew* imagines a Caribbean-wide peasant resistance, and the other the nineteenth-century English "peasant poet" John Clare, writing at a time when England was transforming not just its colonial holdings, but its own landscape into agricultural production zones. Roumain's novel is a great deal more than a nationalist search for an original Haitian culture through a romanticization of its peasant class, which is how it has often been read. Instead, it imagines a community subsisting on the Earth while refusing to define that subsistence as predicated on a collective resource. My reading of Roumain's novel frames, in turn, my reading of Clare. Through Roumain's reenvisioning of global solidarity, Clare's poetry shifts from its common critical valence—a localist poet nostalgic for England's common system—to become a posthuman meditation on the Earth as a commons that facilitates inter-species solidarity. Like Roumain, Clare reimagines the dependence of the social on an unconditional Earth that cannot be owned to craft alliances between various human cultures as well as alliances between those cultures and the *non*human worlds his view of the Earth makes possible. For Clare recognizes, in an act of solidarity predicated on fidelity to the anteriority of the Earth to human law, that once insect and animal worlds are commodified, they too, like many human communities, become threatened by enclosure and ultimately extinction.

Roumain: The New International and the Earth

When Langston Hughes first met him in Haiti in 1932, Roumain was a member of the government and an active participant in the *Indigéniste* movement, a nationalist response to the American invasion of 1915 that aimed to develop a political and literary culture specific to Haiti. The two men corresponded for five years and met again in 1937 after Roumain was released from prison for having helped found the Haitian Communist Party. Many things had changed from the time of their first meeting to the moment Hughes decided, in collaboration with Mercer Cook, to posthumously translate Roumain's final novel. Among them was Roumain's sharp leftward turn away from his original nationalism. As Nicole Willson argues,[14] the two men shared a desire to articulate a new aesthetics that would unite the African diaspora into a shared anti-colonial struggle and identity,[15] and both sought the model for such an aesthetic in the culture of the peasant class.

But what the two writers found in that culture differs significantly. If by their first meeting in 1932, the *Indigéniste* movement was losing steam in Haiti, Roumain didn't simply substitute his emerging Marxist convictions for his prior focus on peasant culture, interpreting the latter as a proletariat in need of a revolutionary vanguard. Rather, he *adapted* his internationalist Marxism to local peasant culture, in which he was seeking a model for an international Caribbean communist movement that could still be local, moving from specific Haitian peasant practices to a broader community not necessarily governed by class or national identities. In *Masters of the Dew* the global and the local meet in a shared water source and in an old agricultural practice called the *coumbite*, which cultivates common peasant land with the help of music to aid with the collective rhythm of the work. This was not exactly what had attracted Hughes to peasant culture. In "The Negro Speaks of Rivers," for example, water is symbolic and mythic: it cultivates a "soul that had grown deep like the rivers" and connects it to a lost self that had once "bathed in the Euphrates when dawns were young."[16] Hughes's *négritude*-style search for a lost origin prior to diasporic dispersion is not the future-oriented unconditionality of the Earth Roumain articulates by way of water. Hughes's water source and his Earth as commons are grounded in the community of a mythic past; Roumain's is directed to a future community that does not yet exist.

Masters of the Dew centers around a small village, Fonds Rouge, where man-made deforestation has left the region nearly completely arid. The main character, Manuel Joseph, returns after a fifteen-year absence working as a sugar plantation laborer in Cuba to find the villagers in bitter dispute over land and property. Manuel's immediate family is in a blood feud with Manuel's cousin, Gervilen and his family. Prior to the action of the novel, Gervilen's father Dorsica clashed with Manuel's grandfather over farming rights to parcels near the village, leading to an internal rift and the loss of village traditions such as the *coumbite* meant to unite the village by cultivating all its lands in common. Many villagers have been forced to leave because of the drought, going to work for large foreign-owned sugarcane farms, offering the only thing they have left to sell: their labor. While the villagers blame the drought on natural forces beyond their control, Manuel recognizes a man-made disaster when he sees one and takes it upon himself to find a water source. As he does, he also falls in love with a young peasant woman, Annaïse, who is from the other side of the blood feud, and in whom Gervilen is also romantically interested. Though Manuel discovers a water source in the nearby mountains, the only way it can be made to irrigate village lands is if the entire village comes together to channel it. As various villagers, including Gervilen and Hilarion, a local moneylender, conspire to monopolize the water source for their own ends, Manuel addresses the rest of the village, asking them to put their differences aside, telling them where the water source is located, and instructing them on how to channel it to become self-sufficient were he to be killed. His prescience pays off, since he is shortly thereafter murdered by Gervilen, while the novel concludes with the villagers working together to channel the water source in the name of Manuel and Annaïse's unborn child, a symbol of the village's potential reconciliation.

More than one critic has read the novel as a Marxist myth of origins,[17] making the peasants' apparent proximity to the Earth a kind of ahistorical premodern origin for a new collectivity capable of resisting the encroachments of global capital on Haitian society. Michael Dash has argued, for instance, that Roumain's novel should be contrasted with more recent Haitian literature, which emphasizes the displacements and *uprootedness* of the Haitian diaspora as central to "resiting" Haitian narratives within "a new relational space" outside of Haiti.[18] Celia Britton has similarly suggested that Roumain's novel entails an attempt to recover a "lost identity" and a "community in which dissension and difference are ultimately superficial."[19] One can certainly see a version of this concatenation of a notion of national identity and the Earth in Roumain's brief text from 1928 printed in *Le petit impartial* titled *Terre des morts* (Land of the dead), which addresses the memory of the Haitian Revolution. The text outlines a relation between the living and the dead through the metaphor of the "tree of liberty" Toussaint L'Ouverture is supposed to have referred to upon his departure for imprisonment in France, declaring "by overthrowing me, they felled only the trunk of the tree of Black liberty in San Domingo; it will grow through its roots because they are deep and numerous."[20] This model of sacrifice for ancestors that died to provide the condition of possibility for new social forms is in 1928 presented by Roumain as a call to arms in the name of a fidelity to the "founding fathers" of the Haitian Revolution. His earlier thinking, which sees the Haitian Revolution as primarily a war for national independence, involves a claim about the rootedness of Haitians to the land figured by the "tree" of liberty. That, coupled with his disillusionment with Haiti's political class during the American occupation of 1915–32 (because of its complacency toward, or its outright collaboration with, foreign interests), led Roumain to imagine the possibility of national emancipation through the peasant class. For this idea he found inspiration in Jean Price-Mars's *Ainsi parla l'oncle* (Thus spoke uncle) (1928), which argued for a genuine Haitian national identity that could be found in elements of Haitian peasant culture, and which also inspired the *Indigéniste* movement more broadly. At a time when Haiti's political classes were compromised by their allegiance to the influx of American capital, proletarian peasant culture seemed to promise the possibility of an autonomous engine for Haitian independence and nationalism.[21] After all, it had happened before: the Haitian Revolution had pitted destitute former slaves against multiple well-armed colonial militaries, and it had won the country's independence.

However, when Roumain was writing *Masters* in 1943, the political and economic conditions that might have fostered the politicization of the peasant class were quickly shifting. As Beverley Omorod suggests, Haitian peasantry was and still is the poorest in the Caribbean. It was also the class "whose material living conditions [had] changed least since the colonial days."[22] In 1943 Haiti remained, as it does today, an agrarian economy that had eliminated the colonial plantation system in the wake of independence in 1804 but had not yet gone through any significant agrarian reform. What emerged after independence was either the *corvée*, a system of forced labor instituted by Jean-Jacques Dessalines during the colonial period that kept former slaves bound to state-managed modes of agricultural production, or a short-lived system of subsistence farming pioneered in the south; the latter was periodically interrupted by the reinstitution of the *corvée*, but it eventually developed into a combination of subsistence farming and migrant *demwatye* (sharecroppers) who would work the land of elite landowners for a percentage of the harvest, and for their own food. They could, as Toni Presseley-Sanon details, interplant for themselves amid the landowners' cash crops.[23]

With the influx of foreign capital, those conditions began to change as the system was beginning to be dismantled during the US occupation at the behest of American sugar interests. While the Americans had instituted their own version of the *corvée* after the invasion, widespread resistance meant that other means had to be found to supply labor as cheaply as possible to the massive American agribusinesses that had begun to flood into the country. These corporations' first step was to overturn the provision in Haiti's original constitution (also instituted by Dessalines after the country's liberation from slavery) prohibiting whites and foreigners from owning Haitian land. Once this obstacle was removed, large landholdings were quickly consolidated into American ownership or into fewer and fewer wealthy Haitian hands. When regional landowners leased their land to American agribusiness for the purpose of growing cash crops, the *demwatye* were expelled. After that, they were often invited back to work the same land for nonsubsistence level wages, which led to the further impoverishment of the peasantry and to their gradual dispossession from the land.

And so when Roumain wrote *Masters* in the 1940s, the shift from subsistence farming in Haiti to mass agriculture underwritten by global capital had largely already taken place, and the peasant class out of which he hoped to project the future of a Haiti liberated from neocolonialism was being further dispossessed, migrating either abroad or into the cities. Since it was not written for Haitian peasants, who largely were and remain illiterate, *Masters* should be read as an address directed primarily to Roumain's own compromised political class. The question the novel asks is: How do we—a "we" temporarily defined as a Haitian bourgeois Left—begin to grasp from within Haitian peasant culture the possibility of another politics, and thus a solidarity between classes capable of mounting a genuine resistance to American neocolonialism *without* returning to older forms of national identity, since this can be quickly co-opted into complicity with foreign capital? The novel is thus less concerned with a romanticization of the past than with finding its way out of Haiti's enmeshment in a rapidly globalizing American neo-imperialism. The fact that Roumain met and worked with many writers, leaders, and activists in various Black liberation movements around the world suggests that his thinking and writing had developed a more international perspective in his later work. Roumain's wager in *Masters* involves an attempt to portray an indigenous form of collectivity that could become the basis of an alternative society no longer dependent on, or under the thrall of, foreign capital. The hope was that this form of collectivity could then be exported to mount a challenge to American hegemony abroad as well. As Omorod suggests, Roumain's focus on the *coumbite* is his attempt to link his postnationalist communist ideals to specific cultural practices found in rural life.[24]

But what, exactly, does the *coumbite* signify for Roumain? It is, of course, connected with a collective project in which a community's combined labor yields greater abundance than it would with individually cultivated plots of land. That component of collective productivity, however, also involves a relation to a past practice inherited from indigenous and African traditions. In the context of the novel, the combination of these two things takes on added significance insofar as the *coumbite* references a social order that is not merely utopian, a form of social collectivity that has never existed before, but a very *real* form of community the conditions of which have ceased to exist. Those conditions are treated less as bygone historical forms than as internal conflicts tearing the community apart from within thanks to its enmeshment in the market, as each faction attempts to maximize its share of resources for itself according to capitalist logics of surplus profit. But they are also environmental: the drought plaguing the village caused by deforestation and extraction has fractured even the *possibility* of a *coumbite*, whether or not social divisions within the community can be reconciled. It is those two elements—a collective project and its relation to an environment that is the condition of its existence—that interests Roumain. The *coumbite* thus exemplifies both a form of collective action *and* the way that action takes shape in the context of a relation to the Earth—to land and water—understood as a commons rather than a collection of resources, whether divided up privately or in some more egalitarian fashion. For Roumain, without a relation to the Earth as commons, no *coumbite* will ever again be possible, whether local or international. And without a collective relation to the Earth predicated on something other than property as a starting point, there are no *other* conditions for social life other than the private labor market.

At the beginning of *Masters*, Délira, mother of Manuel, exclaims simply, "We're all going to die."[25] Her words thrust the story headlong into the threat of extinction that hangs over their entire village. Eroding soil has led to a collapse of the social structures that once defined it; Bienaimé, Manuel's father, staring at the dried-out fields, wistfully recalls the past: "In those days when they had lived in harmony, united as the fingers of the hand, they had assembled all the neighborhood in collective *coumbites* for the harvest or the clearing" (MD 25/269). Celia Britton understands this nostalgia for a past communal unity as Roumain's "origin myth" of the "common being of the past,"[26] the demolished collective cooperation the novel hopes will return with the discovery of water and the restored fertility of the land.[27]

However, Roumain's set-up of the conflict central to the novel emphasizes less a return to or nostalgia for a premodern past than the absence of any sense of a *future* into which the community can project itself. Délira's diagnosis at the opening of the novel—"We're all going to die"—negates the prospect of any posterity. As Valerie Kaussen has argued, Bienaimé's nostalgia also involves a reification of the *present*, which "remains dead, inanimate, out of time."[28] In Roumain's earlier peasant novel, *La montagne ensorcelée* (The bewitched mountain) published in 1931, a similar devastation of the land and its attendant historical stagnancy is the starting point for the narrative. Yet, the sense of despair, resignation, and the eventual scapegoating of others—the villagers of that novel stone a woman to death and behead her daughter on suspicion of witchcraft—stems not from internal social conflict but from their "superstitious" belief in mystical forces at work in nature. In *La montagne*, Roumain portrays a village mired in an inability to understand the source of its poverty through any other means than nostalgia for its religious beliefs, which have stoked internal divisions and violence.[29] Its stagnancy therefore stems from its inability to "modernize."

In *Masters*, however, the past is prelude to the future, becoming a way *out* of the stagnancy of the present and its deteriorating social conditions. While *Masters* engages in similar (patronizing) themes about peasant "superstition," Manuel early on identifies a clear man-made source for the ecological catastrophe that has befallen his village[30]—local deforestation has exposed the Earth to erosion and thereby left the land arid:[31]

> I see that you have cleared the hills of trees. The soil is naked, without protection. It's the roots that make friends with the soil, and hold it. It's the mango tree, the oak, the mahogany that give it rainwater when it's thirsty and shade it from the noonday heat. That's how it is—otherwise rain carries away the soil and the sun bakes it, only the rocks remain. That's the truth. It's not God who betrays us. We betray the soil and receive his punishment: drought and poverty and desolation. (MD 45/285–86)

Unlike *La montagne*, the ecological catastrophe of *Masters* is the result of the abandonment of the knowledge and practices that previously made the land fertile. The translation here is somewhat imprecise: Manuel insists that "it is not God that has betrayed Blacks" (*le nègre*), but rather they who have betrayed the land (*la terre*), identifying Haitian peasantry with racial dispossession, while also suggesting that they already have the tools needed to overcome it. The betrayal of the land leads not to God's punishment ("his punishment"), but rather the *land's* punishment (*sa punition*), the possessive indicating that it is *la terre* being referred to and not *Dieu* or God.[32] Ecological disaster, therefore, must be read not as an act of divine will but as man-made, the only resolution of which can occur through a different relation to the land rather than by abandoning peasant practices and beliefs in favor of "modern" Western ones. That different relation to the land, Roumain suggests, is not radically new, and can be found in the practice of the *coumbite* the village has forsaken. A future is possible, in other words, not by relinquishing the past, but by resituating it within a new context.

Simultaneously native and an outsider, Manuel embodies the *alternative* modernity Roumain imagines emerging out of Haitian peasant culture.[33] While it may be grounded in specific cultural practices of the past, these have a contemporary significance: They point toward a novel kind of modernity different from Western globalization, one that makes a relation to the Earth as commons its central concern. Though Roumain's unfortunate earlier treatment of Vodou as a peasant practice clearly understands it as a premodern vestige that, with proper education, will eventually be cast off,[34] his emphasis on the practice of the *coumbite* suggests a rural version of social relations organized by something other than property—a new kind of community that can be extended beyond village life. This alternative modernity forms the crux of Roumain's articulation of the kinds of resistance peasant culture might be able to muster against Western globalization, represented by an American agribusiness that has privatized water and land at the expense of peasant communities. Describing what locating a water source for the village would mean, Manuel contrasts the possible future of Fonds Rouge with the form of society taking shape on lands appropriated by American capital:

> "To whom does that land belong, and all the water?"
>
> "To a white American, Mr. Wilson by name. The factory, too, everything all around is his."
>
> "And the peasants, are there peasants like us?"

> "You mean with a plot of land, poultry, and a few head of cattle? No, they're only workers who cut the cane for so much and so much. They've got nothing but the strength of their arms, not a handful of soil, not a drop of water—except their own sweat. They all work for Mr. Wilson." (MD 50/289)

As he makes clear, where American agribusiness has taken over, all that the surrounding peasants have left is the commodity of their labor. Jean-Claude Fignolé's argument—that Roumain could not fully relinquish his bourgeois upbringing, and therefore romanticized individual subsistence farming—does not adequately capture what is at stake in the novel.[35] Throughout, Roumain makes clear that the notion of an unpossessable commons, as opposed to individualized subsistence farming, is in fact the only thing preventing the dissolution of peasant society into wage slavery thanks to its creation of a reconceived common purpose independent of market forces.

Using his knowledge of the local landscape, Manuel discovers a source of water in a secluded spot high up in the mountains, and when he later describes his discovery to his family, he makes clear that irrigating the village's land will require the cessation of social divisions, since it will be impossible to access the water without a broad collective effort. The reason, however, stems not just from the labor required, but from the nature of the water itself. As Manuel suggests, the village's collective use of the spring cannot take the form of private property distributed to each member as one might distribute a parcel of land: "Water isn't something that can be divided up into acres. It can't be marked out on a notary's paper—it's everybody's, the blessing of the earth!" (MD 124/348). Langston Hughes and Mercer Cook's somewhat loose translation here doesn't quite capture what is at stake: Manuel is explicitly contrasting water as a form of "property" (*propriété*) with the idea of it being a "common good" (*bien commun*), which is "everybody's" and a "blessing of the earth" (*bénédiction de la terre*).[36] Neither a private nor a collective form of "property" or "good," as a "blessing" the water is the advent of an Earthly gift or surplus that cannot be transformed into a discrete unit or object, a commodity to be exchanged like an item on a notary's leger, preferably for profit, nor like the parceled-out plots of land that have been the source of conflict in the community. Framed in the language of a gift or a "blessing" (though one subtracted here from its religious context), the water is an event, a given, an offering—by no one and for no one—outside of any economy of exchange.

The water's givenness nevertheless creates a common project, organizing the possibility of a different kind of social relation to the Earth no longer founded on property, the proper, or what is one's "own."

The water's "blessing," however, quickly becomes yet another source of potential division and power as it is threatened with enclosure. Bienaimé, unable to relinquish the feud begun by Dorsica's actions many years ago, initially attempts to control the water for his own profit. As Manuel finishes a speech by asking "by what right" the water can be seen as a form of property, Bienaimé immediately responds with the reintroduction of a conception of individual and communal property rights that mirror the village's internal conflicts over land: "'The right that *you* found it!' he cried. 'The right that our enemies haven't got any rights!'" (MD 124/348–49). Organized around the factionalism that divides the village, Bienaimé's attempt to enclose the water source is echoed by other competitors elsewhere in the novel, specifically Hilarion, the local police officer, who conspires to jail Manuel and force him to reveal where the water source is located. Once that has been achieved, Hilarion's plan is to then monopolize the water source as a weapon to accumulate more property and land by leaving "the peasants to dry off in expectation, and when they had lost courage and all hope, he, Hilarion, would seize their fields and become the owner of several fine, well-irrigated plots of land" (MD 140/361). The "gift" or "blessing" of the water outside of any economy of exchange, in other words, is continuously threatened with its reappropriation into an exchangeable *thing* or asset that can be commodified and turned into a source of power.

Since the conflicts and conspiracies to monopolize and commodify the water remain intact even after Manuel's death, the novel turns explicitly "futural" at the end in several ways. Rather than conclude with an actual *coumbite*, the novel leaves us with a series of promises and hints at a couple of newfound threats. One of the symbols of the futural promise of Manuel's acts lies in the existence of his unborn child with Annaïse, a product of both sides of the divisions that plague the village, and a potential figure for a future reconciliation whose ground Manuel has helped prepare but which he will not live to see. Another futural promise lies in the villagers' fidelity to Manuel's vision that the water remain a common good: "They had been working lately right by the spring itself, at the very head of the water. They had followed Manuel's instructions point by point. He was dead, Manuel, but he was still guiding them" (MD 185/394). The villagers' labor in channeling the spring does not turn the water source into a communal form of property, a thing to be distributed; rather it articulates a new kind of collective project—a new kind of collectivity—organized around what none of the villagers can possess, and which nevertheless reorients them as a community toward a future that diverges from the immobility of the present. Manuel himself becomes a figure for a posterity one might never see, but toward which one must work for the good of others and for future generations, organized around a new relation to an Earth no longer viewed as an object to be parceled out. As the peasants put it, "'A day will come—we'll make a great *coumbite* of all the farmers to clear out poverty and plant a new life.' You won't see that day, Chief, you've gone before your time, but you've left us hope and courage" (MD 166/379). Langston Hughes and Mercer Cook here translate *travailleurs de la terre* as "farmers," which limits the *coumbite* to the village, or perhaps to Haitian peasantry more generally. But rather than *fermier, agriculteur,* or *cultivateur,* Roumain chooses a term that is more literally rendered as "workers of the earth," pointing toward a metaphorization of the "great *coumbite*" into something global.

Masters therefore represents an allegorizing of the *coumbite* as a solidarity between various postnational "wretcheds of the earth." The key term in this articulation, however, is Roumain's representation of the Earth as an inappopriable commons rather than, as Lizabeth Paravisini-Gebert suggests, a space that entails "notions of the indigenous or autochthonous in which the 'primeval' forest stands for a precolonial space of 'national' authenticity."[37] Roumain's water source and the villagers' relation to it transcends both social divisions and the language of "rights," including those instituted by national forms of identity, as well as economic disparity. The "great *coumbite*" can only take shape in relation to a different conception of the Earth that, for Roumain, constitutes the only possible ground for collective action capable of addressing the more recent postcolonial forms of exploitation and extraction produced by global capital. Celia Britton's argument, therefore, that the novel attempts to produce a "mythical" community in which "dissension and difference are ultimately superficial" must be contextualized by the *allegorical* dimension of Roumain's novel. What undoes the relative homogeneity of the community Roumain envisions is not only, as Britton suggests, its "incompleteness," but instead the allegory of the "great *coumbite*," which opens the homogeneity or indigeneity of the community to all the others with which it shares a similar relation to the Earth.[38] Like Manuel's sacrifice performed for a posterity he will never see, the Earth in Roumain is an essentially futural concept whereby communities—local and global—are continuously forming themselves anew in relation to what can never become their property, nor properly belong to them, and yet which nevertheless structures social relations through the inheritance and bestowal of a gift to the other and to the future.

Clare: The Earth's "Eternity" and Resistance to Enclosure

To read the poetry of John Clare through the lens of Roumain's overtly Marxist novel might seem at first to be taking sides in the long-standing debate about how to characterize the nature of Clare's politics. Ever since Raymond Williams reintroduced him to modern audiences,[39] and Marxist historian E. P. Thompson declared him the last of the peasant poets,[40] debate has raged about how to understand Clare's "radicalism" or lack thereof.[41] Though it would be going too far to suggest Clare was a Marxist *avant la lettre*, defining his take on class consciousness as unique among his contemporaries is certainly not far-fetched.[42] Clare was a farm laborer who began to write poetry after discovering James Thomson's "The Seasons" (1730) during a period of unemployment. His poems, at first descriptive of his native Helpston and its surroundings, soon began to center on England's agricultural revolution. In 1809, an enclosure act—a series of laws targeting waste lands and common pastures for "improvement," that is, for private ownership—set its sights on Helpston parish.

Witnessing the replacement of one conception of nature (a commons), with another (a zone of profit to be put to human use), Clare's poetry protests the latter's destruction of the peasant class which depended on the commons. And even if Clare's notion of the commons, unlike Roumain's, is organized around a vanishing legal structure giving commoners certain rights to the surplus originating from privately owned land, in his poetry we all the same find similar forms of economic redistribution underway in Roumain's Haiti a century later: a peasantry slowly forced into wage slavery, either in the cities or as laborers in the fields, as more and more common lands were being appropriated by private landowners, and as peasants' right to the commons to supplement their earnings vanished.

And with the help of Roumain's already post-Marxist conception of the Earth as a commons, we can see Clare's understanding of the commons extending well beyond any purely legal definition. Like Roumain, Clare's commons pertains to a redefinition of the community's relation to the Earth: yet while Roumain's focus is on a community beyond national lines, Clare's, when refracted through Roumain's extension of the commons and the gift-structure of the Earth to the entire globe, can be seen as extending "community" beyond species divisions. Like Roumain, Clare understands the Earth in terms of an unconditional gift, an anteriority to every community that cannot be owned by anyone or made the foundation of human law, and that thereby becomes the basis for communal relations beyond the social contract and the human as organizing categories. Ecocriticism has more recently repainted Clare as "green," in contrast to the "red" one that had been the focus of Marxist literary criticism. Jonathan Bate and, James McKusick for instance, present Clare's writing as a precursor to contemporary environmental concerns.[43] However, as McKusick puts it in *Green Writing*, Clare's ecological concerns extend into a poetry dealing with the possibility of community with nonhuman others: "Clare's view of nature departs definitively from the utilitarian view of the natural world that prevailed among his contemporaries. While Clare rejoices in the beauty of the Earth, he does not primarily see it as existing for human purposes, and he resists its appropriation for economic use or even aesthetic contemplation."[44] However, with the help of Roumain as a lens, it becomes impossible to separate the "green" Clare from the "red." Rather than extend the language of "rights" to the natural world,[45] his poetics attests to the mutual imbrication of the social and the natural and shows that a particular conception of nature that arises from it underwrites a politics that, if not exactly "communist" in Roumain's sense, does involve a collective sharing of the Earth with more than one world, including nonhuman others.[46]

In what follows, I trace Clare's trajectory from his understanding of the Earth as temporally prior and indifferent to humans, to the way that notion is connected with his conception of the Earth as a commons. That conception, I argue, as in Roumain, involves a relation to an antecedence and independence of the Earth shared by the variety of worlds on its surface. Unlike Roumain, however, for Clare those worlds include both human *and* nonhuman ones. Because of this temporal priority of the Earth, no single species can own or appropriate it as its exclusive prerogative; no one species—including the human—has any claim to it as its special or private right. I then show how this notion of the Earth as commons underwrites everything in Clare's so-called protest poetry against the dissolution of the *legal* form of the commons, thereby yoking the "green" Clare with the "red." I conclude by articulating how, through the lens of Roumain's understanding of the Earth as commons, we can better see the relation between the global and the local in Clare's poetics: while Helpston may be Clare's "home of homes," it is also treated as a microcosm of a broader planetary commons connecting other peoples and other species with one another. And despite the obvious nostalgia in Clare for the lost legal frameworks that helped sustain the commons system until its dismantling, the elements his work shares with Roumain's conception of the Earth reveal a latent futural dimension in Clare's work. This futural dimension, I argue, involves the possibility of the advent of a new "communism" that includes solidarity with the worlds of nonhuman others through a fidelity to the temporal priority of an Earth no one species can claim as its exclusive birthright. For Clare the Earth's status as a commons flows from its temporal anteriority to humans.[47] While Clare clearly did not have in mind anything like what we now call "deep time," he did articulate an independence of the Earth from human perception or labor that points to its longevity—its existence prior to human needs or desires. And while he clearly understands the Earth to be God's creation, its temporal existence and its antecedence to human society gives it an independence from any human "right" to its possession that is inviolable; the Earth, in short, is not given by God to man *for* man.

In one of his late poems—titled "Obscurity"—he names this temporal priority of the Earth "blank oblivion." In the only extended commentary on this poem, David Collings reads it as figuring a world without the human gaze and "insisting on an aspect of non-human activity that is at once beyond or outside objects per se and that through its blankness evacuates their import."[48] Collings focuses on the poem's opening reflection on an "old tree" whose provenance is "blank & recordless":

> Old tree, oblivion doth thy life condemn
> Blank & recordless as that summer wind
> That fanned the first few leaves on thy young stem
> When thou wert one years shoot—& who can find
> Their homes of rest or paths of wandering now
> So seems thy history to a thinking mind
> As now I gaze on thy sheltering bough
> Thou grew unnoticed up to flourish now
> & leave thy past as nothing all behind
> Where many years & doubtless centurys lie
> That ewe beneath thy shadow—nay that flie
> Just settled on a leaf—can know with time
> Almost as much of thy blank past as I
> Thus blank oblivion reigns as earths sublime[49]

While Collings's interpretation of the first four lines focuses not just on the fact that no human ear or eye was there to witness the tree sprout, he goes on to argue that the poem thereby considers the possibility that human and nonhuman life might itself eventually be condemned to its own "oblivion." But whereas he identifies oblivion with the "blank and recordless" summer wind equated with a "movement of ongoing erasure that leaves no trace,"[50] Collings leaves aside the last line of the poem, which ascribes that process to the Earth: "thus blank oblivion reigns as earths sublime." The last two lines, then, translate that "blank past" into a "blank oblivion," not just an erasure, or an inability to know, but a process of effacement that is part and parcel of the Earth—its very *modus operandi.* What reigns as "earths sublime," its unfathomably *longue durée,* is both irreducible to the tree's past—including its origin—and is nothing but a future effacement of *both* the tree *and* any trace of it. Thanks to the Earth's temporal priority to all living things, they are all threatened with an "oblivion" specific to the Earth that *it* will survive, and which therefore both precedes and supersedes all living creatures.

Clare's "sublime," then, is neither Burke's nor Kant's, both of which presuppose a spectator who rises above and transcends the threat of erasure posed by the powerful forces of nature. In "Obscurity" nothing is external to the Earth's sublime other than the Earth itself, and its effect is more disorienting than aggrandizing. Sarah Houghton has argued convincingly that the sublime in Clare involves an experience of defamiliarization, where nature presents itself to the speaker in new and unknown ways, and where the poet must articulate a sense of disturbance or dislocation poetically, a process referenced in "Obscurity" by the speaker's question "—and who can find / Their homes of rest or paths of wandering now?"[51] Houghton's suggestion that the defamiliarization of Clare's sublime has a temporal dimension is also registered acutely in the Earth's anteriority to everything alive, from the tree to the creatures that call it home. Unable to establish a reliable spectator (other than God) who can witness the Earth's longevity, one is always confronted in Clare with a time and place—an immemorial past—that is never one's own, and that always threatens to relativize and disrupt the stable coordinates of the present.

That temporal dimension of the Earth is found throughout Clare's writing, from his speculative poems on the nature of time to his more political poems about the destruction of the commons. It is the central element of both his conception of the natural world and his understanding of how human communities articulate themselves based on, and in relation to, the Earth. While the commons system tied commoner's rights to a form of nature that was independent of the human privatization of land, Clare's seemingly more theological or speculative poetry radicalizes the antecedence of nature or the Earth in relation to man, which is the basis of its independence from any juridical-political system seeking to annul the separation between nature and law. In other words, Clare's poetry at its core contests two different conceptions of nature: one that recognizes the Earth's temporal anteriority to human needs and desires, and one that denies that anteriority by comprehending the Earth only through the lens of its capacity to produce harvests of goods for human society. In one of Clare's more speculative poems, "Eternity of Time," for instance, a poem written in roughly the same period as "Obscurity," Clare's sublime becomes indistinguishable from the movement of time itself:

> Eternity grand eternity of time
> Where things of greatest standing grow sublime
> Less from long fames & universal praise
> Then wearing as the "ancients of old days"
> The word once speaking seems but half the way
> To reach that night leap of eternal day[52]

Here the "sublime" is again figured as a temporal antecedence where "things of greatest standing" survive effacement, an idea found also in Clare's contemporary Percy Shelley where, in "Ozymandias" for example, the speaker contemplates what "yet survives" the ruins of a statue depicting Ramses II thanks to the artist-sculptor's abilities to "mock" power by outliving it. In Clare, however, poetry or art offers no such respite against the ceaseless wearing-away generated by the passage of time. As "Eternity of Time" puts it, even "Milton centurys" and "shakspears eras" are to the "forest oaks eternal stay / Are but as points & commas in their way" (ET 228). For Clare, nothing human survives the touch of time, neither the "ancients" nor art: "These less then nothings are to ruins doom / When suns grow dark & earth a vast & lonely tomb" (ET 228). Milton and Shakespeare's legacy—works of humanity as opposed to works of nature—are contemplated here from the standpoint of a future barren and lifeless Earth, their own longevity overtaken by it: they collapse into their own "blank oblivion" in the face of the perdurance of the Earth which, even lifeless, is both prior and posterior to all human and nonhuman worlds alike.

What to make then of the "eternity" of the title of the poem, which appears to imply an atemporal Earth read in terms of a Christian conception of God seemingly transposed onto the natural world? Is the Earth's sublime merely a code word for God? Clare wrote several poems featuring "eternity" in their title as part of their thematic focus, including "An Invite to Eternity," "The Eternity of Nature," "Songs Eternity," and "Earths Eternity." In each one, Clare reserves the use of the word "eternal" as signifying "atemporal" for God alone. "Eternity," when applied to the domain of nature or the Earth, however, reflects only the mortal or finite survival of something that exceeds human knowledge. In his early "Address to Time," for instance, Clare distinguishes between human attempts to fathom time, and time from God's standpoint. Human efforts to understand the past are limited by the fact that—unlike God—humans have not always existed:

> Vain to conceive were thy dark burst began
> Thou birthless endless vast stupendity
> To mortal wisdom thourt already ran
> A circled travel of Eternity[53]

God, on the other hand, the only actual "eternal" being in the usual sense, is thereby also the only one capable of fully comprehending time's immemoriality:

> Consuming tyrant of all mortal kind
> & what thou art & what thou are to be
> Is known to none but that immortal mind
> Who reigns alone superior to thee (AT 488)

Time's "eternity" is here less an atemporal stasis than a process of endless effacement no mortal mind can comprehend, marking the limitations, the finitude, of the speaker's perspective. In other words, Clare's poetry operates within a decidedly Christian conception of the world (as *mundus*) that understands the world as distinct from the divine—the only true "eternity" there is. What falls under the category of the world, then, is everything *but* God, all creatures that exist (including humans), all of nature, in whatever shape or form, as well as the Earth. And the Earth, for Clare, is the only thing in the mundane world that approximates the eternity of God since it is the prior condition of all creatures great and small, and all the various forms of nature. Nature is "eternal" for Clare only in the sense that it operates a ceaseless change on anything that is *not* divine, including itself.

"Eternity" in this nondivine sense is thus part and parcel of the finite world: a feature of the Earth that belongs to its temporal anteriority no human—or other creature—can fully grasp. To the extent that the Earth is part of a process that is organized cyclically by death and rebirth—by the seasons—that process involves the incessant erasure of anything solid, stable, or permanent. Despite his perceptive reading, Alan Bewell's claim that Clare "cannot imagine one nature giving way to another" and that he "does not see nature in general as a historical phenomenon" leaves out the extent to which nature and temporality are in fact intimately intertwined for Clare.[54] Even in "Earths Eternity," where Clare contemplates the possibility of something terrestrial that survives the general mutability of the mundane world, the poem concludes with an opposition between the Earth's temporality—the time it takes mountains to decay—and the duration of human epochs or ages.[55] The former approximates the only "eternity" there is in a finite world (the longevity of the Earth), despite that fact that it too will wane. The latter (the human epoch) is even more fleeting and prone to "oblivion," a temporal existence that pales in comparison to the durability of mountain ranges.

How does Clare's theological or speculative poetry set the stage for his articulation of the Earth as a commons? If the Earth's sublime entails a fundamental temporal priority to every human and nonhuman world, then it also remains independent of human ownership or appropriation, and it is here that Clare's theological conception of the "gift" of the Earth departs most significantly from Locke's and even from Genesis. The Earth's precedence and antecedence to every world is the precondition for any commons worthy of the name, insofar as it constitutes a space or reality external to every conception of nature, but also because it escapes the economization of the gift as designating the Earth *for* Man. The Earth is merely given, outside of the economy that gives it to Man as its rightful recipient. That independence, moreover, acts as an unpossessable ground (quite literally) that allows for the interaction of various worlds with each other, human or otherwise, either contemporaneously or across time. And because the Earth precedes every world, none of them have any privilege in relation to it. The Earth, for Clare, is thus "shared" not as a common resource or property, but as a temporal anteriority and irreducible future no single world can make its own. The temporal antecedence of the Earth limits or constrains the privilege of any human "right" to its use because the Earth is shared with other worlds, including those of animals and insects as well as nomadic human communities (such as gypsies) who have no concept of "property rights." In Clare there is no "natural law" deriving from the Earth that condones the right to property; its "eternity" delimits the so-called natural right of human labor to define it in those terms. Yet it paradoxically also grounds the "rights" of those who don't have them, particularly nonhuman others who have been commodified, or deemed as being without value within a world that can see them only in terms of their use or uselessness to humans. The temporal priority of the Earth is thus, for Clare, an index of what is external to every political-juridical domain treating nature as simply available or there for the taking. But as this inappropriable ground, the Earth's independence from every world is also the condition of possibility, as we will see, for a community between humans and nonhumans that would no longer seek to enclose it as their common possession.

It is here where Roumain's conception of the Earth as commons helps sharpen or clarify this aspect of Clare's poetics. As we have seen, the Earth for Roumain is the basis for a new kind of postnational collectivity that predicates social cohesion on something that is not a shared property: water. Because it cannot be owned, it becomes the basis for a new kind of collectivity. What Roumain allows us to see in Clare is the relation between Clare's conceptual or theoretical poems about time, eternity, nature, and God, and his *political* poems about the collapse of the commons system and resistance to enclosure. Though Roumain's understanding of the Earth as a commons does not have an explicit theology informing it, it does emphasize how the inappropriability of the water source is the condition for a community no longer organized around the idea of a shared property. If the Earth is likewise inappropriable in Clare, if it is not simply a store or supply of commodities awaiting human use, then the significance of the idea of the commons is not just its role in a protest against privatization and the loss of commoner's rights, but also its function in the potential articulation of a new form of community extending beyond the human.

How does this other relation to the Earth take shape in Clare, and what politics, or what conception of nature, does it enable? Clare's approach to the antecedence of the Earth and its incorporation into his political poetry takes several forms, including what I will loosely call, harkening back to my discussion of Glissant in the previous chapter, an "aesthetics" of the Earth. Throughout his oeuvre, Clare describes various ways people and animals relate to the same geographical space. He often depicts, for example, how a poet or commoner might interact with a specific field or pasture in contrast to the "clown,"

Clare's epithet for someone who takes no notice of the other worlds cohabiting the space around him. His early poem "Recollections After an Evening Walk," for example, starts with a group of observers wandering the fields of the parish in the evening, noticing the retreat of laborers from the landscape, and reflecting on what kind of nature emerges through the subtraction of humans. After the woodman "ceasd wi his hatchet to hack / & bent a way home wi his kid on his back,"[56] the poem witnesses other sights and sounds that emerge in the absence of human labor, revealing several worlds outside the distinctly human cycle of work and rest:

> & numbers of creatures apeard in our sight
> That live in the silence and sweetness of night
> Climbing up the tall grasses or scaling the bough
> But these were all namless unoticd till now (RA 327)

Though unnamed, these "unoticd" elements of the landscape are contrasted with human rhythms and workdays, and they thus occupy a different temporal relation to the land Clare designates as nocturnal:

> & then we wound round neath the brooks willow row
> & lookt at the clouds that kept passing below
> The moons image too in the brook we could seet
> As if twas the tother world under our feet
> & we listnd well pleasd at the guggles & groans
> The water made passing the pebbles and stones (RA 327)

This nocturnal nature is the corollary, in the present, of the anteriority or eternity of the Earth, an "other world" that emerges *separate* from the human one, that absconds from its enclosure by the human gaze, while nevertheless remaining "under that world's feet" as it were, its unacknowledged cohabitant.

The name Clare gives to the ability to recognize the independence of nature from human needs and desires is the seemingly aesthetic term "taste," which for him describes the pleasure found in an attunement to the typically "unnoticed" or "useless" forms of nature in one's surroundings.[57] For Clare, the inability to perceive this independence of the natural world from human standards of use or purpose is the mark of "vulgar" judgment, whereas the "man of taste" notices the intricacies and overlooked details of a landscape or waste ground.[58] As Clare puts it in his writings on natural history:

> Taste finds pleasure where the vulgar cannot ever find amusement the man of taste feels excessive rapture in contemplating the rich scenery of an autumn Landscape which the rude man passes unnoticed—the rich colours of the forrest trees the wild hurry of the autumn clouds never harmonize his feelings into raptures—he never turns a look to the sky save in the dread of a coming shower—he never gazes on the painted wilderness of woods & hedges unless business leads his occupation thether & then his eye is dead and sees no praise—he tramples thoughtlessly over the wooden brig that leads him on his path & never so much as glances on the stream that seems smothering the little pebbles beneath him with its chafing gurgles he never heeds it or hears it but plods his way to the end of his intentions with a mechanic impulse of uninterrupted selfishness that occupys all his little mind—[59]

The vulgar man can only ascertain nature's beauty through his own "business," plodding his way to the "end of his intentions" as if he were a machine capable only of remaining immured within himself and his own needs or projects. What makes the natural world around him "dead" to his eye is precisely his "selfishness," for Clare the very first form of enclosure, which he then projects outwards, viewing the landscape in terms of his own ego. His taste, or more accurately his lack thereof, thus involves an inability to encounter the otherness of the natural world, confining the independence of the Earth and all the creatures that inhabit it within his *own* world, within what is proper to him, where they go either unheeded or are reduced to human purposes.

"Taste" for Clare is thus much more than a subjective relation to beauty; it is above all a relation to the other, or to others. Yet it is also primarily a relation to the precedence of the Earth as the ground of every world. Which means, ultimately, that "taste" is not just a feature of the human alone: it is as much about creating a sense of home or habitat, a belonging to the Earth, as it is a judgment about beauty. In other words, taste involves the choice of a world or territory—a way of situating oneself on the Earth, a capacity *every* creature, including plants and animals, has. In "Shadows of Taste," Clare goes so far as to suggest that birds, flowers, and insects all "have taste," not in the sense that they are beautiful, but in the sense that they enact—instinctively or unconsciously—a specific relation to the Earth:

> Taste with as many hues doth hearts engage
> As leaves & flowers do upon natures page

Not mind alone the instinctive mood declares
But birds & flowers & insects are its heirs
Taste is their joyous heritage & they
All choose for joy in a peculiar way
Birds own it in the various spots they chuse
Some live content in low grass gemmed with dews
The yellow hammer like a tasteful guest
Neath picturesque green molehills makes a nest[60]

Animal or plant "taste" is informed by the "various spots they chuse" (ST 303) through the way they articulate a relation to the Earth by positioning themselves within a landscape, a site that precedes them and which they do not own but rather *inhabit* within their own particular world. Even flowers, traditionally the object of aesthetic contemplation, enact taste as a "creative choice" (ST 304) and "seem blest with feeling and a silent voice" (ST 304), choosing where to bloom, whether along roadways or in the "melancholly tomb" (ST 304).

This aesthetic relation to place becomes a "world" for Clare, something that goes beyond the exclusive domain of humans.[61] Emphasizing the term "insect world" in Clare's long pastoral "Shepherd's Calendar," Joseph Albernaz argues that Clare's poetry evinces the idea that multiple worlds can occupy the same geographic space.[62] What matters, however, is not just that cohabitation but the way each one takes up its own relation to the antecedence of the Earth. One can see this sense of "world" at work in Clare in a frequently cited passage from his autobiographical writings that emphasizes not just what it means to inhabit a particular place, but also the sense of dislocation that underpins his understanding of taste when it opens itself up to the "wonder" of other worlds. Describing a moment as a child when he wandered away from home for an extended period of time, Clare details an experience of profound dislocation:

> I had often seen the large heath calld Emmonsales stretching its yellow furze from my eye into unknown solitudes when I went with the mere openers and my curiosity urgd me to steal an oppertunity to explore it that morning I had imagind that the worlds end was at the edge of the orison and that a days journey was able to find it so I went on with my heart full of hopes pleasures and discoverys expecting when I got to the brink of the world that I coud look downlike looking into a large pit and see into its secrets the same as I believed I coud see heaven by looking into the water so I eagerly wandered on and rambled among the furze the whole day till

> I got out of my knowledge When the very wildflowers and birds seemd to forget me and I imagind they were the inhabitants of new countrys the very sun seemd to be a new one and shining in a different quarter of the sky still I felt no fear my wonder seeking happiness had no room for it I was finding new wonders every minute and was walking in a new world often wondering to my self that I had not found the end of the old one the sky still touchd the ground in the distance as usual and my childish wisdoms was puzzld in perplexitys night crept on before I had time to fancy the morning was bye when the white moth had begun to flutter beneath the bushes the black snail was out upon the grass and the frog was leaping across the rabbit tracks on his evening journeys and the little mice was nimbling about and twittering their little ear piercing song with the hedge cricket whispering the hour of waking spirits was at hand which made me hasten to seek home I knew not which way to turn but chance put me in the right track and when I got into my own fields I did not know them every thing seemd so different.[63]

Clare's childhood reminiscence highlights the defamiliarizing element of the relation between taste and world. Assuming that the end of his world is the edge of the horizon, the young Clare ventures beyond the space he typically inhabits and moves "out of [his] knowledge" into another sphere where, despite being close to home, he enters the equivalent of a foreign territory. There, the flora and fauna with which he is familiar "forget him." But despite this disorientation, Clare's primary relation to this place beyond his own familiar habitat is "wonder," a relation to the possibility of other "worlds" with which he is unversed, and which extends to the worlds of animals and insects.[64] In one of his early poems, "The Ants," for example, the speaker is in a similar state of "wonder" at the intricate complexity of an anthill:

> What wonder strikes the curious while he views
> The black ants city by a rotten tree
> Or woodland bank—in ignorance we muse
> Pausing amazd we know not what we see[65]

In all of Clare's poetry about animals or insects there is extensive description from the point of view of the spectator, but the description usually concentrates on situating *the animal or insect* within "its world"—within its own connection to the landscape—and on detailing how the human speaker is left to make sense of a way of looking, a way of interacting, and a way of being, that is fundamentally foreign to his own.

The man of taste is therefore not just someone capable of noticing the unheeded, non-useful, nonhuman worlds that surround him. He is also, thanks to their alterity—an alterity founded on how they constitute a different relation or habitation of the Earth—related to them through the Earth's antecedence to both the other's and his own world. A recognition that his is only *one* world among many, only one way of inhabiting an Earth that precedes him temporally, also puts him into contact with the *other's* taste, the other's intuitive or instinctive relation to a particular landscape he shares with that other world. What is thus shared by ants and humans is not the world, but the Earth; like the nocturnal nature of "Evening Walks," there is "another world" beneath the speaker's feet that cannot be integrated with his own. And yet, as an inhabitant of that place or landscape, the ants have as much "right" to it as any human:

> Surely they speak a language wisperingly
> Too fine for us to hear & sure their ways
> Prove they have kings & laws (A 56)

Bestowing what would normally be reserved for humans alone—language and the rule of law—on the insect world, Clare's poem initially articulates what he sees as the ant-world's equivalence to the human. Yet it is more than just an "equality" of worlds that is at stake. Rather, what Clare emphasizes is that the recognition of the other's "taste" forecloses the possibility that there is only *one* world (one's own) that defines the only conceivable relation to the Earth. The Earth as commons, in Clare, is thus above all a way of articulating a solidarity, if not a co-belonging, between incommensurable worlds that does not reduce them to one another, that maintains not just one's own, but also the alterity of the other's relation to the Earth. In other words, it is not just that ants and humans exist in the same space, or on the same planet; rather, their difference from each other is articulated through a relation to what neither of them can fully appropriate or incorporate into their own purposes, needs, and ends. The Earth, in Clare, is thus always a surplus to every world that, by opening each one to something outside its purview, exposes it likewise to a possible community with the other. It is here that the conception of the commons Clare articulates comes into focus: if there are potentially multiple overlapping worlds within a given geographic space, and if the Earth is anterior to all of them, then there is no single world that is either coextensive with the Earth's sublime, or for whom the Earth is uniquely destined.

And yet this is precisely the privilege that enclosure, and its later manifestations in neo-imperial globalization, grant themselves, thereby effacing the many other worlds that inhabit the same geographic space. In short, Clare's speculative poetry about time, the "eternity" of the Earth, and notions of taste form the background for what motivates his political poetry insofar as these ideas articulate an understanding of *how* the Earth is a commons (it is an unpossessable anteriority), as well as how that concept leads to a new conception of community that could potentially take up a different *relation* to that anteriority.[66] To be able to perceive nature as independent of human use, and the Earth as a home for other worlds that share it and have as much "right" to it as any human landowner, is to enter into an understanding of nature and the Earth directly at odds with the system of industrial agriculture that was beginning to emerge. Because of its ability to reflect a taste attuned to other worlds, poetry is for Clare the only space remaining in which something like a genuine commons of the Earth is still possible.[67]

This also explains poetry's unique relation to the Earth's anteriority: Unlike enclosure's reduction of the Earth to raw material for the construction of human worlds, poetry opens a form of taste that remains attuned to the many different worlds and ecosystems enabled by the Earth but *effaced* by enclosure, which seeks to reduce that multiplicity into a single domain of its own sovereignty. The Earth, unlike specific human political formations, precedes their institution and thereby relativizes them, challenging the supposed "natural right" of their authority. As Clare suggests throughout his poetry, the diversity of worlds the Earth makes possible often remains unregistered or unnoticed until poetry gives those worlds a "voice," thereby recognizing their fragility in the face of the Earth's "eternity." It is that sense of giving voice to what or whomever does not have it that constitutes the political, for Clare, which is not simply a contestation over power, but a way of looking, a "distribution of the sensible" to use Jacques Rancière's term, which defines the political around "what is seen and what can be said about it, around who has the ability to see and the talent to speak."[68] To see these unnoticed worlds and give them space—within poetry at least—is to *produce a commons* for Clare, to give shape and visibility to the multiplicity of worlds denied by enclosure. It is thus also, by definition, to give shape to what is violently and systematically occluded by enclosure: not just the "eternity" of the Earth, but the many human and nonhuman ways of looking, of judging, and of existing, that relate to that "eternity" in entirely different ways. To make these forms visible is to grant their independence, but also to articulate the Earth as a commons populated by a community of incommensurable worlds that share the same space, and a relation to something—the anteriority of the Earth—none of them can possess.

In "Lament of Swordy Well," Clare's best-known political poem, the Earth speaks through the personification of a stone quarry that exhibits something like its "eternity" in Clare's sense: First used by the Romans, the quarry significantly predates the present-day parish in which it is enclosed. And by making the land itself the speaker of the poem, Clare poetically gives speech to an Earth lamenting its reduction to the status of a stockpile. At the same time, the quarry also testifies to the interaction between the various worlds that depend on it, from the rabbits that make their dens in its soil, to the bees that feed on the flowers that once used to bloom there. The quarry, in a sense, speaks for all its tenants, all the various human and nonhuman worlds left destitute or threatened with extinction by its enclosure, from the bees that "thrum their almost weary wings / Upon the moss and die"[69] to the gypsies who "further on sojourn / No parish bonds they like" (SW 113) now that the quarry has been privatized. Each world referenced in the poem takes up a relation to the Earth—through the quarry—developing its own taste and thereby resisting its insertion into the human world of enclosure. Swordy Well's complaint about its newfound status as a privatized space in this world stems not from a conception of a commons organized by legal recognition of a common "right," but from the quarry's *antecedence* to every world it makes possible, including that of the parish. As Swordy Well puts it, "These things that claim my own as theirs / Were born but yesterday" (SW 107). The encroachment of enclosure, and its inability to comprehend any world but its own, has fundamentally displaced and silenced all the other worlds with which it coexists. Rabbits "dread a workhouse like the poor / & nibble on the road" (SW 107) instead of inhabiting their dens. Even laborers who once had a different relation to the land based on their recognized common "rights," have now been enlisted, through a new extractive conception of the land, to view it as a landowner might:

> Alas dependance thou'rt a brute
> Want only understands
> His feelings wither branch & root (SW 106)

The "dependance" human laborers have through their poverty to the forms of exploitation now enclosing the quarry makes them unwilling accomplices in its destruction. Clare's use of the idiom of feelings withering "branch and root" is cleverly connected to the actual physical branches and roots that have now fallen "in parish hands," set to be cleared to plant more grain. Clare's poem thus articulates the interconnections between the laborers' affective relation to the land, the collapse of their world, and their enclosure within another that views the quarry as a vast private repository. The laborer's "want" can only "understand," not feel, because his relation to the land has been compelled by poverty to treat it as a means for bare subsistence.[70] Enclosure thus functions to cut off any other way of looking, "enclosing" the quarry in the twofold sense of privatizing it and enframing it in a world that does not allow anything other than its use-value to be perceived, thereby shrouding the "eternity" of the Earth, its irreducibility to human use, in the mantle of profit and productivity.

Enclosure, in other words, effaces the Earth's anteriority *along with* all the other worlds that existed prior to it. By doing so, it claims its own temporary and specific relation to the Earth as universal—part of the natural order of things à la Locke. And while Clare employs the language of common law or "right" throughout the poem, the fact that Swordy Well and its nonhuman inhabitants could not possibly attain legal status within this system suggests another basis underpinning their "right" to exist: the anteriority or independence of the Earth—the givenness of its precedence to every world it makes possible, which is akin to its indifference to any legal system or "law" defining itself as "natural." The quarry frames this antecedence in terms of what it calls its "own" (SW 106), and while this might sound at first like a conception of property, the quarry specifies its independence in terms of something that remains *beyond* appropriation or ownership, a "common good" in Roumain's sense, which provides an alternative form of value superseding general equivalence.[71] In fact, everything in the poem regarding the quarry's "own" pertains to what *preceded* the world of enclosure. As the quarry remarks elsewhere, it is so old it witnessed the rise and fall of the Roman Empire, an assertion that places the quarry within a much longer temporality of the Earth irreducible to present human civilizations. And when Swordy Well begins to lament the specifics of the theft of "its own," nearly all the examples of what has been "taken" from it pertain to how it used to act as a basis for other *nonhuman* worlds as well as other human communities not part of the parish. The quarry's "own" is simply a description of its status beyond its value as commodity—it is instead a *gift* to the other, a bestowal enacted in ways that do not enter into economic exchangeability and yet form the conditions for relation to the wonder of other worlds.

What Swordy Well mourns is thus not just its own independence, but all the other worlds threatened by the rapaciousness of enclosure. The language of "freedom" in the poem thus has a double meaning: on the one hand, it is identified with the property rights that become the means to expropriate non-owners from the land. On the other, "freedom," when referred to the quarry itself, is understood simply as its freedom *from* human exploitation, a freedom the quarry bestows on the many worlds it makes possible thanks to its existence or givenness.[72] When Clare refers to freedom in the former sense, he has in mind the entire system that organizes private property, and that allows surplus value to be extracted from the quarry based on the market price of specific commodities. When he refers to freedom in the latter sense, it tends to take the form of unnoticed nature or waste grounds we have seen as central to his conception of taste, and to the antecedence of the Earth. Swordy Well, for instance, worries what will happen to it should the price of grain rise again:

> & should the price of grain get high
> Lord help & keep it low
> I shant possess a single flye
> Or get a weed to grow
> I shant possess a yard of ground
> To bid a mouse to thrive
> For gain has put me in a pound
> I scarce can keep alive (SW 110)

As with the man of taste capable of seeing the beauty in waste grounds and in the potentially repellant creatures that inhabit it, the quarry fears what will happen when a commodified plant—wheat—becomes so profitable it supplants the value of other less desirable life-forms. The quarry's lament is thus framed in terms of the flora and fauna seen as anathema to profit. Mice that eat grain, flies that are pests, weeds that vie with wheat for available ground, are all relegated to a zone in which their lives become devalued or worthless—and they become slated for removal or eradication.[73]

As "Lament" is all too aware, Earth's "eternity" does not prevent portions of it from becoming an unrecognizable wasteland. By the end of the poem, the quarry's lament turns into a warning about what will happen if, under the new regime of enclosure, unabated extraction is allowed to proceed unchecked. As the last lines of the poem suggest, the landscape itself may become so fundamentally altered that it becomes unrecognizable, coming to exist only as a memory or "name" that occurs solely in poetry:

> Of all the fields I am the last
> That my own face can tell
> Yet what with stone pits delving holes
> & strife to buy & sell
> My name will quickly be the whole
> That's left of swordy well (SW 113–14)

The final lines of the poem make clear that what remains of Swordy Well's "freedom"—its independence from human structures and history—will henceforth only be recognizable through the indexicality of the name "Swordy Well," whose reference ceases to be a place and becomes merely a mark of its passing. What passes, however, is not "the Earth's sublime," its "eternity," or its anteriority; for Clare that is beyond humanity's influence. Swordy Well may indeed at some point once again enjoy its "freedom" in the absence of humans or enclosure. What passes, rather, is the possibility of any *present* relation to the space of freedom Swordy Well currently represents in any way other than through a poem lamenting its loss. Clare's political poetry, thus, is underpinned not merely by a protest against the loss of the legal protection of the way of life of commoners. It is underpinned by a conception of the Earth as a commons that reveals how that way of life, that world, is only one of many threatened with extinction by enclosure. In the absence of a geographical space for a commons that would link these worlds together in a shared struggle against enclosure, poetry, for Clare, becomes the only place remaining in which various worlds—the worlds of insects, gypsies, rabbits, moles, and agricultural laborers, all the wretched of the Earth—come together around the absent center of the Earth's anteriority. What they share is a relation to its inappropriable gift, which is also a promise of the future: the possibility of a world and of worlds beyond enclosure.

Roumain and Clare: An Earth-Commons of the Future

If Clare and Roumain share a conception of the Earth as commons in the sense that it acts as an unpossessable ground uniting various otherwise discordant worlds or communities, including in Clare's case nonhuman ones, the question remains how this conception articulates more than just a resistance to the status quo. In the case of Clare, we know that enclosure eventually won the day, converting the last remaining recognized common lands in England into private holdings, and in the case of Roumain we know that a new international, much less a pan-Caribbean resistance to neoliberal globalization, never really took shape. What would seem to remain of the Earth as commons, then, is at best an ideal and at worst a pipedream. Yet thanks to Roumain's explicit insistence on the futural dimension of his conceptualization of the international—Manuel acts in the name of a future he will never live to see—one can begin to see that in both of these cases, despite the apparent failure of the idea of the Earth as commons to resist its particular historical version of enclosure in each of their respective moments, both authors point toward a *future* that would be required to take up that idea once again. In our own moment of the Anthropocene, the limits of nation-state sovereignty as the framework for negotiations concerning expanding the idea of the Earth as a commons are all too readily apparent. As I write this, only days after the reelection of Donald Trump to a second term in the White House, what clearly awaits us once again is the US's withdrawal from an inadequate, but crucial, international agreement about limiting carbon emissions—the Paris Accord—and the expansion and acceleration of fossil fuel extraction. In a world seemingly doubling down on assertions of nation-state sovereignty in the face of planetary catastrophe, a different model of the commons from the one this chapter started with (outlined in the document by the International Institute for Applied System Analysis) that understands the commons as yet another shared resource and makes as its central "stakeholder" the national governments that preside over them, becomes necessary: A model that places into relation a now global set of communities dispossessed from the land and organized around a conception of the Earth as something other than a source of raw materials. An Earth as commons that is not only the condition for a new kind of solidarity between non-nation-state actors, but also one articulated through a relation to the Earth as gift—as outside of exchange value. It is here that Roumain and Clare's understanding of the Earth as commons comes back to us from the past, as a memory of the future.

In Clare's case, however, this seems to contradict what appears to be his decidedly backward glance at the commons system that was then being torn apart. However, with the help of Roumain's future-oriented conception of community, an element of Clare's geopoetics surfaces that similarly pairs peasant relations to the land with a future. Nearly all of his protest poems such as "Lament" muse on the fact that the only remnant of the commons system may end up being found nowhere on the Earth except in the domain of poetry.[74] Clare's eventual move to Northborough as his family expanded, though it was only three miles from his native Helpston, is usually seen as the moment when mourning for his "home of homes," as "The Flitting," puts it, begins.[75] This middle period, and the subsequent later poetry he wrote while he was confined to a mental hospital in Northampton, contains a great deal of writing mourning Clare's childhood and lost loves. This apparent longing tends to be read through the lens of Clare's biography, suggesting that, in his displacement from Helpston, Clare became gripped by a nostalgic yearning for a past landscape.[76] The fact that this landscape was only a dozen or so miles from his confinement points to an obvious fact: What is being mourned is not just a landscape that has been irrevocably altered, but an entire world, and entire community, which has fallen apart along with the commons system and the view of nature that sustained it.

Which means that Clare's nostalgia is ultimately refracted through the "eternity" of the Earth, where what matters is a confrontation with its capacity for oblivion, *as well as* its capacity to survive even his own world's dissolution by enclosure. It is here that we begin to see the future-oriented dimension of Clare's poetry, which acts as a witness to a collapsing world to point not toward its reconstitution in the future, but instead to the basic condition that made it possible: the continued perdurance of the "eternity" of the Earth. In all of Clare's poetry, worlds come and go, from the Roman Empire to the commons system to animal worlds destroyed by enclosure. What remains, however, is the Earth which, with the help of the memorializing function of poetry, remains and therefore continues to offer the promise of a different relation to it, and thus another form of community for those no longer seeking to possess it for themselves. While this might begin in Clare with a mourning not just for his own world, but for others destroyed by enclosure, the fact that these communities once existed, that they took up their own relation to the Earth according to their own "taste" means that, so long as the Earth remains "eternal," and so long as poetry witnesses the bygone existence of those worlds, they may not succumb to "oblivion" too quickly. Even the late poems that seem to be predicated on personal reflections almost always return to a mourning for a *shared* world predicated on the "eternity" of the Earth. In "Remembrances," for instance, the connection between Clare's personal memories and the world to which they belonged is central.[77] Over its eight stanzas, the poem transitions several times from reflections organized around a lyric "I," which features remembrances framed by the speaker's own subjectivity, to a much broader lament about the loss of the commons. It begins with an elegiac mourning for "summer pleasures that are gone,"[78] but eventually intertwines the speaker's childhood with a meditation on the broader social and historical changes that have fundamentally altered the parish's relation to the land:

> While I see the little mouldywharps hang sweeing to the wind
> On the only aged willow that in all the field remains
> & nature hides her face where theyre sweeing in their chains
> & in silent murmuring complains
> Here was commons for their hills where they seek for freedom still
> Though every commons gone & though traps are set to kill
> The little homeless miners—O it turns my bosom chill (R 132)

"Mouldywharps"—an archaic word for moles—experience the same homelessness as the speaker, having lost their own commons "where they seek for freedom still." The point is not just nostalgia for the speaker's childhood home but a mourning for a whole series of worlds—including the world of moles—that have vanished.[79]

With the help of Roumain, however, we can now see how Clare's apparent nostalgia and mourning is in fact directed to the future. In Roumain's novel that future is represented by Annaïse's unborn child with Manuel, acting as a symbol for the reconciliation of the village. However, it is also represented by the "great *coumbite*" the villagers envision taking place in the future, a past peasant practice that, in a new context, takes on a different meaning and import. In Roumain, what comes back from the past to open a different future is a peasant relation to the Earth, a peasant social form, that does not return without a difference: In his envisioned "great *coumbite*," it becomes postnational in scope. And so long as the Earth remains "eternal" in Clare's sense—inappropriable in Roumain's—there is always the chance, the possibility, that a relation to the Earth evidenced in the peasant world might return once again in a new form.

Clare is under no illusions that the old world of the commons is coming back. But since it was never predicated solely on a legal structure, its oblivion was never seen as absolute. Since the Earth is "eternal" it has no need of memory, unlike every and any world, whether it be built on a conception of the Earth as a commons, or upon a conception of the Earth as property. Poetry is thus given a seemingly impossible task in Clare: finding a way—momentarily since that is all it can hope for—to transform itself into a trace of the Earth as commons, memorializing a bygone human world in its name, emphasizing the fundamentally *asymmetrical* relation between Earth and world to preserve it for a future that might take it up again in its own fashion. There is a sense, then, in Clare of a battle having been lost—and of a desire for something once again familiar: the world to which he once belonged. But that is not to say that the question of the posterity of Clare's writing, and of the "eternity" of the Earth, is absent. Increasingly in Clare's later poetry, the matter of his own legacy is at stake—usually interpreted through the question of which readers would be capable of appreciating him in the future. "Rural Scenes," for instance, projects a future "man of taste" who will share Clare's "common thoughts that all may read / Who love the quiet fields."[80] Imagining his own "rural fame" (RS 585) in a readership of "humble tongues / In the green shadows of some after day" (RS 585), Clare's poetry projects his desire for a readership sympathetic to peasant "taste" into the future. In other moments, his poetry confronts the possibility of succumbing to the same eventual fate as Shakespeare and Milton in "Eternity of Time": oblivion. But even in those moments, his poetry always reflects on what survives or lives on in the face of the Earth's longevity, its capacity to always promise the possibility of another world, and to outlive or survive even those who seek to enclose it.

It is only in the alternative genealogy of the Earth as commons represented by Roumain and Clare that one can see a genuinely "global commons" taking shape that challenges the Earth's enclosure within the parish and ultimately the nation-state. The starting point must be a conception of the Earth that has no regard for national borders—and that sees the Earth as a condition of possibility of multiple worlds rather than a single one. There are essentially four remaining global commons whose existence has been constructed by international agreements such that they are either *res nullius* (owned by no one) or *res communes* (owned by all), and therefore outside the jurisdiction of any nation-state or set of nation-states: the open ocean and deep seabed, the Earth's atmosphere, the space beyond the Earth's atmosphere, and Antarctica. The problem, of course, is how to resituate the Earth as commons when a system or feature of the Earth that is even more significant to the stability of the biosphere than those *recognized* global commons—such as rainforests or wetlands—are *inside* the legal jurisdiction of a nation-state and are clearly seen as nothing more than a resource to be exploited. Take, for instance, Brazil's insistence under Jair Bolsonaro that the Amazon rainforest, one of the Earth's most important carbon sinks, is that country's own resource to dispose of as it sees fit. How does one counter this assertion of enclosure?

Drawing both on Roumain's conception of the Earth as a common good, and on his understanding of the kind of solidarity between communities this idea implies, his suggestion is that any notion of the "commons" worthy of the name must first challenge enclosure by destabilizing the conception of the Earth as property that enclosure is founded upon. However, for Roumain, resistance to enclosure must also articulate new forms of communal solidarity that challenge the hegemony of national configurations. For Roumain, the Earth as commons is the condition for a migrant trans-historical collectivity no longer rooted to a particular place or land. Writing about the African diaspora, and the possibility of its transformation into a historical force operating beyond the goals of any one struggle for national liberation, Roumain identifies not just a different relation to the Earth in their common solidarity, but a different set of political goals. His late poem "Ebony Wood," for instance, concentrates on how the dispersal of the African diaspora introduced a set of struggles that are at first seemingly disconnected, but that become gradually unified by the "ebony wood," a part of the Earth found in a variety of nations that is not a shared resource, but the site of collective suffering and resistance:

> But I also know a silence
> a silence of twenty-five thousand negro corpses
> twenty-five thousand railroad ties of Ebony Wood
> Under the iron rails of the Congo-Océan
> but I know
> the shrouds of silence in the cypress branches
> the petals of black bloodclots on the branches
> in that woods where they lynched my brother of Georgia
> and, shepherd of Abyssinia
> what terror made you, shepherd of Abyssinia
> this iron mask of silence[81]

The "ebony wood" described here is found in several nations and states: among them the Congo, Georgia, and Ethiopia. Roumain moves in these lines from the atrocity of the construction of the Congo-Océan railway, built by France in 1921 using forced labor from Chad and the Central African Republic (tens of thousands were killed in its construction), to the woods of Georgia in the aftermath of a lynching, to Ethiopia in the aftermath of the Italian invasion of 1936. What connects them is an emerging Pan-Africanism, certainly, but also a collectivity framed in terms of the "silence" of the ebony wood, a silence of the dead, the lynched, the oppressed, presented in the poem as all the places on Earth where that domination has been perpetrated. The Earth as commons in the poem is thus not a resource at the disposal of an already defined nation-state, it is the space in which the memory of what Roumain at one point calls the "world's felony" (BE 77/58) is retained, and the place from which the current distribution of the Earth can be contested. Like Glissant's "memory of the Earth community," Roumain proposes an Earth that shatters purportedly "natural" national borders and forms of memory.

His poem thus figuratively resists the carving up of the Earth into discrete commons and instead proposes an unbordered Earth as the ground for a new collectivity. Reorganizing it into a vast network, as opposed to a set of discrete enclosed states or nations, the Earth is figured in "Ebony Wood" as without borders that have been naturalized by political regimes intent on separating peoples within each locale from what *actually* binds them together: their shared oppression and resistance, as well as their shared relation to the Earth as an "ebony woods," a site in which another relation to territory becomes possible. Rather than a shared ownership of common goods creating the collectivity, it is the other way around: a shared collectivity is organized around what *cannot* define a nation-state, becoming a postnational community of those who—located inside the nation's borders like an enclosed commons—acts on behalf of an inappropriable Earth to disrupt the ultimately proprietary model of "shared resources."

Clare's notion of the Earth as commons, despite being defined in local terms, nonetheless extends the solidarity Roumain has in mind to the worlds of animals and insects with which human communities share the Earth. When coupled with Roumain's postnationalism, the broad scope of the struggles taking shape in the name of animal worlds threatened with destruction comes into view, a struggle that to this point has primarily been articulated as a matter of national trust. What matters in Clare is not just recognizing the disjunction between enclosure and the dependence of other worlds for their existence on the same—now enclosed—space. It is also a matter of recognizing in animals, insects, and other nonhumans another relation to the Earth they enact in their own worlds, other forms of "taste" that relativize humanity's claim on the Earth. It is therefore not just a matter of "protecting" or conserving the few wild animals that remain, but of recognizing their "taste" and even adopting it as a new form of rationality, a new way of existing on the Earth. As we have seen, Clare's protest against enclosure is not just in the name of lost common rights but is also a protest on behalf of the many other forms of community that relate to the land in their own unique ways. Clare's poetry constantly suggests a broad solidarity with nonhuman collectives whose disruption by privatization is as extensive as the human communities affected by it. As Clare's poem suggests, other creatures with as much "right" to an Earth now deemed "private property" keep alive—through their instincts—a conception of the Earth as a commons humans would do well to adopt.

Roumain's and Clare's idea of the Earth thus transcends the notion of a simple shared resource. The Earth is not merely an economic base that must be managed—it is what places us into contact with others, including nonhumans, as a shared "ground" that belongs to no one, and by remaining "boundless" or "free" in Clare's sense, creates the condition for forms of solidarity and community transcending identitarian arrangements based on national or even species differences. While Roumain frames this sharing in terms of a global proletariat that must shed national divisions to finally confront the divisive structures of neocolonialism and global capital, Clare frames his commons in trans-species terms, showing how the Earth as a private enclosure entails conceiving it as a uniform world, whereas it is in fact a domain of contact between multiple worlds, human and nonhuman alike. Clare and Roumain thus represent a tradition of thinking that undermines the pretension of the nation-state to be the sole and final arbiter of the commons, whether through enclosure or regulation. Clare's notion of the commons is "local," but his conception of the Earth makes clear its exteriority to human regulation and control more broadly. Any political system, local or national, that fails to take that fact into account or fails to realize that it is only one of many worlds that inhabits, or will inhabit, the Earth, is fated to a "blank oblivion" of its own. Roumain's commons, developed out of the experience of an agricultural economy and peasant culture in conflict with the emerging integration of markets enacted by a newly aggressive American application of the Monroe Doctrine, sought to find a means by which to connect divergent yet interconnected struggles across national lines, a conception that addresses the local situation while situating it within a global context. Clare's own immersion in the peasant culture of his time meant that his poetry was, in effect, a witness for a lost time and a lost world that manifested another relation to the Earth and which might, in some unknown posterity, reconstitute an *ethos* for another one.

In our contemporary moment of the Anthropocene, it is to these earlier models of the commons that we must turn—for it is there that any sense of the Earth as a space shared with other organisms, worlds, and peoples, as opposed to a shared "stock" for various national economies, finds its expression. Any conception of the Earth as commons leaving intact the idea of the Earth as a "resource base" for national economies, or deemphasizing the interconnection between nonstate communities and nonhuman species, is inadequate in the face of the climate-change challenges ahead of us. What would it mean, then, to take this conception of the commons seriously in our present moment? It would mean, first of all, construction of a broad solidarity with dispossessed groups inside nation-state borders that eschew the notion of the Earth as a shared resource. Take, for instance, the resistance to the Dakota Access pipeline project in the US in 2016 mounted by Lakota, Assiniboine, and Gros Ventre tribes (among others). This struggle created for a moment a flashpoint not just for national fossil fuel policy, but also for the question of "land use," "land rights," and "eminent domain" that were central to the pipeline's construction. In the long and ongoing history of Native American sovereignty, this struggle drew sustenance from the Lakota fight for their "land rights" more than a century earlier that culminated in the massacre at Wounded Knee. Even then, pitted against each other were not just two different peoples but two conceptions of what "sovereignty" over the land might imply. Posed against the pipeline's construction, therefore, was not just another set of "stakeholders," but a different conception of the Earth in line with Clare or Roumain's idea of an inappropriable or unownable basis for communal life. In the case of Standing Rock, this meant no negotiation was possible with the TC Energy Corporation—the primary "stakeholder" in the pipeline's construction—no moment at which a supposedly "shared resource" could be parceled out differently to a wider range of participants in its management, which would only amount to a continuation of business as usual. Or take the solidarity between Amazon Watch, an organization devoted to the protection of the rainforest, and its work with indigenous tribes and working-class laborers of the region resisting ongoing deforestation and dispossession. Their struggle does not demand that those tribes or that class of workers be included as stakeholders in the economic management of the rainforest but is focused instead on opposing the view that the forest is a resource and that, in addition to being a repository of pasts, traditions, histories, lives, and worlds, it is also an anteriority that exceeds our human needs and wants. In other words, taking the commons seriously would mean viewing the rainforest not just as a carbon sink we ought to preserve to avoid the disastrous effects of our accelerated carbon emissions, but as a home to millions of species among which are a hundred thousand invertebrates alone, a hundred thousand "insect worlds," as Clare might put it. It would mean resisting the ongoing enclosure of the Amazon not just in the name of our own self-preservation, but in the name of all those worlds we would otherwise consign to oblivion.

The thinking of the Earth as commons Clare and Roumain represent requires a fundamental reconsideration of what "stakeholder" means, whether the Earth can be conceived as "property," and what social structures would be necessary for instituting an Earth-as-commons not already enclosed by capital and national borders. From out of this thinking emerges a geopoetics and a relation to the anteriority of the Earth that supersedes the regulation of competing national interests, even those having to consider the shared management of the biosphere. This would be an Earth-commons whereby so-called peasant communities are not simply archaic throwbacks to a precapitalist past, but repositories of the memory of another relation to the Earth, and thus an opening to a different future.

THREE

EARTH AS "ARCHIVE"

Senior and Günderrode on the Political Ecology of "Life"

IN 2007 OLIVE SENIOR published *Shell*, a remarkable collection of poetry written to commemorate the 200th anniversary of Britain's abolition of the slave trade. In it shells are figures born of land and sea, rock and water and come to symbolize the past and present of Senior's native Jamaica, its history and culture, its tie to the Earth and ocean, and to the island's memory. How the image of the shell conveys that memory, including the question of what it memorializes, however, reveals a decidedly troubled and troubling relation to the past. Take, for example, the uncertain temporality of Senior's poem from the collection titled "Shelter":

> Growth rings inscribe
> inside each shell
> the markers of
> a former life.
>
> This shell, my skin,
> outers a life
> still stretched
> still lived in.[1]

The poem moves in the first stanza from the image of a typical mollusk shell of the kind one would find on the beach, with growth rings that mark the development and eventual death of the creature it housed, to a present "still lived in," but that has transformed the shell into a metaphor for the speaker's skin. What exactly, then, is the relation between the past and the present? And if the shell is both a figure of a "former life" *and* a present one, what exactly is the status of "life" in the poem, the life that the shell represents which can be both former and present at the same time, seemingly both inert shell and organic skin?

In the prior chapter we saw the way Clare's understanding of the Earth's "eternity," its immemorial past, becomes a way of describing the Earth as a commons, something antecedent to human and animal worlds that is their condition of possibility. With Senior, that "eternity" enters the present, giving "voice"—albeit only as a material trace—to a past that would otherwise have been effaced from human memory. Here a different kind of immemoriality is given shape and figured through the image of the shell: as the discarded detritus of meals by the island's native Taíno inhabitants, or the remains of a maroon encampment, or the vanished shells surrounding the sugarcane plants discarded by slaves on Jamaican plantations. The shells in her poetry become traces of what can no longer be found on a map—a past that has been erased, often intentionally. However, her understanding of the Earth—what she calls the "skin of the Earth," itself another shell—becomes the site of a renewed testimony enacted by the various figures of shells in her poems. If Earth processes often appear to *wear away* the memory of the dead in what Édouard Glissant calls a "time marked by these balls and chains gone green,"[2] in the effacement of the bodies of the enslaved by their interment in the Earth or the ocean, for Senior the figure of the shell becomes a way of re-marking that effacement in the present, locating a trace of that memory in the Earth through the figure of the shell as the lithic memory of a "former life."

However, Senior goes further than the notion of a trace of the past located in the present. Her poetry insists on the present-day *life* to which the shells testify; her geopoetics, in other words, challenges the apparently stable border between life and death itself. As a counterpoint, take the role that the discovery of "pooty shells" (or snail shells) plays in the poetry of John Clare. Finding those shells at the base of an excavation near the ruins of a road from the Roman period allows him to reflect on the passage of time in terms of both geological and human history. The fact that they have been discovered under those ruins, Clare suggests, makes a "pygmy of the pride of man," revealing natural structures that have outlived the imperial ambitions of past human civilizations.[3] Olive Senior's poetry adds a different dimension to the way shells depict or encapsulate prior geological or historical moments. For

Senior, shells are "markers of a former life" and yet also intimate the *ongoing* processes of life to which they still belong. They therefore testify to a kind of "afterlife" that resonates from out of the shell, a seemingly dead husk. For Clare, shells are fossils: dead matter and empty stone that had at one time been shaped into a home for life. Through their position in the terrain or the intricacy of their construction, they reveal animal life's anteriority to the works of man. For Senior, the shell is not seen merely as a relic of the past, but as a *current instance of life*, a force that "outers a life / still stretched / still lived in."

In what follows I examine Senior's poetic conchology, which compresses her various explorations of time, life, and death, and which I read as a contemporary geopoetics—a meditation on the Earth, history, and memory. I also articulate how her poetics finds common cause in the uniquely vitalist conception of the Earth articulated in the literary and philosophical writings of nineteenth-century author Karoline von Günderrode, a long-neglected figure of German *Naturphilosophie*. These two writers, separated as they are by vast geographic and temporal distances, share a conception of life that challenges the supposedly impermeable—and for most Western thought of the last two millennia, foundational—border between life and death, the organic and the inorganic, a border that was an important conceptual scaffolding for colonial narratives that relegated non-European cultures to the state of nature or to an embeddedness in the Earth. Senior and Günderrode both conceive of the Earth as a ground (in Senior's case a "shell") in which various forms of life come to be or pass away. But that passing away is relative, as prior assemblages—whether "organic" or "inorganic"—take on new forms and functions through the Earth, "haunting" the present by leaving a trace in and on it.

But this haunting, and the form those traces take, yields a memory distinct from historical or material traces discovered in the soil of an archaeological site wherefrom they are imported into an organized archive, one that safeguards artifacts, documents, texts, and other markers of the past in controlled ways that allow for their rediscovery in the present. As with Freud's "mystic writing pad," collective archives bear traces of memories that are no longer available to consciousness or historical narrative—and yet are retained in archives on some kind of material (and now virtual) surface as a nonconscious vestige or trace.[4] The writing pad, for Freud, is an allegory for the work of the unconscious itself, and for archivization more generally, suggesting that what is required for archival memory is a selfsame, relatively stable, surface of inscription that ensures in some form or another memory's retention and possible retrieval.

For Senior and Günderrode, by contrast, the Earth as archival surface is indifferent to human law and memory, operating as it does outside the structures of the human psyche. As a substratum or support for remembrance, it is therefore decidedly more tenuous: It cannot function as a selfsame inscriptional surface like Freud's mystic writing pad, since it is constantly remaking itself. What emerges in Senior and Günderrode, then, is a "telluric unconscious" that conceptualizes the indifference of the Earth as an archive without stable substrate, foundation, substratum, or subjectivity, thereby disrupting the conceptual scaffolding underpinning ideas of consciousness, memory, and life that inform more conventional notions of the archive. The Earth is an archive that constantly *reconstitutes* the traces it contains. It is thus "material" not in the sense of being merely physical, much less foundational or preservatory, but rather in a sense closer to Louis Althusser's "materialism of the encounter," a materiality that is "not of a subject (be it God or the proletariat), but of a process, a process that has no subject" and that is imposed "with no assignable end."[5] As a process that has no subject, and no assignable end or *telos*, the form of memory the Earth makes possible *can potentially* intersect with human mnemonics, but need not necessarily do so. As a material archive the Earth is structured by processes irreducible to the human psyche. Those processes must therefore become the object of a geopoetics capable of *interpreting* the Earth's geologic memorialization, particularly since traces return only insofar as they are completely reshaped in ways that are not necessarily selfsame, visible, or whole, nor integrated into existing historical narratives.

Senior and Günderrode's geopoetics thus enlists this materiality to reconceive the relation between matter and memory, matter and spirit, consciousness and the absence of consciousness. Traces in Senior do not return as what they were, nor as fragments of the past. They return in new, often unrecognizable ways transformed by their renovation in and through the Earth in a manner her poetry attempts to register. As with Roumain and Clare, the Earth is not a thing; for Senior and Günderrode it is a *process*, a ceaseless reconstitution of traces that potentially gives them a second life in ways that go beyond what we usually mean when we think of life as a biological structure of self-reproduction. The Earth conceived of in this way generates alternative histories, and in the case of Senior memorializes otherwise those who have been consigned to historical erasure. This idea of the Earth also engenders for Senior and Günderrode alternative political ecologies that render indiscernible the processes of memory and erasure at work in the Earth and those that govern culture or politics.

So what does the conchological Earth—the "skin of the Earth"—entail in Senior? And what exactly is her understanding of "life"? As we will see, for Senior, there is no better metaphor of the indiscernibility between the organic and the inorganic than a shell, a nonliving mineral structure that has been shaped by a living creature into a habitat, indexing a *symbiosis* of the inorganic "lithic" element of the Earth and the living creature. The metaphor of the shell, however, begins to proliferate in Senior's poetry, including not just human skin and corn husks, but the "shell" of the Earth's surface itself, thereby suggesting the fundamentally malleable and figurative nature of the animate/inanimate distinction in her work. What matters for Senior is the way the hollow of the shell, apparently denoting the absence of life, in fact gives shape to a different kind of "life" that is not necessarily biological—such as a new organism coming to use the shell as its home, for instance. Shells, rather, become in Senior a figure for the intertwining of the nonliving with the living, the organic with the inorganic. When brought into the cultural and historical realms, this intertwinement functions as a form of survival, a new kind of memory housed quite literally in the Earth, insofar as past, seemingly "dead" or forgotten objects, genres, forms of culture, and people themselves, are reinscribed in the present, either at the level of historical memory or at the level of their interment in the Earth and revival in the present. The shells in Senior's poetry denote not just a rethinking of the border between life and death, but an alternative Earth-based memorialization and revitalization of the past and of the dead, in and through the living.

Take, for example, one of the poems in Senior's collection titled "Shell Blow," which contrasts the relative durability of inorganic shells with organic flesh:

> Flesh is sweet but disposable, what counts
> is shell. Like other objects beached, beyond
> your ken, inert I lie and toneless
> save for ocean song that only visitors claim
> to hear. (S 33)

The apparently "inert" nature of the shell is in fact given shape by the hollow that mimics what a "visitor" might hear as the "ocean song" coming from it. Since organic flesh is "disposable," supplanted by the more durable stone shell, the shell testifies to its own *longue durée*. From out of its hollow, therefore, comes something more than the mere repetition of present-day ocean sounds captured and amplified by it as an empty vessel. If the visitor hears only an "ocean song," the poem goes on to suggest that another kind of singing, this time a historical one, emanates from out of its hollow:

> there would pour out not the croak
> of song soaked up in sea-water and salt
> but the real thing, a blast-out, everybody's
> history: *areíto, canto histórico,* a full
> genealogy of this beach, this island people. (S 33)

What issues out of the shell is not the generic hum of the ocean but an *areíto, a canto histórico*. In other words, it voices another history: *areíto* is a word from the Taíno language, taken over by Spanish colonizers, denoting a ceremonial song and dance praising the ancestors, chiefs, and gods of the past. What survives is the word, while the practice does not, indexing a past effaced by genocide. The shell is thus the symbolic mouthpiece, for Senior, of "everybody's history," not just the colonizer's; it is a hollow out of which something new emerges—a voice, an image, a text:

> You could be blown away by what is held
> custody here, every whorl a book of life,
> a text, a motion picture, a recording,
> or what passes for such in our island
> version. You could begin anywhere. (S 33)

In this sense, life for Senior is not simply organic matter reborn into a new form (though, as we will see, it is that as well). Life—or the "book of life"—is here defined by the nonliving inorganic structures that make it possible: inscriptions, traces, recordings, and images that provide for the possibility of repetition and reiteration, and that operate *like* the reproductive capacities of biological life.

In "Skin of the Earth," a key poem in the collection I will engage with in more detail shortly, Senior uses the word "encoded" to designate the process by which organic and inorganic matter is reshaped and reconstituted, its hereditary code passed on to new formations, as DNA codes are passed on to the next generation of biological life. In "Skin of the Earth" "we" return after death "encoded in found matter" (S 23). In "Shell Blow" the figural texts, motion pictures, and recordings located in the shell likewise "encode" prior moments and existences in ways that allow them to be recombined in the present, as with the *areíto*, a bygone practice, but one that has now become the marker of a past that signifies in new ways an allegedly "dead" genre whose significance has been reconstituted in the present:

> Encoded in are full facilities for fast forward,
> play, playback and dub, reversible though
> not scrubbable (S 33–34)

The musical genre of "dub," which Senior references here, grew out of reggae and designates songs produced from original recordings through the process of remixing and overlaying. In bringing together two very different mediums—music and natural processes—Senior suggests a musical metaphor for what she will go on to explore as the recombinatory processes of the Earth, suggesting that there is little difference for her between "natural" and "cultural" forms of reproduction and recombination. As the poem insists, however, nothing is lost in this recombination—none of the former moments of the "book of life" are entirely "scrubbable" or effaced so long as there is a geopoetics to give it shape. Like the *areíto*, its musical genre lives on in the new forms of syncretism and musical creation it inspires.

When "Shell Blow" transposes this musical metaphor to the historical realm, it takes on a specific political significance:

> For we—as you know—
> are master engineers when it comes to
> scratching out a living on vinyl, on dutty
> or plantation. We is Ginnal at the Controls!
> Nansi Nation. We can rib it up, dibble it,
> rub it, dub it and fracture it. Splice it. Spice
> it up. But like a spite, we still can't find
> a way to erase not one word. They say
> that is how History stay. (S 34)

The "scratching" of the vinyl record that produces dub music, whereby riffs or sections of prior recordings are remixed and incorporated into a new creation, is metaphorically extended into a broader meditation on how Jamaicans of the past "scratched out a living" in the plantation economy. That idea is then extended further into a reflection on how stories and folklore form another element of the recombinatory dimension found in Taíno-Jamaican music. The reference in the poem to the "Nansi Nation" is an allusion to the

"Anansi Stories," which are an amalgam of West African folklore and contemporary renderings that describe interactions between the divine, humans, animals, plants, and even inanimate objects. They are usually told by the figure of Anansi, a god of stories, wisdom, and knowledge, who is sometimes depicted as a spider spinning a web of interconnection between things, people, places, and times. The migration of this oral culture was transformed during the period of slavery when Anansi as a trickster figure became a symbol of resistance: In many of the classic "spider tales," he can outwit more powerful opponents through his cleverness and cunning. In the context of Senior's poem, this figure takes on yet another dimension, functioning as a folkloric analogue of the *bricolage* she finds underway in all matter and culture. Jamaica itself, its folklore and its history, are interpreted as an example of a recombinatory dimension present in all things, where people, plants, animals, and inanimate objects all bear a "history" within them, allowing each to transform itself, to recombine with other elements in the present, and thus to survive in other forms.

Senior's poetry, however, refuses to keep that recombinatory dimension at the level of culture solely. Her poetry suggests that all matter is "alive" in the sense that the indiscernibility of the organic and the inorganic implies that the Earth itself is engaged in a recombinatory process whereby the dead are never fully obliterated. When she articulates this recombinatory dimension of the Earth in relation to the historical and political domains, her poetry develops new forms of memory, a different conception of the archive, and a political ecology that makes apparently natural processes indiscernible from cultural ones. What structures this exploration is the myriad ways in which shells come to figure that process—either as the lithic remnants of past lives, or as organic mulch for new ones. For shells are everywhere in her poetry. Some shells are fragile and prone to immediate decay—such as the organic husks of the sugarcane—a cash crop brought to Jamaica during the colonial period, and for which slaves were worked to death. All of them, however, become examples of the recombinatory process that characterizes the Earth, which is itself a shell, as "Skin of the Earth" suggests. The Earth is the surface wherein the dead become "found matter," metaphorically revitalized in new forms of life:

> So we too could lie, mountains of bones
> beneath the skin of Earth that quietly

fashions our return. Not in that self-same
shell, that edifice of body, but encoded
in found matter like perfume
strong as clove, bittersweet as orange.
Tantalizing essence of what was once the ripeness of ourselves. (S 23)

The skin of the Earth, for Senior, is a shell upon which everything and everyone lives and to which they return upon death. But that "return" is also the return *to* another life that contains not just traces of the dead—vestiges of the organic—but also the possibility of a return or repetition that would, like Jamaican dub music, "encode" the dead in new forms of "found matter." What it means to be a shell, then, is this commemorative process—it is a figure for the absence of a former life, and the return of another in a moment of reconstitution that does not leave the past intact, but which also leaves a mark of its *passing* in the way it takes on a new existence in the present. While this element is present in all the examples of shells found throughout Senior's poetry, it culminates in the figure of the Earth as the shell of shells, the surface upon which the play of life and death, memory and forgetting, is played out.

One of the ways in which the Earth as shell exemplifies a form of life after death, a kind of survival, is in the way it produces an archive for those without one, from the slaughtered indigenous Taíno people of Xaymaca (the island's original name) to the nameless and countless slaves of Jamaica, whose lives had long ago been effaced in the national archives, their villages not even marked on the documents mapping out the plantation system. Actual lives lost, seemingly without a trace, voices silenced and then silenced again in their historical oblivion—this is a version of the "abyss" of absolute historical rupture, trauma, and forgetting Glissant insists is central to the experience of the Middle Passage.[6] But what kind of archive could materialize this abyss without erasing, or worse, participating in it? In the case of the murdered and those worked to death, the rare relics of their domestic lives constitute the traditional archive: pottery shards and tools, bones—and discarded shells. Yet Senior's poetry is not interested in dealing with these traces as an archaeologist might, nor is she drawn to documents, testamentary knowledge, or objects left behind and now monumentalized by museums. That archive exists, but as a colonial institution, situated at the intersection between the narrative the colonists were giving themselves by way of their own archive, and the narrative of the ghosts they harbor between the lines, as it were—vanished villages, numbers of slaves imported, human and nonhuman "cargo" lost to the ocean, and so on. Senior's archive is none of these: her archive is the Earth, as a shell that tells a different story.

What could this possibly mean? In what sense is the Earth an archive, except as a repository of past life, fossils on cliff walls, shells left on the beach? In the absence of a conventional archive, memory takes another form for Senior, and fashions itself as a poetic or creative act that comprehends the "skin of the Earth" as not merely a vast urn for the dead, harboring within its soil fragments or bones, but as an *active* archive—one directed specifically to the future. As the shell of shells, the Earth "fashions our return" (S 23) otherwise, "encoding" the dead not just as remnants of the past, but as a reconstituted present. The shell therefore also gestures toward new forms of life, "found matter like perfume / strong as clove, bittersweet as orange" (S 23). The shells of sugarcane husks, for instance, return as new foliage on the sites of vanished villages continuing to haunt the Jamaican landscape. But whereas we usually tend to think of the Earth as *obscuring* the past, covering it over or helping consign it to historical oblivion, Senior's poetry insists on the Earth's simultaneous capacity for renewal as one of the few places in which an archive of *other histories*, and thus other futures, can be imagined.[7] The Earth, in short, functions in a way similar to the recombination of DNA, while extending that process further into nonbiological structures that include the recodification of inorganic, organic, and even cultural forms of "life."

Senior's conception of the afterlife of matter has to do with the way in which she, much like her vitalist predecessor Günderrode, problematizes the porous border between the organic and the inorganic: the afterlife the shells figure is not simply a rebirth of the dead in new organic forms—but a form of survival that *includes* death, that is predicated on it and cannot be dissociated from it, an idea in Senior that predates *Shell*. In *Gardening in the Tropics*, for instance, the metaphor of digging in the Earth or "gardening" turns up the bones of those killed in recent drug wars on the island. "Brief Lives" focuses on the return of those remains to the surface by Earth processes:

> Gardening in the Tropics, you never know
> what you'll turn up. Quite often, bones.
> In some places they say when volcanoes
> erupt, they spew out dense and monumental
> as stones the skulls of *desapareicidos*[8]

While the Earth inters the bones, it also spits them back out, uncovering the skulls of those who were supposed to remain "disappeared." In *Shell*, this process becomes a kind of memory. The poem that follows "The Skin of the Earth"—"Sailor's Valentine"—describes this memory as a kind of return after death:

> Long after he is gone, a message
> from a further shore arrives, the token
> of a love alive. The wooden box
> that sailors make for sweethearts
> to display the lovingly collected
> tribute shells in disingenuous array (S 24)

The "valentine" of the collection of "tribute shells" brought by ocean currents in the wake of the sailor's death, like the volcanoes in *Gardening*, leaves a trace of the dead, and of a love that was once "alive." Yet as the unnamed woman of the poem "gazes into the open box," this memorialization remains in an ambiguous limbo until "she summons up the tearing that will cauterize, that will flood the shells and speed them back her / valentine, draining back to the grave, the empty sea" (S 24). The fact that the preposition in the phrase "speed them back . . . her valentine" is missing leaves uncertain whether the shells are returning from or *to* the grave or "empty sea." In this sense the shells create an afterlife of the dead—returned momentarily through the forces of the earth (volcanoes or ocean currents), while at the same time being threatened by those same forces with oblivion or forgetting.

That process of death and return mean that the dead haunt the present in insistently material forms, material traces—such as bones or shells—that are always threatened with physical oblivion, but which also persist in their insistent materiality, albeit in other forms. Hannah Regis has argued that Senior's poetry "sees the Caribbean landscape as the original archive," positing "a reliance on a spirit-infused universe."[9] Yet, and this is crucial, Senior's "spirit-infused universe" is *indistinguishable* from matter. Contrary to how Regis interprets them, the dead in Senior's poetry do not return as immaterial "spirits"—they return in and through the Earth in new explicitly physical forms that are inscriptional, and thus effaceable.[10] It is only through a geopoetics aware of the irreducibility of life to death that one can read these inscriptions before they disappear. As with Glissant's "aesthetics of the earth," we are dealing with a poetics of matter and of the depths of the ocean, a poetics which contains the "punctuation of scarcely corroded balls and chains."[11] In

Senior, the dead are "with us" in the sugarcane shells repossessed by the Earth as the detritus of the colonial plantation economy; they are "with us" in the hollow of the discarded shells that becomes a figure for another kind of archive. They are with us, in other words, at once materially and metaphorically.

They are also "with us," as Senior's poem "Shell" suggests, in the remains of the "bones and beads and shell discarded" (S 70) by those who built the "Great House" of the plantations:

> fragments of the true landowners, the ones before us
> the ones whose bones they buried under fill.
> The "Indian" people that once possessed it,
> and possess us still. (S 70)

These are not spirits or ghosts, but *another history* located in the Earth but forgotten by the official archive. Senior's material vitalism is thus a sister to the one Jane Bennett articulates in *Vibrant Matter*, where she describes "the curious ability of inanimate things to animate, to act, to produce effects dramatic and subtle."[12] However, unlike Bennett, Senior insists that what makes things vital is not their place within a broader actor-network theory of agency,[13] but the fact that, because matter is reconstituted by the forces of the earth, the dead or inert cannot be distinguished from their organic counterparts. The dead do not return either as zombies or as themselves, but their *survival* occurs when the Earth re-members them quite literally, reconstituting their fragments into a new code, a new inscription that demands interpretation, an act of memorialization always threatened by the possibility of a definitive oblivion or forgetting. The hollow of the shell is thus a form of life that cannot, strictly speaking, be opposed to death.[14] It is instead conditioned on it, *passed on*, to a form of survival that cuts into, ruptures or shatters the present by leaving the abyss of the past intact while opening it to the possibility either of an even more definitive forgetting, or of another future. As Senior's own note to *Shell* puts it, the hollow of the shell becomes an "emptied space waiting for the choices we make" (S 96).

That emptied space takes multiple forms, including a vacating of the lyric voice in favor of an Earth that "speaks" in its stead. In the first section of "S(h)ift," one of Senior's most formally and linguistically experimental poems, the first stanza is framed around a poetic "I" that, as the poem develops, can eventually no longer be distinguished from the Earth itself, and eventually from the former slaves of Jamaica:

I
dig
here
sift and measure and
keep on miss
          ing me
                    there (S 72)

The first stanza frames a "shift" from digging in a particular place or locale to something that cannot be located or is "missed" by that excavation. The poem's play with the agency of the pronouns—the "I" is searching for a "me"—is reflected in its syntax, as words are split and broken, as if hit by a digging shovel, over multiple lines.[15] The effect is the "shift" that the poem both describes and performs: the words of the poem shift from nouns to verbs, things to actions that are fractured into syllables, as the poem stutters to name what remains adrift yet discoverable in the Earth:

on pathways
unrecorded
ephemeral
as snail trail
ing silver un
der fences by
passing bound
aries evad
ing cartography (S 72)

The fractured syllables render the alluded-to shell in this poem both a noun and a verb—a "snail trail" which easily vanishes and a "trailing," which is a verb that cannot be reduced to a noun. Just as words break up syllabically and run on without punctuation, what is sought by the act of "sifting" is something that evades both lexical meaning and cartographic place. The "pathways" of the excavation, the search for a sense of "me" missing in the first stanza, gives way to an "unrecorded" pathway or trajectory located in the Earth, articulated by a snail shell whose path can be traced, but which "passes boundaries" and "evades cartographies," proving ultimately elusive. The Earth, hence, contains not just fragments of the past, remnants of worlds and peoples that have come and gone, a graveyard of dead "things," but an ongoing activity the poem marks through the figure of an excavation that finds nothing but the ephemerality of a "pathway" of memory that cannot be precisely pinpointed, but that is captured and repurposed by the "shell" of the Earth's surface.

This "sifting" in the Earth focuses initially on hidden pathways of memory it contains; however, once the speaker is identified with the sifted Earth itself, the poem shifts to a focus on the question of the present and its relation to that memory:

> picture me
> as background fill
> black dots inch
> ing stead
> ily for
> ward
> to fill—
>
> ah
> you blinked. (S 73)

In this third stanza, the speaker is identified with the soil itself, with "background fill," but also with the action of filling something in, "black dots inching steadily forward." Yet the filling never takes place—it is interrupted by a momentary lapse of attention ("ah / you blinked") that leads the poem to meditate on the exact nature of the "pathways" of memory that have been "missed":

> missed
> the pathways of the lash
> inscribed on my back
> the calligraphy of burning
> on my fettered wrists (S 73)

The blurring of lines between the speaker as earth and the speaker as former slave connects the "pathways" of the second stanza (which involve the act of digging in the earth) with the "pathways" of the lash. Though buried, the Earth is the site through which what is "missing"—the slave's body—is not exactly discovered, but is encountered *as* missing, an ephemerality that evades full possession. The poem culminates in another shell image, this time an oyster shell that suggests how its hollowness has given shape to a physical "pearl" of memory, a "place where I house a knot / where memory thickens and pearls" (S 72). This "place" is both the body and the Earth, the body not just of the "missing" slave, but of its descendants, as well as a terrain that harbors the possibility of fusing that memory to other legacies prolonged or interrupted.

In the midst of the metaphor of "sifting" the Earth for alternative histories, another darker element of terrestrial memory comes to the fore in Olive Senior's poetry. The Earthly "fill" referenced in "S(h)ift" also acts as a form of forgetting or burial in other poems. In "Shell," for instance, we are again in the act of sifting the earth, except this time the poem's setting is unambiguous—it's a former plantation:

> From the Great House shell, we salvage bricks
> we pick up sticks, we never throw away.
> We use things up as we are used. What can we
> leave to speak of us? (S 70)

The time in which the poem takes place is not identified, but the reference to salvaging bricks from the master's "Great House" implies we are in a moment during or just after the abolition of slavery. The plural speakers of the poem ("we") are the subjects or survivors of that system, who in the first lines of the poem ask the collection's central question: "What can we leave to speak of us?" The list of objects that follow is composed of relics that often constitute an archaeological find (with the exception of the "shells" of the calabashes, which decay too quickly to be preserved): "mortar / a cast-iron pot (from massa's store), a grinding / stone" (S 70). Much like Senior's famous "Meditation in Yellow," this poem also abruptly leaps forward in time to imagine the same physical place today, now occupied by quasi-archaeologists who must dig into the earth to find the remnants of the slaves' "domestic hearth":

> So if in years to come some people
> might be mad enough to search for us
> to trace our passing, they would have
> to dig deep to find us here, sift ashes,
> measure bones and beads and shell discarded. (S 70)

The same sifting that occurs in "S(h)ift" here figures as a link between the present and the past, while the physical remains—"bones and beads and shell discarded"—testify to the lives of former slaves.

The poem goes on, however, to revisit the same quasi-archaeological moment in which those slaves, the remains of whose lives were discovered in the Earth, find the remnants of the island's indigenous inhabitants whose memory was eradicated by the construction of the master's "Great House":

> Just as the men long ago
> digging the foundations of the Great House
> my grandfather did say, came across fragments
> of the true landowners, the ones before us
> the ones whose bones they buried under fill.
> The "Indian" people that once possessed it (S 70)

Here the "fill," the soil deposited at the base of the foundation of the house, signifies the gesture of eradicating both a people and the historical record of their existence, dispossessing them of any trace by consigning them to the Earth in the hope that it will forever withhold evidence of the crime of their extermination. This repetition yokes the dead twice over with the living who, as the last line suggests, "possess us still" (S 70). Reversing the possession of land the plantation economy instituted, the dead claim "possession" over the survivors of the colony not only as part of their past, but as constitutive of their present, just as the enslaved Africans encountered the unrecorded history of Xaymaca while they excavated the grounds of the "Great House." The fact that the present is still "possessed" by the past signifies more than simply being haunted by it: the present is structurally built over top of it, part of the "fill" that obscures its return. The Earth, for Senior, therefore contains layers of living memory by which the present is either consciously or unconsciously defined.

No better example of the kind of memory Senior is describing in her poetry can be found currently than in the discovery of what is estimated to be the remains of roughly eight thousand enslaved Africans in the hills of St. Helena, a former penal island in the middle of the South Atlantic held by the British. Although it was initially a stopover during the Middle Passage for the restocking of slave ships, during the period between 1840 and 1872, after England had abolished slavery, it became the site of a Vice-Admiralty court charging slave ship operators with what had now become a crime. Their enslaved "cargo" was off-loaded in St. Helena in the hope of repatriating them to Africa. The St. Helena National Trust estimates that nearly a third of those offloaded from slave ships during this period perished on the island and were buried in mass graves in the hills of the island's Rupert's Valley.[16] Because their graves remained unmarked, they were essentially forgotten once the Vice-Admiralty court ceased operation, their graves merging back into the landscape. Their remains were only discovered again when the island began excavation to build an airport. Once unearthed, however, the scope and importance of the discovery became clear: Rupert's Valley is not only, as the Helena National Trust suggests, "the most significant physical remaining trace of the transatlantic slave trade on Earth," it is also the only known site to house the remains of enslaved people who were offloaded *directly* from slave ships that had sailed only days or weeks prior from the coast of Africa. The fact that Rupert's Valley has not been immediately declared a national memorial or a world heritage site speaks to the function of memory in relation to national history, particularly given the fact that the original site of Napoleon's tomb—he died in detention on the same island in 1821—remains well marked and a significant tourist attraction. There is, in other words, an official memory, a memory of state that commemorates those proclaimed to be the most important "actors" of (European) history even if, like Napoleon, they sought to restore slavery to liberated former French colonies. There is also, as Senior suggests, another kind of memory of the Earth that comes to undermine and contextualize the latter. Like the "Great House" of Senior's "Shell," the discovery of Rupert's Valley undoes the state's official narrative: it reveals that "fill" in Senior's poetry is not just the backfill one uses to cement the foundation of a house with soil, it is also a historical narrative that gives precedence to some forms of remains—that is, those that now officially lie honored in *Les Invalides* in Paris—over others who remain nameless and numerous, buried in the hills and awaiting recognition and narrativization in the present.

But if "Shell," or even the discovery of the remains in the hills of St. Helena, would appear to treat the Earth as an archaeologist might—a tomb of discarded objects that mark the traces of the past, fossils of the dead that must be rediscovered—why define the Earth as a *living* archive in Senior? First, because for Senior the Earth doesn't re-member the way a museum does, which constitutes a kind of official narrative. Second, however, because that form of remembering, that form of afterlife, treats the dead as mere objects, repeating the injustice of their enslavement in the present. It keeps the dead "alive," but only by treating the past as static; an object to be discovered and preserved. The museum's form of commemoration is thus contrasted with what Senior spells out in the final section of her poem "Auction," which draws a connection between slave auctions and the auctioning off of plantation estates to museums and archives, calling it the "new slavery": "Nothing / can stave off the relentless grinding down by / this new slavery: the collections, the recordings, the writing of history" (S 92). The museum, for Senior, represents an archive of dead artifacts that will be fitted into an already existing narrative, obfuscating the source of wealth that produced the objects themselves.

But through the recombinatory dimension of the Earth, that material also breaks free from this artifactual death as a fine dust settles on the objects of the museum that—symbolically—derives from the shells that testify to a different history:

> Nothing remaining of vanished pride and tower
> except the possessions auctioned, collected in
> other citadels of power: libraries, museums,
> galleries, castles, to gather dust in other empty
> rooms where consumers still consume in loneliness (S92)

Having shifted from the domain of the plantation estate, the collected objects remain housed in other "citadels of power," objects of a different kind of consumption. Yet the dust that settles on them is not impartial:

> Day after day, in gilded halls, the
> servant armies vacuum, and wonder: Whence
> comes this dust?
> O could it have been when
> you introduced into your aristocratic domains,
> for style and decorative effect, those black
> pages?
> Our fragile fetishes of power, our powdered
> fragments, rise now to lightly dust these precious
> artefacts, these hollowed shelves. (S 92)

The play on words in the last line, "hollowed" for "hallowed," suggests that the dust that settles on the objects of the estate comes from the "shells" representing the dead. As the collective pronoun "our" is applied to both the "fetishes of power" and the "powdered fragments" that dust them, the answer to the question "whence comes this dust?" refers to a previous section of the poem where the master of the plantation fondles a "rare book" as he would his slave: "At auction, books and paintings bought and sold / in lots / like slaves / fondled / as my master in far-off England / fondles / the rare book he purchases" (S 84). The book, purchased like all the objects of the estate—including slaves—becomes the occasion for the introduction of the dust that covers the archived artefacts, the moment when "those black pages," like the slaves themselves, "were introduced into your aristocratic domains." The dust reveals for Senior that "none can shackle / passing time that is excavating from within, the / promise of the silenced voices: the resonance of the empty shell" (S 92). That resonance is not buried in the funeral pyre of an eradicated past housed in a museum; rather it is found in the "hollow" of the shell whose resonance actually gives voice to the dead, or in the dust—fine particles of solid matter—whose accumulation overtakes the elision of memory the objects in the museum represent.

This elision of the border between the living and the dead, the organic and the inorganic, as we will see in the next section, is also a means by which to critique colonial conceptions of history and the opposition between nature and culture that underpinned them. The recombinatory aspect of the Earth's "shell" in Senior should not be interpreted as an idealization of the Earth as a righting of historical wrongs. As her poetry continuously suggests, the indifference of the Earth can just as well act as historical "fill" as much as a living "archive," obscuring past life as much as reconstituting it. Its capacity for recombination simply means that there is no absolute point of discernibility between the organic and the inorganic—which in turn means that the past is never completely dead, that it is always in the act of being repurposed, and that the Earth must be seen as an active participant in the formation of historical memory and forgetting. Being an active participant, however, does not mean acting *on behalf* of the dead; it simply means that the divisions that sought to separate the living from the dead also sought to silence them once and for all. Senior's understanding of the Earth as shell and as living archive, therefore, is only a chance or possibility of another thinking of history and of "life," not its realization.

From Senior's Earth to Günderrode via Hegelian Colonial History

We have seen how Senior's Earth entails a recombinatory dimension that disarticulates key distinctions between the organic and the inorganic, allowing the dead to reenter the concerns of the present, as it were, giving them a different kind of "life" that extends beyond biological life. We have also seen how that recombinatory dimension is found, for Senior, at every level; it is both in nature and part of the work of culture, thereby disordering the distinction between them,[17] introducing a new form of history and a new relation to the

Earth as an archive. What is not always made explicit in her work, however, is how and why these disrupted conceptual distinctions matter to Senior's overall contestation of colonial narratives, including their understanding of history and the Earth, both of which constitute elements of the conceptual scaffolding for the slave trade and the plantation economy. If as she insists, "the story is now about us" (S 96), the "us" being inheritors of the legacies of slavery and colonialism and of the resistance to them, how might her poetic reinvention of the Earth as shell, of history as trace that is shaped and molded by the Earth, along with the collapse of the distinction between nature and culture, help contest the ongoing consequences of those legacies?

Senior's Earth as living archive challenges a philosophical tradition—coextensive with colonialism and the slave trade—that understands the Earth as mere inert matter that must be overcome for human history and human consciousness to perfect itself and liberate itself from its Earthbound confines. While there might be a history of the Earth independent of human consciousness, this view understands it as a step on the way from nature to spirit. The Earth is therefore but an inert object, like the dead; it is incapable of life, which involves an autonomous capacity for self-reproduction. Natural history is therefore understood as fundamentally distinct from human history.[18] History begins, in these theories, with the advent of a form of life that has liberated itself from its natural confines by negating its embeddedness in anything external to itself, including and especially the Earth. When Senior connects the indigenous population of Jamaica and the slave communities her poetry memorializes to the Earth, she ostensibly repeats a trope that consigns non-Western populations to the realm of nature and to a space outside of history. However, by doing so, and by insisting that the Earth is a living archive of *other histories* that have been systematically effaced, she destabilizes the teleological framework that interprets the Earth, and non-Western cultures, as the realm of *pre*history.[19]

As Sylvia Wynter has argued, the secularization of "Man" as the (European) subject endowed with natural right entailed a rearticulation of otherness in terms of a normative conception of "Man" and "the human": "the large-scale accumulation of unpaid land, unpaid labor, and overall wealth expropriated by Western Europe from non-European peoples . . . was carried out within the order of truth and the self-evident order of consciousness, a creed-specific conception of what it is to be human."[20] Once the Earth becomes secularized—that is, no longer a mere antithesis of the divine—and therefore naturalized, a new *episteme* comes into being grounding colonial narratives in the Great Chain of Being I examined in the previous chapter that grounds otherness in the human/sub-human binary. A version of this multipurpose colonial narrative is perhaps best exemplified by Hegelian conceptions of history, which privileges history as an affair of consciousness, and relegates non-Western cultures to the status of prehistorical nature. In *Lectures on the Philosophy of World History* Hegel divides the Earth into various *geographically determined* forms of consciousness. The Earth itself, for Hegel, plays the role of marking the border between inorganic and organic forms of nature. On the side of the inorganic, for Hegel, lie natural forms structured as assemblages that have the meaning of their existence outside themselves; in the organic domain, those forms of nature are essentially autonomous and self-reproductive. This moment, which is found in the unfolding dialectic of Hegel's *Naturphilosophie*, returns with a vengeance in his *Lectures on the Philosophy of World History* when that idea of the Earth helps to determine which cultures are still "too Earthly," too entrenched in their inert inorganic stasis to have either full freedom or self-consciousness. It is *precisely this distinction* that Senior's poetry overturns by showing their indiscernibility, short-circuiting the hierarchy of geography and culture that results. Hegel separates culture (and consciousness) from nature, which it ultimately leaves behind. Senior, by poetically articulating the indiscernibility of nature and culture, undermines this conceptual scaffolding, the very source of the exclusion of non-European peoples from freedom and protection of the law.

So how, then, is the Earth presented in Hegel's philosophy of history? Hegel begins the section on "Africa" in *Lectures on the Philosophy of World History* with the following claim: "Man as we find him in Africa has not progressed beyond his immediate existence. As soon as man emerges as a human being, he stands in opposition to nature, and it is this alone which makes him a human being."[21] In other words, what makes "Man" a human being—his separation from the natural world, which is to say, as we'll see, from the Earth—is precisely what Africans lack. From here, one can easily see how Hegel ends up, however circuitously, justifying slavery, for Africans are already slaves to nature: "The basic principle of all slavery is that man is not yet conscious of his freedom, and consequently sinks to the level of a mere object or worthless article" (WH 183). And because "man as we find him in Africa has not progressed beyond his immediate existence," Africans are merely a preliminary step on the way to the full unfolding of human freedom, which for Hegel entails an absolution from spirit's externalization in nature, embodied in and exemplified by Europe and spirit's position in the Christian structure of the Trinity.

Most importantly, though, this conceptualization of the relation between culture and nature is then *spatialized* on the Earth's geography realized, according to Hegel, in the distribution of the continents. On this logic, slavery is neatly coextensive with the organization of the Earth, part of its "natural" make-up of "old world" continents as opposed to continents of the "new world." As Hegel puts it in *The Philosophy of Nature*:

> The Old world exhibits the perfect diremption into three parts, one of which, Africa, the compact metal, the lunar principle, is rigid through heat, a land where man's inner life is dull and torpid—the inarticulate spirit which has not awakened into consciousness; the second is Asia, characterized by Bacchanalian extravagance and cometary eccentricity, the center of unrestrained spontaneous production, formlessly generative and unable to become master of its center. But the third part, Europe forms the consciousness, the rational part, of the earth, the balance of rivers and valleys and mountains—whose center is Germany.[22]

While these categorizations should be easily dismissed, it is not as if one couldn't find examples of their persistence, particularly in Europe's self-understanding of its relation to the rest of the world. Given their centrality to European philosophy and history, it is crucial to situate these characterizations within the broader context that produced them—namely the various definitions of consciousness, spirit, and nature—that constitute the political idea of European exceptionalism. The reason Hegel can even begin to claim that Africa has "not awakened to consciousness" while Europe "forms the rational part of the earth" is that their respective geographical (i.e., "natural") manifestations are seen as reflections of consciousness (or the lack thereof) inherent in the culture that emerges out of a particular topography, while nature is seen as what must be negated for consciousness and culture to come into being. In the *Philosophy of Nature* the Earth constitutes a key moment for Hegel in the transition from dependent inorganic entities to self-generating, autonomous organic entities. This idea of the Earth, however, is then transposed in *World History* into a classification of the cultures that remain caught in the Earth's supposed in-organicity. "Culture" for Hegel has a "natural" basis, but only insofar as a genuinely free civilization exists only once it has negated its natural origins which, according to Hegel, no non-European culture has succeeded in doing. As we will see, the distinction between nature and culture, the organic and the inorganic, becomes a cudgel with which to bludgeon non-Western cultures into the dark night of prehistory, preculture, and precivilization, where the Earth, including its non-Western inhabitants, becomes a vast domain of passive "nature" waiting to be exploited. What destines Africans for slavery, for Hegel, is their inability to dialectically shed or absolve themselves from their "bondage" to the Earth—they are trapped and enslaved by their dependency on it as an exteriority they cannot overcome. As a result, they can be trapped and enslaved by a (European) culture and "consciousness" that has liberated itself from nature. The Earth, in other words, for Hegel, is a vast colony rife for the domination of European "freedom."

In this hierarchy of nature, the Earth plays a central role. In Hegel's *Philosophy of Nature*, for instance, the Earth functions as the crucial transition from inorganic nature to the organism. The organism is part of a process in the development of life that initially includes the Earth, but ultimately supersedes it, starting with plant life and ascending upwards to "spirit": "This life which is a reflectedness-into-self is now established as an independent existence passing through its own cyclic process, and it has its own existence which remains opposed to that other reality [geologic nature] and holds fast to it negative nature, denies its origin, and displays its own becoming" (PN 302). The moment when life—the "organic" properly speaking—denies its geological origins is crucial for most iterations of *Naturphilosophie* because it prefigures the "freedom" or autonomy that is the goal of self-consciousness. The ideality that remains "too immediate" in the plant will, in Hegel, continue to develop into further stages of life that articulate its ever-greater subjectivity. Once the merely biological organism becomes "consciousness," it is on the way to absolving itself of all physical externalities, becoming eventually a rational consciousness on the stage of world history.

It is this idealist conception of nature and life as a series of stages overcome by a spirit liberated from its natural confines that connects Senior and Günderrode. By challenging the opposition between life and death, the organic and the inorganic, they both undermine the basic premises of the idealist tradition and articulate a different conception of the Earth than the one that has come to dominate the present (an Earth that is thought to be merely the inorganic substrate for life, a repository of resources waiting to be "developed" by human civilization). Both Senior and Günderrode's oppose the way the Earth has tended to be understood in Western philosophy: as a nonparticipatory background to consciousness and culture, or as an inert mass waiting to be molded into human uses.[23] What comes undone along with the undoing of the opposition between life and death, the organic and the inorganic, are the historical narratives and ontological categories that consign whole cultures and parts of the Earth to the status of property to be confiscated or to a domain of nature to be dominated. Questioning these oppositions, as Senior and Günderrode do, in turn problematizes the *political* structures justifying the historical narrative of Europe as the best exemplar of humanity's freedom, and the relegation of non-Western cultures to the status of societies not yet sufficiently extricated from the grip of natural forces. Senior's writing, as well as Günderrode's, is a geopoetics that asks, in the tradition of Gayatri Spivak's subaltern: Can the Earth "speak?"—but without comprehending that question as necessarily entailing a personification or anthropomorphization of the Earth in response.[24]

Günderrode and *Naturphilosophie*

The Earth that "speaks" in Senior does so, as we have seen, not as some neo-animist entity or as a premodern pantheism, but as a countercurrent to elements of the Western tradition that had consigned it to a conception of inert nature—an inorganic, dead, or static structure that must be transcended by its opposite, "life." Another writer, and not inconsequentially another woman, had done the same with astonishingly similar conceptual tools at the height of German idealism. Two centuries ago, Karoline von Günderrode also let the Earth "speak," but she did so within the tradition of European Romanticism and German *Naturphilosophie*. And it is precisely Senior's contemporary post-colonial and geopolitical poetics that helps us to sift through the discarded relics of Romantic philosophy and literary history to uncover Günderrode's work on the Earth, and to situate its contemporary relevance.

An avid reader of Johann Gottlieb Fichte and Friedrich Schelling, Günderrode was fully immersed in the idealist tradition that passed through Kant and on to her main interlocutor, Schelling. But unlike her contemporaries, she did not privilege the notion of spirit or self-consciousness as the *telos* of nature and history. Günderrode was also a committed student of Eastern philosophy, including Hinduism and Islam, both of which understood the notion of "spirit" in quite different terms. A writer, philosopher, and poet, she engaged with the philosophical and literary tradition of her moment, but in ways that separated her from the main currents of those ideas. Günderrode had immense difficulty finding publishers for her work, in part because she was a woman engaging with her male contemporaries in the domain of philosophy. Before her suicide in 1806, she published several works under the pseudonym "Tian," the Chinese character signifying heaven or sky in Confucianism, but which came to be associated in Daoism with nature or the cosmos more generally. Her own *Naturphilosophie*, written in dialogue with Schelling, makes the Earth central, and presents it as an unconditionality, something that is the condition of possibility for every Earthbound entity, from natural beings to human political structures.[25] Ungrounded yet silently grounding everything else, the Earth for Günderrode is the precondition for every particular world, human or otherwise. But as a condition of possibility, the Earth necessarily relativizes each world to itself, making it impossible for any of them to understand themselves as detached from the Earth, or as *the* world—solitary and universal. Günderrode articulates these ideas not just in her philosophical responses to idealist contemporaries, but also in the literary works she often—notably—sets in non-Western locales. In her play *Muhammed: Prophet of Mecca*, for instance, she develops a political ecology that extends the claims of her philosophical treatise "Idea of the Earth" into political and religious domains. In all these writings Günderrode's take on the philosophy of nature, and on the Earth specifically, challenges idealist elements of more traditional *Naturphilosophie* by contesting its "natural" hierarchies and racial logics. One wouldn't be too off the mark to claim her political ecology to be strongly, if anachronistically, "Seniorian" as it is precisely the lens of Senior's geopoetics that sharpens the political and philosophical significance of Günderrode's revolution in *Naturphilosophie*.

In the recent turn toward non-human-centered ontologies and alternative cosmologies in ecocriticism,[26] German *Naturphilosophie* has been by and large dismissed as an ecological touchstone, largely on account of its centralization of spirit or consciousness, which in Hegel's encyclopedic system liberates itself from nature and the Earth. If nature is seen as not-yet-spirit or not-yet-consciousness, as idealism declares, then a quasi-secular Great Chain of Being is constituted with all the taxonomic and racial hierarchies it entails. As Nigel Clark asserts, "Hegel goes to great lengths to show that human agents must logically leave the tilting and heaving Earth behind them. Human self-determination or 'freedom,' he will argue, develops potentials that are present but arrested in the natural world, and, once that possibility for freedom has been realized, the blind exertions of nature are consigned to developmental prehistory."[27] *Naturphilosophie*, according to many contemporary ecocritics, must therefore be discarded to make room for ecologies that take seriously the *inhuman* as a central category for understanding the alterity of the natural world to human concerns.[28]

But not all *Naturphilosophie* is idealist. Günderrode's version, as we will see, is a serious intellectual challenge to the separation of spirit and matter because, like Senior, she deactivates distinctions between life and nonlife, the organic and the inorganic.[29] To get a sense of the radicality of Günderrode's intervention, however, it is important to situate her work in relation to the predominantly male context out of which she emerged. Her main interlocutor was Schelling, and she never read Hegel, having committed suicide before his mature *Naturphilosophie* was published in 1817. Yet, as we'll see, Günderrode's criticism of some of Schelling's key positions are precisely the ones Hegel took up from Schelling and developed. Because these trajectories are convoluted and overlapping, it is vital to examine how each of these thinkers understood the Earth to demonstrate how this shaped their quite different corresponding political ecologies. To that end, I will interweave my analysis of Günderrode's philosophical and literary works with an exposition of Schelling's and Hegel's conceptions of the Earth in their own *Naturphilosophie*, to present the specificity and, indeed, the radicality of her long-neglected contribution.

In Schelling's philosophical dialogue *Bruno* (1802), which Günderrode was likely reading at the time she wrote her own *Naturphilosophie* "Idea of the Earth," he separates the Earth into two different modalities: there is the "created" Earth, and the "true Earth." The former is "only the image of the Earth" whereas the true Earth is "uncreated, unoriginated, and never to pass away."[30] This timeless archetype, for Schelling, paradoxically contains all the Earth's life, because on it there is "no man or beast nor plant nor stone whose likeness does not shine brighter in the living artistry and wisdom of archetypal nature than in its lifeless copy, the created world. Within this exemplary life, things never come into being nor will they ever perish, whereas their imaged life under the rule of time begins and ends" (B 125–26). Schelling's conception of the Earth here is idealist to the point of Platonism: The Earth's material reality is the imperfect finite "copy" of the "true Earth," which lies beyond the physical one and constitutes the asymptotic form of perfection toward which it is developing. The relation of life to the Earth is therefore an endless approximation to an ideal: to the extent that the Earth is not yet the abstract *idea* of the Earth, it is not yet capable of life in any genuine sense, which exists for Schelling only in the timeless realm of spirit.

It is precisely this idealist conception of the Earth that Günderrode rejects, but she does so while at the same time retaining two important dimensions of Schelling's *Naturphilosophie*: on the one hand its understanding of the "unconditionality" of nature, and on the other the Earth as an *active force* rather than a static, inert object. Both of these features are generated out of the distinction Schelling makes between the "true" Earth and its material image. But whereas Schelling will insist on the fundamental *difference* between the "true Earth" and its image, Günderrode places that internal tension *on the same immanent plane*, the immanent surface of a completely material, and therefore already existing, nondualistic Earth.[31] Günderrode seems to develop this idea out of a specific interpretation of Schelling's notion of the "indifference" between his two Earths. Sensing that an absolute opposition would produce a dualism that cannot be reconciled, Schelling insists that both Earths—the one material, the other ideal—must form some kind of unity. For that unity to be possible, the "image" of the Earth must operate as something other than a derivation of the "true" Earth, and the true Earth likewise cannot simply exist in some static Platonic utopia—it must exist in the "here and now," in what Schelling calls the "indifference" of the two.[32] That "indifference," for Schelling, produces a tension between the real and the ideal, along with the teleological direction of the Earth as tending always toward its ideal form. But whereas Schelling maintains that the two Earths are essentially different orders, the one existing in time, the other outside of it, Günderrode insists that they are both part of the same *temporally determined* plane of existence, which she calls the Earth's "realized idea."[33] It is that tension, ultimately, that for Günderrode produces an Earth in constant change and development, as opposed to one that is static and atemporal. While the science of plate tectonics, or an awareness of the mobility of continents and land masses, was more than a century away, her conception of the Earth transformed it, albeit in idealist terms, into an *activity* as opposed to an object, a constantly transforming and transformative development as opposed to a fixed or stable ground.

What also follows out of Schelling's quasi-Platonic conception of the Earth is something Günderrode develops as key to her own conception of the Earth and her understanding of the notion of life that develops out of it. Life, for Günderrode, is predicated not on an ideality, but on the Earth's material unconditionality. Schelling had argued that there is nothing that precedes or supersedes nature; it is an unconditional ground. As he puts it in the *First Outline of a System of the Philosophy of Nature* (1799), which Günderrode almost certainly read: "The unconditioned [*das Unbedingte*] cannot be sought in any individual 'thing' nor in anything of which one can say that it 'is.' For what 'is' only partakes of being and is only an individual form or kind of being—conversely one can never say of the unconditioned that it 'is.' For it is *being itself*, and as such, does not exhibit itself entirely in any product, and every individual is, as it were, a particular expression of it."[34] When Günderrode outlines her own definition of the absolute in her notes on the "Philosophy of Nature," she reflects a version of this concept of unconditionality: "That is absolute which is not limited by anything else, which limits itself, and which is in itself the cause and effect at once, and consequently has no ground outside itself."[35]

However, when she applies this conception of unconditionality to the Earth, Günderrode generates an *actual* or "realized" (*realisiert*) unconditional ground that contains all "individual and smallest things" which "only exist through it" (IE 82/446). In other words, the Earth becomes for Günderrode not just a step on the way to other forms of nature, but the absolute itself: a non-ideal, quasi-materialist ground for anything born of the Earth. Furthermore, she reinterprets Schelling's argument that, because it is unconditioned, nature must be thought as an "originary activity" that cannot be reduced to the notion of an "originary being." For Schelling, since nature is unconditional, it is not a being, a static *thing*, but an activity, a process of development. While Günderrode picks up on this idea as well, her application of it to the Earth entails an awareness that it is something more than simply a planet, an inorganic object which particular organisms inhabit. The Earth is an active process, as in Senior, it is *itself alive* in a certain sense. Whereas the activity Schelling associated with nature does not yet amount to his notion of life because that activity could still be blind, without aim or intent, Günderrode, as we will see, extends the activity or movement that characterizes nature to *everything* on the Earth, "inorganic" and "organic" alike.

The difference between organic and inorganic forms of activity introduces a hierarchy of beings in Schelling that is effectively nonexistent in Günderrode's *Naturphilosophie*. Because nature for Schelling is simultaneously homogeneous and heterogeneous to itself, it contains within itself the possibility of its own self-differentiation. This is what ultimately explains the difference between organic and inorganic elements of nature as Schelling describes it in *First Outline*:

> If the universe has been formed by an infinite differentiation of one primal product into an increasing number of novel factors, then every *individual* factor can only = one of these factors, and what belongs to it must be *homogenous* within itself (all material of the Earth, for example). But the condition of the chemical process is *heterogeneity*—if all material of Earth = one matter (their diversity merely a diversity of variety), then there is no real opposition between them, and thus no chemical process is possible. (F 176)

This necessity of an internal heterogeneity—the difference between the ideal and the real—that "animates" the homogeneity of the Earth in Schelling also defines his conception of the opposition between organic and inorganic natures. Since, for Schelling, it is not the Earth that is unconditional but the more indefinite "nature," the Earth becomes just another moment among others in the development of a nature that eventually discards its purely "mechanical" or "chemical" status, transcending itself into a progressively more self-differentiating complexity. In Schelling's *Bruno*, the Earth is merely a moment within a system that is surpassed by an exteriority—the organic—it gives rise to, but from which it has liberated itself: "The earth more or less imperfectly sustains the identity whereby it is itself a substantial reality, yet organic beings stand related to this identity as the ground of their existence, without being identical to it" (B 177). For Günderrode, by contrast, nothing escapes the Earth because the Earth is the basis of all inorganic *and* organic activity. Although plant life, for example, remains quite literally rooted in the Earth, it is, for Schelling—and for Hegel—the starting point for a process that will break life free of its Earthbound confinement.

How does Hegel extend Schelling's conception of the division between the organic and the inorganic to his own conception of the Earth, and in what way does this help to produce his philosophy of history? For Hegel, like Schelling, the Earth is the basis for the emergence of the first organism, the first real moment of fully autonomous life. It therefore functions as a substrate for the hierarchy of organisms that originate out of it. As Hegel puts it in the *Philosophy of Nature*: "The earth is a whole, the system of life, but, as crystal, it is like a skeleton, which can be regarded as dead because its members seem still to subsist formally on their own, while its process falls outside it" (PN 276). He continues: "The members of this merely implicit organism do not therefore contain the life-process within themselves and constitute an external *system* whose forms exhibit the unfolding of an underlying idea, but whose *process of formation* lies in the *past*" (PN 278). In Hegel's system, unlike Schelling's, the Earth is already formed, it is not in a process of endless approximation to an ideal version of itself. For Hegel, therefore, the Earth is no longer an unconditional *activity* nor self-productive like an organism. The Earth, for Hegel, is a *thing*, and a thing of the *past* as the last moment of inorganic nature. The Earth had a history, for Hegel, but that history has now come to an end, and the processes that formed and shaped it reach their conclusion when it "receives its consciousness in Man and so confronts itself as a stabilized formation" (PN 282). For Günderrode, this idea would make no sense, committed as she was to the idea of the unconditional *activity* that characterizes the Earth, and which means that the Earth cannot be reduced to the status of a mere object.

That notion of the Earth as object or inert mass plays a key role in Hegel's philosophy of history. We have already seen how he relegated Africans to the status of mere animals, mere organisms not yet "free" of their natural proclivities. Hegel's conception of the Earth thus plays a central role in his conception of history especially when it comes to non-Western cultures, because his elaboration of global history is in constant dialectical relation to the Earth's geography. When he describes the interrelationship between various world histories, for example, Hegel ties a specific connection to the Earth to the characteristics of the nation that emerges out it:

> Every people which represents a particular stage in the development of the spirit constitutes a *nation*; its natural characteristics correspond to the nature of the spiritual principle within the series of spiritual forms. This natural dimension leads us to consider the influence of geography; for the latter includes all that belongs to the purely natural phase. (WH 153)

In this concatenation of geography and history, Hegel expresses much more than the idea that geography plays an important role in history in the way, say, trade routes along the path of a river might. Rather, he draws conclusions about the way geography *determines* a particular relation to the universal through the culture or history that emerges in that physical geographic space. To the extent that a culture is seen as still enmeshed in the inert Earth, it no longer has a history and has therefore been overcome by those that do. Non-Western cultures become seen as simply tributaries, literally and figuratively, to a Europe that has or will come to dominate the globe because it has realized its independence from the Earth.

The fact that Hegel applies this conception to nearly every non-Western culture as a mark of its subordination is not immaterial. It is ultimately linked to what Malcom Ferdinand in *Decolonial Ecology* calls "colonial inhabitation," which he defines by three structural principles: 1. It is geographical in that it is concentrated in a particular enclosed space on the Earth, but that space remains subordinate to "mainland habitation," Europe in particular. 2. Because it is subordinate in that way, colonial land is a space available for the exploitation of natural resources, including humans seen as simply part of the landscape. 3. It involves what Ferdinand calls *othercide*, "the refusal of the possibility of inhabiting the Earth in the presence of an other."[36] That last feature is a central element of Hegel's understanding of the Earth: What follows out of his arguments is an identification of the flora, fauna, and other occupants of a particular geographic space with "nature as a whole." In other words, indigenous inhabitants all become available for the exploitation described in Ferdinand's second principle, not simply because they are "bare life,"[37] but because they are part of the natural realm from which consciousness has liberated itself. They are therefore available for the same exploitation as the natural world thanks to the vestige of the *inorganic* Earth that continues to persist at their stage of organic life. This stratification of nature, beginning with the Earth as the inorganic origin of life, entails a political ecology that makes the Earth the inert starting point for an ascendent scale of forms of life and culture—ranging from those who are embedded in its inorganic stasis, to those who have, in their specifically Western "freedom," liberated themselves from its confines so as to dominate it and everything on it.

What would it mean, then, from within the context of a tradition that makes the Earth a condition of the hierarchization of life and a prelude to Western imperial domination, to think the Earth otherwise? What happens when a relation to the Earth is no longer the question of proximity to inert matter, but where the Earth becomes once again an indifferent activity of its own, not dependent on self-consciousness to "realize" it? What happens to a political ecology predicated on the notion of a stable, inert Earth when the Earth is seen as having its *own* trajectory independent of human history? While Günderrode was writing from within the tradition of *Naturphilosophie*, her own version of the Earth, as we have already intimated, presents a marked contrast to both Schelling and Hegel. Günderrode, however, weds a very different conception of the Earth with her unique conception of life, one much closer to Olive Senior's than either Schelling or Hegel, separating her own political ecology from traditional *Naturphilosophie*. Though she appropriated elements of Schelling's philosophy, including its language and concepts, she introduces a conception of the Earth that recognizes a *multiplicity of worlds*, including nonhuman and non-Western ones. Her Earth is also *alive* in its own way, remaining independent of the telos of spirit as self-consciousness, while also destabilizing, as Olive Senior's poetics does, the boundary between the organic and the inorganic that defines life in the traditional sense. Günderrode's Earth silently forms the background for the emergence and dissolution of individuals and species, becoming the "all" that constitutes the absolute for Schelling and Hegel.

The Earth's separate trajectory from consciousness in Günderrode stems from its unconditionality; there is no overcoming of the Earth in Günderrode. It is always bound up with, and yet independent from, the "natural" entities it makes possible. In other words, she effectively reverses the opposition in traditional *Naturphilosophie* between the absolute or the universal and its determinations: rather than understanding the absolute as arrived at through a process of the gradual sublation of the particular within a larger whole containing it, Günderrode understands the absolute or the unconditional as always already "realized." As a result, the Earth is a fundamental externality that none of its "products," whether lithic, vegetal, or human, can do without, and to which they all return.

The first sentences of "Idea of the Earth" spell out what is at stake by describing the Earth as a unity of body and soul:

> The earth is a realized idea, one that is simultaneously effective (force) and effected (appearance). It is thus a unity of soul and body. We call the pole of its activity that it turns outward extension, form, body; the one turned inward intensity, essence, force, soul. (IE 82/446)

Since the Earth is an already realized idea, as opposed to an ideal in the process of being approximated (as in Schelling), there is no opposition between body and soul, real and ideal, that must be reconciled. Instead "body" and "soul" are simply two different ways of conceiving the activity of the Earth, stretched out on a single immanent plane in which these twin poles interact and form assemblages. There is the Earth as "effected" (by itself), a "pole" that is linked with a given appearance, arrangement, or physical form, and there is the Earth as an intensity or force that is "inward," an activity that does not produce a particular form but involves the *formation or dissolution* of physical forms, structures, or organisms. Because the Earth is defined by the twin "poles" of body and soul (which makes them initially sound as if they are different in kind), this nonopposition defines all things—humans included—the Earth gives rise to:

> Now, as the whole of the earth only exists through this unification of soul and body, so, too the individual and smallest things only exist through it and cannot at all be conceived as split in two, for an outer without an inner, an essence without form, a force without some sort of effect, is not comprehensible. (IE 82/446)

The Earth, thus, imparts the unification of body and soul to everything that depends on it, whether it be organic or inorganic. At the same time, the Earth remains essentially *external* to every one of its products. While Günderrode doesn't use the language of "unconditionality" in the same way as Schelling, her understanding of the "Earth-essence" (*Erdwesens*) as the coexistence of the twin "poles" of body and soul functions *like* Schelling's unconditional. Since the Earth is a "realized idea," its internal dynamic is found in each and every particular being the Earth makes possible, and while the tension between body and soul may momentarily privilege one pole over the other, it is at work in *everything.* In other words, there is no moment or stage in Günderrode's *Naturphilosophie* that articulates a hard and fast division between inorganic beings and organisms. Everything, including what Schelling and Hegel would define as the inorganic, has an element of life, for Günderrode.

Günderrode's conception of life thus follows from her understanding of the Earth as a "realized idea." The differences between various forms of life have to do not with a notion of autoproduction or self-generation as in Hegel, but simply with the "proportion" (*Verhältniß*) of forces or activity found on both sides of the poles that constitute the Earth. Depending on the form of life, one or the other pole is prioritized. There is therefore no specific hierarchy of life, only a variety of mixtures, all of which are temporary and eventually dissolve. Life thus resides *in the interstice between the two poles,* and in the interrelationships between the various elements that comprise a given individual being: "The most intimate mingling of different elements with the highest degree of contact and attraction [is what] we call life. To whatever perfection it may have developed it is still only the product of the synthesis of the elements that gestate life" (IE, 82/446, translation modified). In other words, life for Günderrode is not an ideality or an autoproductive or reproductive force. It is instead a relationship between elements that are both material bodies (*Leibe*) as well as made up of forces or intensities (*Seele*). There is no opposition between the two, but rather a complex matrix of elements of both kinds, which coexist in a composite relationship with one another.

Life is therefore, as Günderrode provocatively insists, "immortal." But it is immortal only in the sense that it is a continuous movement of dissolution and interconnection between elements, a process or activity that is incessant. The individual beings that are produced by those temporary arrangements, on the other hand, come to an end or die. If life is the interrelationship between various elements, then the form that this relationship takes is capable of dissolution. However, new arrangements of elements take shape thereafter, revealing that individual organisms perish, but the elements out of which they are composed form new relationships through the Earth, as they do in Senior. The Earth thereby prolongs not the life of the individual, but life in the broader sense of the synthesis of different elements, including the inorganic. As Günderrode puts it,

> With the dissolution of this synthesis the product also ends, but the life-principle in the elements is immortal; it requires only contact and connection again like before and new life blossoms with all the blooms that we call thought and sensation, and organism and body and soul. Thus life is immortal and surges up and down in the elements, for they are life itself. (IE 82/446)

Since life is *any* concatenation of elements, including relationships biology would never consider properly alive, there is no teleological development of life in Günderrode except, as we'll see, when it pertains to the Earth itself.

The lack of teleology specific to individual organisms, for Günderrode, rests on the fact that the Earth is both the unconditional foundation of all life, and the unconditional basis for the variety of relationships that constitute every individual being. It is therefore both that *out of which* each thing emerges and that *into which* each thing dissolves. It is both producer and product, that which makes possible a particular arrangement, and that which reconstitutes that arrangement otherwise. Günderrode frames this idea in terms of the death of an individual person: "When a person is dead, their mixture returns to the substance of the earth, but that within them which we called force, activity, or rather that of its materials in which the more active pole predominated, reverts to that which is related to it in the earth; the coarser elements likewise seek what is similar to them according to laws of affinity" (IE 82/447). Rather than escaping the Earth as self-consciousness or soul, the death of the individual involves a "return" to the Earth and a redistribution of the matter, forces, and intensities that formerly constituted it. Every particular being, whether plant, animal, or human, "returns" to the Earth. What constitutes a higher form of life, then, is not the individual, *but the Earth itself.* The Earth is alive rather than inert, not in the sense of a vast organism, but in the sense both that it mobilizes or produces given arrangements of elements that are either organic or inorganic, and that it also reconstitutes dead or bygone arrangements in new ways. The "immortality" of this form of life is thus specific to the Earth, where "life is immortal and surges up and down in the elements, for they are life itself" (IE 82/446), whereas the individual organism is only a temporary instance of this process.

Whereas Hegel and Schelling describe an independent process that produces the organism as a self-regulated entity, Günderrode makes the Earth *itself* the developmental process by which entities or species evolve. Those elements of the individual identified with "soul" find new relations with similar forces and "revert to that which is related to it in the earth" (IE 82/447). This is likewise the case with those elements identified as "body," whose affinity with other bodies implies that they form new connections with similar elements through the Earth. However, Günderrode goes on to insist that this exchange is not a zero-sum game: Having already been in *other* relations of association with other elements, the "life" located in them produces a surplus that reinvigorates the tension between the two poles that governs everything in and on the Earth. As Günderrode insists, "once these elements have been driven to life in the organism, they become different from what they were before they entered into this organic connection" (IE 82/447). This implies, first, that entities can pass back and forth between the completely porous border between what would otherwise be understood as the organic and the inorganic, just as human bodies return, in effect, to their lithic origins as they decay after death, and just as Senior suggests the "skin of the earth" recombines matter into new forms. But it also implies, for Günderrode, that in every connection of elements, there is a surplus of life that, once lived, returns to the Earth and enters into new connections that increase *its* activity, *its* potentiality as the condition of possibility for other arrangements.

This trajectory—I choose this word deliberately to contrast it with the notion of a development or telos—of the Earth toward its own "idea," produces the closest thing there is to a dialectical progression in Günderrode. At the level of the individual organism, the surplus of life over itself has no significance since this is always overcome eventually by death and decay. The Earth, however, which as the basis of all individual organisms is both external to them and acts as their unconditional foundation, is also in a sense an excess irreducible to the life of an individual or species; it is capable of surviving and absorbing the effects of their rise and fall. As Günderrode puts it: "The earth bears the life-material given back to it again in ever new appearances, until through ever new transformations everything capable of life in it has come to life" (IE 82–83/447). While this might sound as if she treats the Earth as a vast superorganism in the process of formation, the important caveat is in the second clause: "when everything *capable of life* (*lebensfähige*) has become living." This qualification implies that not everything in and of the Earth is alive in the same way as it. It also suggests that the Earth, by incorporating the organic arrangements of elements of individual living organisms, becomes *itself* steadily more active in its own way.

This argument, unaware of the mass extinctions that are part of the history of the Earth,[38] or at least interpreting prior extinctions in terms of the development of increasing organic complexity, is predicated on the relationship between the "All" (*Allheit*) and the particular. The "All" is the Earth itself, a decidedly dynamic, yet corporeal and material absolute, which in its own way "sublates" the particular into itself:

> So each mortal gives back to the earth a raised, more developed elemental life, which it [the Earth] cultivates further in ascending forms, and the organism, by assimilating ever more developed elements, must thereby become ever more perfect and universal. Thus the All comes to life through the downfall of the particular, and the particular survives immortally in the All whose life it developed while alive, and elevates and increases even after death, and so by living and dying helps to realize the idea of the earth. (IE 83/447)

The difference between Günderrode's absolute and those of her male counterparts in *Naturphilosophie* could therefore be put this way: Whereas they make every particular form or individual organism a step on the way to an absolute that is not yet realized, Günderrode makes her absolute the "realized

Earth," with its own existence and historical trajectory. To call the Earth an "organism" is thus to suggest not that it functions like an individual organism or collection of elements but that, as the ground in which those elements come together and separate, the Earth is the only "immortal" life there is.

Though the Earth's trajectory is imagined by Günderrode as an "ascension" toward more and more complex organisms rather than the rise and fall of various biota we now understand as central to the Earth's history, she nevertheless makes the Earth (rather than self-consciousness) the telos of that ascension. The Earth is not an ideal virtuality latent in the present; it is instead a materiality or corporeality irreducible to any particular being. It grants location, without itself being localizable, and yet it is also the geographic space in which human, nonhuman, and inhuman forces and bodies emerge and interact.[39] The Earth is an "All" for Günderrode, but not because it is an ideality that surpasses particulars thanks to its supersensuous ideality. Rather, the Earth is an "All" because it is both the basis of, and fundamentally external to, every particular being *while remaining* a physical, actual fact, one as real or "realized" as the ground one walks upon.

Perhaps this is why, when Günderrode attempts to describe the "final" realization of the Earth, her language begins to stumble over the terms it has borrowed from her idealist interlocutors. When she explains the Earth's arrival at its "proper being," for instance, it is described as a point of indistinguishability between "body" and "spirit":

> This perfect unity of essence and form cannot be achieved in *separation* and multiplicity, for through precisely *these* the form is different from the essence, because the essence can only be one but the forms are various. The earth can therefore only attain its proper being when its organic and inorganic appearances dissolve in a collective organism, when both factors—being (body) and thinking (spirit)—penetrate each other to the point of indistinguishability, where all body would also at the same time be thought, all thinking at the same time body, and a truly transfigured body, without lack or illness and immortal, and thus wholly different from what we call body and to which we attribute transcience, inertia, illness and deficiency, for this kind of body is, as it were, only a failed attempt by nature to produce that immortal ideal body. (IE 83/448)

The Earth as an eventual "immortal ideal body," seemingly a contradiction in terms, suggests that the dynamics that organize the interchange between "body" and "soul," appearance and activity, are read in terms of a telos that eventually unites the two, making all appearances, all instances of "body," immortal, since bodies would no longer be prone to mutability or to decay, properly speaking. The Earth's tendency toward perfection appears to reestablish something like the passage from the inorganic to the organic that exists in Hegel and Schelling, since it eventually makes that distinction irrelevant only when the Earth is "immortal," a body without lack or defect.

However, Günderrode is not certain about this aspect of her cosmology and whether this end or telos is a necessary component of the Earth: "I do not assert whether the earth will be altogether successful in organizing itself immortally like this; there may be a disproportion of essence and form in its primal elements that always hinders it from this" (IE 83/448). The possibility of this "disproportion" suggests not just her awareness of the finitude of the Earth (well before any scientific understanding that the Earth will likely cease to exist in roughly another 4.5 billion years!), but also that the Earth's asymptotic trajectory never arrives at, or reaches its fulfillment in, an ultimate equilibrium. This is perhaps why Günderrode expands the conception of immortality presaged here into a wider and wider horizon: "perhaps the totality of our whole solar system is needed to resolve the task of such an equilibrium of essence and form, and perhaps even this does not suffice for it and it is a task for the entire universe" (IE 83/448). This speculative turn to the "entire universe" appears to some extent to be Günderrode chafing at her own insights into the nature of the unconditional ground of every Earthbound being. Among those insights is one that requires a recognition that every "particular" takes up a relation to a ground (the Earth) that is *itself* exposed to mortality and transience in a way that does not diminish its unconditionality. What if, in other words, the Earth were not an "immortal body," but a trajectory without end or completion, except in the "realization" of the universe? Though Günderrode would obviously understand the "end" quite differently as a moment of perfection or harmony between the two poles of body and soul, one could alternately read this "end" as Ray Brassier does, in the heat death of the universe, and the end of any life or activity whatsoever.[40] Since the Earth is its own trajectory independent of consciousness in Günderrode, so too might be the entire universe.

Günderrode's conception of the Earth as a realized idea has several important consequences: the first is an understanding of the organism that does not necessarily privilege self-consciousness or spirit as its highest form of development. Organisms are generated out of a specific arrangement of elements whose form and function need not necessarily be human or coincide with a notion of (inhuman) self-consciousness. Furthermore, without a dialectical or conceptual differentiation between the organic and the inorganic, Günderrode's cosmology makes neither one external to the other; they are simply different aspects or elements within a given arrangement. Finally, the only "thing" external to those arrangements is the Earth itself, which functions as an unconditional ground prior to any claimed unconditionality, including the supposedly self-organizing principles inherent in every organism and, as we'll see, the political formations those organisms produce.

Günderrode, the Earth, and Worlds

This latter point—the inability of any given organism to ultimately liberate itself from the Earth—has political implications Günderrode pursues in her more literary compositions since, as we will see, it implies that any self-declared autonomy, independence, or sovereignty in relation to the Earth is always eventually reappropriated by it. Moreover, Günderrode's interest in and knowledge of Islam, Buddhism, and Hinduism was centered on how those religions and practices differed from traditional Christian-European conceptions of the soul. This allowed her to find touchstones in other cultures that could reinforce the insights of her conception of the Earth in her *Naturphilosophie*. Ideas such as the Buddhist conception of surrendering personhood to the All, or the Hindu notion of the transmigration of souls, provided alternative frameworks through which she could demonstrate how non-Western worlds had their own specific relation to, and understanding of, the Earth along with its production of life or immortality. In other words, those Eastern philosophies and religions were, for Günderrode, better positioned in their denial of the Christian concept of the soul as what rises above the material and remains separate from it to comprehend the thoroughly nonhierarchical sense of life her *Naturphilosophie* elaborates, and to understand how the Earth engages in a form of physical and material re-creation. Just as Hinduism offers a conception of the transmigration of souls, often into other forms of life that are not human, so too does Buddhism offer a form of thinking—in terms of karma—that explains how arrangements can be extended over the course of multiple generations, taking on a life outside of the individual. Something like the "All" of the Earth is required to make those ideas intelligible, for Günderrode. She does more than read these beliefs as allegories—they, in fact, describe actual states of affairs, other possible relations to the Earth.

In "Letters of Two Friends," for instance, which was meant to be published in a collection of other texts under the title *Melete*, and which is framed as an epistolary meditation on friendship and love, Günderrode sets up a dialogue that develops when one of the friends—Eusebio—responds to the other's lament about the reality of death by referencing the Hindu conception of reincarnation.[41] Günderrode describes this conception explicitly in terms of the interplay between force and stasis, soul and body, that characterizes her understanding of the Earth. She frames, for instance, the process by which the individual dies and is reborn in terms of a relation between the "All" and the individual:

> But so that you see more clearly what I mean by this, I am sending you some books about the religion of the Hindus. The wonders of ancient wisdom, set down in mysterious symbols, will touch your soul; there will be moments in which you feel yourself stripped of this personal particularity and poverty and again surrendered to the great whole [*großen Ganzen*]; where you more than just think that everything that is now sun and moon, and flower and gemstone, and ether and ocean, is one thing, a holy thing, which rests unceasingly in its depths, blessed in itself, eternally embracing itself, without desire for the action and suffering of the duality that stirs its surface. In such moments, when we can no longer think reflectively, because that which awakens our individual, earthly consciousness has disappeared to our outer senses under the dominance of inner contemplation—in such moments I understand death, the mystery of religion, the sacrifice of the son and love's unending longing. Is this not nature beckoning us to turn back from particularity to the common All, to leave the divided life in which the creature wants to be something for itself and yet cannot be?[42]

As with "The Idea of the Earth," the All is interpreted here as something that cancels dualities and the "divided life in which the creature wants to be something for itself and yet cannot be." Günderrode's focus in "Letters of Two Friends" centers on the way in which every "individual creature" that wishes to live independently of its relation to the All is incapable of doing so: It is always overcome by its return to it, its relation to something it is not.[43]

Yet precisely that dissolution opens the individual to a *relationality* to other worlds the Earth makes possible and that therefore interact with one another. The fact that Günderrode frames this in terms of non-Western traditions gives a sense of what is at stake: rather than one world, one conception of death, one relation to the Earth predicated on Western Christian notions of immortality, Günderrode attempts to describe how multiple worlds, including non-European traditions, take up a relation to the Earth's productive and reproductive capacities—to the "immortal" life that exists only in and through it. As Günderrode puts it in her *Philosophy of Nature*, "This double being is the principle of all entities. Thus, all the bodies and materials of the earth are each an individual being for themselves and also, at the same time, a universal being insofar as they are an element that belongs to the great whole of the earth."[44] The particular or the individual is thus both "for itself" while also related to the All—the "great whole of the earth." It is thereby placed into relation *via the Earth* with the other: other beings, other humans, other organisms, other generations.[45]

This relationality is figured in various ways in "Letters of Two Friends," including by what Günderrode calls "love's unending longing" (LT 355). By this she means not just the connection between two separate individuals, but also their connection to the alterity to which they both belong: the Earth. What she calls "inner contemplation," as in some schools of Buddhism, yields not an autonomy or a self-reflecting subjectivity, but the realization that one is an individual only temporarily, and is enmeshed in a relationality to something other than oneself. For Günderrode, this alterity is the Earth above all. What appears to be an interiority, in this sense, leads immediately and directly to an exteriority that defines "love's unending longing" by situating it in terms of a law of attraction located in the elements of the Earth, which find themselves temporarily coalesced into individuals who in turn long for one another. As in "Idea of the Earth," individual death in "Letters of Two Friends" is thus not a reincarnation of the same or the prolongation of what Günderrode calls "personhood" (*Persönlichkeit*) across time; rather "a necessity births us all into personhood; a common night devours us all" (LT 358). But in that "common night" what lives on is the attraction, the life, of the elements that defined each individual and which have a decidedly material existence, like the shells in Olive Senior's poetry that continue to live in the Earth as markers of former times and lives. In Eusebio's reply, Günderrode emphasizes the extent to which the "immortality" of love can be found only in what she calls the "primordial matter of the world": "I said that your I and mine [elements] should be dissolved in the ancient primordial matter of the world; then I consoled myself that our befriended elements, obeying the law of attraction, would find each other even in infinite space and join with each other" (LT 358). Günderrode frames even her conception of romantic love and its existence beyond death within the terms of "Idea of the Earth," grounding it in the twin poles of soul and body that characterize her *Naturphilosophie*. In contemplating the mortality and survival of love, the mortality and survival of humanity, what returns constantly in Günderrode are claims about how these are enfolded in the "immortal body" of the Earth.

When, for instance, Günderrode engages with the question of the survival of thoughts and opinions beyond the death of the one who thinks them, it is their dissolution into a greater "whole" that permits not just their survival, but their being carried forward, developed, and reconstituted, in the thinking and actions of future generations, not unlike the "skin of the earth" in Senior, or the metaphor of remixing found in "Shell Blow":

> But what, then, is life? The possession already relinquished and acquired again? I often ask myself this. What does it mean that from the All of nature a being cuts itself loose with such consciousness and feels torn off from it? Why do human beings cling with such strength to thoughts and opinions, as if they were what is eternal? Why can they die for them, when precisely these thoughts are lost to them with their death? And why, if these thoughts and concepts die with individuals anyway, why are they always brought forth from these individuals all over again, to forge ahead, through the ranks of the generations that follow each other, to immortality in time? (LT 359)

Eschewing the notion of the eternity of conceptual thought, Günderrode goes on to situate these questions in terms of the movement of temporary stasis and dissolution that characterizes the Earth and its activity:

> For a long time I did not know an answer to these questions, and they bewildered me. Then suddenly, in a revelation, everything was clear to me and will remain so forever. I know that life is only the product of the deepest contact and attraction of the elements; I know that all its blossoms and leaves, which we call thoughts and sensations, must wither when that contact is dissolved, and that individual life is given up to the law of mortality. But as certain as this is to me, just as much is something else beyond all doubt for me: the immortality of life in the whole. For this whole is just life, it surges up and down in its parts—the elements—and whatever has returned to it through dissolution (which we sometimes call death) mingles with it according to laws of affinity, i.e. the similar mingles with what is similar to it. (LT 359)

Though Günderrode does not name the Earth directly here, the fact that the next sentence repeats verbatim passages from "Idea of the Earth" suggests that the same dynamic that governs "natural" entities operates also in the realm of human consciousness. For thoughts do indeed die with those who think them, or who die for them. What survives, however, is the possibility that another generation, another group, might take up that element in a new form or shape, giving it life again, according to what Günderrode call "laws of affinity."

However, it becomes just as clear that the life that exists in thoughts or ideas, or in the romantic connection between two individuals, can only be "reincarnated" in an entirely *new* form, not the one in which it previously existed, just as Senior suggests in her own poetic examination of earthly afterlives. That is, the life of a thought or idea exists only in the actual physical and *material* existence of concrete individuals. The life it represents is thus entirely grounded in the Earth and its ability to sustain that thought across multiple generations. After restating the passage cited above on the "realization" of the idea of the Earth, Günderrode goes on to frame the survival of love, and the survival of ideas, in the context of a "transmigration of souls":

> Thus, however the elements may be dispersed, when they join to what is already living they will elevate it; when they join to those things whose life resembles death, they will animate them. And it seems to me, Eusebio, that the idea of the Indians of the transmigration of souls corresponds to this opinion; and the elements may wander and search no longer only when the earth has thoroughly attained its proper existence: the organic. (LT 360)

This kind of "transmigration," however, is decidedly material, since no "soul" remains intact after death. What survives is only the relation between various elements understood as life, including "life that resembles death." The survival of any idea, or any "soul" for that matter, is completely tied to its reconstitution in a new (material) assemblage, or in a new individual that is itself fated to die, but which temporarily reanimates that idea. Günderrode describes this process in these terms:

> From this perspective, Eusebio, it also became clear to me what the great thoughts of truth, justice, virtue, love and beauty claim, which germinate in the soil of personhood and, soon overgrowing it, stretch up to the free heavens, an immortal growth that does not perish with the soil in which it developed, but always generates itself anew in new individuals. (LT 361)

Ideas, souls, or anything else are "immortal" only to the extent that they "generate [themselves] anew" out of the Earth, out of a recombination of elements in the formation of "new individuals." What is passed down is both the physical remnants of past lives and their "thoughts," which are inherited and transformed from generation to generation.

Günderrode, History, and the Political

Günderrode's conception of the Earth and the forms of life it contains produces a set of ethical and political consequences she hints at in her more philosophical texts, but which she explores more fully in her literary work, particularly her plays. The tendency of the Earth toward an increasing surplus of life is often couched in spiritual terms, particularly when she frames that life through non-Christian religions. That spiritual language, however, tends to be grounded in the unconditional activity of the Earth as the driving force of what otherwise would be seen as transcendental concepts such as "justice" or "morality," ideas usually associated with social or civil society, rather than the natural world.[46] This blurring of the distinction between the social and the natural in Günderrode, as in Senior, produces a unique political ecology that, among other things, undoes many of the assumptions behind idealism's justification of colonialism as a hierarchy of life-forms and races.

In her short piece *The Story of a Brahmin*, for instance, the main narrator, Almor, details a quasi-spiritual discovery of a sense of the divine that, as with Günderrode's description of life in "Idea of the Earth," is material rather than ideal or spiritual. When Almor defines the sudden awakening of his spiritual sensibility, it is first in relation to the question of justice, morality, and civil society that his experience is described:

> For a long time it had been clear to me that justice is the basis of civil society and morality the basis of human society. These two relations had once satisfied me; I had sought to bring all the points of my mind into contact with them. Now I discovered aptitudes within me that these finite relations would no longer satisfy.[47]

However, those questions about human morality and society quickly transform into a meditation on the concept of life itself:

> In this longing, in this love, the spirit of nature spoke to me. I heard its voice, but I did not yet know where it came from; but the more I listened

> to it, the clearer it was to me that there was a fundamental force in which everything, visible and invisible, was connected. I named this force primal life. (SB 308)

The "primal force" of life Almor refers to here has been interpreted as a kind of pantheism,[48] but if it is a pantheism, it is remarkably similar to the "realized idea" of the Earth found in Günderrode's *Naturphilosophie*, suggesting something more material than divine. That is, the life Almor describes is both producer and product, both material and a *process* that dissolves materiality into other forms:

> It is at the same time the ground of all things and the things themselves, the condition and the conditioned, the creator and the creature, and it divides and separates itself in various figures, becomes sun, moon, stars, plants, animal and human being together. (SB 309)

In *Story of a Brahmin* we begin to see the concept of life developed into a more general principle whereby the unconditioned differentiates itself into the various forms that populate what Günderrode here calls "nature," or "sun, moon, stars, plants, animal and human being."

The fact that human consciousness is included *within* the domain of "primal life," however, suggests that human political, ethical, and moral spheres cannot be fundamentally demarcated from the realm of nature.[49] Nor for that matter can religion. As Günderrode writes, "the intuition of their original primal ground is the deepest soul of religions" (SB 309). As she goes on to suggest, however, it is not evident that self-consciousness is the end point of nature or the telos of the All. Framing this idea in terms of the Brahmin's spirituality, Günderrode suggests that the "spirit of nature" "wanders through all forms," at one point developing "consciousness and thought in human beings" (SB 312). That moment is not conclusive, however, since "from human beings on an infinite series of migrations that lead to ever higher perfection await souls" (SB 312). Since a "soul" in Hinduism, depending on the school of thought, is either endlessly reborn in new physical forms, or ends the cycle of death and rebirth once it has finally achieved karmic perfection, it is not entirely clear that a strictly "spiritual" perfection is being alluded to here. Instead, we are presented with a series of evolutions that are material as much as "spiritual," a progressive formal development. And since a "soul" in the language of "Idea of the Earth" is not a spiritual entity in the typical sense, the implication here is that human consciousness is itself a temporary moment that will eventually be repossessed by the Earth and the "infinite series of migrations" it perpetuates, like everything else.

What follows out of this insistence is not just a rethinking of consciousness or nature, or the relationship between them, but also a recognition that human social formations and thus history are, like the natural world, governed by the same movement of temporary stasis and dissolution affecting the Earth. Rather than conceive of the social and historical realm as a break with nature, Günderrode makes them part of the same process, since they both belong to the "All" of the Earth. Just as particular natural forms come and go, so do human civilizations which are born and die, rise and fall, according to the same dynamics.[50] Voicing her ideas through the figure of the Brahmin, and his relationship to past and present civilizations, Günderrode contextualizes history in terms of a succession of temporary and fragile configurations that dissolve and reform themselves in continuously new ways:

> He taught me the story of his fatherland [India] in greater detail, and with astonishment I say that India's culture reached into an antiquity in which other people's calendars were not yet born. If, he once said to me, the proud Europeans boast of being the midpoint of the civilized and enlightened world, the sun that illumined and warmed the earth rose in the orient; later and paler it sends its beams to the occident. The fog of forgetfulness veils the graves of our primeval world, only a few figures shimmer through; our victorious gods have fled, we are trodden down by the crude Mongols, we die slowly through the profit-seeking Europeans. Each people's greatness appears to be a spring that comes only once and then escapes to bless other areas. (SB 311–12)

It is important to note the extent to which this description of India's past emphasizes something other than a Hegelian history that views non-Western civilizations as having been surpassed and overcome by Europe. The particular Indian "world" (*Vorwelt*) that arose prior to the contemporary one has ceased to exist, although vestiges of it find echoes later on in "other areas" (*andere Zonen*). The implication is that much of the original cultural impetus for that prior world remains alive and well in other forms, other cultures, just not in the geographic space of present-day India. The reference to a "people's greatness," emerging only once but then escaping to "bless" other areas of the globe, suggests something like the forces of decay and rebirth that define the

Earth.

This idea is one of the central concerns of what is perhaps Günderrode's most ambitious literary work, her play *Muhammed: Prophet of Mecca*. Her interpretation of Muhammed as a religious and political figure is prefigured in "Story of a Brahmin" directly after introducing the notion of the way every religion constitutes an intuition of a "fundamental force" (*Grundkraft*) or "primal life" (*Urleben*). Almor claims that he:

> studied Muhammed's teachings and his life. My spirit passed over into contemplation of him: I saw how the consciousness of divine things germinated early in his soul, how a powerful longing drove him to inject this branch from the eternal tree of life into the weather beaten stem of his people, but how this tender plant, which can only bloom and bear fruit in a soil purified by morality and culture, adopted an altered and foreign shape and nature. (SB 308)

Almor's interpretation will end up being one of the main themes of Günderrode's play on Muhammed. The play makes the titular character a representation of the force of change and renovation Günderrode had earlier associated with the Earth.[51] Much of the first part of the play centers on the way Muhammed attracts a following by shifting other's allegiances from the old gods of Mecca to the new one for which he is the prophet. Recounting his loss of faith in the old gods to one of his acolytes, Nahlid, Muhammed makes clear that, despite having been admitted to the "holy establishment" at Kaaba, the "silence" of the old gods leads him to turn away from them:

> I became a youth, and still every morning with ardent prayers I turned my hopeful eyes towards the east, to see whether the new sun would not bring a new fortune to me. In vain! Deaf those false gods remained. Where no deed is, there is no power, where no effect is, there the effective thing is missing.[52]

The "silence" which Mohammed refers to is not simply his inability to "hear" the voice of the old gods; they are not just incapable of speaking to him, they are without any "effect" *(Wirkung)* even in their silence. The world they govern, a world of faith, obedience, and action, and the one into which Mohammed thought he had been initiated no longer has any effectivity; it is not just no longer believed in, it no longer *acts* or is capable of enacting anything as a world. Muhammed, in other words, doesn't simply lose faith, he loses the very world that this faith holds up, its capacity to generate or reproduce itself not just in him, but in others. The gods are not just silent, they are absent. This fact is the starting point of Muhammed's "conversion," opening a space in which other forms of activity, legitimacy, and authority are able to inaugurate themselves.

This is perhaps why Günderrode chooses a prophet from a non-Western monotheism around which to center the play, one whose God would doubtless *not* be recognized or believed in by most of her audience, but whose capacity to generate a new political and religious movement dramatizes the themes of momentary coalescence and eventual dissolution governing her *Naturphilosophie*. Muhammed enacts a new religion that renovates the political and religious domain of a vast area of the Earth, setting into motion a series of revolutions that leave practically nothing in its political and religious domains intact. What Muhammed does, in effect, is reinvent the world from the standpoint of another unconditionality—Allah—one decidedly not of the Earth, but one that also nonetheless mirrors the *effects* of the Earth's unconditionality. While Muhammed and his followers articulate the novelty of Muhammed's intervention in explicitly divine or visionary terms, it is the chorus of the play that acts as the interpreter of the action and frames it in slightly more earthly terms. As the first part of the chorus worries that innocent blood is about to be spilled in the battle for Mecca, the second interprets Muhammed's account of his visions:

> I saw him stray through the desert
> Full of thought and all alone
> Making conversation with his spirit;
> And in the moon's dusky light
> Descend to pyramids,
> Summon there the earth's spirit;
> To show him what is hidden
> And how the stream of time flows. (MP 170/121)

Although the chorus does not claim any knowledge of Muhammed's vision, it does make clear that it interprets that vision in terms of "earth's spirit" which "shows him how the stream of time flows," suggesting a terrestrial rather than a divine or eternal force ultimately at work. As the first chorus goes on to contemplate the extent to which Muhammed is possibly led by "high powers" that are "will-less and unconscious" (*willenlos und unbewußt*) (MP 172/122), the chorus clarifies that Muhammed has become a force of renovation, but in ways that are not necessarily intentional:

But he composes himself,
Brings to life
What he dreamt;
Changes order
Into dream's confusion;
The thing's existence
Into change and flight. (MP 172–74/123)

As Muhammed "brings to life" the dream that he neither reveals nor has direct access to, that dream becomes a way of disordering what already exists, changing "order into dream's confusion." Muhammed's "vision" is therefore not something he "has" in the sense of a definitive conception of the future—instead, it is one that defines itself negatively against what exists, becoming a futurity that coexists within the present, overturning its existing social and religious orders.

Despite the religious element of Muhammed's status as prophet—where he is described as the vessel of higher powers—the play consistently attempts to demonstrate the extent to which he is in fact an *earthly* political figure, a force of change emanating not, strictly speaking, from the divine, but from the finite world of change that connects him to the dynamics of life specific to the Earth. As the second chorus insists:

Such forces, too, must the cosmos have,
Quiet existence is no use to it;
When instead of refreshing earth's children,
Destruction breaks from the womb of clouds;
When enraged waves break on the shore,
The fire's glow churns up the earth's womb,
When loud thunder speaks through the heavens,
And pain, horror fills every breast;
Then the narrow bounds cave in,
The old world is devoured,
Yet from the creaturely mind
A more beautiful is established. (MP 174/123)

Although Muhammed himself claims a divine mission, the chorus understands his status as prophet squarely in terms of the "forces" that govern the cosmos and the Earth. Those forces are initially destructive; the chorus compares Muhammed to "enraged waves" and volcanic eruptions that had long been used in the Romantic period to describe revolutionary potential. As with the processes of dissolution and reconstitution in "Idea of the Earth," the forces Muhammed represents "devour" the old world and its "narrow bounds," opening up a "more beautiful" one in its place.

Muhammed: Prophet of Mecca, then, describes a political upheaval modeled on the natural upheavals that occur in the process of the realization of the "idea of the Earth."[53] Though this might appear to be unique to Günderrode's *Naturphilosophie*, it is not exactly an esoteric or marginal idea. For if the Lisbon earthquake, for instance—which I described in the introduction—can be seen as not just a natural occurrence but also as a political one, then it becomes increasingly difficult likewise to discern the difference between purely natural and purely political forces in human history. In the case of Günderrode's *Muhammed*, what is involved is a supplanting of one regime of authority predicated on the divine with another. Muhammed's attractiveness as a prophet is precisely his claim to speak for the vision of the divine that acts as a direct challenge—culturally and politically—to the old regime. As his message begins to have the effect of rallying others to his cause, the chorus shifts from questioning whether Muhammed is in fact a prophet, to an ode about his grounding of "a new world" (MP 184/130):

> Now the face of the earth
> Will transform itself,
> The old, familiar
> Aged and ugly,
> Full of worn looks;
> Now will unfold itself
> In smiling youth;
> The weakness of age
> Of ailing times,
> Becomes bold youth
> By the deed of enthusiasm
> Awakened to life. (MP 186/130–31)

To the chorus, Muhammed now represents the transformation of the Earth, not simply in terms of the introduction of a new conception of the divine but in terms of the ways in which a new form of life begins to take shape in the unfolding of his and others' "enthusiasm" for the new god. The old world of the past gods has begun to crumble, and Muhammed represents a reconfiguration of this old world—its religious and political institutions—into new ones.[54]

Yet the creation of new life is not all the play is interested in: It also begins to hint at what happens when Muhammed's renovation of the world begins to see itself as permanent and global in scope. The second half of the play examines the potentially totalizing imperial ambitions Muhammed's emergence represents. In other words, the renovation Muhammed brings about also contains the possibility of a calcification that fails to recognize that it, too, is prone to the same processes of dissolution and reconstitution that brought it into being in the first place. The play goes on to suggest that the renovating element of Muhammed's revolution threatens to transform itself into a planetary mission of conversion and conquest, an attempt at a new form of stasis, a conversion of the Earth's ceaselessly renovating force into an inert timelessness. At the end of the play, for instance, Muhammed exhorts his followers to carry their work to the ends of the Earth: "Go! Wander victoriously through the earth from the farthest west, where the sun goes down in an ocean of darkness, to the peoples of the East, over whose heads the sun stands vertically; for you are the conqueror, of whom it is written: He will subjugate sunrise and sunset" (MP 298/200).

Günderrode's interest in Islam and Muhammed, then, also focuses on the way that some nascent religions, revolutions, and political movements are at first a new kind of life and renewal, but then are usually repossessed by their endeavor to universalize themselves, a process that brings about their dissolution through their stagnation. As Mecca is conquered, and the old world destroyed, Muhammed turns to address these global imperial ambitions directly:

> The earth is ripe for our work, illness and inner disquiet unhinge it, we shall breathe into it again a healthy living breath, it is disunited by partisanship and bloody hate, we shall unite the parties, reconcile hate. The age-old, many-headed monster, heathendom, is displaced from the West, in the East it fights despairingly its last fight against Christendom. Christendom has torn itself away from its begetter, Judaism, it abandoned its parental house and wandered out to all four winds, it sends out of the distances the poisoned arrows of persecution against its father's holy head; at the same time it is at odds with itself, its parts dispute in grim strife and its otherwise well-built body is full of wild ghoulish excesses. (MP 238/162)

Framed in terms of the rise and fall of religions and the language of renewal, decay, and health, Muhammed describes a history that understands his own religion as that history's pinnacle, and as the reconciler of divisions governing other histories and traditions, which are either on their way to extinction (heathenism) or are internally divided (Christianity). Muhammed sees the birth of Islam as offering a new undivided global community that can reshape the Earth in its likeness, unlike Christianity, which has been fractured and reconstituted in multiple churches among multiple nationalities. His sense of the uniting capacities of Islam suggests the same kind of universalism that drives Western and Hegelian forms of colonial history, complete with its own missionary task.

What Muhammed fails to consider, for Günderrode, is that there is no religion, political community, or empire on the Earth that remains stable indefinitely. Instead, human history, like the history of the Earth itself, must be conceived as a series of rises and falls, inaugural moments and their calcification into static structures that must be renewed repeatedly. Any imperial ambitions to constitute the Earth *as* a totality, as a single unified world that would "reconcile" all the others, neglects the Earth as process and the fact that it has its own trajectory and is constantly potentializing other worlds and dissolving the contours of present ones. In *Muhammed*, Günderrode turns a lens on the same missionary ambitions that characterize eighteenth- and nineteenth-century Christian colonialism by examining it through the lens of the other. *Muhammed*, then, is not meant to be an accurate portrayal of the origin of Islam, but an examination of the inauguration of a new religion and its concomitant political arrangements, its conditions of possibility and its eventual devolution into an imperial project. Unlike Hegel's conception of history, Muhammed's is not prefaced on a conception of the Earth as the inorganic backdrop to the hierarchy of life that follows from it. But it *is* premised on fidelity to that which stands over and above the Earth (God) and can therefore uniquely sanction Islam's reign over it.[55] In this way, at least, there are structural similarities between the two forms of colonial history: both Christianity and Islam liberate themselves from the Earth in order to dominate it, detaching themselves from its unconditionality by engendering their own. The Earth is, for Günderrode, not just "there"—an object to be colonized—but an active participant in the political formations it makes possible. It is therefore an unconditional ground of a very peculiar kind, one that must be distinguished from any human sovereignty. The only unconditional foundation it offers is one that is constantly at work *overturning* and reconstituting all the assemblages it makes possible.[56]

Senior and Günderrode: Situating the Earth Otherwise

In what way, then, does Günderrode's conception of the Earth, and the political ecology that follows out of it, resonate with Senior's Earth and her political ecology of life, which reanimates the past but also reveals how older forms of colonialism and slavery reconstitute themselves? Günderrode, like Senior, understands that the activity of the Earth reflected in human social formations is not inherently "revolutionary"—older forms resurface, new ones harbor global ambitions. Senior too understands this form of reconstitution of the past, though she is less inclined to identify it with the Earth than with the colonial archive. One of the poems that concludes Olive Senior's *Shell* is a reflection on a trip to the estate of William Beckford Jr., "called by Lord Byron England's richest son" (S 75), and the largest land and slave owner of the former Jamaican colony.[57] As Senior begins to reflect on and "sift through" the remnants of the estate and the period in which Beckford amassed his wealth, the poem dissects all of the *objets d'art*—the paintings and other material goods—that remain archived as the ill-gotten gains of slavery. We begin to see, therefore, how Senior's poetry marks not just the afterlife of peoples and cultures consigned to oblivion by Western colonialism, but also, as in Günderrode, the decay and afterlife of the world that made that oblivion possible. For Senior, as with Günderrode, new forms of life depend on the death of the old world. Describing the neogothic tower on the estate built through the profits of slavery to elicit "sentiments of amazement, shock and awe" (S 91), the poem's fourth section goes on to describe the tower's ruins, its being reclaimed by the Earth and by time:

> How time and distance swallow the vanished
> Ruins, the mock glens and pastures, wild copse
> And groves of pine. How the Wiltshire Downs
> Reclaim the artificiality of the picturesque.
> Nothing remaining of vanished pride and tower
> Except the possessions auctioned, collected in
> Other citadels of power. (S 92)

Using the trope of Romantic picturesque ruins, Senior initially provides a way to read the landscape: The fact that Wiltshire Downs is reclaiming Beckford's estate, while his possessions are auctioned off to museums and art galleries, seems at first to resonate with Percy Shelley's fascination with the same kinds of ruins in his poem "Ozymandias," which is an image of autocratic power having reigned for nothing and having been outdone by time.[58] However, Senior goes further, revealing how that power has reconstituted itself in the aftermath of colonialism in the stockpiling of its spoils, their re-formation into new archives, the accumulation of objects ranging from European art to Greek antiquities to Egyptian antiquities to Persian carpets, "collected in other citadels of power," and decontextualized from their provenance in the genocide and enslavement of non-European peoples.

The other form of archive Senior's poetry envisions, however, clearly resonates with Günderrode's conception of the Earth as constantly reconstituting the past from prior elements that have been dissolved and dispersed. In the epigraph to "Join-the-Dots," for instance, we read the following: "In the sample of 282 plantation maps drawn from the National Library of Jamaica's collection, some 25 percent show the 'village' areas as a blank" (S 68). In a map designed to chart the geography and settlement of Jamaica, the land's relief and its use—the enclosure of the plantation being the primary one—the space of the village housing slaves is not even recorded. It may be there in the landscape, but it has not been reflected in the archive. The poem then proceeds to mark or register the village through a poetics, allowing the absent village to be situated on the landscape:

> We played at Join-the Dots, Grandma and me,
> But never could we win the prize
> For I saw pictures she could not see.
> They said I had clear-seeing eyes.
> Our house was built on land where once
> A village stood. Where fragments
> Floating in the air sometimes cried out
> For personhood.
> They pounded on the rooftop, tore at
> The gutter; "Hush it is the wind,"
> Grandma said, but I knew better
> Though I would never
> Utter a word. For I was sworn to secrets.
> "This is where we once lived too."

The children said. "We'd like
To play with you." (S 68)

The game of "join-the-dots" becomes the central metaphor of the poem, a game where the speaker, a young girl, connects individual points together on a page to reveal an otherwise invisible image. That metaphor is then transposed to the landscape of the absent village, where physical fragments, like the dots on the paper, float in the air and "cry out for personhood." As we've seen, that cry is more than a metaphor for Senior and Günderrode. In Senior's poem, the landscape itself is made up of the *life* of that past, its fragments which float in the air, the wind and rain that pounds on the rooftop, and which the speaker can connect into an image, an afterlife that still has actual material existence. Being kept awake by the "black dots," the girl is then given a cocoa-tea "sweetened / with cane sugar and / a hint of nutmeg," which she shares with her "ghostly friends who said they / lived in land-snail shells" (S 68–69). Those friends are not just a memory, or a "ghost," but are physically located in the cane sugar, cocoa, and nutmeg that flavors the girl's night-time drink:

Their Old One said: "No. You drink up
Child. For this our bodies
Turned to dust. Ground
Into fields of sugar cane, of cocoa-walks,
Of nutmeg groves. Drink.
In remembrance of us." (S 69)

As the elder "ghost" tells the speaker to finish her drink, a new relation to memory is enacted through the Earth. The very bodies of bygone villagers have been ground into the fields that grew the crops that flavor her drink, on the very physical landscape upon which she is housed. The "memory" of the villagers therefore takes not just the form of a mental image but is part of the recombinatory powers of the Earth—their bodies are actually part of the drink, containing not just their memory but their afterlife, like the forms of "personhood" constituted and dissolved in Günderrode's idea of the Earth. In Senior and Günderrode, the Earth is ready to tell a very different story: not one of power, but of survival, or subsistence.

This notion of subsistence and of the reconstitution of the past is central to both Senior and Günderrode's work. Eschewing the hierarchy of organisms and self-consciousness that emerges out of German Idealism's conception of the Earth as an *inert* background for life, Günderrode's thought resonates with Senior's poetics of survival. As in Senior, the Earth tells a different story for Günderrode—every culture, from Western Christian, to Hindu, to Muslim, is embedded in the Earth. The rise and fall of empires cannot, in her philosophy, be rigorously distinguished from the rise of fall of individuals or species. There is no "liberation" from the Earth—no transcendence toward a realm of morality or spirit that would be capable of "freeing" itself from the Earth's gravity. Those Earth-processes also represent for Günderrode, as for Senior, a form of survival, a form of life that allows elements of the past to be reconstituted. In both Senior and Günderrode, the "personhood" or the continuity of the individual cannot be maintained, and so death is indeed inevitable. But the elements that composed that life—at once physical, material, and mental—live on in new forms, constituting a kind of "memory" the Earth bears within it. Elements of past moments, past lives, past civilizations, return, imposing themselves on the present in unforeseen and unforeseeable ways, generating new forms of life that in turn decompose and recompose. In Senior's case, there is a further political dimension to these notions: in the wake of exterminated cultures, destroyed societies, and forced migrations, that new life becomes a means of addressing the way the past is not just memorialized, but continues to have structural effects in the present. To give voice to the dead, the exterminated, the enslaved, is not just to memorialize them, but to recognize the extent to which they are still with us in other forms: their blood and bodies have formed our institutions and shaped our history and our present. To reconstitute the Earth in this way, to see it as alive in the sense Senior and Günderrode understand it, is to think not just the problem of multiple worlds that exist on its surface and the violence implicit in the notion of a *single* totalizing "world history." It is also to open a space in which the survival of the various worlds wiped out by that totalizing history have new possibilities, new "ways of speaking" in the present. Worlds come and go—the Earth remains and anticipates and gives shape to other worlds and histories to come.

FOUR

EARTH WITHOUT WORLD

Ruins of History in Chamoiseau and Hölderlin

> Wherever the essential decisions of our history are made, wherever we take them over or abandon them, wherever they go unrecognized or are brought once more into question, there the world worlds. The stone is world-less.
>
> —MARTIN HEIDEGGER

THOUGH THE VOLCANO THAT destroyed Pompei in 79 AD burst back into life in 1631, it wasn't until more than a century later, in 1763, that the city it had annihilated was fully discovered and identified buried under ancient ash, thanks to the unearthing of an inscription. In a period increasingly fascinated with the grandeur of Greek ruins, Pompei became something of a tourist sensation: the discovery of what had once been a lively city destroyed in an instant, and then just as suddenly preserved by layers of falling ash. The vivid traces of victims' bodies in their death throes were like photographic negatives created nearly a century before early photography. Together they offered a snapshot of a city taken by surprise, not by an enemy at the gates but by the destructive forces of the Earth, unleashed in mere moments to snuff out an entire community. What was perhaps most striking about Pompei, however, was not its grandeur but precisely its banality: Preserved in its ruins was a record of the everyday lives of the victims caught suddenly off guard by the deadly pyroclastic flow that moved too quickly for any escape. The rediscovery of Pompei thus produced an anxiety for the 1800s: Civilizations might rise and fall thanks to historical forces, but they could also disappear without warning—vulnerable and exposed to volatile and uncontrollable Earth systems. That modern Europe was in no better a position to deal with these forces than ancient Greece was surely part of the fascination: Pompei was above all a portent for the present, not unlike interest today in the natural causes—such as a centuries-long period of drought induced by climate change—that had forced the Mayans to abandon their cities prior to conquest. Our historical curiosity is amplified by our anxiety about the effect of global warming on the future of our own civilizations.[1]

At stake, then, is not the question of the *biological* destruction of ancient societies: Indigenous Caribbean Taíno DNA lives on in its surviving descendants, for example. What prompts our fascination is the extinction of a *world*, a way of being, a culture, a cosmology, a mode of existence. If Senior and Günderrode understood the Earth as a vital archive, a reconstitution of life and of the living in new forms, the two writers I turn to now view the Earth through the lens of a succession of *bygone* worlds, the coming and going of civilizations irreducible to the Earth they once inhabited. Whereas Senior and Günderrode emphasize the Earth as a process of constant dissolution and renewal, another seemingly unlikely couple—Martinican author and theorist Patrick Chamoiseau, and German Romantic poet and theorist Friedrich Hölderlin—emphasize a relation to an Earth that bears the traces of worlds that have gone extinct, horizons of meaning that are no longer operative. But for both writers, this relation to a departed civilization is not just a relation to the past. It is also fundamentally a relation to *a present* placed under the threat of its future extinction. As with the example of Pompei, it is not so much the traces interred in the Earth of a bygone civilization that provokes wonder or anxiety: It is that they invoke the fragility of the present, a sense that existing horizons of meaning are in the process of collapse. In other words, the signs of the extinction of the past world become an index of the present one's future disappearance. This in turn provokes a meditation on that future from the standpoint of the contemporary world's disappearance: The Earth, in both authors, reveals itself as potentially *worldless*, either a transition between the collapse of the present world and another that has not yet taken shape, or an opening toward an Earth bereft of meaning or sense entirely. In both Chamoiseau and Hölderlin, in other words, an indifferent Earth emerges in the interstice *between* two historical worlds as the recognition that the present—for better or worse—is in advance faced with its own demise and thus must confront a future no longer defined by its own structures of meaning.

Two key novels in Chamoiseau's oeuvre place the Earth front and center: his rewriting of the Robinsonade in *Crusoe's Footprint* (2012) and his account of a marooning slave in *Slave Old Man* (1997). *Footprint* reinterprets Defoe's Crusoe myth by making the titular castaway an African man—a fact we don't discover until nearly the end of the novel—who eventually overcomes his initial attempt to re-create the old world lost in the shipwreck on this new seemingly uninhabited island. The narrator's initial account of his relation to the island is one of conquest and domination. Upon discovering the footprint of an unidentified other on the beach, his relation to the island changes, invoking what might be called a Glissantian poetics of relation. In seeking out the other across the island, the man who formerly calling himself "the idiot" transforms himself into what he now calls a "small person," someone capable of seeing the land, its flora and fauna, even its very mineral composition, beyond the structuring confines of his previous world: "I found myself facing another self: the whole, entire island; I now perceived it like a multitude that touched me, grabbed me, squeezed me all over, as if I were immersed in a mass of presences, imperious and lively."[2] As opposed to the hierarchical structuring of the world that places the Crusoe character second only to God, with the rest of the inhabitants of the island at his disposal, the footprint and its invocation of a relation to the other transforms him into an "artist." That is, he becomes capable of creating a narrative of his own rebirth in a reconstruction of the world as a recognition of the alterity of the island and all its inhabitants.

Footprint, however, essentially picks up where the earlier novel *Slave Old Man* left off, namely in the question of how a new relation to the Earth becomes the starting point for a transfigured connection with others. Though the terrain of the encounter is the island, and while it is central to the narrator's conversion, the emphasis in *Footprint* is on relations to others encountered only through an Earth reconceived as "another self," that is, as the material precondition of relations to the other as such (as we saw in the first chapter). In *Slave Old Man*, however, the narrative is focused less on relations with others than on how the titular character is *displaced* from his former world of the plantation through an encounter with an essentially worldless Earth represented in a Stone (as it is capitalized in the novel) that is the only vestige of now-disappeared indigenous civilizations. The encounter with the other through the Earth in *Slave Old Man* is therefore less about the reinvention of a new horizon of meaning than about the collapse of a presently existing or prior one. This Earth is thus not just a site for a reinvention of the world, but a worldless space *between* the death of past and present ones. The Earth's liminal status as described in *Slave Old Man* is not only a concept also found in Hölderlin's geopoetics, it similarly generates the critical thrust of Chamoiseau's and Hölderlin's understanding of the relation between literature and history, as well as its encounter with what Chamoiseau calls its "unthinkable" anteriority. Given *Slave Old Man*'s focus on the political and poetic consequences of that anteriority, my analysis focuses on the earlier novel, where the Earth becomes a central motif of the collapse of a horizon of meaning *prior to* another being established.

In *Slave Old Man*, the Earth is compressed metonymically in the motif of an ancient Stone inscribed by extinct Amerindian cultures. Though bearing the traces of multiple past civilizations, the Stone is a marker of *worldlessness*, the irretrievable loss of prior horizons of meaning. However, precisely because it is worldless, it also becomes central to how the novel calls into question the supposed ineluctability of the plantation-world from which the eponymous protagonist escapes, forcing both master and slave alike to face the collapse of their respective horizons of meaning. Similarly, the Earth figures in Hölderlin's articulation of history through the relation between the former world of ancient Greece and modern Europe (or what he calls "Hesperia"). Under the pressure of Chamoiseau's more explicitly political articulation of the Earth's irreducibility to human worlds, we see similar claims emerge in Hölderlin's own obsession with the bygone world of the Greeks. While Hölderlin's contemporaries found in ancient Greece a forerunner of the civilization they envisioned as a model for modern Germany, Hölderlin insisted that the "greatness" of the Greek world could not be reconstituted in the present. Through Chamoiseau's more disorienting Earth, which undoes all horizons of meaning, Hölderlin's idea of the Earth likewise comes into view as a form of worldlessness. However, the Earth in Hölderlin potentially nullifies the possibility of inaugurating *another* world and highlights the inherent fragility and contingency of all worlds, including the contemporary one. That is, when faced with the reality of the unrepeatable bygone world of ancient Greece, Hölderlin's poetry also confronts, as in Chamoiseau, the Earth as an interstice between an extinct world and the present. As a discontinuity between two worlds—one that has collapsed, and another that has not yet been formed—the Earth in Hölderlin exposes the present to a fundamental disorientation, a wandering on an Earth without axis, a "homeland" far stranger and more uprooted than the nationalism of his contemporaries. Since the extinction of the worlds and peoples to which the Amerindian stone testifies in Chamoiseau were not victims of natural forces but of European genocide, his novel gestures toward the possibility of a more humane world he hopes is taking shape in its wake. Hölderlin's encounter with the Earth, however, grounded as it is on sheer historical erasure, leaves open the possibility that no new world might be in the process of formation. In both cases, an essentially worldless Earth not only exposes the present to its future dissolution, but also gestures toward an Earth without any world or horizon of meaning to give it sense or purpose.

Marronage Between Two Worlds

Slave Old Man opens with a statement that seemingly gives away the ending, much like Roumain's novel *Masters of the Dew*: the nameless protagonist—a slave, an old one, and a man—will die:

> When this story gets under way, everyone knows that this slave old man will die. This conviction is based on no evidence at all. He is still vigorous and seems like an indestructible mineral, something *djok*-strong.[3]

The fact that the novel opens with the main character's future death—a character not even given a name, just a description—sets the action of the novel definitively in the past, and more specifically, as the novel puts it, in "slavery times" (SM 3/17). But it also places the reader in the position of an inheritor: How does one accede to this story, which becomes an allegory for all the anonymous slaves of Martinique, whose only traces are not their names but whatever of them remains—what they have left behind after their death?

Slave Old Man narrates the story of a marooning slave whose remains will be discovered a hundred years later lying next to an Amerindian stone such as the one in figure 1 which was found in Martinique's Montravail Forest. The Stone is inscribed with symbols, the engravings of many indigenous peoples, "peoples of whom only it [the Stone] remains" (SM 102/129). Had this rock been discovered by Senior or Günderrode, it would have figured in their writings as a metaphor for the Earth as a living archive. For Chamoiseau, however, the Amerindian stone indexes the *fragility* of such an "archive": The dead do not return. Instead, we encounter their absence in our own historical moment and, a bit like the dead of Dante's *Inferno*, these remainders of a vanished world come to dispute the supposedly undisputed truth of our own. They ask

FIGURE 1. Amerindian stone, Montravail Forest, Martinique, 2020. © Sébastien Pierrot-Minnot.

also how our present has absorbed them into its own self-understanding, particularly since it is responsible for their disappearance. From the outset the novel situates us uncomfortably between two worlds, if not more: between worlds that have evanesced and a present whose self-understanding is crumbling under the pressure of that encounter.

This encounter is staged by the protagonist's escape: as he flees the organized territory of the plantation, he enters the "Great Woods," a vast tropical forest at the edge of his master's home, the disorganized space of noncultivation and the source of myriad tales of maroons' disappearance and death. The slave old man passes from the world ordered by the brutal racial hierarchies of the plantation system into a boundless zone wherein the absence of any human-made structures throws the contours of the master's world into disarray. For the slaves, the world of the plantation condemns them to a timeless present, cutting them off from their own pasts and denying them any relation to a future:

> The Plantation is small, but each link among its memories vanishes into the ashes of time. The bite of the chains. The *rwash* of the whip. The rending cries. Explosive deaths. Starvations. Murderous fatigues. Exiles. Deportations of different peoples forced to live together without the laws and moralities of the Old-world. All of that quickly muddles, for those gathered there, the rippling of recollections and the depth-sounding of dreams. In their flesh, their spirit, subsists only a *calalou*-gumbo of rotting remembrance and stagnant time, untouched by any clock. (SM 6/20–21)

Relations to the past reside only beyond the orderly stagnancy of the plantation in the space outside, in the ancient forests that still bear the vestiges of a time before the plantation existed, and even before contact, a veritable memorial to indigenous cultures exterminated by the world that brought the plantation into existence. In the Great Woods, as the narrator informs us, "the Amerindians of the first times turned themselves into writhing vines of suffering that strangle the trees and stream over the cliffs, like the unappeased blood of their own genocide" (SM 6/21).

Before he runs away, the slave old man is likewise arrested by the ahistorical stagnancy of the master's territory; he is "bound to the Plantation like the air and the earth and the sugar" (SM 8/24), which is why no one notices his departure at first. His absence begins to register only in the breakdown of the plantation machine: a sugar boiler overflows; a mule cannot be calmed down. Intangible, but consequential nevertheless: "Nothing has changed but everything is slipping sideways: a kind of chemical decomposition, impalpable but major" (SM 12/27). The everything that has changed includes the crumbling social structures propping up the plantation system, the sense of fear that kept the slave old man on the plantation in the first place, and the cohesiveness of its functioning. The realization, thanks to the cries of his mastiff trained to hunt down and attack marooning slaves, that it is the silent but forever loyal old man who has "gone marooning," slowly shatters the coordinates that give meaning to the master's world: "The Master abruptly realizes that for a long time already, the mastiff has been howling, and that this howling, all by itself, *défolmante*—is dis-in-te-gra-ting—the substance of his world" (SM 13/29).

The master's world further dissolves as his pursuit of the slave old man enters the forest which, though he views it as a virgin space outside of time, in fact harbors various histories that decenter his world and sense of self. For the master, the Great Woods is outside of time, whereas for the slave old man it is his only possibility of escape from the historical immobility of the plantation, however unaware he is of the variety of temporalities it contains. The slave old man suffers a similar transformation, but one that takes on a very different significance from the destructuring the master experiences.[4] The space outside of the plantation is thus a place *in between* two worlds: it is a space of pure exteriority for the master, outside of the coordinates that define his sense of self. Likewise for the slave old man, who has left the confines of the plantation, but has not yet entered a recognizable territory:

> The forest interior was still in the grip of a millenary night. Like a cocoon of aspirating spittle. Another world. Another reality. The old man could have run with his eyes closed: nothing could orient him. (SM 39/59)

For the slave old man, however, this profound disorientation affects everything; it is generated out of the complete dissolution of any horizon of meaning. He can't make sense of his surroundings:

> His mind warps. Slowly. He glimpses forms: troubled, troubling, all threatening. Impossible to identify. They come from nothingness. They flow toward him. There is this. There is that. They are legion, of all sorts without kinds or categories. (SM 52/72)

In the space of the Great Woods, the slave old man cannot identify anything except the most anonymous forms: a "this" and a "that," things "without kinds or categories." Nothing registers to him as familiar or meaningful, as a point through which he can orient himself or locate himself in a territory: "He no longer even knew where the sky was, where the earth lay palpitating, which side was his left, where to go to the right" (SM 40/61). For both the slave old man and the master, the Great Woods is a vast disorder that functions in two very different ways. For the master, it is a part of the Earth that has not yet been tamed by his historical mission, a space not yet colonized by his imperatives. But though he might *imagine* the Great Woods as virginal or untamed, it in fact contains the traces of his crimes, which will come to haunt his legacy into the future and portend the inevitable collapse of the plantation world he helped create. For the slave old man, the Great Woods is also a disintegration of the world of the plantation—the only one he really knows; but this disintegration becomes a space in which he encounters the traces of the extinct worlds it condemned to death, all of which embody a different way of inhabiting the Earth. The slave old man is, in other words, encountering an Earth absent *both* the plantation world *and* the worlds it exterminated, and it is only in that space and through that encounter that a transition to another world, neither his nor the plantation's, becomes possible. For the slave old man, the Great Woods is an aperture between worlds that invokes a future he will never live to see.

That aperture begins to affect the slave old man as he gradually undergoes a transformation defined by a changed relation to the Earth, understood as the ground of worlds distinct from the plantation, even though such worlds no longer exist. This transformation is at first expressed grammatically: As he ventures deeper into the Great Woods, the slave old man changes from the third person "he" to a narrating "I":

> The things around him were formless, moving, as if seen through very clear water. I opened my eyes wide to see better, and the world was born without any veil of modesty. A vegetal whole in an imperious evening dew. I . . . The leaves were many, green in infinite ways, as well as ochre, yellow, maroon, crinkled dazzling, indulging themselves in sacred disorder. I . . . The vines sought out the ground to mix themselves up some more, try rooting, sprouting buds. I could lift up my eyes and see these trees that had appeared so terrifying to me in the great-robes of the night. I could gaze on them at last. (SM 66/89)

This "I" is now no longer the slave old man but "the old man who had been a slave" (SM 62/84). He opens his eyes, and the Great Woods begins to appear less formless and imposing. As a subject rather than an object, he is finally able to differentiate elements of the forest around him: "I, who had envied their [plants] impassive postures, I recognized them, I tried to name them, create them, re-create them" (SM 67/90). His apparent subjectification at first allows him to open the possibility of a different horizon of meaning from the one to which he is accustomed. His ability to name and differentiate things appears to make the forest suddenly accessible, giving it meaning, articulating it through a set of taxonomies and categorizations that shape it into a world.

But whose world is this, exactly? The sudden transformation of the old man who had been a slave into a narrative "I" entails more than just his freedom from the plantation. In fact, he is not yet a fully free subject: The master is still pursuing him and has conscripted his gigantic terrifying dog—the mastiff—to locate him and reclaim him. What he can suddenly see in the terrain is not a world of his own, but the traces of *other* worlds, some of which are extinct, and for which he becomes the conduit. If his marronage has merely hinted at a space outside the plantation where other worlds are possible, he slowly begins to discern the traces of prior ones. The Great Woods is in fact a site of history that is indiscernible to the master but available to the old man who had been a slave not as "his own" world, but thanks to the collapse of the plantation world to which he formerly belonged. The Great Woods is thus not itself a world of its own—rather it is the trace of other worlds, other cosmologies, that predate the plantation system and render it contingent or conditional and, above all, guilty of genocide. Unlike the dream of the master, who sees the Great Woods as empty, worldless in the sense of an empty space waiting to be conquered or transformed into his world, the old man who had been a slave understands that same worldlessness as housing extinct civilizations. When he names the trees, for example, he does so according to a knowledge he himself could not possibly have, but according to a set of incommensurable worlds to which the landscape testifies: "The immense Gum trees destined for *drivée*, ocean drifting," and "the Breadfruit trees planted by the Maroons" (SM 68/90–91) are a text, referencing the history of early indigenous peoples—the sailing vessels they carved out of gum trees—as well as the food source of maroon communities on the island. The Great Woods, in other words, is not a mere "wilderness" outside the confines of the plantation—it is marked by worlds and peoples the plantation world systematically exterminated and enslaved.[5] The old man who had been a slave is therefore not creating the world anew, but has simply become able to *read* the landscape, to see its status as housing the traces of other modes of existence.

The traces of these other worlds are located only in the Great Woods—a part of the Earth capable of registering the time out of mind that precedes every world. The Earth thereby predates both the plantation *and* the worlds it has consigned to oblivion, and for Chamoiseau, as with Clare, it is not simply a planet; instead the Earth is an unconditional temporal anteriority, a "primordiality" the Great Woods exemplify. Through the Great Woods, the Earth is revealed to the old man who had been a slave as a worldless space that is nevertheless the basis for an encounter with other unfamiliar, albeit vanished, worlds. He does not enter a *new* world by fleeing to the Great Woods. Rather his marronage culminates in an exposure to a multiplicity of prior worlds to which he does not belong. That exposure ultimately imbues him with the worldlessness of the Earth, and he internalizes it both figuratively and literally, giving him a sense of power, a "puissance well beyond life and death"

(SM 68–69/91). This sense of power is linked with a temporality beyond not just his own individual existence, but also with a "constancy" antecedent to every cosmology or horizon of meaning capable of situating him in relation to the Earth:

> I was eating earth [*Je mangeais de la terre*]. It dissolved warm on my tongue with an aroma of caverns and salt. The earth endowed me with a feeling of puissance well beyond life and death. And the earth initiated me into constancies I recognized as august and everlasting. (SM 68–69/91)

The ambiguity of the word *terre* here as both soil or land and as a metaphor for something nearly "everlasting," suggests that the Great Woods is all three: a soil or land laced with a temporality irreducible to the world of the plantation, which thereby relativizes it, revealing the possibility of that world's dissolution while harboring the trace of other relations to the Earth. In turn, this opens the prospect of another world to come, if not now, then in a future beyond the old man's lifetime.

This notion of a world to come is decidedly lacking in the master's experience of the Great Woods, since, unlike the old man, he remains bound to the plantation world—his very sense of self and purpose defined by it. And unlike the old man, the Great Woods' anteriority to that world provokes fear, shame, and terror rather than any sense of possibility:

> He had fought so hard to clear this land, beat back the savages, attend to those *nègres*, present to barbarities the beauty of plantations and the sugar sciences. His life had been nothing but courage and suffering, work and exhaustion, fevered thoughts and heartfelt anxieties. And yet, in spite of these fatigues, the Master slept quite badly. He detected in himself tumultuous shames foreign to the courages he deployed or his heroics as a mighty builder. (SM 79/103–4)

The forest and its silence, its exteriority to the world of his certainties, fundamentally unsettles him. As the mastiff breaks off to pursue the old man's scent, a profound solitude descends on the master: "He was there, alone among those trees, and those places, and the heroism of the personal chronicle he kept no longer carried much weight" (SM 79/104). The beliefs that make up his world, the rightness of his actions and his justified place in it, are contrasted with the "before time" represented by the woods: "the Great Woods that knew the Before, that harbored the communion host of an innocence gone by" (SM 80–

81/105). The very same sense of "constancy" or antecedence of the Earth the old man experiences as a break with the world of the plantation is precisely what deracinates the master's sense of self because it reveals the essential precariousness of his world, opening onto a space he cannot read, and from which his world is absent. In this other space the master begins to question the naturalness or givenness of the assumptions that hold his world together, among them "the divine right that sanctified his actions" (SM 80/105). The Earth's longevity, then, is more than just a primordial past, it is what precedes and thus carries off the master's sense of sovereignty.

As the old man runs deeper into the forest pursued by the mastiff, he discovers the Stone covered with symbols carved into it by past Amerindian inhabitants of Martinique. But unlike the stones located in Montravail Forest that I referenced above, the one in the novel is a palimpsest of *innumerable* past civilizations. When the old man first uncovers it, the Stone is unrecognizable, much like the initially formless forest. Like the Great Woods in general, the Stone is revealed to be of the Earth in a specific way: "It could have been a tree but it climbs to no brightness. No foliage augments it. The thing is compressed, compact, dense with itself, related more to the earth" (SM 98/125). Despite its density and connection with the Earth, the old man does not feel that it is "lifeless": it is, as he later puts it, "the Stone that dreams" (*la Pierre qui rêve)* (SM 100/126), and it provokes in him waking visions through a nebulous relation to a past he cannot fully grasp or understand. The Stone is not the *cause* of these visions, though: As the old man insists, "the Stone does not speak to me" (SM 102/129). Instead, its very existence, and the unknown writing on its surface, constitute the only memory of the vanished worlds the Stone commemorates: It is "the ultimate matter of these existences" (SM 102/130). And so the old man's dreams aren't exactly spirits returning from the dead, coming to fill the silences left in the wake of their departure. They flow instead from the materiality of the Stone itself, from an Earth that harbors an irrecuperable past provoking him to visualize the "before time" of those vanished worlds through the transmission of traces on the Stone in the register of the imagination.[6] As previously, the worlds of which the Stone is the only vestige are not the old man's—which is why they must be visualized or imagined—but as with his relation to the Great Woods, through the Stone he gains access to an impossible knowledge beyond anything sanctioned by his own world.

It is here that Chamoiseau's two main novels highlighting the Earth (*Cru-*

soe's Footprint and *Slave Old Man*) cross paths. In *Footprint*, the main character also undergoes a transformation when he first encounters the footprint of another he initially names "Sunday." Each time he returns to the footprint he engages in a renewed reflection on his relationship with other island inhabitants, both human and nonhuman. However, until the very end the narrator ultimately understands that relationship as contemporary with himself. It is only once he grasps what the old man encounters in the Great Woods (through the Stone) that the narrator's transformation from the "idiot" to the "small man" to "the artist" capable of engendering a new narrative of "origins" takes shape. A relation to the other through the footprint depends on a relation to the Earth that is at least *potentially* noncontemporaneous:

> I no longer looked at the footprint trying to understand it, or even to surmise some origin; it was here, inscribed in the mass of clay coated in sand; the footprint was ageless, had neither beginning nor end; it must have certainly been there even before I lived on this planet; perhaps it came from prehistoric times, and its relationship with the shape of my foot only originated in my poor senses. (CF 147/217)

The footprint, in other words, is suddenly altered in its meaning once it is connected with the anteriority of the Earth. The narrator entertains the possibility that it is not the footprint of a contemporary who shares the new world he is attempting to create, but comes instead from "prehistoric times," predating the slowly shifting horizon of meaning he is just beginning to reconstruct. This belated encounter with the anteriority of the Earth is likewise the central aspect of the old man's encounter with the stone, and it is only once it takes place that something like the creation of a *new* world in the face of an encounter with the past becomes possible.

What begins to take shape in *Slave Old Man*, then, is a gradual opening to another world after the horrors of the plantation, one that combines various aspects of the past: the gods of multiple religions and other traces that take on new resonance in the present. The old man who had been a slave experiences a moment that connects him, through the Earth, to those past worlds via

> A coming together of exiles and gods, failures and conquests, bondage and death. All that . . . whirls in a movement of life: life alive on this earth. The Earth. We are all the Earth [*Nous sommes toute la Terre*]. (SM 101/128)

This "coming together" is not predicated on a knowledge of, or identification with, the past; the old man is not taking on the belief and traditions of the indigenous cultures represented on the Stone. Instead, as this passage suggests, and as is the case with the Great Woods, the Stone invokes a relation to a past in which the old man was never present, a past that nonetheless displaces the contours of the world to which he once belonged by invoking an impossible conjunction of the present with prior cosmologies, prior worlds. The fact that those prior worlds no longer exist suggests that the Stone, like the Great Woods, is a figure for a worldlessness reminding the present that it too can, and perhaps will, cease to exist. The old man experiences a "coming together" emphasizing how the Earth, having hosted worlds that are no more, also promises the possibility of worlds to come. Hence the strange third-person plural identification with the Earth: "We are all the Earth" signifies a collectivity fractured by a temporal disjunction enacted not just by genocide and the violence of the plantation, but also by the Earth as a past prior to each and every world, including bygone ones. As that antecedence, the Earth is both what bears their traces (in the Stone) and invokes the eventual collapse of present horizons of meaning. It thereby promises a world to come through the figure of an Earth that may yet make possible another collective "we."

The Stone itself is marked with a series of discrete non-overlapping languages and temporalities—like the Great Woods, nothing about it is untouched. And it presents a succession of worlds or civilizations with distinct cosmologies and origin stories. In short, rather than a single vanished civilization, it represents several, a sequence that takes place only in a time out of mind. However, that time is not some utopian atemporality. It is the palimpsest of a series of worlds the memory of which has been lost save for the Stone, each one effaced by the next without any continuity between them:

> Not one crumb of the Stone has remained virgin. . . . The engravers succeeded one another for times-without-times. Neither the same peoples, nor the same tools, nor the same intentions. A *ouélélé*- tumult of myths and Geneses. (SM 101/128–29)

Doris Garraway has argued that through the figure of the Stone, the novel generates a "creole myth of origins," an "*ailleurs mythique*"—a mythic elsewhere—in contrast to the present. The intermingling of the old man and the Stone, she claims, "occurs not in the one-dimensional time of history, but that of myth; that is, an atemporal dream-space of supernatural fantasies, visions and folkloric allusions that interact with the historical real without being reducible to it."[7] However, it is not clear at all that the "origins" of the Stone are unified or continuous. In fact, the Stone appears as quite the opposite: It is a "tumult of myths and Geneses" in the unspecified plural rather than a unified origin story. Each epoch represented on the Stone supplants and writes over the next, each world's cosmology and language being effaced by the one that follows it, each origin story ultimately lost in "times-without-times." The Stone unites these worlds, but only to the extent that it is marked by their mere succession and noncontemporaneity with each other. If the novel asks us to consider that "we are all the Earth," then that "we," which is supposed to span the temporal succession of worlds inscribed on the stone, is certainly "mythic," but only insofar as that term supposes an imaginative *act* rather than a timeless origin story. The Stone is not outside of history: each of the worlds represented on its surface were once "alive on the earth." And while it tells a communal story of a "we," it is a "we" not predicated on "a shared cultural heritage traceable to a particular moment and place of origin." Rather, the Stone is a marker of an immemorial past that disorients the presumed continuity between past and present, generating a collectivity that does indeed form around a "loss of origins," as Garraway puts it.[8] But such a loss of origins would have to be understood as an "origin myth" without an origin: a sheer reference to an anteriority that destabilizes the present as something it cannot incorporate into a narrative about itself. As with the Great Woods, it marks a "before" not just of displaced or enslaved peoples, but of the Earth itself—an immemoriality older than not only every contemporary world, but past ones as well. The old man who had been a slave becomes aligned with the Earth through the Stone as an inscription or trace of a past to which he does not—and never did—belong, but which returns to haunt the present world that enslaved him, forecasting that world's eventual future dissolution.

And so the old man dies, and at the moment when he reaches "the rib [*une nervure*] of an alliance between life and death, victory and defeat, time and immobility, space and nothingness" (SM 103/130), his connection with the Stone is solidified by collapsing those oppositions. If the Stone, which the old man sees as a "refuge-being" (*être-refuge*) (SM 103/130) does not save him from death, it does allow him to "dissolve [him]self" (SM 103/130) and to be memorialized in his turn. Though he has escaped the world of the plantation and will die "free," he openly wonders about the posterity of his bones:

> Fixed feeling in my bones. My bones. What will they say about me? Like those peoples sheltering in a stone, I will end up as a few lost bones in the depths of these Great Woods. (SM 107/135)

The old man's last thought is the double question of what kind of narrative might form around him after his death, and whether his physical remains, identified now with the Stone, will remain lost in the depths of the woods, forgotten by time and human memory. That narrative retrospectively becomes the narrative of the novel itself and is thus, as Garraway suggests, a turn toward the future, another present—our own—which succeeds both the plantation world and the exterminated worlds of the past, inheriting the stone and the old man's bones in the name of what she calls a "new composite form of humanity"[9] such as Chamoiseau and others have written about elsewhere.[10] The traces of the past, of other worlds that once existed on the Earth, open up an immemoriality that unsettles the present—whether that present is the world of the plantation or a postemancipation world. "We" are thus—thanks to our own encounter with the Stone—faced with an anteriority that places us between a world in the process of collapse and one not yet fully formed.

Once the old man dies next to the stone, the narrative becomes future-directed, narrating what happens with his remains and to the master after his death. The master returns to the plantation, but the marooning of the old man has set into place a dissolution of the master's world that awaits its consummation in the future:

> In him, now, other spaces were bestirring themselves, spaces where he would never go, perhaps, but where one day no doubt, in a future generation, hopefully in the full radiance of their purity and legitimate strength, his children would venture, as one confronts a first misgiving. (SM 109/138)

Surely, the master does not suddenly convert into a postcolonial penitent; he doesn't throw off the world of the plantation. And yet a "space" is created that awaits a future forced to confront the fact that his world has been made possible through the destruction and genocide of others.

The novel's final section moves forward to a time when an amateur historian is guided to the discovery of the Stone and the old man's remains. Like all sections of the novel, this one begins with a citation of Glissant, which poses the question of succession and inheritance:

> The histories, the stories, the doubles, become fewer, come together. The times are given one to the other. Yet who returns to the slope of the morne and digs in the earth? (SM112/140)

Since the old man's bones are discovered next to the Stone, the historian associates them with each other: "I was set on finding out how a vanished people could inhabit us, in what way and what mystery. But all of them—really serious anthropologists, devotees of science—turned down the adventure into this poetic muck" (SM 114/142). The task of finding out "how a vanished people could inhabit us" is not a scientific but a poetic one: It will not involve forensic identification but, as with the old man, an act of imagination that takes as its starting point the antecedence of the bones and of the Stone.

The historian's relationship to that precedence, like the master's and the slave old man's, begins with a temporal dislocation specific to the Earth. The writer describes the stone as "older than timeless": "A volcanic rock. Imagining it astonishing. Covered with Amerindian signs. Guapoïdes. Saladoïdes. Calviny. Cayo. Suazey. Galibis. Every epoch jostling there together" (SM 114/143). The names of the Amerindian peoples the writer identifies through the inscriptions on the Stone date from the neolithic period to the pre-Columbian Arawaks to the Kalina people, descendants of whom survive in parts of South America, making it impossible to identify its exact historical provenance. The same applies to the discovery of the bones, which the historian cannot identify, but which, as in the tale of the old man and his relationship to the Stone, causes the historian to "dream." His dreams are poetic reconstitutions of the past that cannot be authenticated as fact. Though the first dream the historian has after touching the bones suggests they belonged to a "Carib," their derivation is as potentially wide-ranging as the cultures represented on the Stone:

> There was a reason for those bones to trouble me. They could have been from anyone among us. Amerindian. Nègre. Béké. Kouli. Chinese. They spoke an entire epoch, but one open in its uncertain totality. (SM 116/144)

Having shifted the historical perspective from "slavery times" to the twentieth century, the final section of the novel essentially calls into question its entire preceding narrative and highlights the ongoing act of interpretation required to, as the historian puts it, produce "the infinite renaissance of his bones in a new genesis." Just as the old man "intermingled" with the Stone, the lost worlds of the Amerindian peoples and the old man become in their turn a twentieth-century narrative "molded from the great silences of our mingled stories, our intermingled memories," an "uncertain totality" that promises the birth of another world (SM 116/145).

At the end of the novel the significance of the Stone and the bones becomes entirely a question of posterity and inheritance. Chamoiseau extends the idea of the Great Woods as a space external to the world of the plantation into a vision of a *global* "Great Woods" that precipitates a flight outside of every identitarian social structure:

> Facing the Great Woods of the world busy binding itself together. Great Woods of the peoples who bond as brothers, *Territoires qui font Terre*. Territories that make Terra, tongues that hail harmonies. We are all, like my runaway old-fellow, pursued by a monster. To escape our old certainties. Our so-careful moorings. Our cherished reflexes clock-timed into systems. Our sumptuous Truths. In a heady rush toward the unforeseeable to-be-constructed that opens its dangers to us. (SM 117/146)

Circling back to the epigraph that opens the novel with its question, "Does the world have an intention?," the end of the novel affirms that the "Great Woods" of the present is, like the Earth, which remains irreducible to every world, in a space and time *between* worlds, between the bygone worlds of the Amerindians, the bygone world of slaves and the plantation, and another world taking shape through the un-intelligible measure of that past—a multiplicity of territories that "make Earth" (*font Terre*). While this "making Earth" could be said to be the central focus of the second section of Chamoiseau's *Crusoe's Footprint*, where the narrator newly rediscovers his relation to other inhabitants of the island, in *Slave Old Man* it is only a promise. The Earth is thus, in Chamoiseau's earlier novel, that disorienting space of the *between*—between a world that has ceased to be and one that has yet to take shape in the wake of the collapse of past and present horizons of meaning. Because the Earth is irreducible to every world, its antecedence decenters existing ones by maintaining the traces of those that are prior, intimating that the present may someday share their fate. However, at the same time, the Earth, through its inscription of bygone worlds, also promises a future in which that immemoriality once again shapes the present.

Chamoiseau and Hölderlin on the Question of Origins

Chamoiseau's rewriting of *Robinson Crusoe* in *Crusoe's Footprint* is not just an act of literary revision displacing Defoe's colonial version of the Robinsonade, it also highlights his understanding of the relation between literature and history that was already evident in *Slave Old Man*. Literature comes to fill in history's silences, reconstituting the present through a relation to an "unthinkable" past figured by the anteriority of the Earth. In *Footprint*, however, Chamoiseau insists that the narratives and histories made possible by this anteriority must begin with the idea that those origins do not simply lie in the past but come to us from the future. *Crusoe's Footprint* is a case in point: Chamoiseau's rewriting of Defoe displaces the Crusoe myth in a new narrative placing an African Crusoe in a distinctive relation to the Earth that requires overcoming the original story's decidedly colonial relation to the island. Rather than return to the past as origin, Chamoiseau creates a new one—a Robinsonade for the future.

In the concluding section of the novel titled "The Footprint Workshop," then, Chamoiseau invokes Edgar Morin and Martin Heidegger as philosophical fellow travelers who similarly understand origins not as something confined to the past, but as awaiting reinvention in the future: "The origin is modern, and much more, it is ahead of us, as Edgar Morin, like Heidegger, reminds us. And it's true that all life, all art, is worth something only in its relation to the initial unthinkable."[11] As with the memories inscribed on the Stone in *Slave Old Man*, the "initial unthinkable" Chamoiseau references in *Footprint* cannot be fully narratively recuperated. It is both prior to every world and irreducible to its horizon of meaning, as the narrator's final meditation on the noncontemporary significance of the footprint attests: "These useless creations that I had organized around the footprint were just as much signs toward the unknowable, the uncertain, the unthinkable, in which movements, sounds, and disused radiance were found; it had made *an artist* of me; inclined toward the footprint that now seemed to me like the opening of an infinite beginning" (CF 148/218). The footprint, in short, cannot fully become an object of knowledge. But the poetic reinterpretation of its unthinkability becomes a basis for the creation of another narrative, a new way of dwelling on the Earth directed to the future.

This structure of the future anterior similarly defines Heidegger's interest in Hölderlin, whom he understands as taking up a relation to the unthinkable through the prior world of ancient Greece in order to prepare a "new beginning" in the present. However, while Chamoiseau and Heidegger might initially appear to make similar claims about poetry and the unthinkable, they have quite distinct conceptions of the relationship between the unthinkable and the world. What makes the unthinkable "modern" and futural for Chamoiseau and Heidegger is its reinvention by the artist, or poet. For both, this involves the establishment of a new world fundamentally entwined with an unthinkable anteriority that withdraws from it. Chamoiseau's unthinkable, however, unlike Heidegger's, is merely a narrative impetus that can never ultimately be presented or totalized by a horizon of meaning. Heidegger, on the other hand, attempts to *salvage* the "unthinkable" from its historical dispersal to reintegrate it into a coherent horizon of meaning: the history of the West as the history of the forgetting of Being. For Heidegger, the unthinkable maintains itself across time as a selfsame unity, "sent" historically from a starting point—ancient Greece—that must be repeated each time anew.[12] History is thus a single *envoi*—a historical trajectory of ontological decisions determining "what is" that began in Greece and that, Heidegger claims, defines the sequence of Western conceptions of the world up to the present.

In what follows I examine Heidegger's central interlocutor in his articulation of a "new beginning": German Romantic poet Friedrich Hölderlin. For Heidegger, Hölderlin's poetry, in dialogue with the Greeks, is defined by an attempt to enact a new form of revealing or *poesis* laying the ground for a new relation to "what is," in short, for another world. My own reading of Hölderlin, however, questions some of Heidegger's premises, specifically the role the Earth plays in his poetry. For Heidegger, the Earth is just an aspect of the world, part of what is revealed by that world's ontological decision about "what is." By contrast, Hölderlin situates the Earth *between* the departure of one world—ancient Greece—and the possible, though not guaranteed, arrival of another. This "betweenness" of the Earth, which is irreducible to every world, an idea shared with Chamoiseau, disrupts the presumed continuity upon which Heidegger insists, challenging the supposed unity of a single historical trajectory known as "the West." What comes to the fore in Hölderlin's poetry, then, as in Chamoiseau, is a relation through the Earth to a bygone world. But unlike in Heidegger, ancient Greece for Hölderlin has fundamentally and forevermore departed from the face of the Earth, never to return. Greece, for Hölderlin, represents not just an inimitable civilization of the past, but a dead world, implying not just the contingency of every horizon of meaning, but also an encounter with a fundamentally worldless Earth.

In Hölderlin what is encountered in the bygone world of ancient Greece is thus unthinkable in a quite different sense from Heidegger: not a new horizon of meaning, but the Earth as what remains after the collapse of that horizon. Hölderlin's poetry therefore highlights for me a latent aspect of Chamoiseau's geopoetics: Though the Earth is prior to every world, it's anteriority does not remain "intact" as the selfsame unthinkability that underpins the succession of worlds. The Earth for Chamoiseau and Hölderlin would instead be caught in a dispersal without end—remaining essentially worldless through and through. As such, it makes possible a very different history than the one Heidegger envisions being at stake in his reading of Hölderlin. What takes place instead is a history of the *erasure* or dissolution of worlds, rather than their latent or hidden continuity. With Chamoiseau's help, we can better perceive the political and aesthetic consequences of this understanding of history as the articulation of the relation between world and Earth. The instability of that relation in Hölderlin challenges any notion of historical unity and, as in Chamoiseau, renders every world contingent and dependent on a materiality that escapes every structure of sense and signification. The Earth is therefore unthinkable to every former or currently existing world in a way that makes the conception of a future world to come tenuous. That is, the worldlessness of the Earth lays bare not just the contingency of every world, but also each one's exposure to its future disappearance.

The German-speaking world that existed during Hölderlin's main writing career before his madness and confinement in 1806 was certainly in the midst of contemplating not only the dissolution of an old world, but the possible birth of a new one. Modern Germany did not yet exist, and German-speaking territories were divided up into multiple states—vestiges of the Holy Roman Empire whose final dissolution also in 1806 made the prospect of a unified German nation a sudden possibility. As the intelligentsia gradually became obsessed with that thought, the recent failure of the French Revolution intimated that this new Germany would likely have to be molded along the lines of some nonrepublican image.[13] As Philippe Lacoue-Labarthe and Jean-Luc Nancy have suggested, this image often took the form of myth—specifically the imitation of ancient Greece—as a means by which to produce "models or types . . . in imitation of which an individual, or a city, or an entire people, can grasp themselves and identify themselves."[14] A primary example of this notion of the imitation of the Greeks as the means by which to found a new Germany can be found in the lasting influence of eighteenth-century art historian Johann Winckelmann, who was influential not just for artists interested in neoclassical form, but even for his Romantic-era inheritors who broke with these forms but took seriously his contention that "the only way for us to become great or, if this be possible, inimitable, is to imitate the ancients."[15] This imperative in many ways set the stage for the specific form of Hellenism that was ubiquitous in the Romantic period: for Winckelmann and his heirs, the Greeks in their inimitability must be repeated, revivified, *as* the nascent German nation, and as the unity and historical consistency of "the West." The myth of Greece as a model for Germany, one that could avoid the fate of the French Revolution, would thereby take the form of a repetition not of Greece's political forms (i.e., the city-state), but rather of its inaugural grandeur: the flourishing of its art and culture.

Hölderlin's early works, specifically his early ancient-Greek style tragedies written for modern audiences, aren't immune to this identificatory mechanism. His poetics is largely defined by its engagement with ancient literary forms, from Greek tragedy to the ode. However, the fact that Hölderlin makes an encounter with the Earth central to his relation to the bygone world of the Greeks, separates him from most of his contemporaries. Distinct from all worlds, yet the very condition of their possibility, the Earth for Hölderlin situates us, just as in Chamoiseau, between two worlds in the "between time" (*dürftiger Zeit*)—between a world that has come and gone, and another yet to come. Unlike his contemporaries, Hölderlin questioned the need for Germany's mimetic relationship to ancient Greece.[16] His poetics explicitly reflects on the death of Greek cosmology—the departure of a world that can never return—the effect of which is profoundly disorienting because the void it leaves behind disables easy identification with an ancestor. If his European contemporaries conceived history as a succession of cosmologies from the Greeks to the present—and this is above all how the European West understood its own teleological trajectory—Hölderlin's ideas about history are closer to the palimpsest on Chamoiseau's Stone: history as a series of discontinuous worlds.[17] This space "between" the two worlds is marked for Hölderlin by the collapse of *any* cosmology—each world's conception of the divine. The Earth, to begin with, is opposed both to the multiplicity of Greek gods as well as the Christian monotheism of the contemporary world.[18] What ultimately emerges in Hölderlin's poetry, however, is an Earth that has twisted free *entirely* of its place in any world, ancient or modern. It remains, in short, unthinkable by either the Greeks or the moderns, which is why Hölderlin describes this between time as a "wandering below the unthinkable,"[19] a drifting on an Earth stripped of any orienting cosmology.

Hölderlin's geopoetics, then, as I will argue, portrays a ceaseless historical "drifting" on the Earth without any return to an origin. Thus, while his writing often *appears* to use the language of Greek tragedy or myth, he is aware that these forms and the world that produced them have forever vanished and cannot become the means of identification for another one. The reason he uses Greek forms at all is in fact to convey the finality of that disappearance, and to intimate the necessity of a different relationship to the past based not on imitation but on a fundamental rupture that undoes any identification with it. That historical rupture, for Hölderlin, provokes not just a reconceptualization of the relation between Earth and world, but also a much more disjunctive history that disarticulates any identity of Germany or "the West." The Earth in Hölderlin is displaced from every cosmology: it thereby destabilizes every solid sense of ground, every *Heimat, homeland,* or *habitus,* since these all imply a world in which those words or concepts have a sense or meaning. In an encounter with the Earth, Hölderlin's geopoetics is exposed, as in Chamoiseau, to a reconceptualization of what it means to be a "people" across multiple temporal and historical divides and ruptures.

Hölderlin, the Ancients, and the Earth

The Earth is everywhere in Hölderlin, though often only sporadically. Since it first appears in some of his early works where he revisits Attic tragedy, this is where I start as well: from his early play *The Death of Empedocles* and his outline for it in the prose work "Ground for Empedocles." To provide a kind of road map for these difficult works, however, I begin by unfolding a text from the same period (1799–1800)—"On the Difference of Poetic Modes"—that lays out Hölderlin's main aesthetic and poetic ideas about the relation between Greek and modern literature. The Greeks interested Hölderlin intensely, though not, as one might presume, for their purported originary significance which sparked Germany's nineteenth-century craze for all things Hellenistic. On the contrary, Hölderlin was attracted to the *demise* of the Greeks, in part because by comprehending the finality of a bygone world, one touches upon the potential organizing principles of one's own. Resorting to defunct aesthetic forms, then, allowed him to better grasp not only the relation between the forms of presentation specific to the Greek world and their connection to the collapse of the political, religious, and cultural structures that underpinned it, but also how relations between modern modes of presentation and those other structures might be at work in contemporary art forms. And because every cosmology, including the Greek, articulates a relation between the Earth and the cosmos, the collapse of the ancient Greek world propelled Hölderlin straight to the Earth. This genealogy extends to his later river poems which I also touch on, wherein Hölderlin depicts a "wandering below the unthinkable" as being caught between the death of the Greek world and their gods on the one hand, and the absence of any new forms of presentation—any new world—capable of making sense of humanity's new relation to the Earth on the other. This wandering, far from producing the unity of a world called "the West," leaves the poet adrift, without place or home on an Earth fundamentally withdrawn from any horizon of meaning.

"On the Difference of Poetic Modes" is not just a treatise on aesthetics, it is also Hölderlin's clearest expression of his conception of the relation between art forms, their modes of presentation, and the world to which they belong. "Difference" thus spells out how Hölderlin understands not only the relation between modern and ancient art—and therefore the relation between two different worlds—but also how forms of expression change or alternate across time. There Hölderlin suggests that the "alternation of tones" at work within a particular art form is thus also a theory of history, of the way in which the relation between form and expression reflects a specific historical moment.[20] What distinguishes different genres, along with the historical specificity of a work of art, is the relationship between what Hölderlin calls the work's "underlying tone" or *Grundton*—its basic meaning—and its "mode of presentation" or *Darstellung*. This relationship varies from work to work, but it also varies *within* each work through an oscillation that never arrives at their final "alignment." That is, any particular form of expression can never quite fully be integrated with its content, producing an interminable oscillation between two poles Lacoue-Labarthe has called the Hölderlinian logic of "de-distancing" or *Ent-Fernung*: "the more *x* something is, the more *y* it is," that is, the closer it is, the more distant, the more interior it is, the more exterior.[21] For Hölderlin, that tension between form and content, meaning and expression, defines what might be called the aesthetic regime of a particular world, demarcating not just "what is" but also what can be *said* about what is.

At stake in Hölderlin's theory of the alternation of tones is the relation between ancient Greek modes of aesthetic expression—tragedy in particular, because it represents, among other things, the relation between humanity and the gods—and the way those ancient aesthetic forms need to be rearticulated in the present, given that moderns are no longer grounded in Greek cosmology. The alternation of tones found in Greek tragedy conveys, for Hölderlin, the contours of its world, expressing its vision of the relations between nature and culture, gods and humans, that are specific to its historical moment.

However, each work of art worthy of the name also, thanks to the alternation of tones specific to it, gradually overcomes those distinctions, pushing them to their breaking point, extending them beyond their specific historical form. Located within each art form, according to Hölderlin, is the articulation of the internal contradictions defining a particular world that eventually leads to its dissolution. The Greek world didn't vanish thanks to a natural disaster or foreign invasion, for Hölderlin, but because its internal contradictions, expressed most intensely in its art, were pushed beyond a certain limit, remaining fundamentally unreconcilable. When Hölderlin examines Greek lyric, for instance, he suggests that it, like every aesthetic form, is structured by its failure to resolve the oppositions that define its world, a failure that can be mapped onto the difference between the work's "underlying tone" and its "expression":

> In its *basic mood* the lyric poem is the *more sensuous*, in that this [basic mood] contains a unity which lends itself most easily; precisely for that reason does it not strive in the outer appearance for reality, serenity and gracefulness; it evades the sensuous connection and presentation so much (because the pure basic tone inclines precisely toward it) that it is rather miraculous and supernatural in its formations and assembly of these. (PW 83/889)

Though conveyed in a somewhat convoluted way, the basic principle of the alternation of tones remains the same throughout its various permutations: a work's tendency toward one or another form of presentation is paradoxically the means by which that tendency is refracted or displaced and ultimately overcome. Thus, while Peter Szondi is right to suggest that "the alternation of tones becomes the law of Hölderlin's poetry" and that "the contrasting tension between the underlying tone and the art character becomes its structure," it is not so clear that "the gesture of the voice, which introduces the third (or next) tone becomes the authority that guarantees the resolution of the contradiction."[22] In fact, Hölderlin's theory of poetry, and the theory of history that accompanies it, is organized by a series of oscillations between tone and mode of presentation that *never* resolve.

So where, then, does the Earth enter into Hölderlin's discussion of art as the bearer of the internal contradictions specific to a particular world? If the Earth is encountered in the interstice between worlds or cosmologies, then it comes to the fore only in the death of a world—the moment when its internal contradictions no longer oscillate between form and expression but *collapse entirely*, that is, when no new mode of presentation comes to the fore.

Which brings us to Hölderlin's early attempts to write a tragedy: In a seemingly paradoxical sense, his effort to write an Attic-style tragedy—*The Death of Empedocles*—was not an attempt to imitate the Greeks, but was an endeavor to repeat in the present the relation between tone and expression that brought about that world's dissolution. In "Ground for Empedocles," a prose work detailing the theoretical background defining his attempt to write the play, he outlines the problem in these terms: He did not attempt to write a Greek tragedy or revive the world of the dead Greek gods. Instead, he tried to write a modern tragedy expressed through a Greek mode of presentation to discover its obverse: a tragedy for the modern European, specific to the world to which *he* belongs. *The Death of Empedocles*, in other words, was supposed to bridge the gulf between ancient Greek tragedy and whatever that aesthetic form or mode of presentation could possibly signify for a modern European. By witnessing the death of one world, another, possibly, comes to be born in its wake, out of an alternation of tones and modes of expression specific to modernity, albeit derived from the Greeks.

All three versions of the play Hölderlin composed feature the outcome foretold by the work's title: Empedocles throws himself into a volcano, symbolizing not just his own death, but the death of his world—a return to the Earth in the face of the death of the Greek gods. Hölderlin's *Death of Empedocles* thus unfolds the tension between the initial stability of the Greek world and its eventual dissolution. This undoing brings about the end of Empedocles's world, but it also exposes him to an Earth that has begun to twist free of its place within Greek cosmology. Empedocles embodies the internal contradictions of his world, and therefore Empedocles "is a son of his heaven and his time, of his fatherland, a son of tremendous oppositions of nature and art in which the world appeared before his eyes" (PW 54/2:118–19). But he is also "a victim of his time" (*ein Opfer seiner Zeit*) (PW 57/2:121) because he is unable to reconcile the opposition between nature and art that governs the Greek world. As a sacrifice, his death represents the death of ancient Greece: the destiny of his epoch "demanded a sacrifice where man in his entirety becomes real and visible as that wherein the destiny of his epoch seems to dissolve, where the extremes seem to unite truly and visibly in one but therefore are united too closely" (PW 56/2:121). In other words, by failing to reconcile the tensions that define the world to which he belongs, Empedocles ultimately brings about its end, a process Hölderlin elsewhere defines as "a becoming in dissolution" (*Das Weden im Vergehen*).[23] The "fatherland" Hölderlin references in *The Death of Empedocles* is not a geographic place or spiritual identity; it is the way in which a particular world conceives the relation between art and its conception of nature:

> The declining fatherland, nature and man, insofar as they bear a particular relation of reciprocity, insofar as they constitute a special world which has become ideal and [constitute] a union of things and insofar as they dissolve, so that from the world and from the remaining ancestry and forces of nature, which are the other real principle, there emerge a new world, a new yet also particular reciprocal relation just as that decline emerged from a pure yet particular world.[24]

The "fatherland in decline," in this case is a Greek world that, in Hölderlin's early attempt to write a Greek tragedy, contains at least the *hope* that the alternation of poetic tones, the overcoming of the modes of presentation specific to ancient Greece, will give way to a "new world," a new mode of presentation, a new way of representing the relation between the divine and the human, nature and art and all of the defining features of a particular world specific to modern Germany. We arrive at modern Germany not through an imitation of the Greeks, in other words, but through their overcoming.

What emerges on the other side of the death of ancient Greece in *Empedocles*, however, is not modern Europe, but the Earth. All three versions of the play end with Empedocles's suicide, but the play deals with little else but his world's "dissolution": "For when a country [*ein Land*] is about to die, its spirit at the end / Selects but one among the many, one alone through whom / Its swan song, the final breaths of life, will sound."[25] The play, in other words, doesn't quite yet articulate the transition to a "new world," which is only hinted at toward the end of the third and final version of the play, which breaks off fragmentarily with the chorus proclaiming a "new world" that contrasts with the Earth:

> New World
>   and it looms, a brazen vault
>   the sky above us, curse lames
>   the limbs of humankind, and the nourishing, gladdening
>   gifts of the earth are like chaff, she
>   mocks us with her presents, our mother
>   and all is semblance—(DE 188/1:152)

We are thus left at the end with a heaven that has become an empty "brazen vault," and a Greek world that has become nothing but "semblance" (*Schein*), while the "gifts of the Earth" have become "chaff" (*Spreu*), suggesting an Earth viewed as a mere husk, left over from a former plenitude that has now vanished. Though Hölderlin's notes for the continuation of the third version describe Empedocles as "one in and through whom a world dissolves and in the same instant renews itself" (DE 194/2:154), that renewal is never finally articulated in the play, and so we are left not with a new world, but with a barren sky emptied of the gods, and an Earth that "mocks us with her presents."

The three versions of *Empedocles* all thus promise a "new world" that is supposed to emerge out of Empedocles's sacrifice, but what they in fact articulate is simply the death of Greek cosmology and the emergence of an Earth no longer framed by it. Hölderlin's early attempts to write a tragedy, then, while promising the image of "a new world," in fact lands squarely on the Earth. The Earth interrupts that process and introduces a between that, in the early Hölderlin, creates a rupture in the passage between the old declining "fatherland" of the Greeks and the new world that decline promises. Thus, when Hölderlin finally abandoned the project of writing *Empedocles*—each draft was essentially incomplete—and took on the task of translating Sophocles into German for modern audiences, what came progressively to the fore was the role the Earth plays in that transition, and the way in which it acts as a hiatus—a caesura—that interrupts the continuity between then and now, Greek and modern.[26] An actual translation of existing Greek tragedy—Sophocles's *Oedipus Rex* and *Antigone* specifically—into modern modes of presentation would require understanding how Attic tragedy not only already contains within it the contradictions that will give way to the collapse of the Greek world, but also how it hints at an encounter with the Earth as what emerges in the absence of that world, as it does at the end of the third version of *Empedocles*. Translating Attic forms into modern terms, modern modes of presentation, then, also leads to a "translation" of a reflection on the end of the world, except this time the world in question becomes the possible end of the *contemporary* one. In other words, when Hölderlin moves from attempting to write his own Greek tragedy to unpacking the latent internal contradictions in Sophocles, he surreptitiously reflects on the rupture between the Greeks and the moderns, a rupture figured by a return to the Earth as a space irreducible to either world.

The translations themselves are notoriously difficult and "loose" in the sense that they are so nonliteral one could essentially say that Hölderlin was rewriting Sophocles. However, his notes to both translations ("Notes to Oedipus" and "Notes to Antigone") clarify what is at stake: Both focus on what he calls the point of "real separation" (*wirklichen Trennung*) between the Greek world and modern "Hesperia" or Europe—a point of separation he will later identify with the Earth. To describe the emergence of this moment in each play, Hölderlin introduces the distinction between what he calls "organic" tendencies within a particular form, by which he means its tendency toward a relative stability, and a form's "aorgic" tendency toward formlessness or dissolution. The "organic" represents a tendency toward a more or less stable but regulated order, whereas the "aorgic" represents a tendency toward disorder—the coming undone of a particular temporary equilibrium.

The highest point of the tension between these two tendencies Hölderlin names either the "caesura" of the play, or the "real separation" that brings about, as in his own play, the dissolution of the Greek world:

> And here, in the excess of spirit within unity, in its striving for materiality, in the striving of the divisible, more infinite aorgic which must contain all that is more organic . . . in this striving for separation of the divisible infinite, which in the state of highest unity of everything organic imparts itself to all parts contained by this unity, in this necessary *arbitrariness of Zeus* there actually lies the ideal beginning of the real separation. (PW 85–86/1:892–93)

Identifying the "arbitrariness of Zeus" with the "real separation" or caesura of the play, Hölderlin goes on in "Notes to Antigone" to suggest that "Zeus"—which stands for the central principle organizing a world's cosmology (he is, after all, king of the gods)—is also the point at which that world's limits are reached and overcome. Zeus is both the organizer of a world's cosmology, its religious, social, and natural categories and hierarchies, *and* what, in its absence, causes those categories to dissolve. Moreover, there is no dialectical resolution to this tension, since its main representative (Zeus) is purely "arbitrary"; as a figure for the lynchpin of Greek cosmology, Zeus is unable to reconcile a "striving for materiality" and a "striving for separation of the divisible infinite" with Greek conceptions of the divine. What results is the internal collapse of Greek cosmology, provoked by the irreconcilable organic and aorgic tendencies found within it.

Unlike in *Empedocles*, however, the motif of the Earth does not appear until the collapse of the Greek world has been "translated" into modern modes of presentation. If in the Greek world, "Zeus" is the pivotal cosmological figure, what exactly constitutes the modern "Zeus"? In "Notes on Antigone," Hölderlin addresses this question by framing the "real separation" specific to Europe (or Hesperia) in terms of a "reversal" that occurs in Sophocles's play when Kreon and Antigone both appeal to Zeus as a principle of divine order. Their appeals are to the same god—Zeus as ultimate arbiter of what is just and true—but in each appeal "Zeus" represents something completely different. For Kreon, Zeus represents a traditional form of divine authority, a law giver whose edicts must be followed. For Antigone, Zeus's divine status is inverted into its opposite and given a distinctly earthly significance. For her, Zeus is "father of time or: father of earth, for it is his character, opposing the eternal tendency, to reverse the striving from this world to the other into a striving from another world to this one" (PW 112/2:454). Calling Zeus the "father of time or father of the Earth" encapsulates for Hölderlin the fundamental historical rupture between Greeks and Hesperians. Françoise Dastur's answer to the question "Why did Hölderlin translate the Greek name 'Zeus' by the expression 'father of time'?" is helpful to understand what is at stake: "Simply because the name Zeus no longer means anything to us, whereas it had meaning to the Greeks who still knew what they were saying when they used the name Zeus. For us this name is something conventional, 'positive,' dead."[27] "Zeus" is thus both the Greek world's name for the central figure or principle of its cosmology, *and*, thanks to Hölderlin's "translation" of the play into modern forms of presentation, a gesture toward what "comes next" after the death of the Greek world—what grounds and stabilizes the modern world.

That stability, however, never arrives. Hölderlin's "translation" of Zeus into modern Hesperia does not open another world. Instead, "Zeus" becomes a placeholder, an empty form, standing in for a moment when the name signified something divine, though it no longer does. Antigone's appeal reverses the striving in the play for a transcendent or divine law in favor of one grounded in a strictly temporal order.[28] This reversal, however, makes Zeus the "father of Earth" because he points to the "highest" (the *arche* or organizing principle of the cosmology to which he belongs) as "lawless" (*gesetzlos*):

> Once, that which characterizes the Antitheos, where someone, in the sense of god, acts as if against god and recognizes the spirit of the highest as lawless. Then the pious fear of destiny, thus the praise of god as something

> preordained. This is the spirit of the two impartially contrasted opposites in the chorus. Antigone acting more in the first sense. Kreon in the second. (PW 112/2:455)

Whereas Kreon appeals to Zeus as the representative of divine and tragic destiny, Antigone's appeal to Zeus as an "Antitheos" emphasizes his "lawlessness" or arbitrariness,[29] a divine that has fundamentally absconded. Hölderlin's reading of Sophocles at this point is aligned with Jean-Pierre Vernant's suggestion that "the tragic universe lies between two worlds,"[30] a past age of myth that was still present (Kreon), and the values of the new political order that emerge in and through the collapse of the world of myth (Antigone).[31] Hölderlin's identification of Zeus with the Earth would thus appear to be a name for a juridical-political order no longer founded on theological structures.

However, in a further development of the Earth motif, Hölderlin makes clear that this reversal is not "ours" as moderns. It is not enough to say that the Greeks believed in the divine and we moderns do not. It is not *Hesperians* who are in the midst of a reversal that undoes the configuration of their world—it is the Greeks. In other words, the collapse of the divine, and the turn toward an Earthly "Zeus" read in terms of its opposition to the divine, is a contradiction specific to the collapsed world of *the Greeks*. The reversal from the divine to the Earth brings about the tragic end of *their* world.

For us moderns, by contrast, for whom a "lack of destiny" (*das Schicksallose*) (PW 114/2:456) is our essential attribute, the earthward turn must be understood differently. "Our Zeus" is anything but divine, and anything but a higher principle of order or justice:

> For us, existing under the more real Zeus who not only stays between this earth and the ferocious world of the dead, but who also forces the eternally anti-human course of nature on its way to another world *more decidedly down onto earth*, and since this greatly changes the essential and patriotic representations, and since our poetry must be patriotic so that its themes are selected according to our world-view and their representations, for us, then, the Greek representations change insofar as it is their chief tendency to comprehend themselves. (PW 113/2:456)

Displaced from the opposition between the terrestrial and the heavenly, "our Zeus" abandons any reference to transcendence whatsoever, any reference to "another world"—even one that has been withdrawn.[32] This abandonment has a concomitant effect: the Earth Hesperians are forced to confront is even more alien than the Greek world since it can no longer be comprehended in opposition to the divine. Our Zeus is a "god" in name only, who "forces the eternally anti-human course of nature on its way to another world *more decidedly down to Earth*." This other Earth specific to Hesperians has fundamentally changed our "essential and patriotic representations." That is, because modern poetry must select its themes "according to our world-view and their representations," the bygone Greek modes of presentation no longer function. "Our" Zeus forces nature toward a world that is even more "down to Earth" than the Greek Earth whose significance is still derived from the absence of their gods. While the translator uses the term "anti-human" here for *menschenfeindlichen*, this word suggests something that is not just "anti-human" but also "inhuman," an Earth that is fundamentally distinct from every world or cosmology, every mode of presentation, every poetics that would attempt to present it.[33]

Not unlike the sudden disorientation that afflicts the slave old man and his master upon their journey into the Great Woods, this encounter with an Earth that has slipped the moorings of every mode of presentation, every world that would give it sense or meaning, generates a similar disorientation in Hölderlin's modern "Hesperia." Hölderlin's use of the term "patriotic" (*vaterländisch*) to characterize the representations that follow from this earthward turn should not be misread: any sense of *patria*, of belonging suggested by the word "patriotic" has been entirely upended.[34] Hölderlin's suggestion that the earthward turn of "our Zeus" necessitates a radical change in "the essential and patriotic representations" and that "our poetry must be patriotic so that its themes are selected according to our world-view and their representations" (PW 113/2:456) does not mean that poetry should be nationalistic—only that modernity cannot adopt the modes of presentation specific to the bygone world of the Greeks. Hölderlin's insistence on the possessive "our" throughout this passage—"our Zeus" and "our world-view"—is identified with an earthward turn that leaves us without bearings, without a world or cosmology through which to position the Earth. The term "patriotic," then, does not refer to a "native land" in the traditional sense of a geographic or spiritual space in which a collective sense of belonging, an "us" or a "we," might identify itself. The term "patriotic" here refers simply to what *remains* after the extinction of the world and the modes of presentation specific to the Greeks—the death of their "fatherland" and the nonexistence of our own.

The "patriotic representations" that follow out of the "the eternally anti-human course of nature on its way to another world *more decidedly down to Earth*" unsettle poetry's ability to present or articulate any common world or unified conception of "the West." Whereas the Greek world comes to an end, Hesperian modernity is defined by its complete reversal of *all* forms of representation, which Hölderlin calls a "patriotic reversal" (*vaterlandische Umkehr*):

> For patriotic reversal is the reversal of all modes and forms of representation. However, an absolute reversal of these, as indeed an absolute reversal altogether without any point of rest is forbidden for man as a knowing being. And in patriotic reversal where the entire form of things changes, and where nature and necessity, which always remain, incline toward another form—be it that they transcend into chaos or into a new form—in such a change everything that is necessary favors the change. (PW 114–115/2:457)

This "patriotic reversal," in other words, is not another "representation" of the Earth, its placement within a new cosmology, but the "reversal of all modes and forms of representation" *tout court*. What follows is that "the entire form of things" (*die ganze Gestalt der Dinge*) is altered in the absence of a unified cosmology or ontology. The modern world is not organized like the Greek one, with a hierarchy of beings that includes the divine as its zenith. Instead, Nature is transformed either into "chaos" (*Wildnis*—which also implies that it is an external "wilderness")—or simply "another form" (*einer andern Gestalt*). The fact that nature "inclines toward another form" while threatening to undo every form and representation suggests that it is both inhuman and a *process*. It is a *course* of nature (*Naturgang*), a tendency rather than an object or totality of objects. This also means that what characterizes "eternally anti-human (or inhuman) nature" for Hölderlin is a process that outstrips itself and the modes of presentation that attempt to encapsulate it.

Nevertheless, Hölderlin's assertion that a "complete reversal altogether without any point of rest is forbidden for man as a knowing being" also implies that, despite its complete reversal of "all modes and forms of representation," poetry in fact bears witness to the "real separation" of the Earth. And this is where Hölderlin's geopoetics becomes most acute: the disorienting Earth of "our Zeus" means that no new world or stable cosmology forms itself in the wake of the collapse of the Greek one. There is no unity tying Greeks and ancients together around a shared origin—only a ceaseless historical falling away that leaves the coherence of modern Europe without any ground or foundation. The Earth of "our Zeus" thus locates us in a space without a horizon of meaning, in what Hölderlin will call, in one of his river poems, a "boundless Earth," an Earth on which there is no longer a unified world—or a set of modes of presentation—capable of situating it. The result is an encounter with an Earth that destabilizes the basic coordinates of every world, calling into question the spatial and temporal unity of the West (or "Hesperia"), and forcing it to face its own contingency through the death of the Greeks.

This earthward turn also introduces a discontinuous history—there is no unified sending of "the West" in Heidegger's sense, only a succession of worlds that cannot be reconciled with one another. The "real separation" of the Earth introduces a radical disjunction between the Greeks and Hesperia since it can be integrated into neither world's cosmology, and yet it nevertheless creates the only relation between them. Hölderlin's late river poems, often interpreted as a poetic meditation on history,[35] articulate this relation to a worldless Earth in terms of a wandering—a historical drifting that no longer culminates in an ultimate horizon of meaning, a unified world known as "Europe" or "the West." Heidegger's extensive commentary on these poems—he built entire lecture courses around nearly all of them—inevitably treat what he calls the theme of "historical journeying" in them by suggesting how they are in dialogue with the Greeks. In each one there is often a backward-looking focus of the river toward the past, toward its own source or starting point, usually understood by Heidegger as the world of ancient Greece. The fact that Hölderlin refers to the rivers as "demi-gods" (*Halbgötter*) suggests that they represent a journeying *between* worlds or cosmologies, at certain moments constituting the foundation of a particular world, at others bringing about its dissolution. Heidegger's description of the rivers as "creating paths" on the Earth is helpful insofar as it, at least initially, makes the rivers themselves central figures for the history of the succession of worlds. As he puts it in the lecture course on *Germania*:

> The river violently creates paths and limits on the originally pathless Earth. (Since the flight of the gods, the Earth has been pathless) . . . Through the arrival of the new gods, the entire historical, Earthly Dasein of the Germans is to be pointed on a new path and created a new determinacy and orientation.[36]

What Heidegger misses, however, is the extent to which the "pathless Earth" is never overcome in Hölderlin.[37] For Heidegger, "the arrival of the new gods" creates a new "homeland" or world—a new relation to beings as such. What Hölderlin emphasizes in one of his Pindar fragments titled "The Life Giving" (*Das Belebende*), by contrast, is the way in which the river exemplifies an opposition between (aorgic) fluidity and (organic) solidity, a relatively contained or stable form or direction, and one that overcomes that stability and spills over its banks, changing its course in the process:

> But the more the dry substance of its two banks consolidated itself, and obtained direction from firmly rooted trees, and shrubs and the grapevine, the more the river, too, taking its direction from the banks, must acquire direction, until, urged on from its origin, it broke through at a place where the mountains that enclosed it were more lightly joined.[38]

The river, as a figure for history, does not just carve the Earth as an inert substance preceding it;[39] instead, the Earth first gives direction to the river through resistance to its aorgic tendencies in the interplay between water and land, determination and indetermination. The "pathless Earth" is thus irreducibly prior to any historical progression of worlds for Hölderlin.

The rivers thus operate retrospectively, like the writer in Chamoiseau's *Slave Old Man*. Faced with the mute Stone and the bones found next to it, the writer must narrate the jumble of temporalities and worlds represented there without a stable reference point. Hölderlin's river poems attempt a similar narration, turning back toward a reflection on the vanished world of the Greeks, and an encounter with the Earth and its disorienting effects in the present. But whereas Chamoiseau's writer engages with that disorientation by gesturing *forward* to another world he suggests is in the process of formation, Hölderlin's river poems emphasize the dissolution not just of past worlds, but of the present one as well. The river is thus indeed a figure for the succession of worlds—including their fundamental erasure or extinction. But it is also a relation to an Earth that withdraws so fundamentally from that history that it reveals the possibility of an absolute loss of any cohesive sense or meaning, any new world that would take shape on and through it.

The river poems could thus be considered Hölderlin's third attempt at a modern poetics that centers on the specificity of "our Zeus." Exploring the intricacies of all the river poems would require a book of its own, so my example will be Hölderlin's shorter poem "The Main" (*Der Main*), which invokes a historical and geographical journeying on the Earth from the river's source in the Alps to its emptying out into the Rhine. It opens with a relation to "other lands":

> True, on this living earth there are many lands
> I long to see, and over the hills at times
> My heart runs off, my wishes wander
> Seaward, and on to those shores which more than
> All others that I know have been glorified.[40]

By the third stanza the speaker's longing for "other lands" becomes temporal as he singles out a specific world—ancient Greece—as his focus:

> O once I long to land there, on Sunium's coast,
> Once ask my way to your columns, Olympion! (M 137/1:239)

Once the river "arrives" in Greece—clearly not actually following the geographic course of the Main—and as it recognizes the bygone status of this ancient world, the poem shifts into the "heroic" tone. Desiring to "land" at Sunium, which features several ruined temples including the temple of Zeus (the "Olympion"), the speaker hopes to witness its "columns" before it too is consigned to oblivion:

> And soon, before the northern gale can
> Bury you too in the scattered rubble
> Of temples Athens raised, and their imaged gods
> For long now desolate you have stood, O pride
> Of worlds that are no more! (M 137/1:239)

As the poem goes on to suggest, the speaker's focus on the destruction of the ancient Greek world represented by the temple—the "world that is no more"—introduces a reflection on the Earth, an even more radical "stranger" than the Greeks. The speaker's encounter with the "unbounded" Earth in the rubble of the divine leads him to declare his own "homelessness":

> To you, perhaps, you islands, yet one day shall
> A homeless singer come; for he's driven on
> From stranger still to stranger, and the
> Earth, the unbounded, alas, must serve him
> In place of home and nation his whole life long. (M 139/1:240)

The abrupt shift away from the focus on the gods as the object and source of the speaker's song gradually destabilizes the ground beneath him, disrupting any clear opposition between *Heim* and *Fremde*, home and the strange (or foreign). Faced with the destruction of the temple of Zeus and the collapse of the world to which it belonged, the speaker is instead "driven on" from stranger to stranger, toward an Earth freed (*Erde, die freie*) from its determination by that world, as a prelude to its reconstitution in relation to another.[41]

This "unbounded Earth," however is not another world or "homeland," since, as the passage makes clear, it "serves" the speaker *in place of* home and nation. Rather, the ode ends with the speaker addressing the river, but that takes place only once there is tonal shift after the caesura of the eighth stanza which distinguishes between a human lifespan and the temporality of the river:

> And when he dies—but never, delightful Main,
> Shall I forget you or your banks, the
> Variously blessed, on my farthest travels.
> Hospitably, though proud, you admitted me,
> And, smoothly flowing, brightened the stranger's eye
> And, taught me gently gliding songs, and
> Taught me the strength that's alive in silence. (M 139/1:240)

As the intermediary between the "boundless" Earth and the poet, the Main becomes both the condition of possibility for his poem (teaching "gently gliding songs") as well as what remains unspoken or unpresentable in the poem (teaching "the strength that's alive in silence"). The river has thus made possible this historical-poetic journey by traveling to the bygone world of ancient Greece, but as in Hölderlin's work on tragedy, the speaker is ultimately left in an even more "foreign" place, exposed to a worldless and "unbounded" Earth that substitutes for anything resembling "home and nation."

So what is the upshot, then, for Hölderlin's conception of history, and for his understanding of modern Europe or Hesperia? Like Chamoiseau, the relation to a bygone world is articulated by an Earth that subtends it, destabilizing the coordinates of existing horizons of meaning. The fact that the Earth is worldless does not mean that it is some abstraction. Quite the contrary: It is the condition for every world, past, present or future. But as this basis, it is the only connecting bond between them, including between the present world and those that have ceased to exist. Unlike Heidegger's conception of "the West" as a series of continuous worlds, successive decisions about "what is," there is no "history of Being" binding these decisions together around a common or shared ground. Rather than provide a stable continuity between worlds, the

Earth for Hölderlin marks the radical disjunction between them—a worldless interstice without form and meaning. Thus, Chamoiseau's invocation of Heidegger in *Crusoe's Footprint* does find common cause with the idea that "origins" come to us not from the past, but from the future: except that Chamoiseau's conception of this construction of the origin is closer to Hölderlin's disjunctive history of the Earth than Heidegger's continuous and singular history of Being. The significance of that difference pertains to the *kind* of relation to origins the past vanished civilization makes possible. Heidegger's conception involves the possibility of a repetition of a basic structure of meaning and belonging—a "world"—that both the past and the present share, even if it is only unacknowledged or currently imperceptible. Chamoiseau and Hölderlin, by contrast, through their mutual understanding that it is only a worldless Earth that binds the past and the present to each other, articulate a history that more radically breaks with the past, consigning it to a more fundamental oblivion. Yet by doing so, the question of a future world becomes all the more trenchant; for Chamoiseau, that future must be fundamentally inaugural in the recognition that the prior worlds that have vanished, that have been wiped off the face of the Earth, are not coming back. Yet it is in the name of their erasure that a new world must be constructed. For Hölderlin, however, the possibility that another world is possible is far more tenuous—in the wake of the disjunction between the past and the present, and in the flight of the Greek gods and the cosmology that went with it, we are left with an Earth that no longer provides any orienting point from which to imagine a future world.

The history we encounter in Hölderlin is thus not the history of the West as a unified world enveloping the planet, but a succession of distinct worlds with nothing in common but the disjunctive Earth upon which they stand or once stood. What results is a complete decentering of the present world in the face of one that existed in the past but does no more: for Hölderlin, not only is no modern cosmology or myth of origins possible, but contemporary Europe is also structured by a relation to the Earth that must take into account its irreducibility to *all* modes of presentation—that is, to *any* world whatsoever. "Wandering beneath the unthinkable" thus means being cast adrift without recourse to anything beyond the Earth, that is, without recourse to another cosmology, another "god," that would bring it back into the orbit of the thinkable: the Earth as the place of the mundane as opposed to the sacred, or as a resource base, or as the mother of all life, and so on. This means, ultimately, that for Hölderlin modern Europe is defined by *nothing but* this disorientation. Hesperia is not just another step in the succession of worlds defining the

West, it is an encounter with the essentially contingent and fragile nature of every world, a recognition that each one of them comes to an end, and they all depend on an Earth that precedes them. Worlds come and go; the Earth remains, but is also incapable of providing any historical continuity for their succession. While the profound disorientation the worldless Earth invokes in Chamoiseau has a clearly defined political dimension—disintegrating the coordinates of the plantation world, its racial hierarchies, and its sense of inevitability—the disorientation in Hölderlin is more opaque but no less political. A world fundamentally destabilized by the radical materiality of the Earth cannot claim to be a "homeland" in any usual sense, nor can it claim any sense of historical inevitability. Hölderlin's poetics thus leaves us, we moderns, on a precipice faced with the materiality of an Earth with which we have yet to fully come to terms.

Stone Worlds

Romanticism's fascination with ruins has often been read in terms of a fascination with the past—either as a nostalgia for some golden era, or a meditation on the ability of time to destroy even the most powerful of empires. But the fascination with bygone civilizations often had other political dimensions: For many German writers, the ruins of ancient Greece bespoke a greatness that needed to be imitated for a new (German) world to come about. These were ruins that pointed to something only temporarily decayed that could be restored in the present as a blueprint for the future. That same conception of ruins would, more than a century later, inform Albert Speer in his plans for a postwar Berlin, with buildings designed to decay into picturesque ruins so that future generations would marvel at the greatness of the Third Reich, thereby creating a testament to the grandeur of the past, its purchase on the present, and the power of its status as a model to be repeated in the future.

With the help of Chamoiseau's focus on how a different relation to the ruins and traces of past civilizations *disorients* the present, a very different political dimension of Romanticism's fascination with ruins comes to the fore, particularly in Hölderlin. The past civilizations marked by the Stone in *Slave Old Man* are not just victims of time's passing, they have been willfully exterminated, and their pasts deliberately obliterated. The Stone itself remembers them by inscribing them into a different temporality and narrative—the Earth's—that calls into question the stability and permanence of the present through a relation to an even more immemorial past. Past worlds might be anterior to the present and therefore occluded by, or held up as, models for the now, but the Earth's anteriority undercuts any succession between each world and reinstates each one's relation to an indifferent past it cannot incorporate into a narrative about itself. Because the Earth is anterior to every world, it relativizes them all, forcing the present to encounter a reality it cannot master, a time it cannot claim as its own. To read Hölderlin's apparent Graecomania through Chamoiseau's insistence on that disorienting effect highlights the extent to which a different anti-nostalgic dimension takes shape in Hölderlin, articulating a fascination with the ruins of ancient Greece in different terms from his nationalist contemporaries. As a world that no longer exists, on an Earth that both predates and succeeds it, ancient Greece's bygone nature forces an encounter not with the question of how prior civilizations inform the present, but instead with its own extinction. When Sir John Soane, the architect who built the Bank of England in the late eighteenth and early nineteenth century, commissioned Joseph Gandy, his draughtsman and an artist in his own right, to depict the bank in ruins in a not-too-far-off future, he provided a visual depiction of the temporal disruption the Earth invokes in Hölderlin (figure 2). These are ruins not of the past—they are a projection of the present into a ruined future.

FIGURE 2. Joseph Michael Gandy (1771–1843), "Architectural Ruins, A Vision" (1798). © Sir John Soane's Museum, London.

They are more like the images conjured by Austrian filmmaker Nikolaus Geyrhalter in his film *Homo Sapiens*, where long pans of ruined buildings, empty spaces, and cities (such as Pripyat, abandoned entirely after the 1986 Chernobyl disaster, in figure 3) greet us without commentary, situating us in the spaces of an Earth we currently inhabit, but where humanity has disappeared, having abandoned these sites to a nature that is in the process of reclaiming them.

These are images of a present world that once existed, but which no longer does not only now, but in the future. Hölderlin's geopoetics thus conjures not a revived German world, but the possibility of its present and future ruin. It also conjures the possibility of an Earth without humanity *tout court*, a conception that has grown increasingly relevant in the time of the Anthropocene.

It is on the question of the future of a world to come that Chamoiseau and Hölderlin differ most sharply in their conceptions of the Earth. For Chamoiseau, the fact that the present has had a hand in the prior world's extermination forces a different kind of confrontation with the past. Borrowing Glissant's conception of the "whole-world" (discussed at length in the first chapter), Chamoiseau suggests that his novel proposes what he calls a "Stone World"—the invention of a relation between past and present that ought to

FIGURE 3. Pripyat (Ukraine), Jorge Franganillo, November 4, 2017 (CC BY 2.0).

include those that no longer exist. In *La matière de l'absence* (The matter of absence), Chamoiseau's hybrid text combining personal reflections on the death of his mother with meditations on cultural memory in Martinique, he takes a moment to reflect on the meaning of the Stone in his novel *Slave Old Man*:

> In *Slave Old Man*, I told the story of the old slave who goes marooning, not to attempt to rediscover a real or fantasized Africa, but to dive into a modality of living of which he was not able to conceive. It is this impossibility to conceive that I symbolized (in reference to the philosopher's stone of the alchemists) through a Stone: at the end of his run, the slave old man encounters a symbolic stone that gathers in its impenetrable matter all the presences, the "voices" and "paths" (*les "voix" et les "voies"*) of the world realized as an object of consciousness. For me, this Stone was nothing but a Glissantian Whole-World (*Tout-monde*). Transforming the Whole-world into a Stone-world was my way of saying that the Whole-world emerges from the unknowable, and that we had to, like this old slave, envisage our re-foundations, whether personal or collective, in the shifting stratum of the impossible, the unpredictable or the unknowable.[42]

Chamoiseau's own reading of his novel, and the place of the Stone within it, emphasizes the historical rupture over which the Stone is suspended. To include a relation to the nonexistent worlds that inscribed themselves on it as a version of Glissant's "whole-world"[43] is to transform the Stone into a figure for a "Stone-world" that emphasizes the "unknowability" of those relations—like the unknowable Earth in Glissant I discussed in the first chapter—even as it treats the Stone as still part of *a* world, or of many. As Chamoiseau suggests, the slave old man forms a relation, through the Stone, to the impossible—an impossible "future" or *avenir*,[44] "the impenetrable which for him constituted the future, and which was, for him, strictly unknowable" (MA 229). For Chamoiseau, the impenetrability of the Earth becomes the very opening up of a relation that involves a community with the dead:

> The real maroon, the fundamental maroon, as Glissant was, was thus not the one who ran away in search of new certainties, or of a transparency of the world, but was the one who had the courage, through the Whole-world, through the Stone-world, to accept the great relational mystery and to merge with the irrefutability of what he could not envisage understanding. (MA 229–30)

The Stone-World still entails a "relational mystery," not to the bare materiality or anteriority of the Earth, but *through* the Earth, to a fundamentally unknowable world that is the cipher for relations between existing worlds in the present.

Heidegger famously claimed in *The Fundamental Concepts of Metaphysics* that while Man is "world forming," animals are "poor in world" because they have no relation to it as a basic "accessibility to things." Whereas humans and animals "have" a world in some sense, a stone is "worldless" because "it has no possible access to anything else around it, anything that it might attain or possess as such."[45] While Heidegger may have been wrong about Hölderlin's conception of history, he accurately reflects Hölderlin's conception of a worldless Earth. Except that such a term—"worldless Earth"—has no meaning for Heidegger, who can understand the worldlessness of the stone only from the standpoint of the world. Hölderlin, on the other hand, contemplates the worldlessness of the stone from the standpoint of a geopoetics confronted with the Earth's essential worldlessness, without assuming any "world-forming" capacity to create another world that could gain access to it. Caught between two worlds, we arrive at a "homeland" in Hölderlin that, like the Stone in Chamoiseau, involves an encounter with a fundamental alterity, an *Abgrund* or abyss.

But if Hölderlin leaves us suspended in the face of that abyss, Chamoiseau insists that a new kind of Earthbound-community-in-progress is made possible by it. *The matter of absence* at one point addresses this question through a theoretical framework that takes Hölderlin's conception of the aorgic—the self-overcoming dimension of nature and culture—a step further. Chamoiseau projects a form of disorder onto the Earth as an essential activity through which something unprecedented comes about, where new forms of life and modes of existence materialize:

> Life has been maintained for billions of years throughout structural disturbances, massive volcanic-geologic disasters, gaseous mutations, cosmic bombardments, mass extinctions and climate fluctuations. It has always been continued, renewed, complexified everywhere, specialized here, diversified there, not as opposed to all of that, but in fact with, and thanks to, all of that; lack, disequilibrium, and disorder have reinforced agile dynamics, cleared unpredictable paths, allowed beings who could, to improvise unprecedented horizons. (MA 249)

Describing the anteriority of the Earth and the life that depends on it as vulnerable to disorder and instability, catastrophe and dissolution, Chamoiseau argues that these processes are the means by which life diversifies itself, creating itself anew. Turning to the effects of these forces of disorder on the political domain, Chamoiseau implies that they reveal a set of tendencies in the Earth that undermine desires for permanence and the quest for stable identities: "One will have to wait a long time for the pragmatisms of survival, identitarian ascendencies, to bend creativity toward the riches of this earth-here, its silences, its voids, its ruptures and its lacks" (MA 239). The materiality of the Earth—its silences, voids, and ruptures—becomes for Chamoiseau the very source of its "richness," its capacity to initiate other possible human worlds.

Those silences threaten another possibility in Hölderlin, however: an Earth without any world whatsoever to give it shape. His geopoetics, which contemplates an Earth without a world, becomes all the more relevant as we stumble toward the precipice of another disaster of our own making, exposing ourselves to an Earth that is no longer a stable home, that threatens to disorient, if not make extinct, not just the many worlds of the present, but future ones as well. For Chamoiseau, only a geopoetics of "this earth-here" could conceive another "*lieu*" or "place" on the Earth, another relation to it as an exteriority to each and every world it makes possible: "a 'Place' that is not a territory considered to be exclusive in the old way, but a mixture of lost land, of dreamed land, of imagined land, of constituted land, of land, in the end, that is becoming a project" (MA 239). This "place," of course, is currently no actual locale on the Earth, forcing Chamoiseau to frame it as a question: "Is there a way to inhabit an earth without absolutes, to leave it full of everything, to live it without fixities, without barbed-wire borders?" (MA 239) The skeptical reply comes back: "I think that only its poets have done so . . ." (*Je crois juste que ces poètes l'ont fait . . .*) (MA 239). For Chamoiseau, the worldless Earth solicits a poetics waiting patiently for a promised performative that will bring a new kind of life, a new world, into existence. It is either that, or the more barren worldless Earth of Hölderlin's poetry: a wandering beneath the unthinkable as the end of all possible worlds to come.

CONCLUSION

Toward a Geopoetics of the Future via Maximin and Frankétienne

TWO EARTHQUAKES BOOKEND THIS study: the Lisbon earthquake, one of the strongest in human history, and the earthquake that devastated Haiti in 2010, by far the deadliest—with more than 300,000 dead and nearly a million left homeless. The Lisbon earthquake brought a major colonial power to its knees, setting the stage for the geopoetics I thenceforth examined that challenged the ideologies and beliefs underpinning European exceptionalism, colonialism, and racism. The Haitian earthquake, conversely, revealed the extent to which the neocolonial structures and economies of extraction that took shape in the wake of decolonization have not only remained in place but have taken on new forms. This was not the official narrative of course. In fact, a cynically amnesiac one emerged that accounted for the 300,000 dead by casting blame on Haitians themselves and their poor building codes, echoing Rousseau's earlier argument about the Lisbon earthquake.[1] Such blatantly ahistorical explanations fail (perhaps intentionally) to recognize that Haiti was systematically excluded from trading on the world market until it agreed to take on the crushing debts its former colonial slave masters claimed they were owed because of its independence, including for the former slaves' own bodies, which had formerly been French "property." It ignores the fact that for two centuries Haiti withstood multiple foreign military and multinational invasions, and that for nearly a century it had had its internal political affairs systematically corrupted or overturned by foreign (mainly US) interests. In other words, those poor building codes were merely the nail in the coffin, dramatically revealing that the scope of the earthquake's devastation was by no means an accident of history but the consequence of a series of measures designed to keep in check the legacy of an early example of successful liberation from colonial rule.

But things are not so clear-cut; it's not a game of then and now as the effects of these policies have become global in the age of the Anthropocene, when the difference between natural and man-made disasters is itself not so clear-cut. For the devastation wrought by the Haitian earthquake is in fact part and parcel of the devastation unleashed on the island by neocolonialism. Surely "building to code" is important, but it becomes meaningless in the absence of proper materials and funds. It is also beside the point in the context of the increasingly destructive telluric forces unleashed by anthropogenic climate change, including warming oceans, more destructive storms, higher sea levels, increasing erosion, and the loss of arable land. If the Lisbon earthquake could be said to have measured the speciousness of the ideology of European exceptionalism and its "nomos of the Earth," the Haitian one indexes our own moment and the heightened effects of anthropogenic "natural" disasters, with the global South bearing the brunt. Like the hurricanes that every year ravage the Caribbean with ever greater force and frequency, the Haitian earthquake's devastation foregrounds a new matrix of relations between neocolonialism, global capital, and natural disaster, the three joining forces to become a single global catastrophe.

In the trajectory of the geopoetics I have followed to this point we have seen a variety of different responses to the matrix of nationalism, colonialism, and resource extraction that developed in the colonial period and reestablished itself in new forms after decolonization. These responses address the racial and cultural hierarchies underpinning imperialism and slavery in the eighteenth and nineteenth centuries as well as notions of rootedness to the land that generated exclusionary identities in the twentieth. They challenge the ontologies that structured European dominance then and now and confront the web of concepts and ideas about the Earth that have fueled European expansion and global dominance from the Romantic period to the present day. The authors I have read are part of a historical configuration formulating new kinds of community, new relations to the other, new conceptions of the commons, new articulations of life, and new ways of understanding the relation between the anteriority of the Earth and the various human worlds it makes possible. They all articulate a *poesis*, a mode of making, thinking, and being, a way of envisioning another world and its connection to the Earth, distinct from the present.

But the Haitian earthquake shifts the perspective somewhat and introduces a fault line into that trajectory. Its staggering death toll exposes a new relation between world and Earth that goes beyond the crisis revealed in the Lisbon earthquake addressed by the Romantic authors I have discussed. In the eighteenth century, the Lisbon quake might have revealed that the Earth is not "for" humankind, its indifference casting doubt on European man's dominance over nature and the planet as a whole. In the context of the Anthropocene, the Haitian earthquake reveals a new situation: a distinctly twenty-first century concatenation of neocolonialism, global capital, and natural catastrophe that has begun to threaten the very existence of even a *future* shift in the relation between world and Earth. In short, we are now confronted with a disaster threatening to foreclose even the *possibility* of another world.

In the last chapter, I examined how the worldlessness of the Earth articulates a relation to past civilizations, casting doubt on the perdurance of contemporaneous worlds, whether they be the plantation system, modern Germany, or contemporary Martinique. In the twenty-first century, that worldlessness is not just located in the past but threatens to overtake the future. In the geopoets I have explored to this point, present worlds may be threatened with their end, but there is always at least the *promise* of another, especially in the contemporary Caribbean authors I have examined. But the upheavals of the Anthropocene force a reckoning with an even more destabilizing and destructive Earth that requires "us"—a "we" that has yet to take shape, that can only be postnational, that must reckon with all the legacies of colonialism and racism engaged with here—to contemplate the end of our world *before* it brings about the end of even the possibility of another. The worlds discussed in this book—including those that have ceased to exist such as the Amerindian civilizations represented on the Stone of Chamoiseau's *Slave Old Man*—have been built around more or less stable ocean levels, weather patterns, and temperatures. What confronts contemporary geopoetics, including the contemporary Caribbean authors I have explored in *Adrift on the Earth*, is not just the question of how to produce the conditions for another world, but also how to engage with the end of the one we currently inhabit. For all intents and purposes, in fact, the present world has *already* ended, whether we realize it or not; it too was constructed around predictable ocean levels and rainfall. That more-or-less stable Earth no longer exists, even if the world we created on it remains intransigent in its habits and mode of existence, which is why new ways of addressing the future on a changing Earth have recently emerged, from "climate adaptation" and "green capitalism" to the fever dream of colonizing other planets. Each of these approaches, however, leaves intact the coordinates of the existing world: they either offer products that can supposedly address the climate crisis without any significant lifestyle changes or build structures adaptable to a changing planet that will nevertheless allow existing ways of life to remain in place (and I won't even address the fantasy of conquering other planets). Yet as all the geopoets in this book insist: The Earth can very well do without the worlds humans have created for themselves, but those worlds cannot possibly do without the Earth. What must take place now, with the help of the geopoetics examined here, is a relation to the *end* of our world and the question of how that end forces upon us a new relation to the Earth and a relinquishment of our current horizon of meaning.

To gesture toward this geopoetics of the future and to conclude, I briefly address two Caribbean authors—Guadeloupian writer Daniel Maximin and Haitian artist Frankétienne—who both explicitly and recently pose the question of what it means for a world to end due to natural disaster. Maximin explores the history of natural disasters, from the period of slavery to the present, to imagine a liberatory dimension in the unleashing of telluric forces capable of toppling even the most entrenched regimes of power. He thus develops a geopoetics in which one world is destroyed to make room for another, with the end of the present world opening onto another relation to the Earth. In Frankétienne, on the other hand, those same forces threaten to reduce entire nations to vassal states dependent on foreign assistance, and at the planetary level portend the possibility of the extinction of life on Earth as we know it: His is a geopoetics that entertains the possibility of a new abyss—a worldless Earth without a future of which to speak. And while they both articulate a warning about what may come if we fail to accept the end of our current world, they also point to a moment when the fragile relation between world and Earth in the configuration I call "Caribbean Romanticism" reaches the limits of one of the terms defining that configuration—Romanticism—which as a period could not have foreseen the conjunction of the ruinous capacities of humanity's exploitation of the Earth and the Earth's own destructive potential. This is why neither Frankétienne nor Maximin have a direct Romantic counterpart, although Romantic-era geopoetics might energize aspects of their Earth-eschatology.

Maximin's 1981 novel *L'isolé soleil* (The isolated sun)[2] revolves around the life of Louis Delgrès, a French officer from Martinique who first fought against the British in the Caribbean during the French Revolution, and who then became a leader of the resistance to Napoleon's reinstitution of slavery in Guadeloupe (Maximin's birthplace). Since then, Maximin has published a book of poetry and an autobiography while championing pan-Caribbean culture as a broadcaster and as regional director of cultural affairs in Guadeloupe, later working in the Ministry of National Education and the Ministry of Culture and Communication. *Les fruits du cyclone: Une géopoétique de la Caraïbe* (Fruits of the cyclone: A geopoetics of the Caribbean, 2007) develops a theory of the relation between the Earth and the long history of Caribbean resistance to colonial rule and slavery.[3] Privileging two main figures in the book—the maroon and the peasant—he argues that Caribbean geopoetics, a term he uses to define the distinctive relation to the Earth that unifies all Caribbean literature despite national and linguistic differences, concerns a conflict between two different conceptions of that relation: a Caribbean one that emphasizes subsistence, and the modern European one that emphasizes over-exploitation.

While that aspect of Maximin's argument pertains to the Earth's productive capacities, the other focus of his book is on the "fruits of the cyclone," that is, the way a cyclone's[4] destructive force is intertwined with resistance to the plantation system; by destroying the plantation, hurricanes become a wind of change on the side of emancipation.[5] Maximin draws on Amerindian beliefs about hurricanes acting as figurative retribution for slavery, an idea oddly exemplified in William Gilbert's early Romantic theosophical poem *The Hurricane*,[6] which imagined a storm made up of the spirits of slaughtered Amerindians from the Caribbean overtaking Europe and sweeping away the old order.[7] As Maximin writes: "Hurricanes originate on the African coasts, cross the Atlantic and arrive, according to an ancient Amerindian belief, as revenge or reinforcement to destroy and sweep away all that *should not have been built to begin with*."[8] Thus Maximin's geopoetics makes clear that it is not only the Caribbean's fertility that sustains the maroon community's resistance to the plantation system by providing sustenance in the uncultivated lands outside it; it also makes clear that in the Caribbean hurricanes are powerful enough to lay waste directly to that system.

This emphasis on the destructive forces of the Earth is more acute in Maximin than in other Romantic and Caribbean geopoets. He argues, for instance, that the Caribbean hurricane's destructive capacities must be interpreted differently from the lament over the indifference of the Earth to human suffering one finds in the aftermath of the Lisbon earthquake. In fact, Maximin is very much aware of the significance of the Lisbon quake and comments in *Fruits* on the European reaction to it. For him that reaction was framed through a desire to maintain the contours of a familiar world or horizon of meaning by recuperating exposure to an indifferent and uncontrollable Earth in the idea of man's mastery over nature:

> Voltaire in his century presented the Lisbon earthquake as an unjustifiable scandal of nature, the massacre of innocent humanity. A philosophy of man's mastery over nature can only consider the earthquake as an accident, geologically and morally inexplicable, unjustifiable, an error or fault of nature. And the only way to master this violence is to recover it as the expression of a divine will, of a theological order and not of a *natural causality*, an order of the world independent of the history of men and the anger of the gods. (FC 102)

Europe's confrontation with an indifferent Earth could not in the end, for Maximin, fully face an essentially uncontrollable nature capable of ending entire worlds at a moment's notice.

Maximin's geopoetics, therefore, marshals the destructive forces of the Earth on behalf of liberation; if a hurricane can demolish a plantation overnight, its destructive capacities become a means of inscribing "a hope in the earth and in the memory of a surviving people" (FC 94). The European conception of nature that continues to dominate the globe is of a nature that can be mastered, domesticated, transformed, or terraformed into submission. What natural catastrophes reveal, for Maximin, by contrast, is an *uncontrollable* nature that does not bend to our whims, and that overturns the systems, worlds, and economies predicated on its control—precisely the form of nature European reactions to Lisbon could not adequately face, and that underpinned the slave system:

> From there, two modalities of nature appear: nature dominated by oppressive European man, nature surrounding human habitation, cultivated and exploited nature; and beneath it, beneath this tropical, warm and fertile nature, obscure forces which will have the possibility of destroying what Western Man had come to institute. Hence two levels: a nature that appears hospitable and a willing slave, extremely fertile and productive, and behind that the capacity for violent revolt, unpredictable in time and space, which comes to sweep everything away. (FC 99)

When coupled with the resistance movements Maximin describes in his book—such as the maroon communities central to the many revolts and revolutions throughout the Caribbean during the period of slavery—hurricanes and other natural disasters become a potentially emancipating force as their devastation is capitalized on for the resistance's own ends.[9] Just as in those revolts where seemingly "willing slaves" were suddenly capable of "violent revolt," the destructive force of hurricanes strike a blow—albeit inadvertently—for abolition by introducing a different modality of nature that is no longer acquiescent but instead comes to "sweep everything away."

Linking hurricanes to the image of the spiral, Maximin connects their natural form to the structure of human history where, in a periodic cycle of destruction and regeneration, the hurricane makes something unprecedented suddenly possible. What emerges out of the hurricane as both a destructive force and as an image is:

> A vision of cyclical and spiral time which integrates the idea of unprecedented emergence into cyclical temporality. Nothing goes right, but nothing goes in circles, and the spiral of life reintroduces the *always possible*—for better or worse—by breaking the alliance between the cyclical and fatality. (FC 104–5)

This doesn't just mean that the Earth's destructive capacities are able to break with a "fatality"—the endless reproduction of an exploitative relation to the Earth—but that through its destructive force something else "for better or worse" emerges. That phrase, "for better or worse" is crucial, since it suggests that there is no guarantee that what comes next will necessarily be an improvement. The worst may still come, but the destruction unleashed at least creates the conditions for something else.

Maximin's geopoetics therefore engages with a new aspect of the Earth/world relation in the Anthropocene: The Earth's increasing instability requires more than simply adapting to its changing patterns and systems. It requires addressing how that instability will make specific *kinds* of worlds unfeasible. Global "over-exploitation," Maximin suggests, has unleashed telluric forces that are the starting point for a new kind of resistance. This requires not just the utilization of the effects of the climate crisis on behalf of what one might call "disaster *anti*-capitalism,"[10] but also forms of resistance of the kind exemplified by maroon communities and peasant revolts. Today, this perhaps requires developing a broader "extinction rebellion"[11] operating globally outside of official government institutions, capable of solidarity and coordinated action with other movements—nonviolent or insurrectional as the case may be—around the world. A tall order, in other words, but likely the only possibility for a future after the end of the world we currently inhabit, especially in the face of the climate catastrophes we *will* face in the future.

There is, of course, another way of conceiving of the Earth/world connection through the Anthropocene's destructive forces, one with a decidedly foreclosed relation to the time that remains. The early works of Haitian author Frankétienne (who unfortunately passed away in February 2025) tackle the corruption and brutality of the dictatorships under which he lived, including both Duvalier regimes. His more recent work, however, has taken on a more global focus, addressing questions of Haiti's relation not just to its colonial and neocolonial past, but its vulnerability to the forces unleashed by climate change. *Melovivi ou le piège* (Melovivi or the trap)[12] is a minimalist play written in December 2009, just weeks before the 2010 Haitian earthquake. Its first rehearsal, in fact, wrapped up on January 12, 2010, minutes before the ground began to shake.[13] With remarkable prescience, it outlines a world and planet spiraling out of control, heading toward an unprecedented catastrophe, raising the possibility of a futureless Earth—its capacity to support life in its current form progressively destroyed. Frankétienne's geopoetics thus takes Chamoiseau's and Hölderlin's idea of a worldless Earth to its breaking point, where the Earth spirals into a lifelessness no longer able to sustain not only current worlds, but any worlds to come. Frankétienne's play is more than merely a warning: It is a *cri de coeur* to avoid this scenario before it is too late, suggesting as it does that a future Earth without a world is already presaged in what he calls the "non-world" of capitalist modernity, which empties out every horizon of meaning in advance. It is only by resisting the effects of that non-world, the play suggests, that the finality of a worldless Earth can be averted.

The drama features two voices identified simply as "A" and "B" who are interred in the Earth after some unspecified natural catastrophe. Cut off from the world, they strike up a conversation and try to identify the forces that have entombed them.[14] From this bare, apocalyptic, almost Beckettian setting there emerges a meditation on all kinds of devastations—from ecological to cultural and political—instigated and accelerated by twenty-first century global capital: "Can't you see that they destroyed everything. They disrupted the planet. They have disrupted all the planets in the system. They wreaked havoc on the climate" (MV 30). That disruption is figured through the play's structure, which is divided into eight "sequences" rather than acts. Rather than a plot or any interconnection between them, the play instead develops a growing sense of purposelessness, a drift toward what the play calls "nothing" (*rien*), shorthand for the "non-world" of ecological catastrophe.

Like Maximin, Frankétienne articulates the action of the play through the figure of the spiral, which is a central motif throughout his oeuvre and is usually identified with the logic of life and creation, as it is in Maximin, who suggests that even the hurricane's cyclical movement figures a historical opening that institutes the "always possible."[15] In a 1992 interview, Frankétienne defines the spiral in terms of its overcoming of binary oppositions and the movement of life:

> At the beginning was the Word, i.e. the vibration, the original pole of the spiral, the movement of which is everlasting in the dialectical unity of spirit and matter, in the dynamic of conscience and energy, in the interaction of Yin and Yang (as Tao has demonstrated). . . . In biology, life, whatever its form, develops a spiral structure during its evolution. The phenomena of fertilization, of cellular multiplication and reproduction unfold in the dynamic of the spiral motion. . . . The general impulse of life has an upward nature.[16]

This spiral movement, the development of more and more intricate structures, is contrasted with linear or binary forms of thought: "This movement does not progress along a straight line which would symbolize the sterility of nothingness, nor does it follow a circle which would symbolize death. It is rather a movement in the shape of a spiral which reproduces some aspects of the past but at an infinitely superior level."[17] The spiral as the very engine of life is thus opposed to "nothingness" and death.

In *Melovivi* the spiral is identified with the Earth. Trapped in their cave, A and B discuss the "nothingness" into which they and the planet are descending, as B suggests that they are "at the bottom of the abyss, in the realm of nothingness" (*jusqu'au fond de l'abîme dans le royaume du rien*). "Nothingness," however, is more than just the cave or space in which they have been interred; it is a regime of power as A's retort—"The hegemony of nothingness!" (*L'hégémonie du rien!*) (MV 18)—makes clear. That hegemony is eventually identified by B with "the leading experts on corruption and planetary pollution" (*les grands experts de la corruption et de la pollution planétaire*) and by A as "the virtuosos of the abyss" (*les virtuoses de l'abîme*) (MV 22).

"Nothingness" takes on a more concrete form in the third sequence, when the play connects it with the disruption of the spiral movement of the Earth: "They modified our vibrations. They have disturbed the frequency of our vibrations. They have unbalanced the musical clockwork of our earth" (MV 30). By the end of the play, the tendency toward "nothingness" is connected to intergovernmental forums, "the different summits of the G7, G10, G17 and G20 etc." that are tasked with deciding economic and climatic policies, and do nothing:

> A: See you next summit!
>
> B: Until the next summit!
>
> A: At the next summit? Are you sure? But the planet is swaying. The planet oscillates. Pendulum planet. The planet is toppling. The planet is staggering. The planet stumbles. The planet veers and capsizes in tremors of fear and derailments of terror. No gleam. You don't sense that the Earth is tilting. The Earth is slanted. (MV 51)

The Earth, knocked off its axis, is in a death spiral, teetering toward the brink of catastrophe, while none of the decision-making bodies tasked with addressing the crisis are able to, or have enough will to, do so. This is why, throughout the play, "natural" catastrophes cannot be distinguished from political ones, nor logical collapse from the ecological. The spiral movement of the Earth in its very capacity to support life has become unbalanced, a vessel blown off course toward a new abyss: "Our vessel is caught in a whirlwind . . . we are lost. We are at the borders of the abyss, at the borders of non-sense. We are on the borders of the infernal void . . . on the borders of death. We are on the borders of non-being and non-life" (MV 31). This death or "abyss" is not just "our death"—or the death of A and B; it is not even the death of the human or other species. It is a geocide: the death of the Earth itself. As both voices put it "our beautiful / very beautiful / little planet / may perhaps die" (MV 46). We are confronted, therefore, with the possibility of a lifeless Earth spiraling over the border between life and death, entering an "infernal void" of nonmeaning or "non-sense" where no world, no being, and no life is possible any longer.

The final passage of the last sequence closes on the idea of an impossible future:

I decrypted
the aura
the it-will-work-out
the it-will-happen
the it-will-return
the it-will-be
of the impossible[18] (MV 55)

The question, however, is whether the play articulates the prophecy of the impossibility of the future—any future—or whether it gestures toward a posterity that would *be* the arrival of what now seems "impossible." It is unclear, in other words, whether the "impossible" is the arrival of a dead Earth, or whether the voices are in fact opening themselves to something *seemingly* impossible that in fact "will-be," perhaps a future world that breaks with the impasses of the current one.[19]

The anguished cry of the play, it must be noted—barely—preceded the earthquake with which it will be forever identified, the quake's horrifying death toll now imposing a measure of the play's force. The Haitian earthquake, unlike the Lisbon quake, signals a further turning point in our being adrift on the Earth—we can either take up the injunctions of the geopoetics explored here, recognize that the world as we knew it has ended, that we must move past "rooted" conceptions of community and privatized conceptions of the Earth, or we can double down on trying to maintain that world—what Frankétienne calls the "non-world" of the global extraction economy. This is a choice, in other words, between the Earth's spiral movement of life in Frankétienne and Maximin's sense, or a passage across the border of sense into the abyss of nonbeing and nonlife: A choice between a future and a world without one. A choice between a geopoetics that either ends in a cry of despair, or an act of resistance. A decision on the side of life or the exposure of various worlds and peoples to the mass death embodied by the Haitian earthquake.

What exactly does a geopoetics of the future signify, then? Neither a fatality, to use Maximin's term, nor a seemingly passive form of hope. Any notion of "the future" implies *some* relation to at least the *possibility* of a world that would give that future its meaning. And the only way for that world to come into being is through a new relation to the Earth. Adrift on the Earth, or nothing.

NOTES

Introduction

1. These facts and the testimony of the captain of the *Nancy* are part of a new account of the disaster of the Lisbon earthquake by Mark Molesky. See Mark Molesky, *This Gulf of Fire: The Destruction of Lisbon, or Apocalypse in the Age of Science and Reason* (Alfred A. Knopf, 2015).

2. Two of these "waves," the tsunami and the fire, are painstakingly documented in "An Unexpected Horror" and the "Great Firestorm" in Molesky's *This Gulf of Fire*, 117–53 and 154–85 respectively.

3. Daniel Maximin, *Les fruits de la cyclone: Une géopoétique de la Caraïbe* (Éditions du Seuil), 2006.

4. Though the field of ecopoetics is vast, "geopoetics" in the sense I'm using the term here is allied with ecopoetry or writing concerned less with the question of ecological ethics or the capacity of human language to adequately portray nonhuman others, than with questions about how ecology entails an encounter with the *inhuman*. This encounter ruptures existing conceptions of the distinction between culture and nature and exposes poetry to a fissure in the coherence of the world to which it once belonged and for which it has not yet generated new modes of representation. Geopoetics stresses less the *oikos*—the home or habitat implied in the term "ecology"—and more a disruption of existing forms of habitation. For an example of the former, see Scott Knickerbocker, *Ecopoetics: The Language of Nature, the Nature of Language* (University of Massachusetts Press, 2012). For the latter, see Cary Wolfe's recent redefinition of ecological poetics, which emphasizes how conceptions of the "world" must be conceived as cocreated with other nonhuman beings: Cary Wolfe, *Ecological Poetics, or Wallace Stevens's Birds* (University of Chicago Press, 2020). Timothy Morton's conception of ecopoetics as a form of writing that breaks with "ecomi-

mesis" or the representation of the surrounding environment to stir the reader from their immersion in a particular "lifeworld" is also an important example: Timothy Morton, "The Art of Environmental Language," in *Ecology Without Nature* (Harvard University Press, 2009), 29–78.

5. The terms "Enlightenment" and "Romanticism" are effectively shorthand for shifts of emphasis and concern in what one might call the "long eighteenth century." But at this point an important qualification is needed: the Romantic authors who make the indifference of the Earth a central motif in their works do not represent "Romanticism" as a whole, a moniker that, as Arthur Lovejoy long ago demonstrated, should be understood in the plural: "Romanticism" is an invention required for literary historical periodization, whereas "Romanticism*s*" is more apt to characterize the actual complexity of the period. See Arthur O. Lovejoy, "On the Discrimination of Romanticisms," in *Essays in the History of Ideas* (Johns Hopkins Press, 1948), 228–53.

6. Maximin, *Les fruits de la cyclone*, 81–119.

7. Voltaire, "Poem on the Lisbon Disaster," in *The Portable Voltaire*, ed. Ben Ray Redman (Penguin Books, 1977), 560–69; Jean-Jacques Rousseau, "Letter to Voltaire," in *The Discourses and Other Early Writings*, ed. Victor Gourevich (Cambridge University Press, 2011), 232–46; Immanuel Kant, "On the Causes of Earthquakes on the Occasion of the Calamity that Befell the Western Countries of Europe Toward the End of Last Year," in *Natural Science*, ed. Eric Watkins (Cambridge University Press, 2012), 327–36.

8. Immanuel Kant, "History and Natural Description of the Most Noteworthy Occurrences of the Earthquake That Struck a Large Part of the Earth at the End of the Year 1755" in *Natural Science*, ed. Watkins, 363.

9. For in-depth analysis of the development of the concept of the sublime in Burke and Kant as a way of responding to the Lisbon earthquake, see Alexander Regier, *Fracture and Fragmentation in British Romanticism* (Cambridge University Press, 2010), 75–94.

10. In Edmund Burke's theory of the sublime, which entails the spectator maintaining psychological coherence in the face of terror at the spectacle of nature's awesome power, the spectator is kept behind a wall of contemplation, which in turn allows him to escape unscathed from the natural catastrophe before him, while nature is ultimately "called up to heighten the awe and solemnity of the divine presence." Edmund Burke, *A Philosophical Enquiry into the Origins of Our Ideas of the Sublime and the Beautiful*, ed. James T. Boulton (University of Notre Dame Press, 1968), 69. There is no such "divine presence" in Kant's conception of the sublime; his version situates the individual's sense of being overpowered by natural forces in relation to a purely "internal" recognition of humanity's "super-sensuous vocation."

11. Immanuel Kant, *Critique of the Power of Judgement*, trans. Paul Guyer and Eric Matthews (Cambridge University Press, 2000), 144.

12. For the strong correlations between Kleist's depiction of the earthquake in Chile and the Lisbon earthquake, see Christoph Weber, "*Santiagos Untergang—Lissabons Schrecken: Heinrich von Kleists 'Erdbeben in Chili' im Kontext des Katastrophendiskurses im 18 Jahrhundert*," *Monatschefte* 104, no. 3 (2012): 317–36.

13. These experiences range widely and include among others the extreme forms of violence the titular character Michael Kohlhaas is willing to perform in the name of his pursuit of justice. For a reading of that extremity, see Kir Kuiken, "Impasse, Promise and Impossible Community: Kleist's *Michael Kohlhaas* and Blanchot's Community of Lovers," *Comparative Literature* 72, no. 2 (2020): 128–43. For a broader exploration of the role of violence in Kleist, see Andreas Gailus, "Breaking Skulls: Kleist, Hegel and the Force of Assertion," in *Heinrich von Kleist and Modernity*, ed. Berndt Fischer and Tim Mehigan (Camden House Publishing, 2011), 243–57.

14. *Heinrich von Kleist, "Earthquake in Chile," in Selected Writings*, ed. David Constantine (Hackett Publishing, 2004), 312. Heinrich von Kleist, *Sämtliche Werke und Briefe* (Carl Hander Verlag, 1993), 144. All further references will be cited in text as (EC) with English pagination followed by the German.

15. This is how Isak Holm largely interprets the story, framing it in terms of nineteenth-century and contemporary "disaster discourse." See Isak Winkel Holm, "Earthquake in Haiti: Kleist and the Birth of Modern Disaster Discourse," *New German Critique* 39, no. 1 (2012): 49–66.

16. Alan Bewell, "Of Weeds and Men: Evolution and the Science of Modern Natures," in *Natures in Translation* (Johns Hopkins Press, 2017), 296–326.

17. James Hutton, *The Theory of the Earth, 2 vols.* (Edinburgh, 1795). Charles Lyell, *Principles of Geology: Being an Attempt to Explain the Former Changes of the Earth's Surface, by Reference to Causes Now in Operation, 3 vols.* (John Murray, 1830). For a fuller discussion of the ideas and relationships between James Hutton and Charles Lyell, see Stephen Jay Gould, *Time's Arrow, Time's Cycle: Myth and Metaphor in the Discovery of Geological Time* (Harvard University Press, 1987). For an examination of the continued philosophical relevance of the notion of deep time in the present, see David Wood, *Deep Time, Dark Times: On Being Geologically Human* (Fordham University Press, 2019).

18. Lyell explicitly rejects the notion of catastrophism in part because it was still compatible with a biblical view of the Earth's formation.

19. Charlotte Smith, "Beachy Head," in *The Poems of Charlotte Smith*, ed. Stuart Curran (Oxford University Press, 1993), 232.

20. For a careful examination of the way Charlotte Smith integrates the historical and the geological, see Kevis Goodman, "Conjectures on Beachy Head: Charlotte Smith's Geological Poetics and the Ground of the Present," *English Literary History* 81, no. 3 (Fall 2014): 983–1006.

21. For an examination of the geological background to Shelley's poem, see Bryon Williams, "Process and Presence: Geological Influence and Innovation in Shelley's 'Mont Blanc,'" in *Romantic Ecocriticism: Origins and Legacies*, ed. Dewey W. Hall (Lexington Books, 2016), 87–104.

22. Percy Shelley, "Mont Blanc," in *Shelley's Poetry and Prose*, ed. Donald H. Reiman and Neil Fraistat (W. W. Norton, 2002), 99.

23. Frédéric Neyrat, *The Unconstructible Earth: An Ecology of Separation*, trans. Andrew S. Burk (Fordham University Press, 2019), 105–17.

24. I draw here on Jean-Luc Nancy's definition of "world" in Jean-Luc Nancy, *The*

Creation of the World or Globalization, trans. François Raffoul and David Pettigrew (State University of New York Press, 2007), 33–55. For a thorough exploration of the philosophical notion of the world from Kant to the present, see Sean Gaston, *The Concept of the World from Kant to Derrida* (Rowman and Littlefield, 2013).

25. John Keats, "Ode to Psyche," in *John Keats: The Major Works*, ed. Elizabeth Cook (Oxford University Press, 2001), 279, 280.

26. Phil Macnaghten and John Urry, *Contested Natures* (Sage Publications, 1998), 1.

27. Bewell, *Natures in Translation*, 13.

28. Louis Althusser, "Ideology and Ideological State Apparatuses," in *Lenin and Philosophy*, trans. Ben Brewster (Monthly Review Press, 1971), 162.

29. Nicholas Roe clearly demonstrated some time ago, in an argument that contests historicism's claims that Romanticism retreats from history to the supposedly ahistorical realm of nature, that "nature could never suffice as a Romantic escape from history because . . . nature as an idea and as a physical actuality was fundamental to contemporary interpretations of history and to the political theory of the age of revolutions." See Nicholas Roe, *The Politics of Nature: William Wordsworth and Some Contemporaries*, 2nd ed. (Palgrave Macmillan, 2002), 11.

30. By this term I mean something akin to the conception of the Earth Derrida describes in his introduction to Husserl's *Origin of Geometry*—that is irreducible to a mere object or thing, and provides the condition of locality or space: "The Earth is, in effect, both short of and beyond every body-object—in particular the Copernican earth—as the ground, as the here of its relative appearing. But the Earth exceeds every body-object as its infinite horizon, for it is never exhausted by the work of objectification that proceeds within it." See Jacques Derrida, *Edmund Husserl's "Origin of Geometry": An Introduction*, trans. John P. Leavey (Nicholas Hays Limited, 1978), 85.

31. I use this term to some extent similarly to Heidegger. The "world" is not the act of a subject but is a prior ontological determination of "what is." When describing how a field of research opens up, whether it is in nature or history, Heidegger describes a "projecting groundplan" (*Grundriss*): "[The essence of research] consists in the fact that knowing (*das Erkennen*) establishes itself as a procedure within some realm of beings in nature or history. Procedure, here, does not just mean methodology, how things are done. For every procedure requires, in advance, an open region within which it operates. But precisely the opening up of such a region constitutes the fundamental occurrence in research. This is accomplished through the projection within some region (for example, natural) beings—of a ground plan (*Grundriss*) of natural processes." Biology as a field of research, through a "decision" about what is, first opens up a region of being called "biological entities" that it then proceeds to analyze. See Martin Heidegger, "Age of the World Picture," in *Off the Beaten Track*, trans. Julian Young and Kenneth Haynes (Cambridge University Press, 2002), 59. In "Origin of the Work of Art," Heidegger defines the world that the artwork discloses as something other than "a collection of mere things that are present at hand" or a "imaginary framework added by our representation to the sum of things that are

present." The world is not an object that stands before us, but a prior decision about what is that makes things appear *as* natural, etc. He then goes on to define the world in contradistinction to "the Earth," which he describes as that which comes forth as concealed in relation to the world: "It [the Earth] shows itself only when it remains undisclosed and unexplained. Earth shatters every attempt to penetrate it. It turns every merely calculational intrusion into an act of destruction. Though such destruction may be accompanied by the appearance of mastery and progress in the form of the technological-scientific objectification of nature, this mastery remains, nonetheless, an impotence of the will." See Martin Heidegger, "Origin of the Work of Art," in *Off the Beaten Track*, 22, 25.

32. This is too brief a gloss on John Locke's theory of property, which originates from each man being a "property in his own person." That self-possession allows his labor to mix that property with "the Earth and all inferior creatures" such that "whatsoever then he removes out of the State that Nature hath provided, and left it in, he hath mixed his *Labour* with, and joined to it something that is his own, and thereby makes it his *Property*." See John Locke, *Two Treatises of Government*, ed. Peter Laslett (Cambridge University Press, 2004), 287–88.

33. I have in mind here in particular Lyotard's conception of the sublime "after" its foregrounding by Kant in the eighteenth century, which for Lyotard designates an unprecedented relation between art and matter: "Matter does not question the mind, it has no need of it, it exists, or rather *insists*, it sists, 'before' questioning and answer, 'outside' them. It is unpresentable to the mind, always withdrawn from its grasp." Jean-François Lyotard, *The Inhuman*, trans. Geoffrey Bennington and Rachel Bowlby (Stanford University Press, 1991), 142.

34. Bruno Latour makes this sense of enmeshment in the Earth, what he calls the "terrestrial," the basis for a new sense of global politics predicated on a recognition of the finitude of the Earth, and of our dependence on it. See Bruno Latour, *Down to Earth: Politics in the New Climatic Regime*, trans. Catherine Porter (Polity Press, 2018). Isabelle Stengers puts this sense of terrestrial enmeshment even more bluntly: "And it is precisely because she [the living planet] is not threatened that she makes the epic versions of human history, in which Man, standing up on his hind legs and learning to decipher the laws of nature, understands that he is the master of his own fate, free of any transcendence, look rather old." Isabelle Stengers, *In Catastrophic Times: Resisting the Coming Barbarism*, trans. Andrew Goffey (Open Humanities Press, 2015), 47.

35. Dipesh Chakrabarty, "The Planet Does Not Return Our Gaze," *Alienocene*, December 4, 2020, https://alienocene.com/2020/12/04/the-planet-does-not-return-our-gaze/.

36. I write this in the wake of the increasing effects of drought and global warming that have significantly amplified the scale and devastation of forest fires that have begun to impact life in major Western financial centers, such as New York City.

37. "*Les lois secrètes d'une logique du vivant, à côte des malheurs causées par les humains.*" Daniel Maximin, *Les fruits du cyclone: Une géopoetique de la Caraïbe* (Éditions du Seuil, 2006), 102 (translation mine).

38. For a recent collection of essays exploring the relation between Romanticism

and the Haitian Revolution, see Kir Kuiken and Deborah Elise White, eds., *Haiti's Literary Legacies: Romanticism and the Unthinkable Revolution* (Bloomsbury Press, 2022).

39. Immanuel Kant, *Conflict of the Faculties*, trans. Mary J. Gregor (University of Nebraska Press, 1992), 153.

40. Alvaro S. Pereira, "The Opportunity of a Disaster: The Economic Impact of the 1755 Lisbon Earthquake," *Journal of Economic History* 69, no. 2 (2009): 466–99.

41. A recent study of Black and indigenous writers of the Atlantic world during the period that coincides with Romanticism makes a convincing argument that authors such as William Apess, Samson Occom, Mary Prince, and Robert Wedderburn engaged in their own "world-making alternatives" in the face of the obliteration of non-Western cosmologies. Though its conception of the relation between that world-making and the Earth remains primarily focused on the Earth as commons (a concept I deal with in chap. 2), its argument in many ways complements my own, suggesting another trajectory of Romantic-era writing that could be said to be interested in developing a kind of geopoetics. See Shelby Johnson, *The Rich Earth Between Us: The Intimate Grounds of Race and Sexuality in the Atlantic World, 1770–1840* (University of North Carolina Press, 2024), 7.

42. Seanna Sumalee Oakley, *Common Places: The Poetics of African Atlantic Postromantics* (Rodopi Press, 2011), 17.

43. Mary Modeen and Iain Biggs, *Creative Engagement with Ecologies of Place: Geopoetics, Deep Mapping and Slow Residencies* (Routledge Press, 2021), 3.

44. The English version of a description of Kenneth White's "International Institute of Geopoetics" can be found at https://www.institut-geopoetique.org/en/.

45. Of course, most of the archipelagoes immediately threatened with disappearance are located in the Indian and Pacific Oceans. While not threatened by disappearance, Caribbean Island nations are experiencing increasing coastal erosion as a result of global warming.

46. Bruno Latour, *The Politics of Nature*, trans. Catherine Porter (Harvard University Press, 2004), 37.

47. It is this sense of a loss of bearings and a loss of a "native ground" that distinguishes Romanticism's conception of the Earth from Kelly Oliver's philosophical account of the relation between Earth and world, where the explicit goal is to develop a new sense of our "belonging to earth as home." Kelly Oliver, *Earth and World: Philosophy After the Apollo Missions* (Columbia University Press, 2015), 139.

48. I have in mind here Gilles Deleuze and Félix Guattari's conception of the Earth not as a stable ground, but as a movement of "deterritorialization." In other words, the Earth is constantly opening territories and worlds "onto an elsewhere" while simultaneously reconstituting territories otherwise: "The Earth constantly carries out a movement of deterritorialization on the spot, by which it goes beyond any territory: it is deterritorializing and deterritorialized." Gilles Deleuze and Félix Guattari, *What Is Philosophy?*, trans. Hugh Tomlinson and Graham Burchell (Columbia University Press, 1994), 85. For a careful and illuminating reading of Deleuze and Guattari's geo-

philosophy, see Zsuzsa Baross, "Geophilosophy," in *On Contemporaneity, After Agamben* (Sussex University Press, 2020), 99–119.

49. This trope is ubiquitous in Rousseau and is most prominent in "Discourse on the Origins of Inequality," where the "savage" is understood as another name for Man in a state of nature, and where "natural compassion" has not yet been surrendered in the civil polity. See Jean-Jacques Rousseau, "Discourse on the Origin of Inequality Among Men," in *The Discourses and Other Early Political Writings*, trans. Victor Gourevich (Cambridge University Press,1997), 113–222.

50. Jean Bernabé, Patrick Chamoiseau, and Raphaël Confiant, *Éloge de la Créolité/ In Praise of Creoleness*, trans. M. B. Taleb-Khyar (Johns Hopkins University Press, 1990).

51. Jean-Luc Nancy, *After Fukushima*, trans. Charlotte Mandell (Fordham University Press, 2015), 5.

52. From a very different perspective, Evan Gottlieb has recently argued that what he calls "Romantic globalism," which had its origin in the Scottish Enlightenment, also sought to challenge aspects of the existing colonial order. See Evan Gottlieb, *Romantic Globalism: British Literature and Modern World Order 1750–1830* (Ohio State University Press, 2014).

53. Gayatri Spivak, "Imperative to Re-Imagine the Planet," in *An Aesthetic Education in the Era of Globalization* (Harvard University Press, 2012), 338.

54. Édouard Glissant, *The Poetics of Relation*, trans. Betsy Wing (University of Michigan Press, 1997), 33.

55. Olive Senior, *Shell* (Insomniac Press, 2007), 73, 96.

56. Patrick Chamoiseau, *Slave Old Man*, trans. Linda Coverdale (The New Press, 2018), 102.

57. Frankétienne, *Melovivi ou le piège* (Riveneuve Éditions, 2010), 51, 30 (translation mine).

58. Maximin, *Les fruits du cyclone (translation mine).*

Chapter 1

1. William Wordsworth, *The Thirteen-Book "Prelude,"* vol. 1, ed. Mark Reed, 2 vols. (Cornell University Press, 1991), 186 (6:354). All citations from Wordsworth's *Prelude* are from this edition, vol. 1, and will henceforth be cited in text by book number, followed by line numbers.

2. Carl Schmitt argues that the founding act of law in the period of colonization is the original constitutive act of land appropriation and the spatial ordering of the planet. As he insists, "all subsequent developments [in law] are either results of and expansions on this act or else redistributions (*anadasmoi*)—either a continuation on the same basis or a disintegration of and departure from the constitutive act of the spatial order established by land-appropriation, the founding of cities, or colonization." See Carl Schmitt, *The Nomos of the Earth*, trans. G. L. Ulmen (Telos Press Publishing, 2006), 78.

3. John Drabinski argues that Glissant develops a cosmopolitanism "at the level of

ontology," thereby refusing "the ethno-nationalist state from the beginning, breaking with that feature of the nation form in a postmodernity that is simultaneous with the emergence of modernity." See John E. Drabinski, "Reproduction and the Universal in Glissant's Later Work," *New Centennial Review*, 18, no. 3 (Winter 2018), 16.

4. Schmitt, *The Nomos of the Earth*, 45, 42, 43.

5. William Wordsworth insists in the "Preface to Lyrical Ballads" that the poet "considers man and nature as essentially adapted to each other, and the mind of man as naturally the mirror of the fairest and most interesting qualities of nature." "Preface to Lyrical Ballads," in *The Prose Works of William Wordsworth*, vol. 1, ed. W. J. B. Owen and Jane Smyser (Oxford University Press, 1974), 140.

6. Alexander Koch, Chris Brierly, Mark M. Maslin, and Simon L. Lewis, "Earth System Impacts of the European Arrival and Great Dying in the Americas After 1492," *Quaternary Science Reviews* 207, no. 1 (March 2019): 13–36. https://www.sciencedirect.com/science/article/pii/S0277379118307261?via%253Dihub.

7. Homi Bhabha, *The Location of Culture* (London: Routledge Press, 1994), 146, 143.

8. See, for instance, Benedict Anderson, "Memory and Forgetting," in *Imagined Communities* (Verso Books, 2006), 187–206.

9. Édouard Glissant, *Caribbean Discourse: Selected Essays*, trans. J. Michael Dash (University Press of Viginia, 1989), 165.

10. Jean Bernabé, Patrick Chamoiseau, and Raphaël Confiant, *Éloge de la Créolité/In Praise of Creoleness*, trans. M. B. Taleb-Khyar (Gallimard, 1989).

11. John E. Drabinski argues convincingly that this term is central to all Glissant's thought, articulating the simultaneity of here and elsewhere, self and other. My argument is also thoroughly indebted to his interpretation of Glissant's concatenation of geography and thought, which Drabinski calls a "geography of reason." The difference between our two readings concerns the centrality of the Earth in Glissant as the primary "elsewhere," a fundamental alterity to every "world" or community that is the basis for articulating the *form* that community takes. See John E. Drabinski, *Glissant and the Middle Passage: Philosophy, Beginning, Abyss* (University of Minnesota Press, 2019).

12. Édouard Glissant, *Poetics of Relation*, trans. Betsy Wing (University of Michigan Press, 2010), 7. Édouard Glissant, *Poétique de la Relation* (Gallimard, 1990), 19. Henceforth cited in text as (PR) beginning with English pagination, followed by French pagination.

13. François Noudelmann and Celia Britton argue that the historical "abyss" of the Middle Passage is an essential component to an understanding of Glissant's conception of creolization, since it constitutes a structure "that emerges from the loss, the break with all origins in the chaos of heterogeneous, jumbled identities." See François Noudelmann and Celia Britton, "Édouard Glissant's Legacy: Transmitting Without Universals?" *Callaloo* 36, no. 4 (Fall 2013): 869–74. Stanka Radović similarly argues that the historical "abyss" of the Middle Passage constitutes for Glissant a "void" out of which a new culture emerges by being "narrated into a particular place—the Caribbean." See Stanka Radović, "The Birthplace of Relation: Édouard Glissant's *Poétique de la Relation*: For Ranko," *Callaloo* 30, no. 2 (Spring 2007): 475–81.

14. John E. Drabinski suggests that "the world" for Glissant signifies "a series of temporal, spatial, geographic and cultural folds that do the work of liberation in the context of the world as such rather than flirting with the truncated notion of totality one finds in levelling visions of nationalism and fixation on the state." See John E. Drabinski, "Sites of Relation and Tout-Monde: Reflections on Glissant's Late Work," *Angelaki* 24, no. 3 (2019): 164.

15. For a reading of the sea as an "opening upon a world of endless possibilities," see Beverley Omorod, "Beyond Négritude: Some Aspects of the Work of Édouard Glissant," *Contemporary Literature* 15, no. 3 (Summer 1974): 360–69.

16. Glissant seems to have in mind Gilles Deleuze and Félix Guattari's concept of the Earth as a "plane of immanence" that acts as a unitary surface upon which encounters take place between bodies, affects, and other matter, and where there is no exteriority or transcendence. See Gilles Deleuze and Félix Guattari, "10,000 B.C.: The Geology of Morals (Who Does the Earth Think It Is?)," in *A Thousand Plateaus: Capitalism and Schizophrenia*, trans. Brian Massumi (University of Minnesota Press, 1998), 39–74.

17. John E. Drabinski, for example, argues that for Glissant, "geography proves decisive, as the figures of landscape, earth, and the historical experience that inform the given and its possibilities condition subjectivity's content and structure." See Drabinski, *Glissant and the Middle Passage*, 133. Peter Hitchcock has likewise suggested a geographical situatedness as central to Glissant poetics: see Peter Hitchcock, "Antillanité and the Art of Resistance," *Research in African Literatures* 27, no. 2 (Summer 1996): 33–50. See also Lorna Burns, "Landscape and Genre in the Caribbean Canon: Creolizing the Poetics of Place and Paradise," *Journal of West Indian Literature* 17, no. 1 (November 2008): 20–41. Michael Dash's early examination of Glissant's "archipelagic thinking" also attempts to understand the way it is "directement liée à la distance" (directly related to distance) and to a thinking of the other. See Michael Dash, "*Île Rocher Île Mangrove: Éléments d'une pensée archipélique dans l'oeuvre d' Édouard Glissant*," in *Poétiques d'Édouard Glissant, ed. Jacques Chevrier* (Presses Universitaires de Paris-Sorbonne, 1999), 17–24.

18. See G. W. F. Hegel, "The Natural Context or the Geographical Basis of World History," in *Lectures on the Philosophy of World History*, trans. H. B. Nisbet (Cambridge University Press, 1996), 152–220.

19. Édouard Glissant, *Poetic Intention*, trans. Nathalie Stephens and Anne Malena (Nightboat Books, 2010), 7. Édouard Glissant, *L'intention poétique* (Éditions du Seuil 1969), 11, henceforth cited in text as (PI) with English pagination followed by French pagination.

20. Jacques Rancière, "The Distribution of the Sensible," in *The Politics of Aesthetics*, trans. Gabriel Rockhill (Continuum Press, 2004), 12.

21. For an analysis of different conceptions of the unity or wholeness of the Earth in Glissant, see Raphael Lauro and Emily Maguire, "Édouard Glissant's Excursions and Detours," *Discourse* 36, no. 1 (Winter 2014): 3–30.

22. The difference between the "whole-world" and the Earth pertains not just to two modalities of totality, but to the irreducibility of Earth and world. While the Earth,

for Glissant, is the precondition for any world or "culture," it remains irreducible to all of them. The "whole-world," however, is the space and time of their interaction, a different space and time than the ancestrality of the Earth. As John E. Drabinski suggests, "*Tout-monde* [whole-earth] is already a curved space (the physical form of the globe) and a curved time (composed of divergent, incompatible historical narratives that nonetheless touch), and so that term itself bears many of the characteristics of the circular nomad and its rhizome-identity." That is, the "whole-world" is a way of describing the space and time of the interaction of cultures, whereas the Earth is Glissant's way of articulating the situatedness and conditions of possibility of that interaction. Drabinski, *Glissant and the Middle Passage*, 134.

23. Glissant characterizes the "whole-world" as also a "chaos-world," by which he means a world or totality that cannot be made consistent with itself. For a reading of this term in Caribbean literature in general, and Glissant in particular, see Jeannine Murray-Roman, "Reading in the Diminutive: Caribbean Chaos Theory in Antonio Benítez-Rojo, Édouard Glissant, and Wilson Harris," *Small Axe: A Caribbean Journal of Criticism* 19, no. 1, special issue 46 (2015): 20–36.

24. Celia Britton has argued that Glissant's conception of a community in relation, along with his idea that each community or culture has an element of "opacity," prevents any community predicated on notions of fusion rather than difference. See Celia Britton, "Past, Future and the Maroon Community in Édouard Glissant's *Le quatrième siècle*," in *The Sense of Community in French Caribbean Fiction* (Liverpool University Press, 2010), 36–54.

25. As John E. Drabinski has demonstrated, by locating a certain kind of cosmopolitanism (or "Caribbeanness") at the ontological level, Glissant "refuses the techno-nationalist state from the beginning, breaking with that feature of the nation form in a postmodernity that is simultaneous with the emergence of modernity." See John E. Drabinski, "Reproduction and the Universal in Glissant's Later Work," *New Centennial Review* 18, no. 3 (Winter 2018): 1–18.

26. Édouard Glissant, *Treatise on the Whole-World*, trans. Celia Britton (Liverpool University Press, 2020), 119.

27. See Deleuze and Guattari, *A Thousand Plateaus*, 1–25. Glissant's use of "rhizome" has received extensive critical attention. For an argument that claims it is a central feature of Caribbean thought, see Richard L.W. Clarke, "Root vs. Rhizome: An Epistemological Break in Francophone Caribbean Thought," *Journal of West Indian Literature* 9, no. 1 (April 2000): 12–41. For an argument that articulates the important differences between Deleuze and Guattari's and Glissant's use of the term, see Neal Allar, "Rhizomatic Influence: The Anti-genealogy of Glissant and Deleuze," *Cambridge Journal of Postcolonial Literary Inquiry* 6, no. 1 (2019): 1–13.

28. Nick Nesbitt has argued that Glissant's conception of relation as a poetics or aesthetics "definitely abandons the Fanonian struggle for an alternative structuration of social reality (as nation)." See Nick Nesbitt, "Édouard Glissant: From *Poétique de la Relation* to the Transcendental Analytic of Relation," in *Caribbean Critique: Antillean Critical Theory from Toussaint to Glissant* (Liverpool University Press, 2013),

231–50. Nesbitt's reading, however, fails to consider the extent to which Glissant understands poetics as performative, and relation as the realization of that performativity. A similar argument about Glissant's "utopian" and depoliticized late work can be found in Chris Bongie's *Islands and Exiles* (Stanford University Press, 1998). For a clear and cogent critique of these positions, see Celia Britton, "Globalization and Political Action in the Work of Édouard Glissant," *Small Axe: A Caribbean Journal of Criticism* 13, no. 3, special issue 30 (2009): 1–11.

29. For a careful elaboration of the relations Glissant establishes between identity and malleability, see Celia Britton, "Identity and Change in the Work of Édouard Glissant," *Small Axe: A Caribbean Journal of Criticism* 21, no. 1 (March 2017): 169–79.

30. For a reading of this term as an "archipelagic" form of memory, see Bonnie Thomas, "Édouard Glissant and the Art of Memory," *Small Axe: A Caribbean Journal of Criticism* 13, no. 3 (November 2009): 25–36.

31. Édouard Glissant, *Mémoires des esclavages* (Gallimard, 2007), 22. All translations of the text are mine.

32. "*Une pensée archipellique, qui invente à chaque moment les effets de la Relation, disperse et éclabousse les identités en rapport, les renforce chacune cependant et les garantit de l'autisme identitaire, et tremble avec le monde éblouissant . . . par la mémoire de la collectivité Terre, nous pensons avec le monde.*" Glissant, *Mémoires des esclavages*, 166.

33. "*Indépendente de l'action officielle des Etats*," Glissant, *Mémoires des esclavages*, 167.

34. As John E. Drabinksi insists in his analysis of this term, "the meaning and significance of a *Caribbean* loss thus appeals, from the very first, to a geographically rooted *poeisis* with roots in a wounded earth, a tortured geography." The term "tortured geography" pertains not just to the extent to which the Caribbean has been transformed in the service of cash crops, but also to the legacies of the violence and brutality committed in its construction. See Drabinski, *Glissant and the Middle Passage*, 190.

35. This theme can, of course, also be found in many of Glissant's own novels, though in far less of a direct or allegorical form. The opening of *The Overseer's Cabin*, for instance, begins with the following meditation on the relation between a communal "we" and the island of Martinique: "Pythagore Celat went around loudly trumpeting 'we' though there was not a soul who could guess what he meant by it. A 'we' that perhaps, when all was said and done, we could never ever form, this unique body that would make it possible for us to begin entering into our spread of earth or the violet sea around it . . . or into the protracted repercussions weaving the faroffness of the world for us; we who act so crazily scattered; we who rolled our separate selves around, bumping up against each other without ever managing to adjust and settle into this belt of islands." See Édouard Glissant, *The Overseer's Cabin*, trans. Betsy Wing (University of Nebraska Press, 2011), 5.

36. Erna Brodber's work helps clarify Glissant's conception of "territory" and its relation to an understanding of a community's unique filiation as a myth of origins, a story about a unilinear identity predicated on a rooted relation to land. For a reading

of this relation between myth and land in Glissant, see Wilbert J. Roget, "Land and Myth in the Writing of Édouard Glissant," *World Literature Today* 63, no. 4 (Autumn 1989): 626–31.

37. Erna Brodber, *The Rainmaker's Mistake* (New Beacon Books, 2007), 2. Henceforth cited in text as (RM) followed by page number.

38. For a reading of the shifting temporal and spatial coordinates of the novel, see Kelly Josepha, "Beyond Geography, Past Time: Afrofuturism, *The Rainmaker's Mistake*, and Caribbean Studies," *Small Axe: A Caribbean Journal of Criticism* 17, no. 2 (2013): 123–35.

39. See Elizabeth De Loughrey, "Yam, Roots and Rot: Allegories of the Provision Grounds," *Small Axe: A Caribbean Journal of Criticism* 15, no. 1 (March 2011): 58–75; quote at 62.

40. Although Brodber's novel plays with unfixed temporalities and spatialities in the era of myth, Candace Ward argues that these shifts and displacements are nevertheless "grounded in the soil." See Candace Ward, "'In the Free': The Work of Emancipation in the Anglo-Caribbean Historical Novel," *Journal of American Studies* 49, no. 2 (May 2015): 377.

41. I place this term in quotation marks to suggest that what has changed is not a relation to lineage as such, but to the notion of origin as a single patrilinear structure. The former would be something approximating Kamau Brathwaite's concept of a "literature of reconnection" with the African lineage present in Caribbean cultures, a term he uses to describe Caribbean writing that entails a "recognition of the African presence in our society not as a static quality, but as root living, creative, and still part of the main." See Kamau Brathwaite, *Roots* (University of Michigan Press, 1993), 255.

42. See W. E. B. Du Bois, "The Souls of Black Folk," in *Writings* (Library of America, 1986), 357–547.

43. See Frantz Fanon, "The Negro and Psychopathology," in *Black Skin White Masks*, trans. Charles Lam Markmann (Grave Press, 1967), 141–209.

44. Saree Makdisi, *Making England Western: Occidentalism, Race and Imperial Culture* (University of Chicago Press, 2014), ix, xi.

45. Makdisi argues that the ballad form, and Wordsworth's use of it, was too wedded to the notion of the individual subject central to the hegemonic radicalism of the 1790s. As a result, "Wordsworth's attitude to the common people of England and their cultural and political forms was (however sympathetic it may have been) on the same wavelength as the Orientalist's attitude toward his Oriental objects of representation." See Makdisi, *Making England Western*, 108. While I don't disagree with Makdisi's argument in its totality, I do claim that there is another Wordsworth at work here and there, particularly in "Home at Grasmere," where a relational model to the other through the landscape short-circuits the question of representation, and as such offers a more nonhegemonic radicalism I am terming Wordsworth's "geopoetics."

46. Though it is not foregrounded as strongly in Glissant as in Wordsworth's "Home at Grasmere," Carine Mardossian has suggested that Glissant's conception of totality does in fact extend to the nonhuman world. See Carine Mardossian, "Poetics

of Landscape: Édouard Glissant's Creolized Ecologies," *Callaloo* 36, no. 4 (Fall 2013): 983–94.

47. As Ron Broglio has argued, cartography itself involves an attempt to homogenize the geographic space of the nation: "As those who issue and control maps create an ordering of affairs out of the sprawling terrain, Nature becomes a calculable sum. To plot a course between cities, to measure the amount of land held, to mark private property lines, to provide guidelines for tithing and taxes, in brief to mark lived transactions of a people, a country provides national, standardized maps. National maps constructed by a government serve the stability and longevity of the nation." See Ron Broglio, "Mapping British Earth and Sky," *Wordsworth Circle* 33, no. 2 (2002): 70–76.

48. For an example, see Simon White, "Wordsworth and Community," in *Romanticism and the Rural Community* (Palgrave Macmillan, 2013), 41–78. John Rieder had earlier argued that "the interior of Wordsworth's community of recognition crystalizes civil society into a consolatory image where sympathetic virtue claims to restore the lost presence of a 'natural' immediacy in the very act of reading its traces." See John Rieder, *Wordsworth's Counterrevolutionary Turn: Community, Virtue, and Vision in the 1790s* (University of Delaware Press, 1997), 229. For a reading of landscape and solitude in Wordsworth's *The Excursion* which argues that interpretations of landscape constituted an engagement with the political for Wordsworth, see Alex Benchimol, "Debatable Geographies of Romantic Nostalgia: The Redemptive Landscape in Wordsworth and Cobbett," in *Romanticism's Debatable Lands*, ed. Claire Lamont and Michael Rossington (Palgrave Macmillan, 2007), 92–104.

49. See Jean-Jacques Rousseau, "Discourse on the Origin and Foundations of Inequality Among Men," in *The Discourses and Other Early Political Writings*, ed. Victor Gourevich (Cambridge University Press, 2011), 113–231.

50. I am here arguing that Wordsworth, in "Home at Grasmere," is engaged in precisely the opposite of what James M. Garrett calls "writing the nation," which he claims Wordsworth developed through a " 'prospect view,' a vision of the world where everything and everyone is reduced to abstraction, where the particulars of the local landscape, people and manner are coerced into a national sameness." That is precisely the "view" Wordsworth avoids in his early poem. See James M. Garrett, *Wordsworth and the Writing of the Nation* (Routledge Press, 2008), 69.

51. Wordsworth's humanism is one of the many ways in which his project remains fundamentally distinct from Glissant's, suggesting that something like the universal takes shape once again at the level of relations between various landscapes and other "nooks of earth."

52. William Wordsworth, *Home at Grasmere, Part First, Book First of the Recluse*, ed. Beth Darlington (Ithaca: Cornell University Press, 1977), 40, lines 42–46. All further citations of the poem will be made in text using Manuscript B—the earlier version—as (HG) followed by page and line numbers.

53. James Engell helpfully distinguishes between Wordsworth's conception of Nature and his conception of the earth. See James Engell, "Wordsworth's Earth, Nature, Strength," *Wordsworth Circle* 50, no. 2 (2019): 166–79.

54. For a reading of this phrase in *The Prelude*, see Kir Kuiken, "'To the Great Ends of Liberty and Power': Community and the Problem of Sovereignty in Wordsworth's *Prelude*," in *Imagined Sovereignties: Toward a New Political Romanticism* (Fordham University Press, 2014), 121–68.

55. Tim Fulford reads the poem in terms of Wordsworth's disinheritance by Lord Lonsdale of his estate, viewing poetry as a usurpation of the power of land ownership. As he puts it, Wordsworth "has to struggle with his desire to replace the landlord's exclusive possession with his own, to struggle to share with his sister, his friends and his readers a landscape by involvement with which a dispersed community can be renewed." See Tim Fulford, "Fields of Liberty?: The Politics of Wordsworth's Grasmere," *European Romantic Review* 9, no. 1 (1998): 69.

56. Joseph Albernaz has argued that "Home at Grasmere" presents an example of what he calls, following Jean-Luc Nancy, a "groundless community" founded on an experience, "detached both from older metaphysical certainties that would ground collective identity and from newer modern regimes of totalizing equivalence." While he finds this groundless community in the everyday domesticity upon which the poem focuses, my own reading of the unpossessable landscape in the poem resonates with the difference Albernaz articulates between a community located in its "proper rooted place" and one "constituted by its sharing out." Though I would describe the latter more in terms of Glissant's conception of relation, there are important affinities between Albernaz's reading of the poem and my own. See Joseph Albernaz, "Fragmentary Domesticity: Wordsworth's Image of the Common," *New Literary History* 51, no. 3 (Summer 2020): 523–47.

57. See, for example, James Castell, "The Society of Birds in 'Home at Grasmere,'" in *Grasmere 2010: Selected Papers from the Wordsworth Summer Conference*, ed. Richard Gravil (Humanities E-Books, 2010), 65–76; Bruce Clark, "Wordsworth's Departed Swans: Sublimation and Sublimity in 'Home at Grasmere,'" *Studies in Romanticism* 19, no. 4 (1980): 355–74.

58. Raimonda Modiano, "Blood Sacrifice, Gift Economy and the Edenic World: Wordsworth's 'Home at Grasmere,'" *Studies in Romanticism* 32, no. 4 (Winter 1993): 483.

59. The book of *The Prelude* that follows the description of Wordsworth's disenchantment with the French Revolution is titled "Imagination: How Impaired and Restored," a pattern of loss and recuperation that arguably structures the entire *Prelude*.

60. In other words, this is the opposite of Derrida's "*tout autre est tout autre*" or "every other is completely other," a turn of phrase meant to capture the extent to which the otherness of the other cannot be abstracted or universalized. The notion is formulated, among other places, in *The Gift of Death*. See Jacques Derrida, "*Tout autre est tout autre*," in *The Gift of Death, 2nd ed.*, trans. David Wills (University of Chicago Press, 2008), 82–116.

61. Wordsworth uses this phrase to describe the anonymity of the city, and the extent to which the form community takes within it is purely haphazard, organized by commercial relations that have no other purpose to them. William Wordsworth,

The Thirteen-Book Prelude, vol. 1, ed. Mark L. Reed (Cornell University Press, 1991), 210 (7:705).

62. Dorothy Wordsworth, *The Grasmere and Alfoxden Journals* (Oxford University Press, 2002), 92.

63. William Wordsworth, *Poems in Two Volumes and Other Poems, 1800–1807*, ed. Jared Curtis (Cornell University Press, 1983), 563. Henceforth cited in text as (WJ) followed by page number and line numbers.

64. The Cumbrian museum webpage for the Wordsworth Museum and Dove Cottage still features a hike to this site, which is still named "John's Cove." See http://www.trailsoftheunexpected.org.uk/trails/wordsworths-grasmere.

65. It is something of this injunction that Latour addresses in his distinction between "humans" and "Terrans," where the former remain immured in conceptions of human exceptionalism and are therefore incapable of living with others on the Earth, whereas the latter have fallen back "down to Earth" as an absolute limit to endless economic growth. See Bruno Latour, *Down to Earth: Politics in the New Climatic Regime*, trans. Catherine Porter (Polity Press, 2018).

Chapter 2

1. Nebojsa Nakicenovic, Johan Rockström, Owen Gaffney, and Caroline Zimm, "Global Commons in the Anthropocene: World Development on a Stable and Resilient Planet." https://pure.iiasa.ac.at/id/eprint/14003/#:~:text=We%20argue%20that%20humanity%20must,Global%20Commons%20in%20the%20Anthropocene" (Creative commons license), 2016, 27.

2. Nakicenovic et al., 32–36.

3. As J. M. Neeson carefully details, "commoners" were a legal category of persons who had "common right," that is, rights to certain foraging or other land use on owned land. See J. M. Neeson, "Who Had Common Right?," in *Commoners; Common Right, Enclosure and Social Change in England 1700–1820* (Cambridge University Press, 1993), 55–80.

4. My analysis in this chapter is informed by the recent publication of Joseph Albernaz's book *Common Measures*, which traces a theory of the commons in Romanticism to the present, and extends its meaning beyond its legal definition to explore "what happens to the experience of community when the grounds of community dissolve" and where a "groundless" community comes into being through a "sharing that precedes identity and displaces protocols of property." Though I define that sharing differently—as predicated on the Earth's temporal anteriority—there are several affinities between Albernaz's conception of the commons and my own use of the term here, particularly when it comes to the formation of a community predicated on something that cannot be shared in the usual sense of a collective identity or essence, or a rootedness in the land. See Joseph Albernaz, *Common Measures: Romanticism and the Groundlessness of Community* (Stanford University Press, 2024), 1–2.

5. I draw here on Derrida's conception of a gift that exceeds the restricted economy of exchange and is instead an "unforeseeable *exception* (without general rule, without

program, and even without concept)." See Jacques Derrida, *Given Time: 1. Counterfeit Money*, trans. Peggy Kamuf (University of Chicago Press, 1992), 129.

6. King James Bible (Gen. 1:26).

7. Though this formulation is found throughout Heidegger, his most focused elaboration of its relation to the gift is in Martin Heidegger, *On Time and Being*, trans. Joan Stambaugh (University of Chicago Press, 2002).

8. Derrida, *Given Time*, 13, 54.

9. A version of this idea can be found in Derrida's discussion of the relation between the Earth and the lifeworld in his *Introduction to the Origin of Geometry*, trans. John P. Leavey (Nicolas Hays, 1978), 83–85. Husserl claims that the Earth is not just an object or planet, but what he calls a "primordial body," a material object unlike any other that is the condition of appearance of objects in general. What Derrida questions is Husserl's identification of this ground for the human "lifeworld" with the Earth itself.

10. John Locke, "Property," in *Two Treatises of Government*, ed. Peter Laslett (Cambridge University Press, 2004), 285–302.

11. Locke, "Property," 286, 287–88.

12. In the "Ends of Man," Jacques Derrida insists that this notion of the "proper of man"—what constitutes the essential characteristic of the Man or the human—must be deconstructed along with the very concept of Man itself. See Jacques Derrida, "The Ends of Man," in *Margins of Philosophy*, trans. Alan Bass (University of Chicago Press, 1982), 111–36.

13. John Locke, *Two Treatises*, 288. As Locke insists: "Among those who are counted the Civiliz'd part of Mankind, who have made and multiplied positive Laws to determine Property, this original Law of Nature for the *beginning of Property*, in what was before common, still takes place" (289).

14. Nicole Louise Willson, "People Without Shoes: Jacques Roumain, Langston Hughes, and Their Transnational *Ti Nèg* Aesthetic," *Comparative American Studies* 15, no. 3–4 (2017): 146–61.

15. Anita Patterson argues that this alliance was part of the emergence of a distinctly Caribbean modernism. See Anita Patterson, "'I've Known Rivers: Langston Hughes, Jacques Roumain, and the Emergence of Caribbean Modernism," *Langston Hughes Review* 27, no. 1 (2021): 12–28. For a detailed reading of the cultural practice of forming this diaspora, see Brent Edwards, *Practice of Diaspora: Literature, Translation and the Rise of Black Internationalism* (Harvard University Press, 2003).

16. Langston Hughes, "The Negro Speaks of Rivers," in *Collected Poems of Langston Hughes*, ed. Arnold Rampersad (Vintage Books, 1994), 23.

17. See, for instance, Fritz Calixte, "*Le 'retour' dans Gouverneurs de la Rosée*," in *Revolte, subversion et développement chez Jacques Roumain*, ed. Michel Acacia (Éditions de l'Université d'État d'Haïti, 2007), 65–72, and Celia Britton, "Restoring Lost Unity in Jacques Roumain's *Gouverneurs de la Rosée*," in *The Sense of Community in French Caribbean Fiction* (Liverpool University Press, 2008), 19–35.

18. Michael Dash, "Fictions of Displacement: Locating Modern Haitian Narratives," *Small Axe: A Caribbean Journal of Criticism* 12, no. 3 (2008): 41.

19. Britton, "Restoring Lost Unity," 33.

20. "*En me renversant, on n'a abattu à Saint-Domingue que le tronc de l'arbre de la liberté des noirs; il poussera par les racines parce qu'elles sont profondes et nombreuses.*" J. C. Dorsainvil, *Histoire d'Haiti*, 119, as cited in *Jacques Roumain: Oeuvres complètes*, 447 (translation mine).

21. For a detailed analysis of the way Roumain positioned himself between two different class identities, see Kathy Richman, "Whose Other?: The Centrality of Language to Identity and Representation in Roumain's *Gouverneurs de la Rosée*," in *Empire Lost: France and Its Other Worlds*, ed. Elisabeth Mudimbe-Boyi (Lexington Books, 2009), 105–24.

22. Beverley Omorod, *Introduction to the French Caribbean Novel* (Heineman Educational Books, 1985), 19.

23. Toni Presseley-Sanon, "*Masters of the Dew*, the Peasant, the Environment, and the Oral Tradition," in *Haitian Peasantry Through Oral and Written Literature* (Caribbean Studies Press, 2016), 65–83.

24. Omorod, *Introduction*,19.

25. Jacques Roumain, *Masters of the Dew*, trans. Langston Hughes and Mercer Cook (Heinmann Press, 1947), 23; Jacques Roumain, *Gouverneurs de la Rosée*, in *Jacques Roumain: Oeuvres complètes*, ed. Léon-François Hoffmann (Collection Archivos, 2003), 267. All further citations will be made in text as MD, beginning with the Hughes and Cook's English translation, followed by the French pagination.

26. Britton, "Restoring Lost Unity," 22.

27. For a careful elaboration of the relation between Roumain's "indigenism," eroticism, and patriotism, see Jean Michael Dash, "*Jacques Roumain Romancier*," in *Jacques Roumain: Oeuvres complètes*, ed. Léon-François Hoffmann (Collection Archivos, 2003), 1359–77.

28. Valerie Kaussen, "Slaves, *Viejos*, and the *Internationale*: The Marxist Novels of Jacques Roumain and Jacques-Stephen Alexis," in *Migrant Revolutions: Haitian Literature, Globalization, and U.S. Imperialism* (Lexington Books, 2008), 133.

29. For a careful analysis of Roumain's use and avoidance of religious motifs in the novel, see Ulrich Fleischmann, "*Jacques Roumain dans la littérature d'Haïti*," in *Jacques Roumain: Oeuvres complètes*, 1229–65.

30. For an in-depth analysis of the relation between ecological destruction, conceptions of nature, and the syncretic religions of the Caribbean, see Lizabeth Paravisini-Gebert, "'He of the Trees': Nature, Environment and Creole Religiosities in Caribbean Literature," in *Caribbean Literature and the Environment: Between Nature and Culture*, ed. Elizabeth DeLoughrey, Renée Gosson, and George Handley (University of Virginia Press, 2005), 182–96.

31. Gérard Barthélemy questions this explanation of erosion, showing that colonialism's deforestation and climate change are the source. However, Roumain is dealing with an allegory, not describing the actual source of ecological decay. See Gérard Barthélemy, "*Voyage au pays des Gouverneurs*," in *Jacques Roumain: Oeuvres complètes*, 1266–96.

32. "*Je dis vrai: c'est pas Dieu qui abandonne le nègre, c'est le nègre qui abandonne la terre et il reçoit sa punition: la sécheresse, la misère et la désolation*" (I speak the truth: it is not God who abandons the Blacks, it is they who abandon the land, and so receive its punishment: drought, poverty and desolation) (MD 45/286; my translation).

33. As Jean Michael Dash has argued, Manuel "cannot be seen as one's ideal proletarian hero" because Fonds Rouge is essentially a "closed world," making it "difficult to see it as a universal model for proletarian revolt" (148). And yet, I would argue that, to the extent that Fond Rouge is "closed," this immurement stems for Roumain from the village's inability to cast off its internal conflicts. See Jean Michael Dash, "Jacques Roumain: The Marxist Counterpoint," in *Literature and Ideology in Haiti: 1915–1961* (Macmillan, 1981), 129–55.

34. For a close examination of Roumain's misunderstanding of Vodou, see Guy Maximilien, "Jacques Roumain et le vodou," in *Revolte, subversion et développement chez Jacques Roumain*, 261–68. For a brief interpretation of the (perhaps unintended) survival of Vodou in the plot of Roumain's *Masters*, see Colin Dayan, *Haiti, History and the Gods* (University of California Press 1995), 84.

35. Jean-Claude Fignolé, "*Sur Governeurs de la Rosée de Jacques Roumain: Hypothèse de travail dans une perspective spiraliste*," in *Jacques Roumain: Oeuvres complètes*, 1519–31.

36. "*Et puis l'eau, c'est pas une propriété, ça ne s'arpente pas, ça ne se marque pas sur le papier du notaire, c'est le bien commun, la bénédiction de la terre*" (Water is not a form of property, it can't be parceled out, it can't be marked on a notary's leger, it's a common good, the blessing of the Earth) (MD 124/348, my translation).

37. Lizabeth Paravisini-Gebert, "Deforestation and the Yearning for Lost Landscapes in Caribbean Literatures," in *Postcolonial Ecologies*, ed. Elizabeth DeLoughrey and G. B. Handley (Oxford University Press, 2011), 109.

38. Britton, "Restoring Lost Unity," 33, 35.

39. John Clare, *Selected Poetry and Prose*, ed. Merryn Williams and Raymond Williams (Methuen Publishing), 1986.

40. E. P. Thompson, *The Making of the English Working Class* (Vintage Books, 1966).

41. For more recent arguments in this debate, see John Lucas, "Clare's Politics," in *John Clare in Context*, ed. Hugh Hughton, Adam Phillips, and Geoffrey Summerfield (Cambridge University Press, 1994), 148–77. See also P. M. S. Dawson, "Common Sense or Radicalism? Some Reflections on Clare's Politics," *Romanticism* 2, no. 1 (1996): 81–97. The most extensive examination of this question, framed by the historical context of the Swing Riots and by the fact that Clare published in both Whig and Tory newspapers, can be found in Alan Vardy, *John Clare, Politics and Poetry* (Palgrave Macmillan, 2003).

42. As Simon Kövesi suggests, "as a working-class critic of human activity and social structure, there was much he would like to have changed, and much he thought should change. Not radically, not violently, and ostensibly not at the macro-level of the state; still, the sheer amount and tenor of protest in Clare's work overall means we have at least to accept him broadly as an agitator for progress and change." Simon Kövesi, "John Clare & . . . & . . . & Deleuze and Guattari's Rhizome," in *Ecology and the*

Literature of the British Left: The Red and the Green, ed. John Rignall, H. Gustav Klaus, and Valentine Cunningham (Routledge Press, 2012), 78.

43. See respectively John Barrell, *The Idea of Landscape and the Sense of Place 1730–1840* (Cambridge University Press, 1972); Jonathan Bate, *The Song of the Earth* (Harvard University Press, 2000), and James C. McKusick, *Green Writing* (Harvard University Press, 2000).

44. McKusick, *Green Writing*, 81.

45. As Bate suggests, Clare viewed "the 'rights of man' and the 'rights of nature' as co-dependent." Bate, *Song of the Earth*, 164.

46. Making a case for a "radical Clare" located in the structures of his poetry, Simon Kövesi also suggests that his radicality stems from the "de-centered connections" he makes across the traditional divide between man and nature, nature and culture: "Clare's levelling connections—applied to human natural life and natural life without recourse to the staple division of man from nature—is indeed radical, because it posits a root-level sociality between all subjects and bodies in the material world." Kövesi, "John Clare," 79. In his argument for reading Clare's poetry as "ecological" in the more radical sense that he understands the ideological scaffolding of certain concepts of nature, Kövesi convincingly argues that the collapse of the nature/ culture distinction is the key feature of Clare's poetics: "Closing the distance between man and nature has meant the poet is not only implicit in the natural world, but also suggests a rare achievement: the distinctions between man and nature, between nature and culture, have dissolved. The poet has abrogated these manmade categories" (138). Simon Kövesi, "Finding Poems, Making Text: John Clare and the Greening of Textual Criticism," *Romanticism* 17, no. 2 (2011): 135–47.

47. Richard Irvine and Mina Gorji convincingly argue that Clare sought, in contrast to John Locke's theory of labor and property, to develop a theory of the value of nature's "independence of human labour" (129). See Richard D. G. Irvine and Mina Gorji, "John Clare in the Anthropocene," *Cambridge Anthology* 31, no. 1 (2013): 119–32.

48. David Collings, "Blank Oblivion, Condemned Life: John Clare's 'Obscurity,'" in *Romanticism and Speculative Realism*, ed. Chris Washington and Anne C. McCarthy (Bloomsbury Press, 2019), 78.

49. John Clare, "Obscurity," in *Poems of the Middle Period, vol. 4*, ed. Eric Robinson, David Powell, and P. M. S. Dawson (Oxford University Press, 1998), 256.

50. Collings, "Blank Oblivion, Condemned Life," 78.

51. Sarah Houghton, "Enkindling Ecstacy: The Sublime Vision of John Clare," *Romanticism* 9, no. 2 (2003): 176–95.

52. John Clare, "Eternity of Time," in *Poems of the Middle Period*, 4:227–28. All further citations of the poem in the text (ET) will be from this edition.

53. John Clare, "Address to Time," in *The Early Poems of John Clare, vol. 2*, ed. Eric Robinson and David Powell (Oxford University Press, 1989), 487–88. All further citations of the poem (AT) will be in text from this edition.

54. Alan Bewell, "John Clare and the Ghosts of Natures Past," in *Natures in Translation* (Johns Hopkins University Press, 2017), 557.

55. John Clare, "Earth's Eternity," in *Poems of the Middle Period*, 4:568.

56. Clare, *Early Poems*, 2:326–328, here lines 11–12. All further citations of the poem (RA) will be in text from this edition.

57. For a recent analysis of Clare's conception of taste, see Sarah Weiger, "'Shadows of Taste': John Clare's Tasteful Natural History," *John Clare Society Journal* 27, no. 1 (2008): 59–71. See also Timothy Brownlow, "Rich Instincts Natural Taste," in *John Clare and Picturesque Landscape* (Oxford University Press, 1983), 116–33.

58. For a close reading of Clare's understanding of the relation between poetry and botany, see M. M. Mahood, "John Clare: Bard of Wildflowers," in *The Poet as Botanist* (Cambridge University Press, 2008), 112–46.

59. John Clare, "Taste," in *The Natural History Prose Writings*, ed. Margaret Grainger (Oxford University Press, 1983), 283–84.

60. John Clare, "Shadows of Taste," in *Poems of the Middle Period, vol.* 3, ed. Eric Robinson, David Powell, and P. M. S. Dawson (Oxford University Press, 1998), 303–10, lines 1–10. All further citations of the poem (ST) will be in text from this edition.

61. The idea that animals have their own worlds is emphatically rejected by Heidegger, who famously declares in part 2, chapter 3 of *The Fundamental Concepts of Metaphysics* that the stone is without world, the animal is poor in world, and Dasein is world-forming. See Martin Heidegger, *The Fundamental Concepts of Metaphysics*, trans. William McNeill and Nicholas Walker (Indiana University Press, 1995), 186–99. As Joseph Albernaz has argued, Clare's understanding of the multiplicity of worlds means that, rather than a single all-encompassing world, "we are left with the scattered fragments of an infinite play and plurality of worlds—worlds which simultaneously are given and must be made, or formed. Worlds that bump up and push against each other, and overlap at times (and places)." See Joseph Albernaz, "John Clare's World," *European Romantic Review* 27, no. 2 (2016): 189–205.

62. Albernaz, "John Clare's World," 195.

63. John Clare, *Autobiographical Writings*, ed. Eric Robinson (Oxford University Press, 1986), 33–34.

64. For an analysis of the way "wonder" figures in Clare's poetics (in a quite different way from my own argument), see Erica McAlpine, "Keeping Nature at Bay: John Clare's Poetry of Wonder," *Romanticism* 50, no. 1 (2011): 79–104.

65. John Clare, "The Ants," *Early Poems*, 56. All further citations of the poem (A) will be in text from this edition.

66. As Mina Gorji has argued, Clare's poetics concerns itself with things and areas otherwise seen as rebarbative or useless, such as weeds, "because they represent wild freedom—freedom from human control and domination, but also imaginative freedom" (62). See Mina Gorji, "John Clare's Weeds," in *Ecology and Literature of the British Left*, ed. H. Gustav Klaus, John Rignall, and Valentine Cunningham (Routledge Press, 2012), 61–73.

67. Joseph Albernaz has convincingly demonstrated that a key element of Clare's poetics is the way it constitutes "an operation of dis-enclosure, of *de-commensuration* or better, incommensuration: making the commensurable incommensurable (again).

Poetry has a tendency to ruin the enclosures of language, to 'repudiate measuring'" (125). In other words, poetry itself becomes its own form of commons. See Joseph Albernaz, "The Commons: Ruin and Romance," *Social Research: An International Quarterly* 88, no. 1 (2021): 115–50.

68. Jacques Rancière, "The Distribution of the Sensible: Politics and Aesthetics," in *The Politics of Aesthetics*, trans. Gabriel Rockhill (Continuum Press, 2004), 13.

69. John Clare, "Lament of Swordy Well," in *Poems of the Middle Period, vol.* 5, ed. Eric Robinson, David Powell, and P. M. S. Dawson (Oxford University Press, 2003), 105–14; 107. All further citations of the poem (SW) will be in text from this edition.

70. For a study examining the changing relations between farmers and field laborers during the period of enclosure, see Simon J. White, *Romanticism and the Rural Community* (Palgrave Macmillan, 2013).

71. Albernaz argues that Clare's poetics "opens up alternative pathways of thought and praxis that would be directly counter to what we could call the ontology of globalization, with its desire for homogeneity and abstract equivalence under one World" (190). Though I'm not convinced by the claim about Clare's relation to globalization, the idea of "general equivalance," where a single system or measure articulates the place and value of everything, is clearly the main form of homogeneity (and economics) Clare is contesting. See Albernaz, "John Clare's World," 190.

72. Katey Castellano has argued convincingly that Clare's notion of freedom goes even further than questioning the notion of liberal "rights," arguing that "Clare's anthropomorphic identification with nonhuman life establishes a collective among forms of life that are being appropriated into property (land, trees, animals, the poor)" (11–12). See Katey Catellano, *The Ecology of British Romantic Conservatism, 1790–1837* (Palgrave Macmillan, 2013).

73. This multiplicity found within the landscape was for John Barrell one of the key elements of Clare's overall aesthetics that expressed a preference for "multiplicity and particularity . . . over order and generality" (138–39), a key feature likewise of Clare's understanding of the multiplicity of animal worlds that occupy a single landscape. See John Barrell, *The Idea of Landscape and the Sense of Place (Cambridge University Press, 2011).*

74. Though this point is not her main focus, Mina Gorji's study, which makes a case for Clare's sense of place being articulated through his local dialect, suggests another way in which the commons is found only in Clare's poetry. See Mina Gorji, *John Clare and the Place of Poetry* (Liverpool University Press, 2008).

75. John Clare, "The Flitting," in *Poems of the Middle Period*, 3:479–89.

76. See Shalon Noble, "Homeless at Home: John Clare's Uncommon Ecology," *Romanticism* 21, no. 2 (2015): 171–81.

77. Michael Nicholson argues compellingly that Clare's poem "defies the era's new economies of privacy by connecting the poetic 'I' to something other than individuality" and that "Clare's speaker reanimates the entirety of a past local culture and way of life and reaches beyond it to highlight the solidarity of all agricultural laborers" (648). See Michael Nicholson, "John Clare's Lyric Defiance," *ELH* 82, no. 2 (2015): 637–69.

78. John Clare, "Remembrances," in *Poems of the Middle Period*, 4:130–34, line 1. All further citations of the poem (R) will be in text from this edition.

79. Katey Castellano has shown how the moles are not just like agricultural laborers engaging in their common right of subsistence, but that the moles "mark a topography of animal territory that undermines private property" (160). See Katey Casellano, "Moles, Molehills, and Common Right in John Clare's Poetry," *Studies in Romanticism* 56, no. 1 (2017): 157–76. She makes a similar point about the labor that is already present in the landscape as figured in Clare's many poems about bird's nests. See Katey Castellano, "Multispecies Work in John Clare's 'Birds Nesting' Poems," in *Palgrave Advances in John Clare Studies*, 179–97.

80. John Clare, "Rural Scenes," *Poems of the Middle Period*, 4:585. All further citations of the poem (RS) will be in text from this edition.

81. Jacques Roumain, "Ebony Wood," in *When the Tom-Tom Beats: Selected Prose and Poetry*, trans. Joanne Fungaroli and Ronald Sauer (Azul Editions, 1996), 77. For the French, see Jacques Roumain, "*Bois-d'ébène*," in *Jacques Roumain: Oeuvres complètes*, 55–60. All further citations will be made in text as (BE) with English translation followed by French pagination.

Chapter 3

1. Olive Senior, *Shell* (Insomniac Press, 2007), 16. All further references will be made in text (S) to this edition.

2. Édouard Glissant, *Poetics of Relation*, trans. Betsy Wing (University of Michigan Press, 2010), 6.

3. John Clare, "Hunting Pooty Shells," in *John Clare: Major Works*, edited by Eric Robinson and David Powell (Oxford University Press, 2008), 478.

4. Sigmund Freud, "A Note upon the Mystic Writing Pad," in *The Standard Edition of the Complete Works of Sigmund Freud, vol. 19*, trans. James Strachey (Hogarth Press, 1961), 227–32.

5. Louis Althusser, "The Underground Current of the Materialism of the Encounter," in *Philosophy of the Encounter: Later Writings, 1978–1987*, trans. G. M. Ghoshgarian (Verso Press, 2006), 190.

6. For an in-depth analysis of the notion of the "abyss," an experience of absolute loss and reconstitution in Glissant, see John E. Drabinski, *Glissant and the Middle Passage: Philosophy, Beginning, Abyss* (University of Minnesota Press, 2019).

7. Focusing on Thoreau's conception of the archive, Branka Arsić provides an apt description for this kind of memorialization which does not offer itself as a narrative: "Rather than being the site of power, the archive reveals itself as a site of weakness, for it hosts not memory but forgetting, and contains only unrelated fragments. The story or meaning that would relate them into a whole is precisely what is missing; the archive, then, is a story-less void hollowed out by what is no more" (170). Branka Arsić, "'Our Things': Thoreau on Objects, Relics, and Archives," *Qui Parle* 23, no. 1 (2014): 157–81.

8. Olive Senior, *Gardening in the Tropics* (Insomniac Press, 2005), 85. All further references will be made in text (GT) to this edition.

9. Hannah Regis, "Subjection and Resistance: Landscapes, Gardens, Myth and Vestigial Presences in Olive Senior's *Gardening in the Tropics*," *eTropic* 19, no. 1 (2020): 151–66, quote at 153.

10. Olive Senior, in my view, engages similarly in a form of what Édouard Glissant calls an "aesthetics of the earth," which he describes as a rhizomatic "aesthetics of disruption" that eschews a sense of rootedness in place, and challenges the notion that Earth processes are outside the domain of history. See Édouard Glissant, *Poetics of Relation* (University of Michigan Press, 1997), 149–52. For an important account of this notion, see Elizabeth DeLoughrey and G. B. Handley, "Introduction: Towards an Aesthetics of the Earth," in *Postcolonial Ecologies*, ed. Elizabeth DeLoughrey and G. B. Handley (Oxford University Press, 2011), 1–32.

11. Glissant, *Poetics of Relation*, 6.

12. Jane Bennett, *Vibrant Matter: A Political Ecology of Things* (Duke University Press, 2010), 6.

13. Bennett's conception of vitality is derived in part by an extension of Bruno Latour's actor-network theory. See, for example, Bruno Latour, *An Inquiry into Modes of Existence*, trans. Catherine Porter (Harvard University Press, 2013).

14. I draw here from Jacques Derrida's deconstruction of the opposition between life and death. As he writes, "what we call life, the thing or object of bio-logy and biography, has only the complication of not being simply opposed to—as to a contrary—something that would be for it an opposable ob-ject, namely death, the thanato-logical or thanato-graphical over against the bio-logical and bio-graphical." See Jacques Derrida, *Life Death*, trans. Michael Naas and Pascale-Anne Brault (University of Chicago Press, 2020), 27.

15. For an analysis of the way Olive Senior incorporates what she calls "topopoetic" dimensions into her poetry, that is, poetry that emphasizes the connections between landscape and language, see Samantha Stephens, "Caribbean Basins: Containing the Im/material in Kei Miller's 'Quashie's Verse' and Olive Senior's 'Gourd,'" *Journal of West Indian Literature* 29, no. 2 (2021): 13–28.

16. For a detailed account of importance of the site, see https://www.trust.org.sh/shnt-conservation-programmes/cultural-heritage/st-helena-trans-atlantic-slave-memorial/. For an even more developed exploration of the difficulties involved in establishing a memorial and reburial, see the documentary "Buried": https://www.theguardian.com/world/video/2024/mar/27/buried-how-we-choose-to-remember-the-transatlantic-slave-trade.

17. This notion of problematizing the division between nature and culture has become a central motif of contemporary ecocriticism. See, for example, Bruno Latour, *Politics of Nature*, trans. Catherine Porter (Harvard University Press, 2004), and Philippe Descola, *Beyond Nature and Culture*, trans. Janet Lloyd (University of Chicago Press, 2014).

18. For a careful examination of the relationship between human history and natural history, see Dipesh Chakrabarty, "The Climate of History: Four Theses," *Critical Inquiry* 35, no. 2 (2009): 197–222.

19. For a close reading of the way Hegel articulates European "consciousness" in relation to African "pre-history," see Susan Buck-Morss, *Hegel, Haiti and Universal History* (University of Pittsburgh Press, 2009).

20. Sylvia Wynter, "Unsettling the Coloniality of Being/Power/Truth/Freedom: Towards the Human, After Man, Its Overrepresentation—An Argument," *New Centennial Review* 3, no. 3 (Fall 2003): 291.

21. G. W. F. Hegel, *Lectures on the Philosophy of World History*, trans H. B. Nisbet (Cambridge: Cambridge University Press, 1996), 177. All further references will be cited in text as (WH).

22. G. W. F. Hegel, *The Philosophy of Nature*, trans. A.V. Miller (Oxford University Press, 1970), 285. All further references will be cited in text as (PN).

23. Leif Wetherby develops a broad and wide-ranging analysis of Romantic and Idealist conceptions of the "organ" by articulating a theory of "Romantic Organology," by which he means the study of elements with variable functions that are infra-objects, "usable parts that might be repurposed depending on the body or process at hand" (9). This notion of the organ, however, is still only latent in its inception and becomes self-forming in Schelling only in its differentiation from the inorganic. See in particular Leif Wetherby, "Electric and Ideal Organs: Schelling and the Program of Organology," in *Transplanting the Metaphysical Organ: German Romanticism Between Leibniz and Marx* (Fordham University Press, 2016), 171–205.

24. Gayatri Spivak, "Can the Subaltern Speak?," in *Can the Subaltern Speak? Reflections on the History of an Idea*, ed. Rosalind Morris (Columbia University Press, 2010), 21–78.

25. For an excellent analysis of the nature of unconditionality in Günderrode's poetry and its relation to the Earth as a form of gravity that resists transcendence, see Gabriel Trop, "Arts of Unconditioning: On Romantic Science and Poetry," in *The Palgrave Handbook on German Romantic Philosophy*, ed. Elizabeth Millán (Palgrave Macmillan, 2020), 421–48.

26. A wide range of approaches is represented here, including object-oriented ontology, which sees itself as breaking with correlationism, or the assumed correspondence between thought and being, to approaches that attempt to utilize Amerindian cosmology to relativize the West's conception of the difference between the natural world and humans. For an example of the former, see Quentin Meillasoux, *After Finitude*, trans. Ray Brassier (Continuum Press, 2008). For an example of the latter, see Deborah Danowski and Eduardo Viveiros de Castro, *The Ends of the World*, trans. Rodrigo Nunes (Polity Press, 2017), 61–78.

27. Nigel Clark and Bronislaw Szerszynski, *Planetary Social Thought* (Polity Press, 2020), 100–101.

28. For a particularly cogent (and science-based) interpretation of the in-human, see Nigel Clark, "The Earth in Physical and Social Thought," in *Inhuman Nature* (Sage Publishing, 2011), 1–26.

29. Günderrode's idea in this regard in many ways anticipates elements of Jacques Derrida's deconstruction of the (non)opposition between life and death. See Jacques

Derrida, *Life Death*, trans. Pascale-Anne Brault and Michael Naas (University of Chicago Press, 2020).

30. F. W. J. Schelling, *Bruno, or on the Natural and the Divine Principle of Things*, trans. Michael G. Vater (State University of New York Press, 1984), 125. All further references will be cited in text as (B).

31. To some extent, Günderrode's theory of the Earth can be compared with a Spinozistic monism, which eliminates dualism by making all attributes, mental, physical, or otherwise, operate on a single plane of immanence. For a development of the consequences of this immanentism, see Gilles Deleuze, "Spinoza and Us," in *Spinoza and Practical Philosophy*, trans. Robert Hurley (City Lights Book, 1988), 122–30.

32. For a clear articulation of the notion of "indifference" in Schelling's *Naturphilosophie*, see Gabriel Trop, "Mythological Indifference in Schelling and Nerval," *Wordsworth Circle* 50, no. 1 (2019): 108–26.

33. Karoline von Günderrode, "Idea of the Earth," in *Women Philosophers in the Long Nineteenth Century: The German Tradition*, ed. Dalia Nassar and Kristin Gjesdal (Oxford University Press, 2021), 82. Karoline von Günderrrode, *Sämtliche Werke und ausgewählte Studien. Historisch-Kritische Ausgabe*, vol 1., ed. Walter Morgenthaler (Stroemfeld/Roter Stern, 1990–91), 446. All further references will be cited in text as (IE) with the English pagination followed by the German.

34. F. W. J. Schelling, *First Outline of a System of the Philosophy of Nature*, trans. Keith R. Peterson (State University of New York Press, 2004), 13. All further references will be cited in text as (F).

35. Karoline von Günderrode, "Philosophy of Nature," in *Women Philosophers*, 76.

36. Malcom Ferdinand, *Decolonial Ecology*, trans. Anthony Paul Smith (Polity Press, 2022), 29.

37. While it is tempting to equate Hegel's insistence that non-Western cultures are variously confined to the natural world as a focus on the exploitable "bare life" they seem to represent, Agamben's notion of "bare life" is not adequate here to explain Hegel's argument. "Bare life" is not a natural category for Agamben, but the result of the state of exception and the suspension of law. "Bare life" is thus a political category through and through. See Giorgio Agamben, *Homo Sacer*, trans. Daniel Heller-Roazen (Stanford University Press, 1998).

38. Though they would have been unknown to Günderrode, the Earth had seen five mass extinctions, the most recent being the Cretacean extinction roughly 65 million years ago that exterminated the dinosaurs. We are currently in the midst of the sixth mass extinction in the planet's history, caused by human activities. See Elizabeth Kolbert, *The Sixth Extinction: An Unnatural History* (Picador, 2014).

39. While it might be tempting to compare aspects of Günderrode's idea of the Earth with the concept of the Earth presented in Deleuze and Guattari's "geo-philosophy," there are important differences. Whereas in Günderrode the forces of dissolution and reconstitution active in the Earth always promise another world (whether human or nonhuman), the world is not a key component for Deleuze and Guattari; the conception of "territorialization" and "deterritorialization" do not necessarily apply to worlds

but to the Earth as a series of discontinuous, *inhuman* planes. See Gilles Deleuze and Felix Guattari, "Geophilosophy," in *What Is Philosophy?*, trans. Hugh Tomlinson and Graham Burchell (Columbia University Press, 1994), 85–113. For a clear articulation of Deleuze and Guattari's conception of the Earth in relation to their notion of the "world," see Zsuzsa Baross, "Geophilosophy," in *On Contemporaneity, after Agamben* (Sussex University Press, 2020), 105–19.

40. Imagining the endpoint of "life" in any sense, Ray Brassier takes us a far as the "trillion, trillion, trillion years from now" when the "accelerating expansion of the universe will have disintegrated the fabric of matter itself." See Ray Brassier, *Nihil Unbound: Enlightenment and Extinction* (Palgrave Macmillan, 2007), 228.

41. Dorothy Figuiera describes Günderrode's interest in Indian philosophy and religion as an "idealization." While this may be true, her interest in the way that it constitutes a different relation to the Earth is an important one within the idealist tradition. See Dorothy Figuiera, "Goethe and Günderrode: German Poetic Readings of Indian Fatalism," in *Gendered Encounters Between Germany and Asia: Transnational Perspectives Since 1800*, ed. Joanne Miyang Cho and Douglas T. McGetchin (Palgrave Macmillan, 2017), 41–64.

42. I am grateful to Anna Ezekiel for making a draft version of her translation of Karoline von Günderrode's "Letters of Two Friends" available in advance of its publication in *Karoline von Günderrode: Philosophical Writings*, trans. Anna Ezekiel (Oxford University Press, 2025). Günderrode, *Sämtliche Werke*, 1:354–55. All further references to this work will be in text as (LT), citing first Ezekiel's unpublished translation, followed by the published German.

43. For a clear discussion of the problem of "personhood" throughout Günderrode's oeuvre, see Anna Ezekiel, "Metamorphosis, Personhood, and Power in Karoline von Günderrode," *European Romantic Review* 25, no. 6 (2014): 773–91.

44. Karoline von Günderrode, "Philosophy of Nature," in *Women Philosophers*, 76.

45. For a reading of Günderrode's conception of self, which she argues is framed in terms of a constitutive relation with others, see Anna Ezekiel, "Narrative and Fragment: The Social Self in Karoline von Günderrode," *Symphilosophie: European Journal of European Romanticism* 2 (2020). chrome-extension://efaidnbmnnnibpcajpcglclefindmkaj/https://symphilosophie.com/wp-content/uploads/2020/12/4_Symphilosophie-2_2-Ezekiel.pdf.

46. For a reading of Günderrode's conception of the relation between her *Naturphilosophie* and morality, see Dalia Nassar, "The Human Vocation and the Question of the Earth: Karoline von Günderrode's Philosophy of Nature," *Archiv für Geschichte der Philosophie* 104, no. 1 (2022): 108–30. Nassar argues that Günderrode charts her own distinct understanding of the relation between morality and nature by critically evaluating, and departing from, both Fichte and Schelling's philosophies of morality and nature respectively.

47. I am grateful to Anna Ezekiel for making a draft version of her translation of Karoline von Günderrode's "Story of a Brahmin" available in advance of its publication in *Karoline von Günderrode: Philosophical Writings*, trans. Anna Ezekiel (Oxford

University Press, forthcoming). Günderrode, *Sämtliche Werke*, 307–8. All further references will be cited in text as (SB), with Ezekiel's unpublished translation followed by the published German.

48. See Annette Simonis, "'*Das verschleierte Bild': Mythopoetik und Geschlechterrollen bei Karoline von Günderrode,*" *Deutsche Vierteljahrsschrift für Literaturwissenschaft* 74, no. 2 (2000): 254–78.

49. This is one of the key elements that differentiates her not only from Schelling and Hegel but from Kant.

50. For a clear and cogent reading of Günderrode's political philosophy as read through her dramatic works, *Muhammed: Prophet of Mecca* included, see Anna Ezekiel, "Revolution and Revitalisation: Karoline von Günderrode's Political Philosophy and Its Metaphysical Foundations," *British Journal of the History of Philosophy* 30, no. 4 (2022): 666–86.

51. For a reading of *Muhammed: Prophet of Mecca* that emphasizes Günderrode's largely positive portrayal of Muhammed over and against her contemporaries, including Goethe, see Stephanie Mathilde Hilger, "Staging Islam: Karoline von Günderrode's *Mahomed, der Prophet von Mekka*," in *Women Write Back: Strategies of Response and the Dynamics of European Literary Culture, 1790–1805* (Rodopi Press, 2009), 91–118.

52. Karoline von Günderrode, *Muhammed: Prophet of Mecca*, in *Poetic Fragments*, trans. Anna Ezekiel (State University of New York Press, 2016), 160. Günderrode, *Sämtliche Werke*, 1:114. All further references will be cited in text as (MP) with the English pagination followed by the German.

53. This point is explored as well in Ezekiel, "Revolution and Revitalisation."

54. For an elaborate and clear reading of the possibility of community with nonhuman others in Günderrode, see Anna Ezekiel, "Earth, Spirit, Humanity: Community and the Nonhuman in Karoline von Günderrode's 'Idea of the Earth,'" in *Romanticism and Political Ecology*, ed. Kir Kuiken, *Romantic Circles* 1, no. 2 (2024): http://romantic-circles.org/index.php/praxis/political_ecology.

55. I have in mind here a particular form of fidelity: Rather than fidelity to a realized deity, Muhammed seems to offer something closer to a "fidelity to the event" in Badiou's sense, where faith is not predicated on fidelity to something "realized," but to something ongoing. See, for example, Badiou's analysis of having fidelity to the event of the Paris Commune, in Alain Badiou, *Polemics*, trans. Steve Corcoran (Verso Press, 2006), 278–90.

56. My analyses in this chapter have benefited from the argument Joseph Albernaz makes about the relationship between Hölderlin and Günderrode's conception of the Earth. Albernaz views this conception as being centered on an idea of the Earth that "exists in non-relation to the mediated forms of division and connection, but it still moves, it moves against and shatters (*zerbricht*) these forms and what is separate from it, thereby undoing any separation" (135). Albernaz thinks Günderrode's Earth in terms of a "world" that is nontotalizing. My own reading emphasizes its unconditional status, which I argue is anterior to any constitution or deconstitution, division or separation, of any world. See Joseph Albernaz, "Earth Unbounded: Division and

Inseparability in Hölderlin and Günderrode," in *Nothing Absolute: German Idealism and the Question of Political Theology*, ed. Kirill Chepurin and Alex Dubilet (Fordham University Press, 2021), 124–43.

57. For a detailed reading of Olive Senior's relation to Beckford, see Shirley Chew, "'The Story Is Now About Us': Olive Senior to 'England's Wealthiest Son,'" in *Citizens of the World: Adapting in the Eighteenth Century*, ed. Samara Anne Cahill and Kevin L. Cope (Bucknell University Press, 2015), 69–84.

58. Percy Shelley, "Ozymandias," in *Shelley's Poetry and Prose*, ed. Donald H. Reiman and Neil Fraistat (W. W. Norton, 2002), 109–10.

Chapter 4

1. A good starting point for recent research on the relations between the collapse of past civilizations and climate change can be found at NASA's website, "Climate Change and the Rise and Fall of Civilizations," *Climate NASA* (2014): https://climate.nasa.gov/news/1010/climate-change-and-the-rise-and-fall-of-civilizations/.

2. Patrick Chamoiseau, *Crusoe's Footprint*, trans. Jeffrey Landon Allen and Charly Verstraet (University of Virginia Press, 2022), 105. In the original French: Patrick Chamoiseau, *L'empreinte à Crusoé* (Gallimard, 2012), 156. All further citations will be made in text as CF, with the English pagination followed by the French.

3. Patrick Chamoiseau, *Slave Old Man*, trans. Linda Coverdale (The New Press, 2018), 4. In the original French and Creole: Patrick Chamoiseau, *L'esclave vieil homme et le molosse* (Gallimard, 1997), 18. All further citations will be made in text as SM, with the English pagination followed by the French.

4. Renée Gosson has traced the figure of the maroon in Chamoiseau's *Chronicle of the Seven Sorrows*, arguing that many of his characters repeat, in various ways, the "resistant gesture of the primordial maroon" (222). See Renée Gosson, "For What the Land Tells: An Ecocritical Approach to Patrick Chamoiseau's *Chronicle of the Seven Sorrows*," *Callaloo* 26, no. 1 (2003): 219–34.

5. In a careful and meticulous rebuttal of Andreas Malm's argument that the concept of "wilderness" was a key element of maroon resistance to slavery, Malcom Ferdinand argues that those spaces were not a "wilderness," a concept implying a dualist conception of nature separate from the social, but instead were "the material sites of non-modernist cosmogonies and ontologies that did not follow the occidental divide between nature and culture" (185). See Malcom Ferdinand, "Behind the Colonial Silence of Wilderness: 'In Marronage Lies the Search of a World,'" *Environmental Humanities* 14, no. 1 (2022): 182–201; and Andreas Malm, "In Wildness Is the Liberation of the World: On Maroon Ecology and Partisan Nature," *Historical Materialism* 26, no. 3 (2018): 3–37.

6. Milena Fučikova has argued convincingly that Chamoiseau's fiction is in part about the transmission of what would otherwise be "invisible" to historiography. See Milena Fučikova, "*Pourquoi le romancier-poète imagine-t-il un invisible mémoire?*," *Svět Literatury* 30 (2020): 148–59.

7. Doris Garraway, "Toward a Creole Myth of Origin: Narrative, Foundations and

Eschatology in Patrick Chamoiseau's '*L'esclave vieil homme et le molosse*,'" *Callaloo* 29, no. 1 (2006): 151–67, quotes at 159.

8. The earthly element of the Stone and the slave old man's relation to it generates a discontinuous history. Garraway reads that history through colonialism and "in the case of Africans, a dehumanizing rupture with their cultural, social linguistic and geographical origins" as a "spiritual and material" unmaking of the world "through life's return to mere matter." However, as I argue, the Stone itself constitutes a moment when matter insists, and therefore resists, that effacement. See Garraway, "Toward a Creole Myth," 154, 159, 153.

9. Garraway, "Toward a Creole Myth," 163.

10. See Jean Bernabé, Patrick Chamoiseau, and Raphaël Confiant, *Éloge de la Créolité/In Praise of Creoleness*, (Gallimard, 1990).

11. Bernabé, Chamoiseau, and Confiant, *Éloge de la Créolité/In Praise of Creoleness*, 164.

12. Derrida reads this unified "sending" in Heidegger's "Age of the World Picture" as a presumed and problematic unity: "Even if there is dissension (*Zweispalt*) in what Heidegger calls the great Greek epoch and the experience of *Anwesenheit* this dissension groups itself in the *legein*, escapes, preserves itself and thus assures a sort of indivisibility of what it destines" (322). See Jacques Derrida, "Sending: On Representation," *Social Research* 49, no. 22 (1982): 294–326.

13. Though not the only one, a quintessential example of this theoretical formulation can be found in Fichte's *Addresses to the German Nation* where, in the midst of French-occupied Prussia, he describes a need to create a new German world out of a former one (which in this case involves a German, rather than Greek, antecedent): "From this state, in which its former world lies wholly beyond reach of its self-active intervention and in the present one only the glory of obedience is left, it could raise itself only on the condition that a new world dawn for it, with whose creation would begin, and further development fill, a new epoch of its own. Yet since it is subject to an alien power, this new world would have to be so constituted that it remained unnoticed by that power and in no way aroused its jealousy. . . . Now if there is to be a world thus constituted as the means of creating the new self and a new age, for a race that has lost its former self, its former age and its former world, then it would fall to a thorough interpretation of such a possible age to account for the world thus constituted." See Johann Gottlieb Fichte, *Addresses to the German Nation*, ed. Gregory Moore (Cambridge University Press, 2008), 10.

14. Philippe Lacoue-Labarthe and Jean-Luc Nancy, "The Nazi Myth," *Critical Inquiry 16, no. 2* (Winter 1990): 297.

15. Johann Joachim Winckelmann, *Reflections on the Imitation of Greek Works in Painting and Sculpture*, trans. Elfriede Heyer and Roger C. Norton (Open Court Press, 1987), 5.

16. For a clear analysis of Hölderlin's critique of traditional classicism, see Peter Szondi, "Hölderlin's Overcoming of Classicism," *Comparative Criticism* 5, no. 1 (1983): 251–70.

17. Anja Lemke addresses the problematic of "transition"—historical or otherwise—in Hölderlin by characterizing it as a passage between "the possible and the real" which "remembers by dismissing what is past and, precisely by doing so, open[s] a space that enables one to experience the transition itself, the in-between being and not-being, between that which is no longer and that which is not yet" (174). Anja Lemke, "The Transition Between the Possible and the Real: Nature as Contingency in Hölderlin's 'The Declining Fatherland,'" in *Hölderlin's Philosophy of Nature*, ed. Rochelle Tobias (Edinburgh University Press, 2020), 164–77. For a broader analysis of temporality in Hölderlin's poetics, see Johann Kreuzer, "*Zeit, Sprache und Erinnerung: Die Zeitlogik der Dichtung*," in *Hölderlin Handbuch, Leben-Werk-Wirkung*, ed. Johann Kreuzer (Metzler, 2002), 147–61.

18. The quintessential example of a misreading of Hölderlin's language of the divine can be found in Jean-Luc Marion's interpretation of Hölderlin, which effectively transforms the theme of the "withdrawal" of the gods into a negative theology. See Jean-Luc Marion, "The Withdrawal of the Divine and the Face of the Father: Hölderlin," in *The Idol and Distance*, trans. Thomas A. Carlson (Fordham University Press, 2001), 81–138. The opposite and far more interesting approach to the question of Hölderlin's use of divine or sacred terminology is represented by Maurice Blanchot, who argues that Hölderlin's "sacred speech" testifies to an anteriority, an attempt to witness the unpresentable. The unpresentable, of course, is not necessarily a *theos*. See Maurice Blanchot, "The 'Sacred' Speech of Hölderlin," in *The Work of Fire*, trans. Charlotte Mandel (Stanford University Press, 1995), 111–31.

19. Friedrich Hölderlin, *Essays and Letters on Theory*, trans. Thomas Pfau (State University of New York Press, 1988), 110. See also Friedrich Hölderlin, *Sämtliche Werke und Briefe, vols. 1–2* (Carl Hanser Verlag, 1970), 889. Prose texts by Hölderlin will henceforth be cited in text from this edition as (PW) with English pagination, followed by German volume number and pagination.

20. Peter Szondi long ago analyzed the historical dimension of Hölderlin's theory of the alternation of poetic tones, linking that theory directly to Hölderlin's December 4, 1801, letter to Casimir Böhlendorff where he describes the relation between modern or "Hesperian" poetry and Greek poetry and tragedy. See Peter Szondi, "*Gattungspoetik und Geschichtsphilosophie*," in *Hölderlin-Studien* (Insel Verlag, 1967), 105–46. For a more recent reading that treats the "alternation of tones" in terms of musical character as well as in terms of "the challenge of expression and articulation, whereby the spiritual context of the poem is translated into the fabric of its language in order to reproduce and communicate this experience to its readers" (311), see Cyrus Hamlin, "The Philosophy of Poetic Form: Hölderlin's Theory of Poetry and the Classical German Elegy," in *The Solid Letter: Readings of Friedrich Hölderlin*, ed. Aris Fioretos (Stanford University Press, 1999), 291–320.

21. Philippe Lacoue-Labarthe, "Caesura of the Speculative," in *Typography*, trans. Christopher Fynsk (Stanford University Press, 1998), 231.

22. Szondi writes: "*So wird der Wechsel der Töne zum Gesetz von Hölderlins Dichtung, die Gegensatzspannung von Grundton and Kunstkarakter zu deren Struktur und*

der Geist des Gedichts, der den jeweils dritten Ton einführt, zu der Instanz, welche die Auflösung des Widerspruchs verbürgt." See Szondi, *Hölderlin-Studien*, 112 (translation mine).

23. This is also the title of an important essay by Hölderlin, "Becoming in Dissolution" (PW 96–100/1:900–905).

24. Friedrich Hölderlin, "Becoming in Dissolution," in *Essays and Letters on Theory*, 96. Hölderlin, *Sämtliche Werke und Briefe*, 1:900.

25. Friedrich Hölderlin, *The Death of Empedocles*, trans. David Farell Krell (State University of New York Press, 2008), 186. Hölderlin, *Sämtliche Werke und Briefe*, 2:150. All citations of this work will henceforth be cited in text as (DE) followed by English pagination, then German pagination.

26. "Caesura" in Hölderlin has received a variety of interpretations, one of the most important of which is Lacoue-Labarthe's argument that Hölderlin's theory of tragedy involves the "caesura of the speculative." See Lacoue-Labarthe, "Caesura of the Speculative."

27. "*Simplement parce que le nom de Zeus ne signifie plus rien pour nous, tandis qu'il avait un sens pour les Grecs qui savaient encore ce qu'ils disaient quand ils nommaient Zeus. Pour nous ce nom est quelque chose de conventionnel, de 'positif,' de mort.*" Françoise Dastur, *Hölderlin: Le retournement natal* (Encre Marine, 1997), 59 (translation mine).

28. Though Hölderlin would never have had access to Hegel's reading of *Antigone* in *The Phenomenology of Spirit*, both authors and former friends read the opposition between Kreon and Antigone as appeals to different laws. For Hegel, Antigone's insistence on the burial of her brother makes her a representative of the (private and particular) laws of family or kinship, whereas Kreon is a representative of the universal laws of the state. The notion of Kreon and Antigone both appealing to the *same* law or authority under different guises, however, is uniquely Hölderlinian. See G. W. F. Hegel, *The Phenomenology of Spirit*, trans. A. V. Miller (Oxford University Press, 1977), 266–78.

29. Françoise Dastur reads this term "Antitheos" as an opposition that takes place at the level of the divine: "*L'Antitheos, c'est en grec celui qui est semblable à Dieu, mais aussi le Dieu contraire ou ennemi, selon le double sens de anti, qui signifie à la fois contre, en face de, ou à la place de, à l'égal de*" (The Antitheos in Greek is one who is similar to God, but also the contrary or enemy of God, according to the double meaning of "anti," which means at once against, in front of, instead of, equal to). In this case, however, given that Zeus has been interpreted as the "father of time, or father of the Earth," the sense of "anti" as opposition, and therefore as anti-theology, seems predominant. Dastur, *Hölderlin*, 77 (translation mine).

30. Jean-Pierre Vernant and Pierre Vidal-Naquet, *Myth and Tragedy in Ancient Greece, vol. 1*, trans. Janet Lloyd (Zone Books, 1990), 7.

31. The quintessential reading of the overcoming of myth in Hölderlin is and remains Walter Benjamin's early essay, where he argues that the "poetized" (*das Gedichtete*) which constitutes the limit-concept of the poem—what it says without

knowing that it says it—is also its "truth." As Benjamin put it, "contemplation of the poetized . . . leads not to the myth but rather . . . only to mythic connections, which in the work of art are shaped into unique, unmythological, and unmythic forms that cannot be better understood by us." See Walter Benjamin, "Two Poems by Friedrich Hölderlin," in *Selected Writings, vol. 1*, ed. Marcus Bullock and Michael W. Jennings (Harvard University Press, 1996), 35.

32. Beda Allemann makes this "*Vaterländische Umkehr*" or "patriotic reversal" the central motif of his interpretation of Hölderlin. However, he still interprets "our Zeus" and the Earth in terms of its opposition to the divine, a turn away from "heavenly fire" to the Earth. See Beda Allemann, *Hölderlin und Heidegger* (Atlantis Verlag, 1954), 31.

33. Beda Allemann focuses extensively on the term "*Der menschenfeindliche Naturgang*," interpreting it in opposition to the conception of nature specific to the Titans and Hölderlin's work on Empedocles: "*Was Empedokles als legitime Sehnsucht nach der Mutter Natur empfunden hatte, wird zum ewig menschenfeindlichen Naturgang die Natur selbst zur Wildnis und zum Abgrund, in dem die Titanen hausen*" (What Empedocles had felt as a legitimate longing for mother nature becomes an eternally anti-human course of nature, nature itself becomes a chaos and an abyss in which the titans dwell). See Allemann, *Hölderlin und Heidegger*, 65 (translation mine).

34. For a brilliant reading of the misconstrual of this term in Hölderlin by many critics, but most notably by Heidegger, see Jennifer Bajorek, "The Offices of Homeland Security, or, Hölderlin's Terrorism," *Critical Inquiry* 31, no. 4 (2005): 874–902. There she shows how the language of "home," *Heim, Vaterland, patriotisch*, etc. in Hölderlin is marked by its displacement within a language of distance and departure that deracinates the "homeland" or "fatherland" as an origin to which one can return. Bajorek demonstrates clearly how Heidegger, by making Hölderlin's Earth part of the threefold (and eventually fourfold) *unity* of "earth, sky, divinities and mortals," ends up eliding the way Hölderlin's poetics displaces "not simply place but something approaching the *place of place* in the very definition of the earth, which can henceforth no longer be circumscribed by a rootedness in place, at least insofar as our interpretations of rootedness, as of place, remains caught up in notions of immanence and identity" (891).

35. The question of the river as a poetized historical "sending" constitutes the primary focus of nearly all of Heidegger's interpretations of Hölderlin's river poems. See, for instance, Martin Heidegger, *Hölderlin's Hymn "The Ister,"* trans. William McNeill and Julia Davis (Indiana University Press, 1996).

36. Martin Heidegger, *Hölderlin's Hymns "Germania" and "The Rhine,"* trans. William McNeill and Julia Ireland (Indiana University Press, 2014), 84.

37. In the background of this comment about the rivers creating a "path" on a "pathless Earth" is the opposition between world and Earth Heidegger elaborates on in "Origin of the Work of Art," where he reads this relation in terms of *aletheia*, or truth as a revealing-concealing. As Heidegger puts it: "On and in the earth, historical man founds his dwelling in the world. In setting up a world, the work sets forth the earth. 'Setting forth' *[Herstellen]* is to be thought, here, in the strict sense of the word. The work moves the earth into the open of a world and holds it there. *The work lets the*

earth be an earth" (24–25). Though there are clearly similarities between Heidegger's and Hölderlin's conceptions of the Earth (Heidegger seems to import much of his commentary on Hölderlin into his notion of the "fourfold," for instance) given that Heidegger describes the Earth as that which remains "undisclosed and unexplained," the key difference is that Heidegger insists that it is only through the world, through the work of the world-disclosive possibilities of art, that the Earth becomes an Earth. As I have been arguing, Hölderlin's Earth is fundamentally irreducible to every "world." See Martin Heidegger, "The Origin of the Work of Art," in *Off the Beaten Track*, trans. Julian Young and Kenneth Haynes (Cambridge University Press, 2002), 1–56.

38. Friedrich Hölderlin, "Das Belebende/The Life-Giving," in *Poems and Fragments*, trans. Michael Hamburger (Anvil Press, 2005), 721; Hölderlin, *Sämtliche Werke und Briefe, 2:233–324.*

39. Rochelle Tobias suggests this reading of the role of the rivers when she insists that "without the labour of rivers, the earth would be what he calls in the 'Notes on *Antigone*' 'the eternally living unwritten wilderness and world of the dead', that is an endlessly expanding but also spiritless mass." Rochelle Tobias, "Untamed Earth," in *Hölderlin's Philosophy of Nature*, 91.

40. Friedrich Hölderlin, "*Der Main/The Main,*" in *Poems and Fragments*, trans. Michael Hamburger (Anvil Press, 2005), 137–39; Hölderlin, *Sämtliche Werke und Briefe, 1*:239–40. The poem will henceforth be cited in text as (M) followed by the English and then German pagination.

41. Joseph Albernaz interprets these lines (and this poem) in a slightly different fashion, emphasizing the emergence of an Earth that is "unbounded" in the sense of being an "indifferent non-separability" that is the "refusal of enclosure and insistence on the immanence of the common" (130). Except for this last phrase, which would seem to imply its repositioning within a "common" world of some kind, I am in complete agreement. See Joseph Albernaz, "Earth Unbounded: Division and Inseparability in Hölderlin and Günderrode," in *Nothing Absolute: German Idealism and the Question of Political Theology*, ed. Kirill Chepurin and Alex Dubilet (Fordham University Press, 2021), 130.

42. Patrick Chamoiseau, *La matière de l'absence* (Éditions de Seuil, 2016), 229 (translation mine). All further citations will be made in text as MA followed by the French pagination; all translations are mine.

43. This concept is at work throughout Édouard Glissant's oeuvre and signifies a rethinking of the nature of totality as something other than a homogeneous "globe." See especially Édouard Glissant, *Tout-monde* (Éditions Gallimard, 1993). As John E. Drabinski succinctly puts it, Glissant's conception of the "whole-world" implies not a totality, but that the world itself is "creolizing." See John E. Drabinski, *Glissant and the Middle Passage: Philosophy, Beginning, Abyss* (University of Minnesota, 2019), 169.

44. There is an element here of what Jacques Derrida has called in *Spectres of Marx* and elsewhere a "messianism without the messiah," or a relation to the future that involves the "irreducible paradox" of "a waiting without horizon of expectation." See Jacques Derrida, *Spectres of Marx*, trans. Peggy Kamuf (Routledge Press, 1994), 168.

45. Martin Heidegger, *The Fundamental Concepts of Metaphysics*, trans. William McNeill and Nicholas Walker (Indiana University Press, 1995), 176–273; quotes at 197.

Conclusion

1. While the claim about building codes was no doubt true, little historical context was provided for this claim in the media, implying that more lives could have been saved if only the Haitian government had enforced stricter laws. By contrast, a report issued by the United States Geological Society establishes clear connections between the lack of properly supervised building codes and Haiti's colonial history: Reginald Des Roches, Mary Comerio, Marc Eberhard, Walter Mooney, and Glen J. Rix, "Overview of the 2010 Haiti Earthquake," *Earthquake Spectra* 27, no. 1 (2001): 1–21.

2. Daniel Maximin, *L'isolé soleil* (Éditions de Seuil, 1987). His first novel is part of a trilogy that includes *Soufrières* (Éditions de Seuil, 1987) and *L'île et une nuit* (Éditions de Seuil, 1998).

3. For a close and careful reading of Maximin's relinquishment of any notion of ancestral origins, see Chris Bongie, "The (Un)exploded Volcano: Creolization and Intertextuality in the Novels of Daniel Maximin," *Callaloo* 17, no. 2 (Spring 1994): 627–42.

4. Maximin uses the term "cyclone" and "hurricane" interchangeably, although cyclones are technically storms formed in the Indian Ocean whereas hurricanes form in the Atlantic. Both are the product of warm water, low atmospheric pressure, and the Coriolis effect caused by the Earth's rotation.

5. Daniel Brant argues that Maximin articulates a "disasterscape" in his novels, that is, he formulates a cosmopolitanism where responses to natural disasters become a crucial connection between cultures. See Daniel Brant, "Disaster Cosmopolitanism: Catastrophe and Global Community in the Fiction of Daniel Maximin and Maryse Condé," *International Journal of Francophone Studies* 17, no. 2 (2014): 215–37.

6. See William Gilbert, "The Hurricane," in *William Gilbert and Esoteric Romanticism*, ed. Paul Chesire (Liverpool University Press, 2018): 103–62.

7. The Romantic period was not without its share of tales of vengeance originating in the natural world to right the wrongs done to it and to various others. For an example of this in Romantic pastoral, see Amanda Goldstein, "Utopian Pastoral and the Inhuman Trade," *Romantic Circles 1, no. 2 (2024)*: https://romantic-circles.org/praxis/publication/romanticism-and-political-ecology.

8. Daniel Maximin, *Les fruits de la cyclone: Une géopoétique de la Caraïbe* (Éditions du Seuil, 2006), 92. All further citations will be in text as (FC); all translations are mine.

9. In a sense, then, Maximin is proposing a left-wing version of what Naomi Klein calls the "shock doctrine," the means by which neoliberal organizations utilize the chaos of various disasters to implement economic reforms and other policies favorable to their interests. See Naomi Klein, *The Shock Doctrine: The Rise of Disaster Capitalism* (Picador Press, 2008).

10. A play on the term "disaster capitalism," which Naomi Klein coined to characterize how global capital utilizes natural or man-made disasters for profit. See Klein, *Shock Doctrine.*

11. "Extinction Rebellion" is a blanket organization attempting to coordinate various climate actions across the globe. I use the term here loosely to suggest a more robust international coalition of partners capable of responding to the slow violence of climate catastrophe. See https://rebellion.global/.

12. Frankétienne, *Melovivi ou le piège suivi de brèche ardente* (Riveneuve Èditions, 2010). All further citations will be in text as (MV); all translations are mine.

13. As Rachel Douglas suggests, on January 12, 2010, at 4:53 p.m., "Frankétienne had just a few minutes earlier finished rehearsing a new play" (394). And while *Melovivi* does not specify exactly what kind of natural disaster has occurred, it does leave both voices interred in the Earth. See Rachel Douglas, "Writing the Haitian Earthquake and Creating Archives," *Caribbean Quarterly* 62, nos. 3–4 (2016): 388–405.

14. As Genevieve Waite has argued, Frankétienne's language reflects the violence of both the natural catastrophes and the political violence plaguing Haiti. See Genevieve Waite, *"L'Haïti métaphorique de Frankétienne: Un écosystème engagé et spiraliste,"* *Journal of Haitian Studies* 26, no. 2 (2020): 128–48.

15. For a thorough and extensive reading of "spiralism" and its significance, see Kaiama Glover, *Haiti Unbound: A Spiralist Challenge to the Postcolonial Canon* (Liverpool University Press, 2010).

16. Frankétienne, "Haitian Literature and Culture, Part 1," interview in *Callaloo* 15, no. 2 (Spring 1992): 390.

17. Frankétienne, "Haitian Literature and Culture, Part 1," 389–90.

18. *"J'ai décrypté / l'aura / le ça-ira / le deviendra / le reviendra / et le sera / de l'impossible!"* Frankétienne, *Melovivi*, 55.

19. As Derrida has suggested, "the impossible" as an unprecedented or unforeseen event occurs every day, and part of the task of "deconstruction" entails thinking the impossible in its possibility. See Jacques Derrida, "A Certain Impossible Possibility of Saying the Event," trans. Gila Walker, *Critical Inquiry* 33, no. 2 (2007): 441–61.

REFERENCES

Agamben, Giorgio. *Homo Sacer.* Translated by Daniel Heller-Roazen. Stanford University Press, 1998.

Albernaz, Joseph. *Common Measures: Romanticism and the Groundlessness of Community.* Stanford University Press, 2024.

Albernaz, Joseph. "The Commons: Ruin and Romance." *Social Research: An International Quarterly* 88, no. 1 (2021): 115–50.

Albernaz, Joseph. "Earth Unbounded: Division and Inseparability in Hölderlin and Günderrode." In *Nothing Absolute: German Idealism and the Question of Political Theology*, ed. Kirill Chepurin and Alex Dubilet, 124–43. Fordham University Press, 2021.

Albernaz, Joseph. "Fragmentary Domesticity: Wordsworth's Image of the Common." *New Literary History* 51, no. 3 (Summer 2020): 523–47.

Albernaz, Joseph. "John Clare's World." *European Romantic Review* 27, no. 2 (2016): 189–205.

Allar, Neal. "Rhizomatic Influence: The Anti-genealogy of Glissant and Deleuze." *Cambridge Journal of Postcolonial Literary Inquiry* 6, no. 1 (2019): 1–13.

Allemann, Beda. *Hölderlin und Heidegger.* Atlantis Verlag, 1954.

Althusser, Louis. *Lenin and Philosophy.* Translated by Ben Brewster. Monthly Review Press, 1971.

Althusser, Louis. *Philosophy of the Encounter: Later Writings, 1978–1987.* Translated by G. M. Ghoshgarian. Verso Press, 2006.

Anderson, Benedict. *Imagined Communities.* Verso Books, 2006.

Arsić, Branka. "'Our Things': Thoreau on Objects, Relics, and Archives." *Qui Parle* 23, no. 1 (2014): 157–81.

Badiou, Alain. *Polemics.* Translated by Steve Corcoran. Verso Press, 2006.

Bajorek, Jennifer. "The Offices of Homeland Security, or, Hölderlin's Terrorism." *Critical Inquiry* 31, no. 4 (2005): 874–902.

Baross, Zsuzsa. *On Contemporaneity, After Agamben*. Sussex University Press, 2020.

Barrell, John. *The Idea of Landscape and the Sense of Place*. Cambridge University Press, 2011.

Barthélemy, Gérard. "*Voyage au Pays des Gouverneurs*." In *Jacques Roumain: Oeuvres complètes*, ed. Léon-François Hoffmann, 1229–65. Collection Archivos, 2003.

Bate, Jonathan. *The Song of the Earth*. Harvard University Press, 2000.

Benchimol, Alex. "Debatable Geographies of Romantic Nostalgia: The Redemptive Landscape in Wordsworth and Cobbett." In *Romanticism's Debatable Lands*, ed. Claire Lamont and Michael Rossington, 92–104. Palgrave Macmillan, 2007.

Benjamin, Walter. *Selected Writings. Vol. 1*. Edited by Marcus Bullock and Michael W. Jennings. Harvard University Press, 1996.

Bennett, Jane. *Vibrant Matter: A Political Ecology of Things*. Duke University Press, 2010.

Bernabé, Jean, Patrick Chamoiseau, and Raphaël Confiant. *Éloge de la Créolité/In Praise of Creoleness*. Translated by M. B. Taleb-Khyar. Gallimard, 1989.

Bewell, Alan. *Natures in Translation*. Johns Hopkins Press, 2017.

Bhabha, Homi. *The Location of Culture*. Routledge Press, 1994.

Blanchot, Maurice. *The Work of Fire*. Translated by Charlotte Mandel. Stanford University Press, 1995.

Bongie, Chris. *Islands and Exiles*. Stanford University Press, 1998.

Bongie, Chris. "The (Un)exploded Volcano: Creolization and Intertextuality in the Novels of Daniel Maximin." *Callaloo* 17, no. 2 (Spring 1994): 627–42.

Brant, Daniel. "Disaster Cosmopolitanism: Catastrophe and Global Community in the Fiction of Daniel Maximin and Maryse Condé." *International Journal of Francophone Studies* 17, no. 2 (2014): 215–37.

Brassier, Ray. *Nihil Unbound: Enlightenment and Extinction*. Palgrave Macmillan, 2007.

Brathwaite, Kamau. *Roots*. University of Michigan Press, 1993.

Britton, Celia. "Globalization and Political Action in the Work of Édouard Glissant." *Small Axe: A Caribbean Journal of Criticism* 13, no. 3, special issue 30 (2009): 1–11.

Britton, Celia. "Identity and Change in the Work of Édouard Glissant." *Small Axe: A Caribbean Journal of Criticism* 21, no. 1 (March 2017): 169–79.

Britton, Celia. *The Sense of Community in French Caribbean Fiction*. Liverpool University Press, 2010.

Brodber, Erna. *The Rainmaker's Mistake*. New Beacon Books, 2007.

Broglio, Ron. "Mapping British Earth and Sky." *Wordsworth Circle* 33, no. 2 (2002): 70–76.

Brownlow, Timothy. *John Clare and Picturesque Landscape*. Oxford University Press, 1983.

Buck-Morss, Susan. *Hegel, Haiti and Universal History*. University of Pittsburgh Press, 2009.

Burke, Edmund. *A Philosophical Enquiry into the Origins of Our Ideas of the Sublime and the Beautiful.* Edited by James T. Boulton. University of Notre Dame Press, 1968.

Burns, Lorna. "Landscape and Genre in the Caribbean Canon: Creolizing the Poetics of Place and Paradise." *Journal of West Indian Literature* 17, no. 1 (November 2008): 20–41.

Calixte, Fritz. "*Le 'retour' dans Gouverneurs de la Rosée.*" In *Revolte, subversion et développement chez Jacques Roumain*, ed. Michel Acacia, 65–72. Éditions de l'Université d'État d'Haïti, 2007.

Castell, James. "The Society of Birds in 'Home at Grasmere.'" In *Grasmere 2010: Selected Papers from the Wordsworth Summer Conference*, ed. Richard Gravil, 65–76. Humanities E-Books, 2010.

Castellano, Katey. *The Ecology of British Romantic Conservatism, 1790–1837.* Palgrave Macmillan, 2013.

Castellano, Katey. "Moles, Molehills, and Common Right in John Clare's Poetry." *Studies in Romanticism* 56, no. 1 (2017): 157–76.

Castellano, Katey. "Multispecies Work in John Clare's 'Birds Nesting' Poems." In *Palgrave Advances in John Clare Studies*, ed. Simon Kövesi and Erin Lafford, 179–97. Palgrave Macmillan, 2020.

Chakrabarty, Dipesh. "The Climate of History: Four Theses." *Critical Inquiry* 35, no. 2 (2009): 197–222.

Chakrabarty, Dipesh. "The Planet Does Not Return Our Gaze." *Alienocene*, December 4, 2020. https://alienocene.com/2020/12/04/the-planet-does-not-return-our-gaze/.

Chamoiseau, Patrick. *Crusoe's Footprint.* Translated by Jeffrey Landon Allen and Charly Verstraet. University of Virginia Press, 2022.

Chamoiseau, Patrick. *La matière de l'absence.* Éditions de Seuil, 2016.

Chamoiseau, Patrick. *L'empreinte à Crusoé.* Gallimard, 2012.

Chamoiseau, Patrick. *L'esclave vieil homme et le molosse.* Gallimard, 1997.

Chamoiseau, Patrick. *Slave Old Man.* Translated by Linda Coverdale. The New Press, 2018.

Chew, Shirley. "'The Story Is Now About Us': Olive Senior to 'England's Wealthiest Son.'" In *Citizens of the World: Adapting in the Eighteenth Century*, ed. Samara Anne Cahill and Kevin L. Cope, 69–84. Bucknell University Press, 2015.

Clare, John. *Autobiographical Writings.* Edited by Eric Robinson. Oxford University Press, 1986.

Clare, John. *The Early Poems of John Clare. Vol. 2.* Edited by Eric Robinson and David Powell. Oxford University Press, 1989.

Clare, John. *John Clare: Major Works.* Edited by Eric Robinson and David Powell. Oxford University Press, 2008.

Clare, John. *The Natural History Prose Writings.* Edited by Margaret Grainger. Oxford University Press, 1983.

Clare, John. *Poems of the Middle Period. Vol. 3.* Edited by Eric Robinson, David Powell, and P. M. S. Dawson. Oxford University Press, 1998.

Clare, John. *Poems of the Middle Period. Vol. 4*. Edited by Eric Robinson, David Powell, and P. M. S. Dawson. Oxford University Press, 1998.

Clare, John. *Poems of the Middle Period. Vol. 5*. Edited by Eric Robinson, David Powell, and P. M. S. Dawson. Oxford University Press, 2003.

Clare, John. *Selected Poetry and Prose*. Edited by Merryn Williams and Raymond Williams. Methuen Publishing, 1986.

Clark, Bruce. "Wordsworth's Departed Swans: Sublimation and Sublimity in 'Home at Grasmere.'" *Studies in Romanticism* 19, no. 4 (1980): 355–74.

Clark, Nigel. "The Earth in Physical and Social Thought." In *Inhuman Nature*. Sage Publishing, 2011.

Clark, Nigel, and Bronislaw Szerszynski. *Planetary Social Thought*. Polity Press, 2020.

Clarke, Richard L. W. "Root vs. Rhizome: An Epistemological Break in Francophone Caribbean Thought." *Journal of West Indian Literature* 9, no. 1 (April 2000): 12–41.

Collings, David. "Blank Oblivion, Condemned Life: John Clare's 'Obscurity.'" In *Romanticism and Speculative Realism*, ed. Chris Washington and Anne C. McCarthy, 75–91. Bloomsbury Press, 2019.

Dash, Michael. "Fictions of Displacement: Locating Modern Haitian Narratives." *Small Axe: A Caribbean Journal of Criticism* 12, no. 3 (2008): 32–41.

Dash, Michael. "*Île Rocher/Île Mangrove: Éléments d'une pensée archipélique dans l'oeuvre d'Édouard Glissant*." In *Poétiques d'Édouard Glissant*, edited by Jacques Chevrier, 17–24. Presses Univérsitaires de Paris-Sorbonne, 1999.

Dash, J. Michael. "Jacques Roumain: The Marxist Counterpoint." In *Literature and Ideology in Haiti: 1915–1961*, 129–55. Macmillan, 1981.

Dash, Jean Michael. "*Jacques Roumain Romancier*." In *Jacques Roumain: Oeuvres complètes*, ed. Léon-François Hoffmann, 1359–77. Collection Archivos, 2003.

Dastur, Françoise. *Hölderlin: Le retournement natal*. Encre Marine, 1997.

Dawson, P. M. S. "Common Sense or Radicalism? Some Reflections on Clare's Politics." *Romanticism* 2, no. 1 (1996): 81–97.

Dayan, Colin. *Haiti, History and the Gods*. University of California Press, 1995.

De Loughrey, Elizabeth. "Yam, Roots and Rot: Allegories of the Provision Grounds." *Small Axe: A Caribbean Journal of Criticism* 15, no. 1 (March 2011): 58–75.

DeLoughrey, Elizabeth, and G. B. Handley, eds. *Postcolonial Ecologies*. Oxford University Press, 2011.

Deleuze, Gilles. *Spinoza and Practical Philosophy*. Translated by Robert Hurley. City Lights Books, 1988.

Deleuze, Gilles, and Félix Guattari. *A Thousand Plateaus: Capitalism and Schizophrenia*. Translated by Brian Massumi. University of Minnesota Press, 1998.

Deleuze, Gilles, and Félix Guattari. *What Is Philosophy?* Translated by Hugh Tomlinson and Graham Burchell. Columbia University Press, 1994.

Derrida, Jacques. "A Certain Impossible Possibility of Saying the Event." Translated by Gila Walker. *Critical Inquiry* 33, no. 2 (2007): 441–61.

Derrida, Jacques. *Edmund Husserl's Origin of Geometry: An Introduction*. Translated by John P. Leavey. Nicholas Hays Limited, 1978.

Derrida, Jacques. *The Gift of Death. 2nd ed.* Translated by David Wills. University of Chicago Press, 2008.

Derrida, Jacques. *Given Time: 1. Counterfeit Money.* Translated by Peggy Kamuf. University of Chicago Press, 1992.

Derrida, Jacques. *Life Death.* Translated by Michael Naas and Pascale-Anne Brault. University of Chicago Press, 2020.

Derrida, Jacques. *Margins of Philosophy.* Translated by Alan Bass. University of Chicago Press, 1982.

Derrida, Jacques. "Sending: On Representation." *Social Research* 49, no. 22 (1982): 294–326.

Derrida, Jacques. *Spectres of Marx.* Translated by Peggy Kamuf. Routledge Press, 1994.

Descola, Philippe. *Beyond Nature and Culture.* Translated by Janet Lloyd. University of Chicago Press, 2014.

Des Roches, Reginald, Mary Comerio, Marc Eberhard, Walter Mooney, and Glen J. Rix. "Overview of the 2010 Haiti Earthquake." *Earthquake Spectra* 27, no. 1 (2001): 1–21.

Douglas, Rachel. "Writing the Haitian Earthquake and Creating Archives." *Caribbean Quarterly* 62, nos. 3–4 (2016): 388–405.

Drabinski, John E. *Glissant and the Middle Passage: Philosophy, Beginning, Abyss.* University of Minnesota Press, 2019.

Drabinski, John E. "Reproduction and the Universal in Glissant's Later Work." *New Centennial Review* 18, no. 3 (Winter 2018): 1–18.

Drabinski, John E. "Sites of Relation and Tout-Monde: Reflections on Glissant's Late Work." *Angelaki* 24, no. 3 (2019): 157–72.

Du Bois, W. E. B. *Writings.* Library of America, 1986.

Edwards, Brent. *Practice of Diaspora: Literature, Translation and the Rise of Black Internationalism.* Harvard University Press, 2003.

Engell, James. "Wordsworth's Earth, Nature, Strength." *Wordsworth Circle* 50, no. 2 (2019): 166–79.

Ezekiel, Anna. "Earth, Spirit, Humanity: Community and the Nonhuman in Karoline von Günderrode's 'Idea of the Earth.'" In *Romanticism and Political Ecology*, ed. Kir Kuiken, *Romantic Circles* 1, no. 2 (2024). http://romantic-circles.org/index.php/praxis/political_ecology.

Ezekiel, Anna. "Metamorphosis, Personhood, and Power in Karoline von Günderrode." *European Romantic Review* 25, no. 6 (2014): 773–91.

Ezekiel, Anna. "Narrative and Fragment: The Social Self in Karoline von Günderrode." *Symphilosophie: European Journal of European Romanticism* 2 (2020), chrome-extension://efaidnbmnnnibpcajpcglclefindmkaj/https://symphilosophie.com/wp-content/uploads/2020/12/4_Symphilosophie-2_2-Ezekiel.pdf.

Ezekiel, Anna. "Revolution and Revitalisation: Karoline von Günderrode's Political Philosophy and Its Metaphysical Foundations." *British Journal of the History of Philosophy* 30, no. 4 (2022): 666–86.

Fanon, Frantz. *Black Skin White Masks.* Translated by Charles Lam Markmann. Grave Press, 1967.

Ferdinand, Malcom. "Behind the Colonial Silence of Wilderness: 'In Marronage Lies the Search of a World.'" *Environmental Humanities* 14, no. 1 (2022): 182–201.

Ferdinand, Malcom. *Decolonial Ecology*. Translated by Anthony Paul Smith. Polity Press, 2022.

Fichte, Johann Gottlieb. *Addresses to the German Nation*. Edited by Gregory Moore. Cambridge University Press, 2008.

Fignolé, Jean-Claude. "*Sur Goverteurs de la Rosée de Jacques Roumain: Hypothèse de travail dans une perspective spiraliste*." In *Jacques Roumain: Oeuvres complètes*, ed. Léon-François Hoffmann, 1519–31. Collection Archivos, 2003.

Figuiera, Dorothy. "Goethe and Günderrode: German Poetic Readings of Indian Fatalism." In *Gendered Encounters Between Germany and Asia: Transnational Perspectives Since 1800*, ed. Joanne Miyang Cho and Douglas T. McGetchin, 41–64. Palgrave Macmillan, 2017.

Fleischmann, Ulrich. "*Jacques Roumain dans la littérature d'Haïti*." In *Jacques Roumain: Oeuvres complètes*, ed. Léon-François Hoffmann, 1229–65. Collection Archivos, 2003.

Frankétienne. "Haitian Literature and Culture, Part 1." Interview in *Callaloo* 15, no. 2 (Spring 1992): 390.

Frankétienne. *Melovivi ou le piège suivi de brèche ardente*. Riveneuve Èditions, 2010.

Freud, Sigmund. *The Standard Edition of the Complete Works of Sigmund Freud. Vol. 19*. Translated by James Strachey. Hogarth Press, 1961.

Fučikova, Milena. "*Pourquoi le romancier-poète imagine-t-il un invisible mémoire?*" *Svět Literatury* 30 (2020): 148–59.

Fulford, Tim. "Fields of Liberty?: The Politics of Wordsworth's Grasmere." *European Romantic Review* 9, no. 1 (1998): 59–86.

Gailus, Andreas. "Breaking Skulls: Kleist, Hegel and the Force of Assertion." In *Heinrich von Kleist and Modernity*, ed. Berndt Fischer and Tim Mehigan, 243–57. Camden House Publishing, 2011.

Garraway, Doris. "Toward a Creole Myth of Origin: Narrative, Foundations and Eschatology in Patrick Chamoiseau's '*L'esclave vieil homme et le molosse*.'" *Callaloo* 29, no. 1 (2006): 151–67.

Garrett, James M. *Wordsworth and the Writing of the Nation*. Routledge Press, 2008.

Gaston, Sean. *The Concept of the World from Kant to Derrida*. Rowman and Littlefield, 2013.

Gilbert, William. "The Hurricane." In *William Gilbert and Esoteric Romanticism*, ed. Paul Chesire, 103–62. Liverpool University Press, 2018.

Glissant, Édouard. *Caribbean Discourse: Selected Essays*. Translated by J. Michael Dash. University Press of Virginia, 1989.

Glissant, Édouard. *L'intention poétique*. Éditions du Seuil, 1969.

Glissant, Édouard. *Mémoires des esclavages*. Gallimard, 2007.

Glissant, Édouard. *The Overseer's Cabin*. Translated by Betsy Wing. University of Nebraska Press, 2011.

Glissant, Édouard. *Poetic Intention*. Translated by Nathalie Stephens and Anne Malena. Nightboat Books, 2010.

Glissant, Édouard. *The Poetics of Relation*. Translated by Betsy Wing. University of Michigan Press, 1997.

Glissant, Édouard. *Poétique de la Relation*. Gallimard, 1990.

Glissant, Édouard. *Tout-monde*. Éditions Gallimard, 1993.

Glissant, Édouard. *Treatise on the Whole-World*. Translated by Celia Britton. Liverpool University Press, 2020.

Glover, Kaiama. *Haiti Unbound: A Spiralist Challenge to the Postcolonial Canon*. Liverpool University Press, 2010.

Goldstein, Amanda. "Utopian Pastoral and the Inhuman Trade." *Romantic Circles* 1, no. 2 (2024). https://romantic-circles.org/praxis/publication/romanticism-and-political-ecology.

Goodman, Kevis. "Conjectures on Beachy Head: Charlotte Smith's Geological Poetics and the Ground of the Present." *English Literary History* 81, no. 3 (Fall 2014): 983–1006.

Gorji, Mina. "John Clare's Weeds." In *Ecology and Literature of the British Left*, ed. H. Gustav Klaus, John Rignall, and Valentine Cunningham, 61–73. Routledge Press, 2012.

Gosson, Renée. "For What the Land Tells: An Ecocritical Approach to Patrick Chamoiseau's *Chronicle of the Seven Sorrows*." *Callaloo* 26, no. 1 (2003): 219–34.

Gottlieb, Evan. *Romantic Globalism: British Literature and Modern World Order 1750–1830*. Ohio State University Press, 2014.

Gould, Stephen Jay. *Time's Arrow, Time's Cycle: Myth and Metaphor in the Discovery of Geological Time*. Harvard University Press, 1987.

Günderrode, Karoline von. "Idea of the Earth." In *Women Philosophers in the Long Nineteenth Century: The German Tradition*, ed. Dalia Nassar and Kristin Gjesdal, 82–84. Oxford University Press, 2021

Günderrode, Karoline von. *Karoline von Günderrode: Philosophical Writings*. Translated by Anna Ezekiel. Oxford University Press, 2025.

Günderrode, Karoline von. *Muhammed: Prophet of Mecca*. In *Poetic Fragments*, ed. and trans. Anna Ezekiel. State University of New York Press, 2016.

Günderrode, Karoline von. *Sämtliche Werke und ausgewählte Studien. Historisch-Kritische Ausgabe*. Vol. 1. Edited by Walter Morgenthaler. Stroemfeld/Roter Stern, 1990–91.

Hamlin, Cyrus. "The Philosophy of Poetic Form: Hölderlin's Theory of Poetry and the Classical German Elegy." In *The Solid Letter: Readings of Friedrich Hölderlin*, ed. Aris Fioretos, 291–320. Stanford University Press, 1999.

Hegel, G. W. F. *Lectures on the Philosophy of World History*. Translated by H. B. Nisbet. Cambridge University Press, 1996.

Hegel, G. W. F. *The Phenomenology of Spirit*. Translated by A. V. Miller. Oxford University Press, 1977.

Hegel, G. W. F. *The Philosophy of Nature*. Translated by A. V. Miller. Oxford University Press, 1970.

Heidegger, Martin. *The Fundamental Concepts of Metaphysics*. Translated by William McNeill and Nicholas Walker. Indiana University Press, 1995.

Heidegger, Martin. *Hölderlin's Hymn "The Ister."* Translated by William McNeill and Julia Davis. Indiana University Press, 1996.

Heidegger, Martin. *Off the Beaten Track.* Translated by Julian Young and Kenneth Haynes. Cambridge University Press, 2002.

Heidegger, Martin. *On Time and Being.* Translated by Joan Stambaugh. University of Chicago Press, 2002.

Hilger, Stephanie Mathilde. "Staging Islam: Karoline von Günderrode's *Mahomed, der Prophet von Mekka.*" In *Women Write Back: Strategies of Response and the Dynamics of European Literary Culture, 1790–1805*, 91–118. Rodopi Press, 2009.

Hitchcock, Peter. "Antillanité and the Art of Resistance." *Research in African Literatures* 27, no. 2 (Summer 1996): 33–50.

Hölderlin, Friedrich. *The Death of Empedocles.* Translated by David Farell Krell. State University of New York Press, 2008.

Hölderlin, Friedrich. *Essays and Letters on Theory.* Translated by Thomas Pfau. State University of New York Press, 1988.

Hölderlin, Friedrich. *Poems and Fragments.* Translated by Michael Hamburger. Anvil Press, 2005.

Hölderlin, Friedrich. *Sämtliche Werke und Briefe. Vols. 1–2.* Carl Hanser Verlag, 1970.

Holm, Isak Winkel. "Earthquake in Haiti: Kleist and the Birth of Modern Disaster Discourse." *New German Critique* 39, no. 1 (2012): 49–66.

Houghton, Sarah. "Enkindling Ecstacy: The Sublime Vision of John Clare." *Romanticism* 9, no. 2 (2003): 176–95.

Hughes, Langston. *Collected Poems of Langston Hughes.* Edited by Arnold Rampersad. Vintage Books, 1994.

Hutton, James. *The Theory of the Earth. 2 vols.* Edinburgh, 1795.

Irvine, Richard D. G., and Mina Gorji. "John Clare in the Anthropocene." *Cambridge Anthology* 31, no. 1 (2013): 119–32.

Johnson, Shelby. *The Rich Earth Between Us: The Intimate Grounds of Race and Sexuality in the Atlantic World, 1770–1840.* University of North Carolina Press, 2024.

Josepha, Kelly. "Beyond Geography, Past Time: Afrofuturism, *The Rainmaker's Mistake*, and Caribbean Studies." *Small Axe: A Caribbean Journal of Criticism* 17, no. 2 (2013): 123–35.

Kant, Immanuel. *Conflict of the Faculties.* Translated by Mary J. Gregor. University of Nebraska Press, 1992.

Kant, Immanuel. *Critique of the Power of Judgement.* Translated by Paul Guyer and Eric Matthews. Cambridge University Press, 2000.

Kant, Immanuel. *Natural Science.* Edited by Eric Watkins. Cambridge University Press, 2012.

Kaussen, Valerie. "Slaves, *Viejos*, and the *Internationale*: The Marxist Novels of Jacques Roumain and Jacques-Stephen Alexis." In *Migrant Revolutions: Haitian Literature, Globalization, and U.S. Imperialism.* Lexington Books, 2008.

Keats, John. *John Keats: The Major Works.* Edited by Elizabeth Cook. Oxford University Press, 2001.

Klein, Naomi. *The Shock Doctrine: The Rise of Disaster Capitalism*. Picador Press, 2008.

Kleist, Heinrich von. *Sämtliche Werke und Briefe*. Carl Hander Verlag, 1993.

Kleist, Heinrich von. *Heinrich von Kleist: Selected Writings*. Edited by David Constantine. Hackett Publishing, 2004.

Knickerbocker, Scott. *Ecopoetics: The Language of Nature, the Nature of Language*. University of Massachusetts Press, 2012.

Koch, Alexander, Chris Brierly, Mark M. Maslin, and Simon L. Lewis. "Earth System Impacts of the European Arrival and Great Dying in the Americas After 1492." *Quaternary Science Reviews* 207, no. 1 (March 2019): 13–36.

Kolbert, Elizabeth. *The Sixth Extinction: An Unnatural History*. Picador, 2014.

Kövesi, Simon. "Finding Poems, Making Text: John Clare and the Greening of Textual Criticism." *Romanticism* 17, no. 2 (2011): 135–47.

Kövesi, Simon. "John Clare & . . . & . . . & Deleuze and Guattari's Rhizome." In *Ecology and the Literature of the British Left: The Red and the Green*, ed. John Rignall, H. Gustav Klaus, and Valentine Cunningham: 75–88. Routledge Press, 2012.

Kreuzer, Johann. "*Zeit, Sprache und Erinnerung: Die Zeitlogik der Dichtung*." In *Hölderlin Handbuch, Leben-Werk-Wirkung*, ed. Johann Kreuzer, 147–61. Metzler, 2002.

Kuiken, Kir. *Imagined Sovereignties: Toward a New Political Romanticism*. Fordham University Press, 2014.

Kuiken, Kir. "Impasse, Promise and Impossible Community: Kleist's *Michael Kohlhaas* and Blanchot's Community of Lovers." *Comparative Literature* 72, no. 2 (2020): 128–43.

Kuiken, Kir, and Deborah Elise White, eds. *Haiti's Literary Legacies: Romanticism and the Unthinkable Revolution*. Bloomsbury Press, 2022.

Lacoue-Labarthe, Philippe. *Typography*. Translated by Christopher Fynsk. Stanford University Press, 1998.

Lacoue-Labarthe, Philippe, and Jean-Luc Nancy. "The Nazi Myth." *Critical Inquiry 16, no. 2* (Winter 1990): 291–312.

Latour, Bruno. *Down to Earth: Politics in the New Climatic Regime*. Translated by Catherine Porter. Polity Press, 2018.

Latour, Bruno. *An Inquiry into Modes of Existence*. Translated by Catherine Porter. Harvard University Press, 2013.

Latour, Bruno. *Politics of Nature*. Translated by Catherine Porter. Harvard University Press, 2004.

Lauro, Raphael, and Emily Maguire. "Édouard Glissant's Excursions and Detours." *Discourse* 36, no. 1 (Winter 2014): 3–30.

Lemke, Anja. "The Transition between the Possible and the Real: Nature as Contingency in Hölderlin's 'The Declining Fatherland.'" In *Hölderlin's Philosophy of Nature*, ed. Rochelle Tobias, 164–77. Edinburgh University Press, 2020.

Locke, John. *Two Treatises of Government*. Edited by Peter Laslett. Cambridge University Press, 2004.

Lovejoy, Arthur O. *Essays in the History of Ideas*. Johns Hopkins Press, 1948.

Lucas, John. "Clare's Politics." In *John Clare in Context*, ed. Hugh Hughton, Adam Phillips, and Geoffrey Summerfield, 148–77. Cambridge University Press, 1994.

Lyell, Charles. *Principles of Geology: Being an Attempt to Explain the Former Changes of the Earth's Surface, by Reference to Causes Now in Operation. 3 vols.* John Murray, 1830.

Lyotard, Jean-François. *The Inhuman*. Translated by Geoffrey Bennington and Rachel Bowlby. Stanford University Press, 1991.

Macnaghten, Phil, and John Urry. *Contested Natures*. Sage Publications, 1998.

Makdisi, Saree. *Making England Western: Occidentalism, Race and Imperial Culture*. University of Chicago Press, 2014.

Mahood, M. M. *The Poet as Botanist*. Cambridge University Press, 2008.

Malm, Andreas. "In Wildness Is the Liberation of the World: On Maroon Ecology and Partisan Nature." *Historical Materialism* 26, no. 3 (2018): 3–37.

Mardossian, Carine. "Poetics of Landscape: Édouard Glissant's Creolized Ecologies." *Callaloo* 36, no. 4 (Fall 2013): 983–94.

Marion, Jean-Luc. *The Idol and Distance*. Translated by Thomas A. Carlson. Fordham University Press, 2001.

Maximilien, Guy. "Jacques Roumain et le vodou." In *Revolte, subversion et développement chez Jacques Roumain*, ed. Michel Acacia, 261–68. Éditions de l'Université d'État d'Haïti, 2007.

Maximin, Daniel. *L'île et une nuit*. Éditions de Seuil, 1998.

Maximin, Daniel. *L'isolé soleil*. Éditions de Seuil, 1987.

Maximin, Daniel. *Les fruits de la cyclone: Une géopoétique de la Caraïbe*. Éditions du Seuil, 2006.

Maximin, Daniel. *Soufrières*. Éditions de Seuil, 1987.

McAlpine, Erica. "Keeping Nature at Bay: John Clare's Poetry of Wonder." *Romanticism* 50, no. 1 (2011): 79–104.

McKusick, James C. *Green Writing*. Harvard University Press, 2000.

Meillassoux, Quentin. *After Finitude*. Translated by Ray Brassier. Continuum Press, 2008.

Modeen, Mary, and Iain Biggs. *Creative Engagement with Ecologies of Place: Geopoetics, Deep Mapping and Slow Residencies*. Routledge Press, 2021.

Modiano, Raimonda. "Blood Sacrifice, Gift Economy and the Edenic World: Wordsworth's 'Home at Grasmere.'" *Studies in Romanticism* 32, no. 4 (Winter 1993): 481–521.

Molesky, Mark. *This Gulf of Fire: The Destruction of Lisbon, or Apocalypse in the Age of Science and Reason*. Alfred A. Knopf, 2015.

Morton, Timothy. *Ecology Without Nature*. Harvard University Press, 2009.

Murray-Roman, Jeannine. "Reading in the Diminutive: Caribbean Chaos Theory in Antonio Benítez-Rojo, Édouard Glissant, and Wilson Harris." *Small Axe: A Caribbean Journal of Criticism* 19, no. 1, special issue 46 (2015): 20–36.

Nakicenovic, Nebojsa, Johan Rockström, Owen Gaffney, and Caroline Zimm. "Global Commons in the Anthropocene: World Development on a Stable and Resilient

Planet." https://pure.iiasa.ac.at/id/eprint/14003/#:~:text=We%20argue%20that%20humanity%20must,Global%20Commons%20in%20the%20Anthropocene" (Creative commons license), 2016.

Nancy, Jean-Luc. *After Fukushima*. Translated by Charlotte Mandell. Fordham University Press, 2015.

Nancy, Jean-Luc. *The Creation of the World or Globalization*. Translated by François Raffoul and David Pettigrew. State University of New York Press, 2007.

NASA. "Climate Change and the Rise and Fall of Civilizations." *Climate NASA* (2014). https://climate.nasa.gov/news/1010/climate-change-and-the-rise-and-fall-of-civilizations/.

Nassar, Dalia. "The Human Vocation and the Question of the Earth: Karoline von Günderrode's Philosophy of Nature." *Archiv für Geschichte der Philosophie* 104, no. 1 (2022): 108–30.

Neeson, J. M. *Commoners: Common Right, Enclosure and Social Change in England, 1700–1820*. Cambridge University Press, 1993.

Nesbitt, Nick. "Édouard Glissant: From *Poétique de la Relation* to the Transcendental Analytic of Relation." In *Caribbean Critique: Antillean Critical Theory from Toussaint to Glissant*, 231–50. Liverpool University Press, 2013.

Neyrat, Frédéric. *The Unconstructible Earth: An Ecology of Separation*. Translated by Andrew S. Burk. Fordham University Press, 2019.

Nicholson, Michael. "John Clare's Lyric Defiance." *ELH* 82, no. 2 (2015): 637–69.

Noble, Shalon. "Homeless at Home: John Clare's Uncommon Ecology." *Romanticism* 21, no. 2 (2015): 171–81.

Noudelmann, François, and Celia Britton. "Édouard Glissant's Legacy: Transmitting Without Universals?" *Callaloo* 36, no. 4 (Fall 2013): 869–74.

Oakley, Seanna Sumalee. *Common Places: The Poetics of African Atlantic Postromantics*. Rodopi Press, 2011.

Oliver, Kelly. *Earth and World: Philosophy After the Apollo Missions*. Columbia University Press, 2015.

Omorod, Beverley. "Beyond Négritude: Some Aspects of the Work of Édouard Glissant." *Contemporary Literature* 15, no. 3 (Summer 1974): 360–69.

Omorod, Beverley. *Introduction to the French Caribbean Novel*. Heineman Educational Books, 1985.

Paravisini-Gebert, Lizabeth. "Deforestation and the Yearning for Lost Landscapes in Caribbean Literatures." In *Postcolonial Ecologies*, ed. Elizabeth DeLoughrey and G. B. Handley, 99–116. Oxford University Press, 2011.

Paravisini-Gebert, Lizabeth. "'He of the Trees': Nature, Environment and Creole Religiosities in Caribbean Literature." In *Caribbean Literature and the Environment: Between Nature and Culture*, ed. Elizabeth DeLoughrey, Renée Gosson, and George Handley, 182–96. University of Virginia Press, 2005.

Patterson, Anita. "'I've Known Rivers: Langston Hughes, Jacques Roumain, and the Emergence of Caribbean Modernism." *Langston Hughes Review* 27, no. 1 (2021): 12–28.

Pereira, Alvaro S. "The Opportunity of a Disaster: The Economic Impact of the 1755 Lisbon Earthquake." *Journal of Economic History* 69, no. 2 (2009): 466–99.

Presseley-Sanon, Toni. "*Masters of the Dew*, the Peasant, the Environment, and the Oral Tradition." In *Haitian Peasantry Through Oral and Written Literature*, 65–83. Caribbean Studies Press, 2016.

Radović, Stanka. "The Birthplace of Relation: Édouard Glissant's *Poétique de la Relation*: For Ranko." *Callaloo* 30, no. 2 (Spring 2007): 475–81.

Rancière, Jacques. *The Politics of Aesthetics*. Translated by Gabriel Rockhill. Continuum Press, 2004.

Regier, Alexander. *Fracture and Fragmentation in British Romanticism*. Cambridge University Press, 2010.

Regis, Hannah. "Subjection and Resistance: Landscapes, Gardens, Myth and Vestigial Presences in Olive Senior's *Gardening in the Tropics*." *eTropic* 19, no. 1 (2020): 151–66.

Richman, Kathy. "Whose Other?: The Centrality of Language to Identity and Representation in Roumain's *Gouverneurs de la Rosée*." In *Empire Lost: France and Its Other Worlds*, ed. Elisabeth Mudimbe-Boyi, 105–24. Lexington Books, 2009.

Rieder, John. *Wordsworth's Counterrevolutionary Turn: Community, Virtue, and Vision in the 1790s*. University of Delaware Press, 1997.

Roe, Nicholas. *The Politics of Nature: William Wordsworth and Some Contemporaries*. 2nd ed. Palgrave Macmillan, 2002.

Roget, Wilbert J. "Land and Myth in the Writing of Édouard Glissant." *World Literature Today* 63, no. 4 (Autumn 1989): 626–31.

Roumain, Jacques. *Gouverneurs de la Rosée*. In *Jacques Roumain: Oeuvres complètes*, ed. Léon-François Hoffmann, 249–396. Collection Archivos, 2003.

Roumain, Jacques. *Masters of the Dew*. Translated by Langston Hughes and Mercer Cook. Heinmann Press, 1947.

Roumain, Jacques. *When the Tom-Tom Beats: Selected Prose and Poetry*. Translated by Joanne Fungaroli and Ronald Sauer. Azul Editions, 1996.

Rousseau, Jean-Jacques. *The Discourses and Other Early Political Writings*. Translated by Victor Gourevich. Cambridge University Press, 1997.

Schelling, F. W. J. *Bruno, or on the Natural and the Divine Principle of Things*. Translated by Michael G. Vater. State University of New York Press, 1984.

Schelling, F. W. J. *First Outline of a System of the Philosophy of Nature*. Translated by Keith R. Peterson. State University of New York Press, 2004.

Schmitt, Carl. *The Nomos of the Earth*. Translated by G. L. Ulmen. Telos Press Publishing, 2006.

Senior, Olive. *Gardening in the Tropics*. Insomniac Press, 2005.

Senior, Olive. *Shell*. Insomniac Press, 2007.

Serres, Michel. *Natural Contract*. University of Michigan Press, 1995.

Shelley, Percy. *Shelley's Poetry and Prose*. Edited by Donald H. Reiman and Neil Fraistat. W. W. Norton, 2002.

Simonis, Annette. "'*Das verschleierte Bild*': *Mythopoetik und Geschlechterrollen bei*

Karoline von Günderrode." Deutsche Vierteljahrsschrift für Literaturwissenschaft 74, no. 2 (2000): 254–78.

Smith, Charlotte. *The Poems of Charlotte Smith*. Edited by Stuart Curran. Oxford University Press, 1993.

Spivak, Gayatri. *An Aesthetic Education in the Era of Globalization*. Harvard University Press, 2012.

Spivak, Gayatri. *Can the Subaltern Speak? Reflections on the History of an Idea*. Edited by Rosalind Morris. Columbia University Press, 2010.

Stengers, Isabelle. *In Catastrophic Times: Resisting the Coming Barbarism*. Translated by Andrew Goffey. Open Humanities Press, 2015.

Stephens, Samantha. "Caribbean Basins: Containing the Im/material in Kei Miller's 'Quashie's Verse' and Olive Senior's 'Gourd.'" *Journal of West Indian Literature* 29, no. 2 (2021): 13–28.

Szondi, Peter. "Hölderlin's Overcoming of Classicism." *Comparative Criticism* 5, no. 1 (1983): 251–70.

Szondi, Peter. *Hölderlin-Studien*. Insel Verlag, 1967.

Thomas, Bonnie. "Édouard Glissant and the Art of Memory." *Small Axe: A Caribbean Journal of Criticism* 13, no. 3 (November 2009): 25–36.

Thompson, E. P. *The Making of the English Working Class*. Vintage Books, 1966.

Trop, Gabriel. "Arts of Unconditioning: On Romantic Science and Poetry." In *The Palgrave Handbook of German Romantic Philosophy*, ed. Elizabeth Millán, 421–48. Palgrave Macmillan, 2020.

Trop, Gabriel. "Mythological Indifference in Schelling and Nerval." *Wordsworth Circle* 50 (2019): 108–26.

Vardy, Alan. *John Clare, Politics and Poetry*. Palgrave Macmillan, 2003.

Vernant, Jean-Pierre, and Pierre Vidal-Naquet. *Myth and Tragedy in Ancient Greece. Vol. 1*. Translated by Janet Lloyd. Zone Books, 1990.

Voltaire. *The Portable Voltaire*. Edited by Ben Ray Redman. Penguin Books, 1977.

Waite, Genevieve. "*L'Haïti métaphorique de Frankétienne: Un écosystème engagé et spiraliste*." *Journal of Haitian Studies* 26, no. 2 (2020): 128–48.

Ward, Candace. "'In the Free': The Work of Emancipation in the Anglo-Caribbean Historical Novel." *Journal of American Studies* 49, no. 2 (May 2015): 359–81.

Weber, Christoph. "*Santiagos Untergang—Lissabons Schrecken: Heinrich von Kleists 'Erdbeben in Chili' im Kontext des Katastrophendiskurses im 18 Jahrhundert*." *Monatschefte* 104, no. 3 (2012): 317–36.

Weiger, Sarah. "'Shadows of Taste': John Clare's Tasteful Natural History." *John Clare Society Journal* 27, no. 1 (2008): 59–71.

Wetherby, Leif. *Transplanting the Metaphysical Organ: German Romanticism Between Leibniz and Marx*. Fordham University Press, 2016.

White, Simon J. *Romanticism and the Rural Community*. Palgrave Macmillan, 2013.

Williams, Bryon. "Process and Presence: Geological Influence and Innovation in Shelley's 'Mont Blanc.'" In *Romantic Ecocriticism: Origins and Legacies*, ed. Dewey W. Hall), 87–104. Lexington Books, 2016.

Willson, Nicole Louise. "People Without Shoes: Jacques Roumain, Langston Hughes and Their Transnational *Ti Nèg* Aesthetic." *Comparative American Studies* 15, nos. 3–4 (2017): 146–61.

Winckelmann, Johann Joachim. *Reflections on the Imitation of Greek Works in Painting and Sculpture.* Translated by Elfriede Heyer and Roger C. Norton. Open Court Press, 1987.

Wolfe, Cary. *Ecological Poetics, or Wallace Stevens's Birds.* University of Chicago Press, 2020.

Wood, David. *Deep Time, Dark Times: On Being Geologically Human.* Fordham University Press, 2019.

Wordsworth, Dorothy. *The Grasmere and Alfoxden Journals.* Oxford University Press, 2002.

Wordsworth, William. *Home at Grasmere, Part First, Book First of the Recluse.* Edited by Beth Darlington. Cornell University Press, 1977.

Wordsworth, William. *Poems in Two Volumes and Other Poems, 1800–1807.* Edited by Jared Curtis. Cornell University Press, 1983.

Wordsworth, William. *The Prose Works of William Wordsworth.* Vol. 1. Edited by W. J. B. Owen and Jane Smyser. Oxford University Press, 1974.

Wordsworth, William. *The Thirteen-Book "Prelude." Vol. 1.* Edited by Mark L. Reed. Cornell University Press, 1991.

Wynter, Sylvia. "Unsettling the Coloniality of Being/Power/Truth/Freedom: Towards the Human, After Man, Its Overrepresentation—An Argument." *New Centennial Review* 3, no. 3 (Fall 2003): 257–337.

INDEX

The authorized representative in the EU for product safety and compliance is:
Mare Nostrum Group
B.V Doelen 72
4831 GR Breda
The Netherlands

www.ingramcontent.com/pod-product-compliance
Lightning Source LLC
Jackson TN
JSHW021135190226
98286JS00003B/3

* 9 7 8 1 5 0 3 6 4 6 8 2 7 *